MW01711539

The Journal of the Association for Nepal and Himalayan Studies

HIMALAYA

HIMALAYA
The Journal of the Association of Nepal and Himalayan Studies

Editorial

Expanding Horizons, Deepening Engagement

Michael T. Heneise

DOI: https://doi.org/10.2218/himalaya.2025.10883

In a year already marked by complex transformations across the Himalayan region—including the deeply troubling military escalation between India and Pakistan in May 2025, which rekindled long-standing tensions in Jammu and Kashmir—it is more important than ever to foster spaces for thoughtful scholarship, nuanced dialogue, and inclusive representation. HIMALAYA continues to offer such a platform: one committed to rigorous, regionally grounded research; to innovative, multimodal approaches; and to expanding our network of scholars, reviewers, and readers, particularly across South and Central Asia.

This issue of HIMALAYA appears at a moment of vibrant institutional growth and editorial transition. Our move to the Open Journal Systems (OJS) platform in 2022 significantly streamlined our editorial processes and increased global accessibility through full open-access publishing. In 2023, we deepened our collaboration with the University of Edinburgh, now our official publishing partner. This strategic partnership has enabled broader indexing and long-term archiving, while allowing us to adopt IngramSpark for print-on-demand services. As a result, HIMALAYA is no longer confined to a mainly North American readership but is now more accessible to readers, libraries, and institutions across the Himalayan region and beyond.

As part of this evolution, we also celebrate important editorial transitions. Dr Jeevan R. Sharma, who graciously invited me to join him as Co-Editor in 2020, now steps into the esteemed role of Editor-at-Large. His vision and collaborative leadership were instrumental in guiding the journal through the OJS transition, steering our partnership with Edinburgh, and shaping our global distribution model. In 2024, Dr Shubham Sapkota joined the team as Associate Editor. Based at the University of Colorado Boulder, Shubham has already played a pivotal role in shaping our distribution strategy, increasing accessibility, and fostering emerging scholarship from underrepresented areas of Himalayan studies.

We are equally pleased to introduce Dr Zezhou Yang (Asia Research Institute, NUS) as our new Reviews Editor. Joining in November 2024, Zezhou brings extensive editorial experience and a commitment to encouraging critical dialogue through

CC BY NC ND
This work is licensed under a Creative Commons Attribution-Noncommercial-No Derivative Works 4.0 License.

the reviews section. His forthcoming innovations include author-reviewer interactions and expanded book forums. Shortly after Zezhou's arrival, we welcomed a new team of in-region Assistant Editors: Haidamteu Zeme (IIT Delhi), Gulal Salil (Independent researcher and graphic designer), and Dr Yatin Batra (University of Delhi). In addition to their own research contributions, they bring deep regional expertise and a keen curatorial eye that will influence the journal's evolving design, visual culture, and author and reviewer networks. Most recently, we welcomed our new Assistant Editor Fatma Matar (UiT The Arctic University of Norway), a visual anthropologist assisting us in exploring multimodal content. With her expertise, we aim to further develop the journal's engagement with multi-sensory scholarship and non-textual forms of expression.

Our current editorial team builds on the formidable legacy of past editors, particularly the many decades of stewardship by colleagues at Macalester College. That team's design sensibility, editorial excellence, and commitment to Himalayan scholarship helped establish HIMALAYA as one of the few academic journals to successfully blend peer-reviewed research with arresting visuals and elegant design. In a publishing landscape increasingly polarized between traditional and digital formats, we continue to experiment with hybrid models that retain the tactile pleasures of print while embracing the fluidity of digital access.

This issue reflects the editorial team's commitment to thematic curation and disciplinary breadth. The opening article by Deepsikha Chatterjee, "Bhairab Nach and Navadurga: Masked Rituals of Nepal," is a visually rich, ethnographically grounded exploration of ritual performance in the Kathmandu Valley. Her detailed study of mask-making, embodied pedagogy, and Tantric cosmology exemplifies our vision for multimodal scholarship. Following this, Paola Tiné's sensitive narrative, "The Difficult Art of Parenting," offers a rare glimpse into domestic moral instruction among middle-class families in Nepal, weaving textual and painted accounts into a vivid ethnographic canvas. Sanjay Barbora's article, grounded in fieldwork across Northeast India, interrogates upland agriculture and entrepreneurship as developmental ideologies, while Sushan Bhattarai provides an innovative archival ethnography of conservation efforts in Ladakh.

Parjanya Sen's work revisits Charles Bell's photographic archive through the lens of native agency, offering a critical historiography of colonial visuality in Tibet. Menia Taba's contribution, "Vkur Nukuj (Let Us Return)," is a powerful autoethnographic account of visual repatriation among the Nyishi people of Arunachal Pradesh, bridging photography, identity, and memory. Bhoomika Joshi contributes a striking analysis of landscape aesthetics and colonial remoteness in the Indian Himalayas, while Patrick Kaplanian probes the socio-political boundaries of communal identity among Buddhists and Shi'as in Ladakh.

We are also pleased to publish a rare and timely interview between linguistic anthropologist Dr. Mark Turin, former editor of HIMALAYA, and Dr. Lava Deo Awasthi, the first Chairperson of the Language Commission of Nepal. Their conversation addresses the complex terrain of language policy, recognition, and representation in post-monarchical Nepal—a vital issue given the country's linguistic diversity and its constitutional commitment to inclusion.

The reviews section features three significant contributions. Navneet Kaur assesses Rubina Nusrat's *Sustainability of Van Gujjars*, a critical monograph on pastoral Muslim communities in Uttarakhand. Tanka Subba offers a deeply personal and scholarly reading of *Through the India-China Border* by Prem Poddar and Lisa Lindkvist Zhang, situating Kalimpong as a dynamic node of Himalayan geopolitics. Ina Zharkevich's review of *Nepal's Dalits in Transition*, edited by David Gellner and Krishna Adhikari, affirms its significance as a landmark intervention in Dalit studies and caste politics in contemporary Nepal.

Together, these contributions offer a compelling cross-section of contemporary Himalayan studies. They span thematic domains of ritual performance, ecological transformation, visual culture, linguistic justice, and socio-political memory. We thank our readers for their continued engagement, our contributors for their trust, and our editorial team for their tireless work. As HIMALAYA continues to grow as a premier outlet for research in and on the Himalayan region, we remain committed to fostering a journal that is both accessible and rigorous, rooted and global, traditional and experimental.

Michael T. Heneise
Editor, HIMALAYA

HIMALAYA
The Journal of the Association of Nepal and Himalayan Studies

Research Article

Bhairab Nach and Navadurga: Masked Rituals of Nepal

Deepsikha Chatterjee

Hunter College, CUNY

DOI: https://doi.org/10.2218/himalaya.2025.9978

Abstract

Nepal and surrounding regions in India are known for resplendent masked performances. Often ritual in nature, they serve as tools for spiritual belonging, community cohesion, ties of kinship, and artistic expression. Research on Nepal's culture and performance traditions has been smaller compared to neighboring South Asian countries such as India, Bangladesh and Sri Lanka. Nepal's performance traditions are complex, with centuries of history, culture, and religious beliefs attached to them. In Nepal, many of these traditional performances are called Pyakhan or stories/parables. They are deserving of in-depth study, much like their other South Asian counterparts. This paper takes a deep dive into masked dance forms of Nepal, especially the making and use of masks in Bhairab Nach, and Navadurga performance.

Keywords

mask, costume, ritual images, Pyakhan, tantrism, religion

Recommended Citation

Chatterjee, Deepsikha, (2025). Bhairab Nach and Navadurga: Masked Rituals of Nepal. HIMALAYA 44(1): 5-28.

This work is licensed under a Creative Commons Attribution-Noncommercial-No Derivative Works 4.0 License.

Nepal and surrounding regions in India are known for resplendent masked performances. Often ritual in nature, they serve as tools for spiritual belonging, community cohesion, ties of kinship, and artistic expression. Research on Nepal's culture and performance traditions has been smaller compared to neighboring South Asian countries such as India, Bangladesh and Sri Lanka. Nepal's performance traditions are complex, with centuries of history, culture, and religious beliefs attached to them. In Nepal, many of these traditional performances are called *Pyakhan* or stories/parables. They are deserving of in-depth study, much like their other South Asian counterparts. This paper takes a deep dive into masked dance forms of Nepal, especially the making and use of masks in *Bhairab Nach*, and *Navadurga* performance.

In 2022, I had the opportunity to immerse myself in the study of mask and costume making of Nepal's Kathmandu valley's *Bhairab Nach*. There are 29 forms of masked dances in the area.[1]

Bhairab Nach is a generic term for masked dances in this region. My research was centered on the mask making traditions of Bhaktapur area of Kathmandu valley.[2] The potter community performed their ritual dance *Bhairab Nach* for this research project. They perform this regularly during ritually potent times of the year, particularly after the monsoon months into the autumn. In my research I looked at mask and costume use by the Jetha Ganesh Bhairab troupe from the Pottery Square area of Bhaktapur. Simultaneously I focused on the mask-making tradition by the Chitrakar community. Here, the Chitrakar community is involved in ritual mask-making and ritual image-making at temples. Their work is visible as mask displays and ritual exhibitions at their home as well as activated by the *Navadurga* ritual dance genre. They are performed by the indigenous Newari people of the area (Koizumi 1983, 4; Davis 2019, 15). The Dasain festival takes place during such a potent time, before the harvest season. The performances are dedicated for the community's wellbeing (Davis 2019, 12).

Even as Nepal is a syncretic mix of the old and new, the modern and the ancient, beautiful nature and everyday bustle, the serene and the hectic, Nepal Mandal region in general and Bhaktapur specifically is built geographically and spiritually around the mother Goddess deities. Around the end of September (after the monsoons), a festival called Indra Jatra dedicated to the god of rains Indra takes place. It marks the end of the rainy season and the beginning of a potent time of Dasain. A symbolic staff called the *yasin* is processed around town and then immersed in water in the Hanumante river. Dedication to these Goddess deities is part of the festival. It includes offerings to a prepubescent-aged girl of Buddhist Shakya community (also called a kumari) as the center of the ceremony. The dance drama is based on the sacred text of the *Devi Mahatmya*, an important part of the *Markandeya Purana*, believed to have been penned around the 4th-5th century CE (Coburn 1984).[3] The performance tradition has primarily been passed down orally through the centuries.

This paper and my larger research project are focused on traditional performances that utilize masks. Masks in such traditional settings, as seen in Nepal, India, Indonesia, Japan, and among Yoruba communities in Africa, and other places, are often associated with religion and spiritual practices. Some scholarly books and anthologies have discussed masked performances such as by John Emigh, Margaret Coldiron, Donald Cordry, Deborah Bell, Richard Kohn, Wendy Meaden and Michael Brown, Bruce Kapferer and Georges Papigny, Laurie Margot Ross, and others. While these works are comprehensive in nature, they have not examined in detail the meanings, making, or activation of Nepal's rich performance traditions. There are three prior comprehensive studies on Nepal's performance, history, and religion that are accessible in English. The first is Carol Davis' book *Theatre of Nepal and the People Who Make It*, the second is an older Japan Foundation Publication *Dance and Music in South Asian Drama - Chhau, Mahakali Pyakhan and Yakshagana,* and the third is Gregory Price Grieve's *Retheorizing Religion in Nepal.* Davis's project takes on the commendable task of documenting Nepal's performances. Yet it tackles a lot of breadth, and all that is limited to modern and activist Nepali theatre. It does not delve into traditional performances other than mentioning them.[4] However the first chapter provides important information on the genesis of *astamatrika* dance dramas (invoking eight goddesses), originally conceived by Srinivasa Malla (1649-1685 CE) which is in practice now (Davis 2019, 11-12). These dramas are now under the umbrella of *Bhairab Nach.* Davis also details the cleansing abilities of such ritual performances. The Japan Foundation publication, although several decades old now, did go into depth with documentary details of *Bhairab Nach,* specifically the *Mahakali Pyakhan* genre within that, the conditions of performance, and the artistic style. Yet even that did not fully address the making of the masks. their meanings, how they are used, and most importantly, how they are activated alongside costumes in performance. Gregory Price Grieve discusses the complexity of understanding religion in Bhaktapur Nepal. However, his work does not go into performance traditions in detail other than some references to *Navadurga* performance (Grieve 2006, 17). The goal of this paper is to document the complex performance practice of *Bhairab Nach,* and *Navadurga,* how the masks are made and how they are used. In this pursuit, one publication, Alka Hingorani's *Making Faces,* discussing image-based religious practice in the Garhwal region of Himalayan north India is valuable (Hingorani 2012). Much like these case studies, Hingorani shows us how the images of gods—similar to the masks—possess spiritual potency around which the community comes together. This concept of spiritual potency will be valuable throughout this paper and my larger project.

Masked characters are often embodied in theatre practices that are anchored to the community and its religious beliefs, image-based beliefs, and routines of everyday life. Such everyday life is, by extension, connected to religious practice that is multi-sensorial in modality. This type of everyday life activity might include daily prayers and offerings at a home altar. It may also include annual festivities. I refer to this world an 'umbrella of tradition', a concept encompassing the conditions that enable the performance traditions to continue. In the next section, I will explore the contours of this umbrella of tradition. What is important to note is that this umbrella sustains the performance traditions.

When this umbrella of tradition is meticulously anatomized it can be observed that various segments or conditions allow the genres to be practiced and maintained. The different segments are the following: religious anchors; series of rituals; cyclical time; geographical space on the fringe; access to artistic materials; practice through lineage (caste, normative gender, and division of labor); proximity between mask, movement, and music; embodied acquisition; and a triad of efficacy, culture, and entertainment. These segments are interrelated and influence and inform each other. None of these segments are exclusive of each other. As will be discussed below, it is evident that one condition allows for another condition to exist. If imagined as a multicolored umbrella, each section has ombré coloration, such that red flows into blue, blue flows in yellow, with continuation in between. Sometimes considered traditional, sometimes backward, or primitive—together—these conditions allow room for practice.

Religious Anchors

The genres discussed in the larger project, as well as in *Bhairab Nach* and *Navadurga* here have strong religious backgrounds. They are connected to Hindu-Buddhist tantric practice. I will discuss the salient features of this later in the paper and explain how it helps shape the images and masked performances we study here.

Life, sustenance, culture, and community have been centered around this faith for centuries. In Nepal's *Bhairab Nach*, the performances are rooted in a celebration of Goddess Mahakali from Hindu, pre-Hindu, and non-Aryan beliefs and concepts (Koizumi 1983, 8-14).[5] In Nepal, they also merge with Buddhist tantrism to take on a new conceptual and material avatar. Nepal's Kali goddess and Bhairab look different from the Kali and Bhairab rendition of in parts of Indian performance traditions, in terms of materiality and iconography. The performances and visual renditions adhere to the religious roots of the genres. Diversion from the religious roots is not the norm and a negligible part of the genres. In all these cases, the religious belief systems inform the practices and in turn shape the material aspects of the religions.

In these performance genres, everyday life, defined as mundane or secular life, and sacred life, are intermingled. It is impossible to demarcate where secular practices end, and sacred practices begin. This is observable in visual art, theatre and performance, belief systems, and artistic practice. This phenomenon is especially prominent in Hindu practice, but to some extent this is observable in South Asian Buddhism and Jainism and is present to a lesser degree in South Asian Islamic and Christian contexts. As art historian Vidya Dehejia has written, sacred and profane art forms in South Asia are interspersed (Dehejia 2009, xi). This is particularly notable in premodern art. These forms lack a clear delineation. David Mason, who studied devotional Hindu performances, made similar observations. He wrote, "the image in the temple, or in the household shrine, is both an art object and a manifestation of divinity at the same time." And people make "little distinction between religion and art" (Mason 2009, 5).

In my experience, when consumers come to Bhaktapur's Pottery Square in Nepal and purchase masks of the goddesses, they are aware they are purchasing a goddess's representation for their home, whether they place this on their altar or their living room wall as an artistic piece. These buyers, even as tourists, are aware of a potency carried by the image. Along the same lines, when art historian Kajri Jain wrote about the circulation of religious images in the marketplace, she indicated "majority Hindu deities" [with images of other religions] coexist alongside the mundane "all in vivid, saturated colors" in locations as diverse as "elite living rooms, middle class kitchens, urban slums, village huts" and more (Jain 2007, 2-3).[6] Thus the religious imagery and its many inspirations from the religious roots continue to inspire performance and visual art and everyday life, way beyond the formal religious spaces and activities. We will observe this aspect in the different segments of the umbrella of tradition. This coexistence is chaotic, and within that chaos, there is room for community, cohesion, and creativity.

The Sakti[7] goddesses are the primary deities in the region. Through the ritual and festive masked performances and the everyday worship practices, these performance genres concretize a complex and secretive Tantric version of the religious faith that community adheres to. Religious studies scholar David Gordon White traces the origins of tantrism to "Tantra"—a textual pedigree from before the fifth century BCE—the *Asvalayana Srauta Sutra*, a "ritual framework" that "applies to both Hindu and Buddhist texts" (White 2003, 16-17). Put simply, it connects to what is known as "Kaula-Kula" practice, referring to kinship systems rooted in family and bloodline, often transmitted through initiation, and often involving offerings to Yogini goddesses in rituals of sexual symbolism for achieving well-being and occasionally to achieve magical powers (White 2003; Craig 2020).[8] Art historian Vidya Dehejia, who researched tantrism in India, defines yoginis as female counterparts of yogis who had immense potency and worshipped Siva in the fearsome aspect of Bhairava.[9] These goddesses belong to the Hindu faith on the surface, but the complex Tantric faith crosses beyond, into Buddhism and has a particular local flavor to it. The faith is framed through performances and oral practices in everyday life. Many

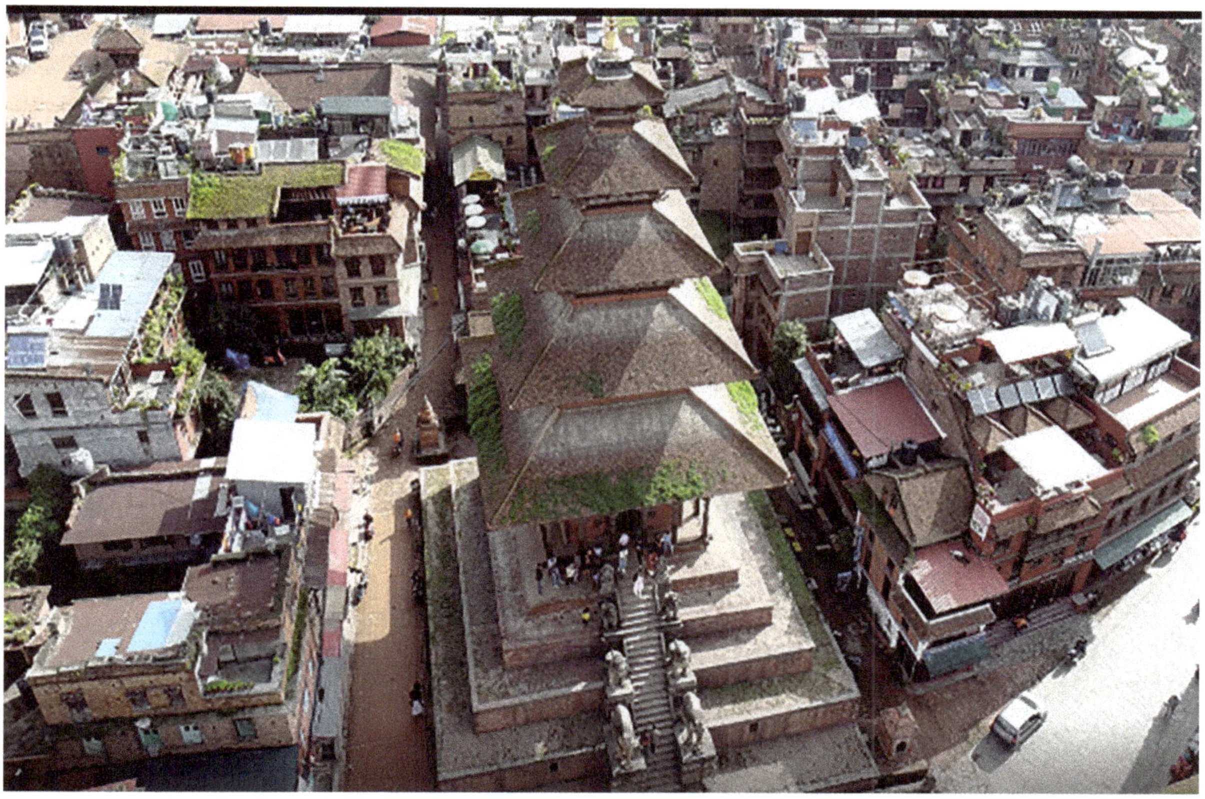

Figure 1: Aerial view of Nyatapola Temple in Bhaktapur. Built around 1701 CE, the temple enshrines a tantric goddess and is open to the public only once a year. It faces Taumadhi Square which includes a community space known as a *dabali* (ritual platform), regularly used for performances such as *Bhairab Nach* and *Navadurga*, as well as other gatherings. Directly opposite stands the Bhairab Temple, where Lord Bhairab (Shiva) is the presiding deity. Considered a fearsome entity, his image is revealed to the public only once annually. Together, the temples and square are imbued with spiritual potency and remain active sites of devotion. *(Photo by Sammit Acharjee)*

temples dot the region such as the Nytapola temple in Figure 1 above. Goddesses offer spiritual protection and benedictions for the eager devotees. But in the case of Bhaktapur, the temples were built around the city in a circular shape providing a boundary of protection. On one side of the city is the Hanumante river—with a goddess temple on its riverbank marking the area's funeral bank. A snake is carved around the city's boundaries, around the temples to further demarcate the space. Bhaktapur is a UNESCO World heritage site, as part of the Kathmandu valley heritage sites and remains protected.[10] The area was affected by the 2015 earthquake, but a majority of the buildings had been rebuilt by 2022.

While the tantric belief system is present in parts of India as well, the performance genres are unique to the Nepal valley. The tantric faith and performance genres lend themselves to an elaborate mask making practice in the region. As religious studies scholar David Gordon White wrote, tantric practice could never be understood through textual exegesis, and its vibrant practice is often seen as the dominant religion in Nepal, Bhutan, and Tibet. Gordon White argued that tantric practice was both elite and vernacular in South Asia (White 2003, 2). The elite presence is perceptible in Nepal valley in the way tantric sculptures are highly visible in grand temple architecture in the region as seen in Figure 1 (Gutschow and Basukala 2011).[11] The royal kingdoms practiced tantrism and supported the practice. Tantric practice's vernacularity is perceptible through the faith practice of the people even now, whether through daily obeisance at such temples by the local population, buffalo procession or *gai jatra* before Dasain and subsequent sacrifice to the goddesses or through the ritual performances that take place throughout the year. The masked dances are part of this vernacular practice. Yet in the context of greater South Asia now, tantrism is the "occulted face" of the religions of the region, in a subaltern position, one among many within a "multiplicity of practices"(White 2003, 4-7).[12] In most cases these goddesses are seen as village deities in India often including the pacification of female ancestors, ghosts, ghouls, and imps who may be angry and hungry, while they remain the prevalent deities in the Kathmandu region, and have been the "perennial" religion of the region (White 2003, 4-5)

Art historian Vidya Dehejia, who investigated art and architecture of tantric Yogini temples of Odisha in the east of India described how Tantric temples differ from mainstream ones in spatial arrangement and goddess iconography (Dehejia 1986, 6-29). Highly decorated Yogini sculptures are arranged around a central Siva deity in this temple in Odisha, India. Yet, resonating the idea of "occult", as mentioned by David Gordon White, Dehejia shows in Odisha, the sensuous and adorned female bodies could have a head of a horse, a large snake hood, the head of a rabbit with particular potencies of their own. Dehejia wrote how Yogini temples are meant to inspire "a deep sense of awe born of fear" (1986, 8). White reminds of the subaltern nature of tantric practice in India and Nepal. White argues that Vishnu centric practice (as seen in Bhaona and other spiritual practices in India I have written about), practiced by the intelligentsia, aristocracy, and merchant class are considered mainstream because it has overshadowed vernacular tantrism. Through this ethnography, I trace a material rendering of the tantric practice, but as will be evident, not all aspects are revealed to outsiders.

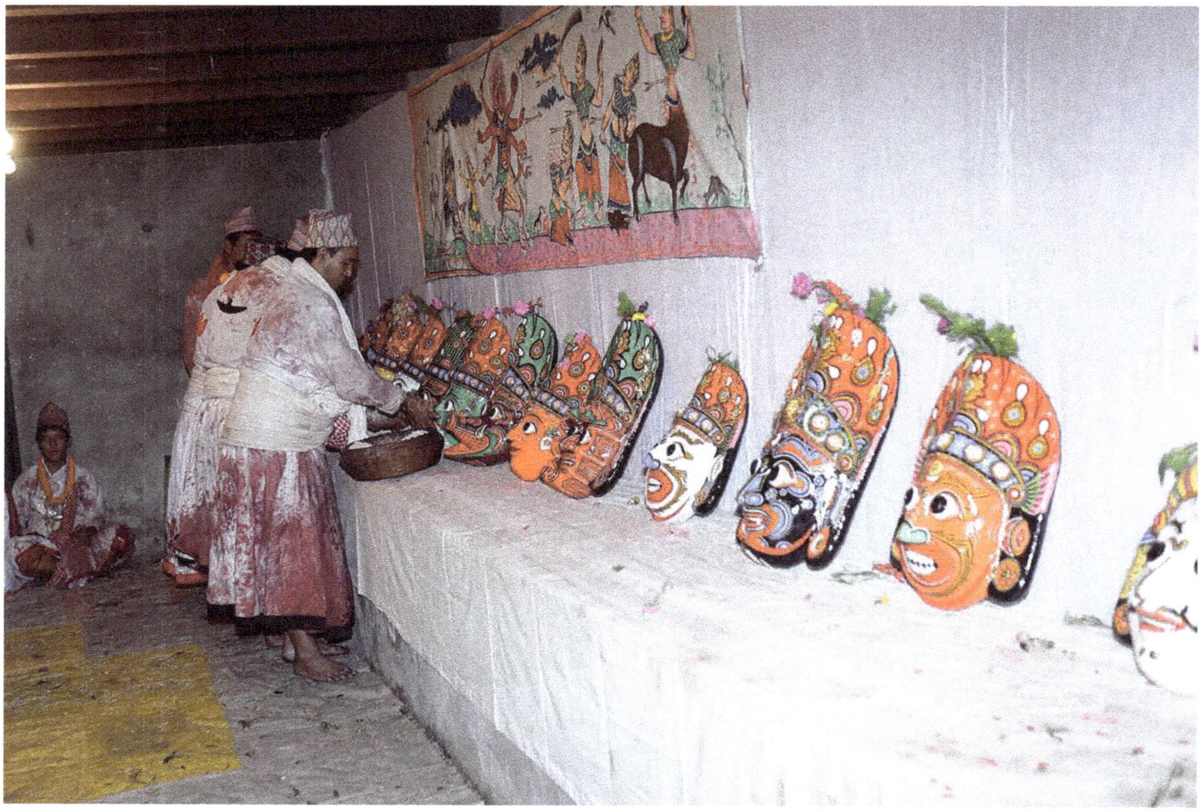

Figure 2: Offerings made to the Navadurga masks—potent religious figures—during the Dasain festival in September–October (autumn), at the home of Purna Chitrakar. *(Photo by Arbindra Prajapati.)*

Series of Rituals, Big and Small

Within these religious practices, there is a series of ritual performances. These ritual practices are both simple everyday practices at homes and temples, as well as significant festivals for large numbers of people. The performances studied here are part of these rituals, performed regularly either in small ways or for larger festivities. In the genres of masked performances, the performances are often rituals themselves. Such rituals are practiced and performed for their efficacious value for the communities that support them. Through artistic practice and performance, an aura of auspiciousness is created for the community through a public offering or gifting process.[13] These rituals are enacted daily, biweekly, seasonally, or annually. Rituals in South Asia are based on a variety of calendar cycles—lunar, solar, seasonal-agrarian, or annual. In some instances, they may be based on the secular Gregorian calendar as well. Most often, the masked performances in Nepal, with large programs and many masks with detailed designs, are part of large annual festivals such as Indra Jatra and Dasain. Yet these large festivals are supported by smaller festivities throughout the year. The smaller festivities may not have masked characters. Yet one festival is interrelated to another, even though they may not be celebrating the same occasion. They reinforce each other. Daily and seasonal prayers and offerings at goddess temples on the perimeter of Bhaktapur are one such everyday activity. The daily, smaller activities inculcate a way of thinking, doing, and performing. The devotee-performer understands that daily ritual performance is essential for sustaining and disseminating the auspicious aura that emanates from the sacred deity and temple space. This understanding is shared by local spectators, pilgrims, and visitors alike. These daily, ritualized performances are believed to be necessary and are conducted for their efficacy and auspiciousness for the community. On the complementary end, receiving and observing these performances becomes second nature for the community members—even when they are not visiting a temple or praying every day. It also defines a way of doing because a devotee-performer with this task of a regular performance has to commit themselves to this irrespective of audience or devotee presence.[14] Most often responsibilities are held by male-identifying members of the community. They have to perform whether there is an audience, another devotee, or a large group present, or no one at all. Each of these practitioners is committed to this "mini" performance irrespective of how he feels on a particular day, thereby making it *his* second nature. Likewise, it requires a method of repeated performances (what we might call warm-up activities or rehearsals in modern theatre) under low-stakes conditions that the devotee-performer must commit to. All together, these mini performances saturate the place and the people such that the annual masked performances, as seen during Dasain, are like condensed, deep, and materially significant versions of these smaller, dispersed performances everyone is used to. Thus, the ongoing rituals ensconce repeatable practices through the festival cycles that occur at predictable intervals. They outlast a bracketed time frame of a day, month, or year to continue into the foreseeable future.

Rituals have to be predictable. In a study of rituals, Claire Sponsler, an American scholar investigating Catholic rituals in Europe, the United States, and the Global South by building on seminal scholars such as Schechner, Turner, and others provided such a definition (Sponsler 2004; Schechner 2011; Turner 1982). This definition is applicable to these heterogeneous ritual performances. In *Ritual Imports: Performing Medieval Drama in America*, Sponsler stated how rituals are "seasonal; not occasional; they are repeated on a regular, usually annual, basis; they are tied, often in an unarticulated way, to the belief systems and deepest values of their communities; and they survive in unwritten forms, passed on from performer to performer through practices, not documents" (Sponsler 2004, 8). While ritual theorists such as Catherine Bell, Christiane Brosius and Ute Hüsken, and aforementioned Sponsler have studied this pattern in rituals in the context of religious, as well as non-religious activities, it is the repetition that becomes a powerful tool in ritual and in these case studies (Bell 1992; Brosius and Hüsken 2010). The length of the activity is not as much of concern, but it is its predictability that is reiterative and restorative for the community it serves. In *Between Theater and Anthropology*, Richard Schechner described the term "restoration of behavior," which is applicable in this context. Under a very broad rubric, restored behavior includes dance, theatre, social dramas, rites, and many more, where such behavior is "expected" and is "'twice-behaved behavior'" (Schechner 2011, 35-36). Such predictability allows for the performance traditions to continue in South Asia.

As we see in Figure 2, offerings to *Navadurga* masks are made annually in this way. Alongside the process of making the masks, and the ritual annual sacrifice of the masks is part of the whole experience. The community members look forward to this rhythm.

Cyclical Time

The ritual practices establish a connection to a cyclical concept of time in these genres. Through daily, biweekly, biannual, or lunar/solar/agriculture/nature–based calendars, performances are repeated. And through such repetition, a relationship to past, present, and future is established. This concept also relates to Hindu-Buddhist concept of time through birth, death, and rebirth. A little child in a family may see regular performances in a nearby temple or in the community right from infancy. This young person may hear of such activities from the elders of the family—grandparents, parents, or uncles and aunts and see such performances in their childhood. The child then develops a sense of the past that is threaded through the memories of his immediate elders. These elders in turn remember and through their memory create a sense of a foregone past when such performances were practiced. In the present, the child observes the immediate family, parents, and grandparents maintaining the genres of performance. And through this, the child projects, or the elders project, a future where the child must carry on the practices. Thus, a sense of the past is threaded through memory and ancestors, an idea of the present is established through embodied experience, and a future is projected that has not yet arrived but promises and/or demands a familiar repetition.

Children from the Prajapati community learn to dance and play the instruments consisting of drums, gongs and windpipes from an early age (Koizumi 1983, 11, 47-48). If they have an inclination, they go deeper into the learning. Once the children learn the steps, they are assigned ancillary roles—such as kawaan (goblin), bhocha (ghost), or betaal (demon)—in the performances. As they grow up and learn the steps of the principal characters, they are able to take on the principal roles.

On the surface this may seem like a heavy burden to bear for a young child. However, through the growing years the child experiences different iterations of the performances and develops an embodied familiarity.[15] Whether or not the child carries on the activities or passes the responsibility to another, the community, through elders, youngsters, and neighbors, all play a part in this familiarization process that helps to sustain the tradition into the future. In turn, they also project a concept of time that is different from the modern city-based calendar. Similar to Sponsler's aforementioned repetition, this phenomenon can be understood as Schechner's restored behavior, where the child expects the ritual to continue, much like with the ancestors, and who in the future may play a part in the process. This contribution may be through the re-creation of the ritual with close-enough authenticity or with funds or other resources for the community. Irrespective of the way in which the ritual continues, there is an expectation of the aforementioned twice-behaved behavior that ensures continuity from day to day, month to month, or year to year. Most often predictability is something the community

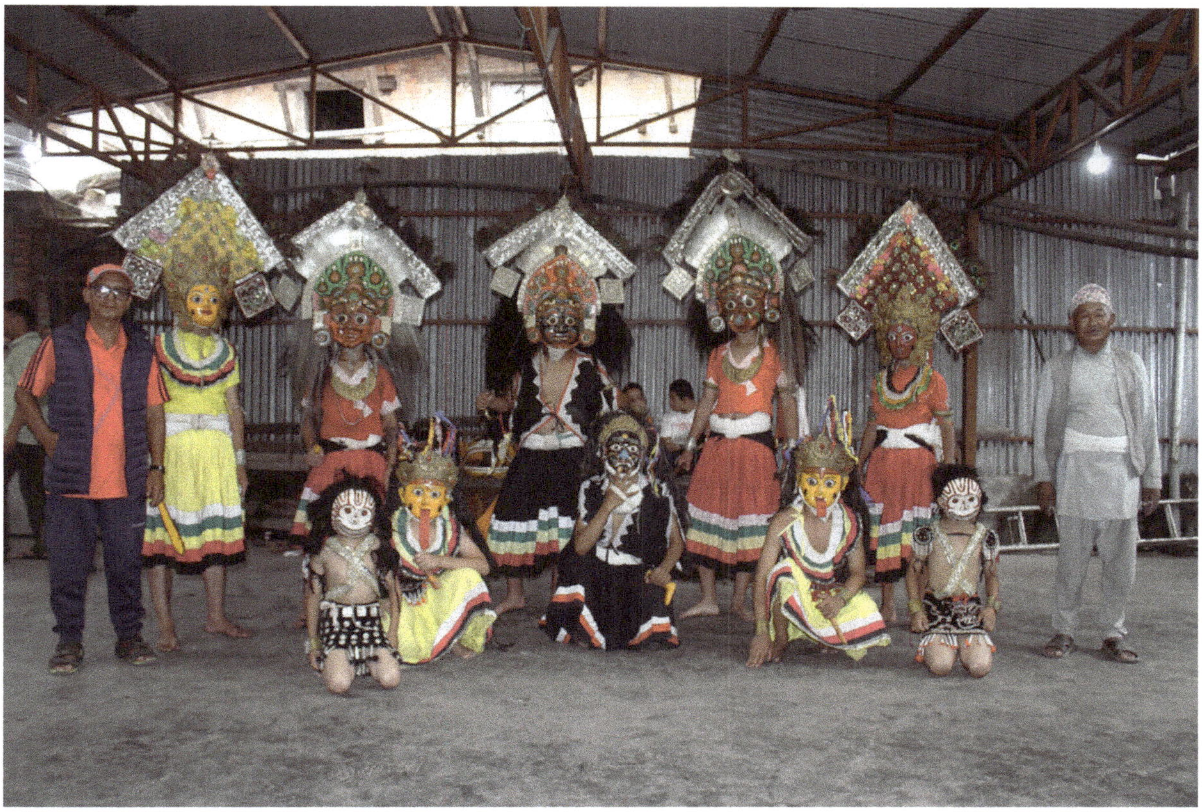

Figure 3: Jetha Ganesh Bhairab Nach Group performing *Bhairab Nach*. Characters identified from left to right. **Back row**: Brahmayani (yellow), Mahayani/Mahakali (red), Bhairab (primary character, black), Barahi (female counterpart of Baraha or boar god, red), Mahalakshmi (red). **Front row:** Kawaan/goblin (child performer), Bhocha, Betal, Bhocha, second Kawaan/goblin (child performer). (*Photo by the author*)

anticipates and enjoys, the local administrations (such as Bhaktapur Nagarpalika or Municipality) organize, governments capitalize on, and artists create for, ensuring flow of funds and festivity.

Bhairab Nach, and the specific roles as gods and goddesses the dancers render include jumps, leaps, synchronized pirouettes, and other vigorous movements while the dancers are in full costume. This means each performer wears the heavy masks, the clothing, some accessories such as necklaces and bracelets, waist bells, ankle bells, and hold hand props while moving. The heavy costume has to work with all these demands on the body. Given the ritual context of these performances, when performing for the religious festivals, the dancers fast to cleanse their body, abstain from sex, avoid certain foods, perform under all types of weather conditions, accompanied by loud drumming, sound of heavy cymbals and gongs, incense smoke—all together creating demanding circumstances. In a few cases, given the demands, some dancers enter a trance-like state. A trance-like state is required in *Lakhe* performances (not part of this research, but part of the 29 aforementioned masked dances of Nepal valley). A trance-like state is *not* required in *Bhairab Nach.* Some artists may enter a trance state in *Navadurga*. If compared, *Navadurga* is more ritually demanding than *Bhairab Nach*. The ritual requires demanding conditions such as all elements of the heavy costume and every musical instrument for accompaniment. Only when all accompaniments are present can the performance achieve its intended efficacy. Yet these conditions sometimes induce a trance-like state because of the physical demands on the body. As tantric scholar Saroj Shrestha explained to me, these conditions are required in order to purify the body, the community, and mother earth with each deity associated with a specific purpose.[16] This is the primary purpose of the performances. He referred to the dance as "making of a temple in the body." Hence most of the performers I met are young, in their teenage years or in their twenties, capable of handling the demanding circumstances. Senior artists such as Lakshmi Sundar Prajapati (on the extreme right in grey in Figure 3), now in his eighties, serves as a guru to the company or Pasupati Prajapati (on the left in Figure 3), now in his fifties, serves as the company manager, but do not perform under such demands themselves. The youth years are when the artists train and learn all the parts. For example, my informant Padmodhar Prajapati, in his 40s living in US, outlined that from his childhood he picked up the assigned role for all the characters of *Bhairab Nach* other than the central ones of Bhairab, and Barahi.

Senior artists ensure the rituals are complete and are compliant to all the expectations of tantric methods. They ascertain that all the masks and costumes are worn as per regulations, and all associated regulations are followed. In some cases, it is necessary to hold back. The seasonal aspect of these performances is also crucial because only at the right timing is the performance valid and efficacious. I had visited Nepal in the summer. This is not considered an efficacious time. As several Prajapatis explained to me, it is considered a "rest period" of the year. There are a series of rituals that take place after monsoons, around late August, starting with Ganesh puja. Following that is a vital ritual called *gai jatra*. This is a procession of water buffalos. Based on tantric practice, these animals are sacrificed for the goddesses the following day. Subsequently the season of Dasain begins. Dasain is the same as Dussehra festival dedicated to the goddess in India. Dasain can also be repeated in spring (around April) when a smaller festivity takes place. Several masked dances take place during this season. The late fall into winter months are considered potent for goddess worship and associated masked performances. After this period a ritual called *jal samadhi*, or burial in water takes place. There are many ritual elements that are then figuratively buried. The ritual masks of *Navadurga* the Chitrakars make once a year are also placed in *samadhi* and thereby destroyed. Subsequently the period of rest begins, where potency is withdrawn and no masked performances can take place. I had requested a performance during this time. Some of the younger people in the group told me it was possible. However, when Lakshmi Sundar Prajapati was informed, he advised against a full performance. He believed it was important to preserve the ritual efficacy of the performance. Thus, the performance I had commissioned did not include some of the ritual gongs that are part of the festival. While I got to experience the material elements of the performance including masks and costumes, by omitting one musical component, the elders ensured that it did not constitute a full performance during an inauspicious time. While there are some, particularly the younger members, who were motivated by the compensation I offered, the seniors made sure no essential ritual rule was violated.

Similar to the Prajapatis, the Chitrakars shoulder the responsibility of all religious imagery in Bhaktapur. Their artistic work beyond mask making includes painting temple portals and divine imagery inside and outside temples, all types of seasonal ritual imagery for use in household altars, Hindu-Buddhist style landscape paintings called *thanka*, and other similar objects. For most of these purposes, printed imagery does not suffice, and the Chitrakar involvement with handmade objects is necessary.

Geographical Space on the Fringe

Masked performances are often practiced outside big cities, urban centers, areas beyond the onslaught of modernity. Bhaktapur, 12 km outside main Kathmandu is suburban to the city. The primary reason the different segments of the aforementioned umbrella of tradition are maintained is because of geographical locations. Bhaktapur is a heritage city that is on the outskirts of the capital. This location (much like others I have observed in India), by being away from the direct onslaught of modernity, play a role in keeping alive some of the conditions under which the ritual performances are continued. It does not mean things are always pastorally romantic for these areas. Issues of poor infrastructure, such as water, power, roadways, and reduced access to education and healthcare, are a given (in all the case studies I have researched)—yet the locals have an interest in continuing the arts, especially the ritual arts. This is done by maintaining traditional communities of performers and audiences and by allocating access to performance space and having artistic materials easily accessible. Their geographical locations are a unique reason why these artistic and theatrical roots developed and continue to be practiced. Unlike other modernized-traditional societies, such as Japan, till now the people of the areas discussed here, have been able to maintain these practices. We see this in Bhaktapur in the goddess temples that surround the town (Birkenholtz 2018).[17] To some extent, the community holds on to the traditions *because* they see these ritual arts and associated performance traditions are ways of pivoting towards modernity, by harnessing travel and tourism. Performers can receive visibility, income through tourism, awards (in India and Indonesia) that they cannot achieve through traditional sustenance activities, such as agriculture and traditional occupations. Thus, the communities and the artists enjoy their locations and the associated visibility from these locations.

The artists create and display their work in public spaces such as temple squares and town squares. The potters, for example, have workshops and retail spaces beside the Jetha Ganesh temple. People walk and drive past them. Similarly, the dance performances take place here. The artists create their work in visible areas. Given that most of these spaces are religious or semi-religious in spirit, outsiders have long been welcomed.[18] Further, this kind of space also invites observers, neighbors, visitors, or audience without creating a sense of intrusion. Such a space is visible in Figure 2, where devotees can come and make offerings to the masks in an open patio in the mask maker's home. These spaces are usually somewhat separated from domestic spaces, such as bedrooms, kitchens, or bathrooms, but are within walking distance. While for an art community this type of a spatial arrangement may seem strategic or promotional, within the folk-arts genres, this is common. Folk artists are typically not ones who commute to work hours away but rather work in spaces close to home. It allows an openness. We will see this further down in the discussion of Bhaktapur's Pottery Square. Through this setup, students who do not belong to the immediate family but those who are in close proximity also get a chance at observation, and if interested, even a chance at experiencing, participating in, and creating the art forms. While interested outsiders were allowed no or limited access in earlier decades, the current conditions have opened possibilities for immersion.

Access to Artistic Materials

As a study of design, materiality, and fabrication processes, part of this research is aimed at understanding artists and their relationship to their artistic materials. Hence, my fieldwork began in workshops, ateliers, or makers' spaces. Upon entering these spaces, it is easy to spot materials strewn around, half-used materials, raw materials with which the artists create, open jars of trim and notions, or partly used paint jars and brushes. One can see how artists work with their materials—how they build, mold, weave, shape and construct their finished objects. Observing artists actively working in such spaces, one can glean a lot of information about their working process. The designer-makers work in family spaces in which they have grown up and so to which they have a long-established relationship. These spaces are also where the artists build up a familiarity with the materials. Whether these artists use clay, bamboo, wood, straw, jute, or softly worn cotton, they all have had access to these types of materials from their childhood. During fieldwork, I have observed children as young as four and five playing with these materials, as their fathers, uncles, or cousins make more "formal" or "finished" objects. Eventually as they grow up, this familiarity allows them to approach the materials without fear or distance, helping them get drawn into or develop a closeness with the process of making. Having acquired basic skills associated with the art early in life, they grow to develop more advanced skills and an eye for both artistic process and final product. This proximity and familiarity allows them to develop into chief or lead artists if they have such an inclination.

Alongside the issue of familiarity is the issue of access to materials for the artists. This access establishes the sense of materiality in these genres. Children in Pottery Square for example, as seen in Figure 3, have access to clay, a potter's wheel, and shaping tools from an early age. They grow up surrounded by these materials. The raw materials that are used to shape masks, puppets, and other performing objects are all locally sourced. The performing objects in *Bhairab Nach* of Nepal are made of clay, cotton fiber, hand-made paper, buffalo fat, flour-based glue, and then painted. In India's different masked genres clay, bamboo, wood, cow dung, straw, jute, pliable wire, homemade flour-based glue and softly worn cotton are used. In Indonesia masks are made from pule wood, with ornamentation in fabric and leather are attached. Additionally, there are paints, brushes, cloth, trims, needles and thread, and other tools. The materials vary slightly from place to place and between the genres. However, what is notable is that the artists primarily use inexpensive, local, and naturally sourced materials. During fieldwork, I often entered workspaces that had such raw materials strewn around in haphazard and messy ways yet were at arm's length for the artists. If I asked artists about this proximity, they were caught off guard because access to materials was not something they ponder about. Such immediate access observed in these genres allows the artists to be physically very close to their materials and build easily. Occasionally they *do* bring in larger quantities through more complex procurement systems. For example, Purna Chitrakar shared how his bright blue paint pigment is acquired from a manufacturer in the UK. However, for artistic work that they engage in on an ongoing basis, their path to their resources is short. This accessibility helps build a proximity to the art form, the materials, and the ability for creativity. As performance scholar Arnab Banerji has illustrated in his research of urban theatre in India, and as I have also noted in my experience, access to materials have an impact on the ultimate creative outcome (Banerji 2020). I would like to assert that such easy access has a very positive outcome on creativity in the genres and in the integration of the materials into the performance.

Practice through Lineage and Embodied Acquisition

As discussed in the section on cyclical time, these genres are maintained through lineages, following what is known in South Asia as the *guru-shishya* model of training. In Nepal, the aforementioned *guthi* system is one such institution for intergenerational knowledge transfer. This has been examined in early cultural policy documents (Amatya 1983), described in official institutional sources (Guthisansthan), and framed as intangible heritage by scholars such as David Gellner (2019). Most often these lineages are family-based, where young children learn from their parents and grandparents. On occasion, these teachers are neighbors or distantly related family. In some instances, students may train as apprentices, even if they are not biological relatives. Resembling the guild models of medieval Europe, lineage-based practice fosters a very strong relationship to materials, belief systems, and maintenance of traditions. Senior teachers instruct young children and junior learners. The juniors then grow up and play a part in maintaining the tradition and teaching new generations.

Such lineage-based systems are not simply linear, passing from father to son. They

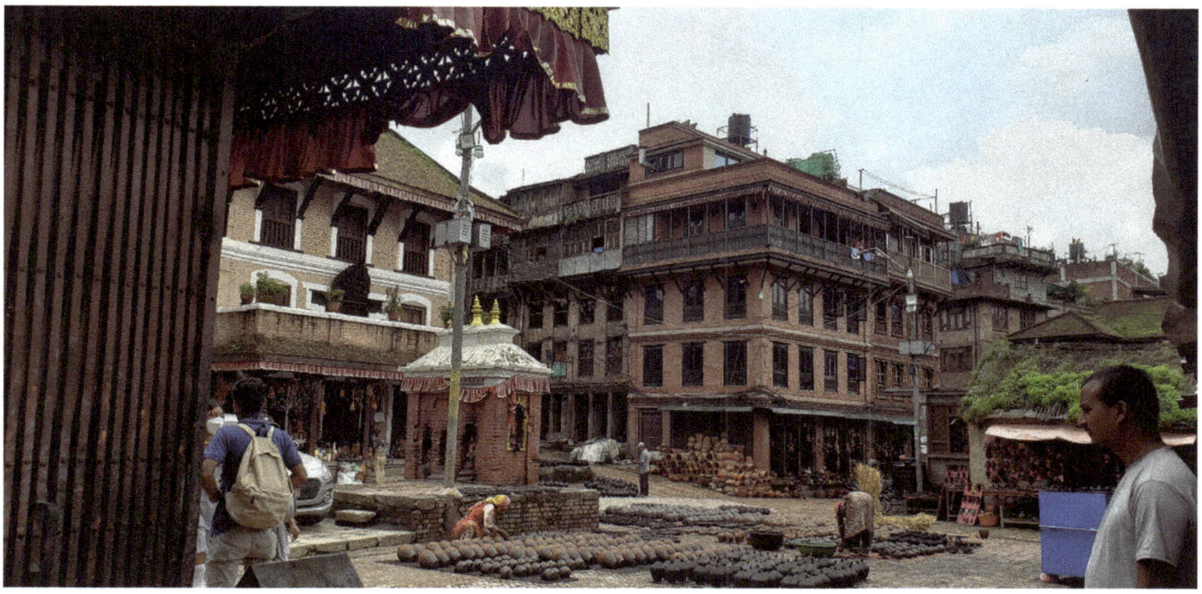

Figure 4: Pottery Square in Bhaktapur. This area is home to many pottery families belonging to the Prajapati community. Traditionally, potters by profession, they are organized into *guthi* (ritual guilds) and continue this work for their livelihood. While some members have moved away for education or employment, many remain engaged in pottery and ritual performance. Community members also participate in *Bhairab Nach*, offering ritual performances for the well-being of the community. *(Photo by the author)*

can be open ended. One can visualize them as rhizomatic systems where the community operates as a network. There is a wraparound effect within which a child from the locality or family learns. Such a child never forgets the system. Children are permitted low stakes learning through mimicry, playing with materials/movements, and developing a taste for the genre. And once they develop this interest, through a system of familiarity, they go on to participate in the genre with inclination and ease.[19] Many of my interviewees have suggested that even though they have moved away from these locations for many years because of work or school, they still have a fondness for and an embodied memory of the genres. One US-based interviewee, Padmodar Prajapati, who grew up in Bhaktapur, Nepal, and learned and performed *Bhairab* dance in his childhood narrated this. Even now, many years later, if he hears that particular set of percussion beats, his heart and body want to dance immediately. Thus, the cocooning effect within the community and muscle memory helps build an intimacy with the genres. I have noticed that the gurus or teachers of local forms of performance are all from a nearby region, district, or locality and/or have family/training-based lineages from the region. Living through and practicing such lineage-based genres comes with significant baggage, such as expectations, tradition-bound lifestyles, and other challenges. There may also be reasons for such exclusivity.

David Mason, in his observation of ritual performances in India, also notes this embodied form of experience. Mason has written about folk-ritual performances in northern India, around Vrindavan. There, devotional performances centered on Lord Krishna are an important part of everyday life. Mason discusses witnessing devotion-based theatre and how the audience is trained in viewing it from childhood—in other words, both the performer and audience have been trained in performing from childhood (2009). The performer learns to enact roles such as Krishna, Radha, or Krishna's kin and devotees. The audience simultaneously learns to take in such performances, react in an expected manner to the performances, make

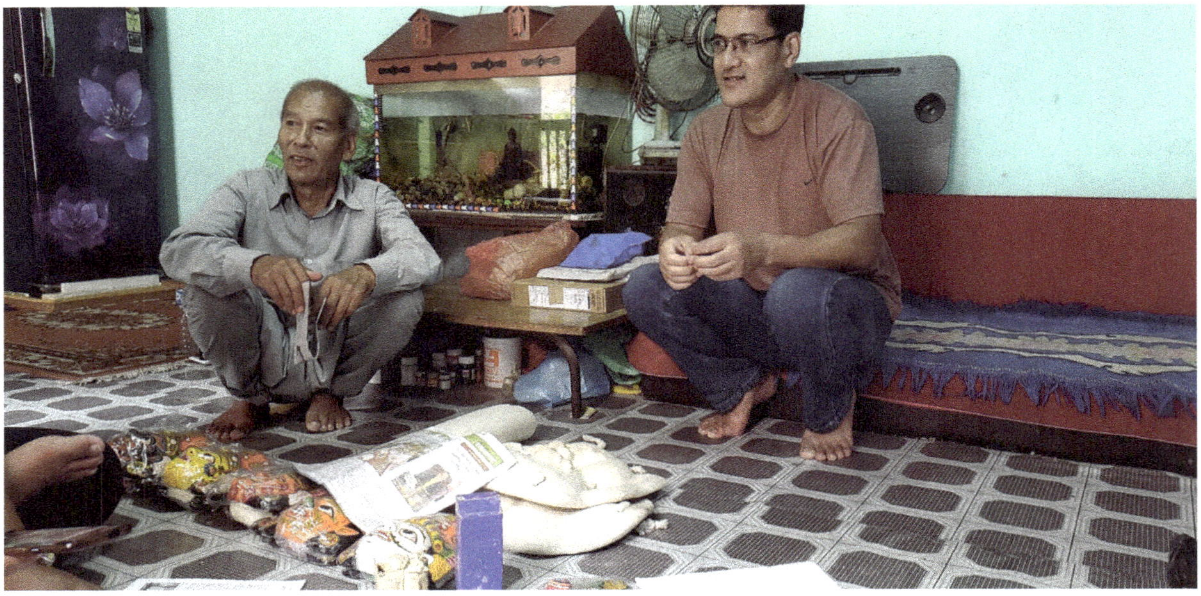

Figure 5: Expert mask makers from Bhaktapur, Purna Chitrakar and his son Rajesh Chitrakar. They belong to the Chitrakar *guthi*, a lineage assigned ritual artist duties. Members of this *guthi* are responsible for producing various forms of decorative art used in ritual contexts. *(Photo by the author)*

expected offerings to the performers, and participate in the devotional experience. Mason compares these performances with Stanislavskian actor-training systems. He notes how the actors are aware they are actors but at the same time are absorbed into and become part of the elevated storytelling. The audience, too, through their embodied-reception experience receives these performances differently than those in formal theatres. In my observation, this is true for the local artists and audiences who are steeped into this tradition from their childhood. While they are exposed to other performances, such as TV, film, and even social-media entertainment, they place the ritual performances on a pedestal. This elevated understanding of the performances is also true for members of the community who have moved away from the region but attach the same value to the ritual performances such as my informants Arbindra Prajapati and Padmodhar Prajapati. And to some extent this sweeps over tourists who come to the area, even if they have not grown up seeing such performances, because they experience it wrapped within a temple and cultural atmosphere that is difficult, if not impossible, to subtract from such events.

Caste, Normative Gender, and Division of Labor

In the various segments of the umbrella of tradition mentioned till now, I have written about how the roots, the rural, the folk, and the preindustrial environment is maintained through community. Yet one of the byproducts of such a wraparound community is that it is maintained through lines of stratification. Such lines of stratification are visible in caste-based and normative gender–based forms of tradition. Such stratification is created through communal classifications and hierarchies. They allow for a division of labor that in turn allows the traditions to continue. Such divisions can easily be perceived as systemic problems. As might be apparent by now, these genres and many others in South Asia perpetuate caste-based training systems. Various subgenres of Nepal's *Bhairab Nach* is the ritual responsibility of *guthis*, or houses/clans from the community in Nepal. Given the system of intergenerational training, *guthi*- or caste-defined training allows artists to specialize in their art form. Yet, much like the disapproval or non-absorption of outsider gurus or teachers, closed caste-based systems of practice can be unyielding.

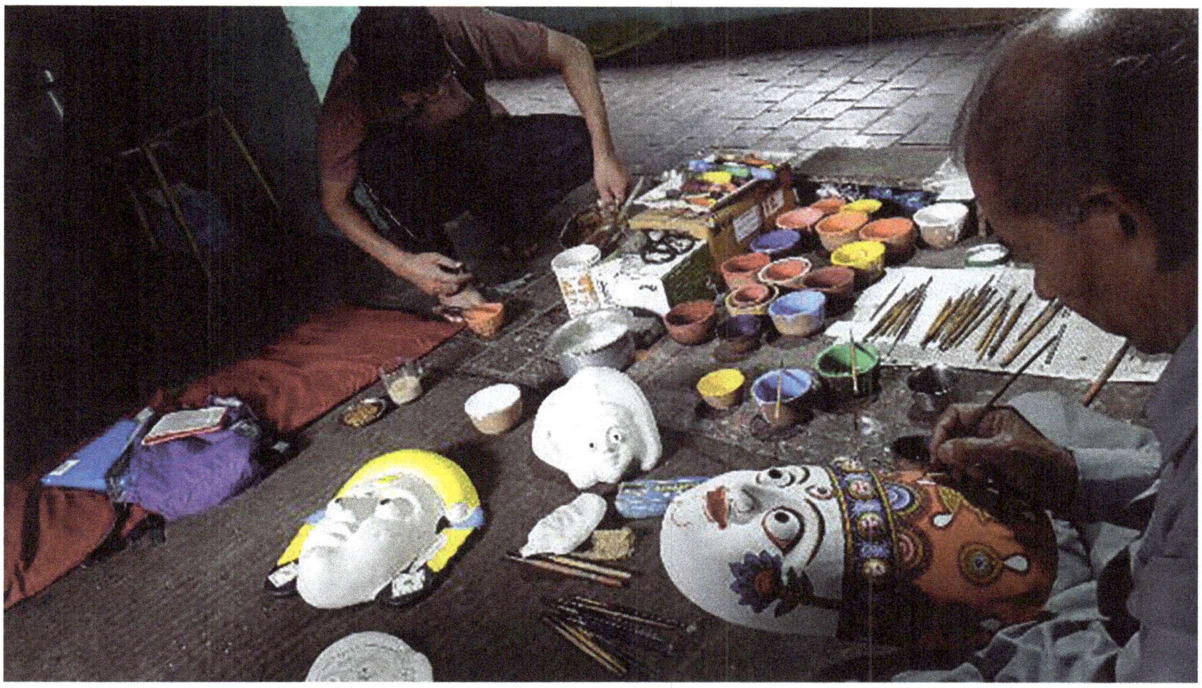

Figure 6: Goddess masks in progress, constructed by Purna Chitrakar and Rajesh Chitrakar. A smaller, unpainted decorative mask—non-ritual in use—is visible at the center. ***(Photo by the author)***

Within these genres, there is a clear delineation between heteronormative male and female roles. Primarily it is the male members of the community who carry the traditions on, and female members remain less visible in public life. They take care of maintaining home and hearth. On occasion, I have seen women participate in the practices, but they are relegated to a secondary position. However, women are present as audience members in all the genres I have studied. While this could be seen as a negative aspect of these traditions, women by maintaining the boundaries of the tradition also help the male members practice, maintain, and specialize in the ritual performances. Mask makers in all the genres I have studied in India, Nepal, and Indonesia are primarily male members. Women do get involved in the costume-making (flexible textile-based parts of the costume) process. Through a gendered division of labor and resulting methods of gaining visibility, the genres maintain continuity. Yet through such maintenance systems, problematic aspects in the traditions can be perpetuated. Within such systems of maintenance, strong lines of knowledge acquisition, as well as boundaries for such acquisition, are clearly drawn out and are a given. In Nepal's Chitrakar community this may lead to extinction of the art form for their family. Purna Chitrakar has trained his son Rajesh Chitrakar. But when I asked Rajesh's son Sandesh (who in 2022 was in his late teens) he was not interested in continuing the family tradition. The other children are females and will not be allowed to continue. And in *Navadurga* tradition, even though sons-in-laws are male members they are not allowed access to the information. This is because of the purity of bloodlines and kinship ties that need to be maintained. Thus, the performance traditions can at times be insular in the flow of knowledge.

Proximity between Mask, Movement, and Music

Given the close-knit communities within which these performance genres are practiced and maintained, there is a very deep relationship between mask-making practices, movement that uses masks, and music that propels such movement. Often the artists are related to each other or are distant relatives or neighbors. They are never outsiders in these genres in Nepal. This creates an atmosphere where it is easy for the masked dance and music to work in synchronization. A musical artist might practice his songs, drumming, or wind instruments on a regular basis. Similarly, a dancer might practice his steps daily. By being close to each other, they might decide to practice together. While practicing, a dancer may choose to use an easily accessible mask for an informal session. And given their familiarity with practicing their art form in open and inviting spaces, such mingling is possible and encouraged. The community-based system of sharing allows the different areas of the genres to work in tandem. Many times, the artists are trained in two or three different areas. Even though they may not excel in all areas, they have knowledge of the other areas. A mask maker may have been a dancer at one point in his life, while a singer could also be a drummer and a mask maker. Through such systems of borrowing, and sharing, ritual mask performances continue in their original locations. It is important to note that the learning process through such immersion is not that of a commercialized give-and-take system but rather is subtler. There is devotional, as well as artistic respect that ties these artists back to the origins. Another clear benefit of such a system is for the young learners. This system also allows youngsters the possibility to observe and experience embodied acquisition. A child can experience all three aspects—music, movement, and mask-making—and decide to specialize in one. Often young children are recruited to perform roles of child characters, and they pick up the character-specific details through observation and practice. Thus, children and new participants do not have the pressure to conform to only one area very early in their learning process. They have the flexibility to dabble in different areas, apprenticing in them, building interdisciplinary knowledge before committing themselves to one.

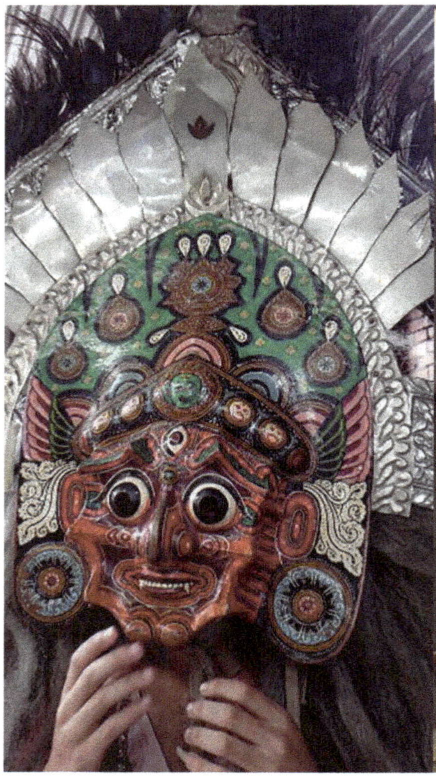

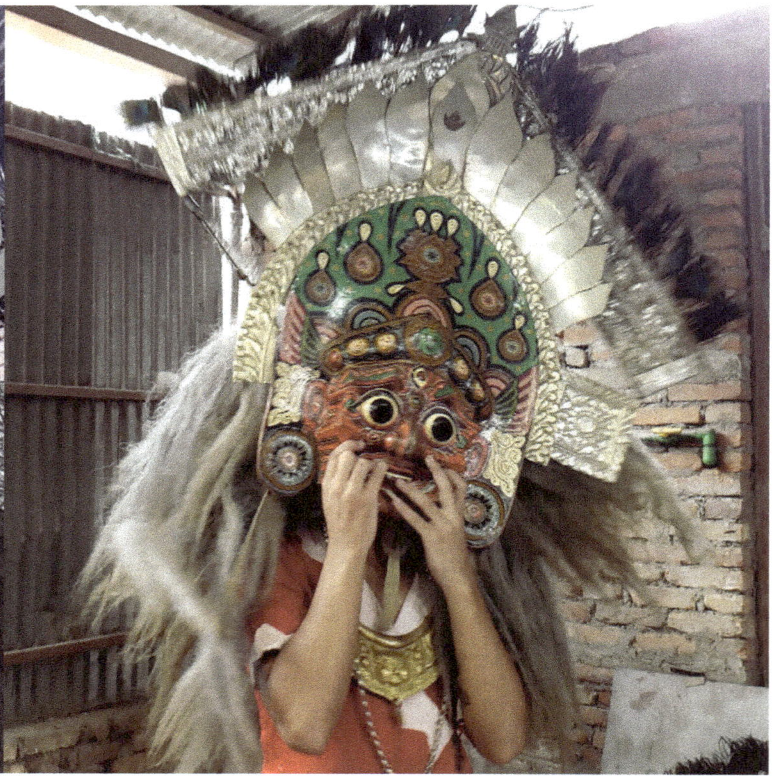

Figures 7 and 8: A finished *Bhairab Nach* Mahakali character mask in use. The performer is seen moving his neck to assess the fit and mobility of the mask before the performance. Dancers perform barefoot, occasionally wearing ankle bells for rhythmic accompaniment. *(Photo by the author)*

Triad of Efficacy, Entertainment, and Culture

These genres of performance operate on multiple valences. When performed during ritual cycles such as Dasain they provide opportunities for community engagement. They also serve as ready entertainment. Audience members who choose to attend the performances know of them through word of mouth, through predictable calendar cycles, and on occasion, through advertisements. They know such performances serve greater and/or imperceptible benefits to the locality and people. They also come simply because they are entertained by the exciting material aspects, bright costumes and props, lights, live music, and a community gathering. Even though the community is aware of other competing entertainment sources through TV, film, other media, and social media, actively consuming such entertainment at other times, they are aware that the ritual performances during specific times of the calendar allow a kind of local and social cohesion the other entertainments do not offer. This community cohesion aspect is a surplus to the efficacy of the rituals already discussed. People come together across generations, genders, and insider/outsider lines to simply take part in the activity. Sometimes tourists and urbanites are specifically invited to such performances, even though they are outsiders, and aware of the rich heritage aspect of these performances, join in.

Simultaneous to the issue of efficacy and entertainment runs the realization within the community that these genres are cultural treasures. UNESCO has recognized several masked dance genres of India and Indonesia as Intangible Cultural Heritage.[20] Nepal could pursue the same for Nepal Mandal's *Bhairab Nach* and *Navadurga* traditions. Nepal's performance genres have not been granted such status beyond space assigned as a UNESCO label 'heritage site'. Only the locations, the heritage cities of Bhaktapur, Kathmandu, and Patan in the Kathmandu valley are designated as a World Heritage Centre.[21] This does not mean a seamless, unified attempt at continuity has taken shape, but a general interest in the continuity of the genre has risen, even from resources outside the community provided by other funding agencies. While the way the practice is continued in the community does not change due to this status, it changes the way opportunities come to the artists, how many opportunities come, and the relevance of their life, art, and culture beyond their local confines. The educated and culturally inclined Nepali citizens are interested in investing more in tourism.[22] And tourism brings a lot of opportunities for *Bhairab Nach* artists. My interviewees Arbindra Prajapati and Padmodhar Prajapati both cited opportunities created by hotels and other tourist facing venues. Artists across South Asia and Indonesia are aware of the effect of tourism. Beyond the simplistic issues of livelihood, such status adds more responsibilities on them but they are simultaneously afforded more cultural and economic capital. Artists are constantly attempting to create new stories, new masks, and new costumes. In *Bhairab Nach*, the focus has been on stronger lines of continuity, smaller and portable masks for tourists and reaching larger audiences.

Here, it is worthwhile to ponder on how efficacy is established through masks and costumes in use here. While we discussed the potency of masks as seen in Navadurga displays and performances, as well in *Bhairab Nach* performance, their costumes also further the efficacy. There are several symbolic elements in the costumes that establish efficacy in *Bhairab Nach*. Typically, a dancer's costume includes a surplice style (tied and crossed over) blouse and a gored skirt with a wide circumference. The color of each costume is connected to the character they play. Black is for Bhairab, red for Mahakali, yellow for Brahmayani such that the mask color and the costume matches. The costumes are usually stock items for the troupe. New costumes are made as and when needed. Tantric scholar Saroj Shrestha explained that the four points where a shirt is tied are iconic of the four cardinal directions. The northeast direction is called Ishan,

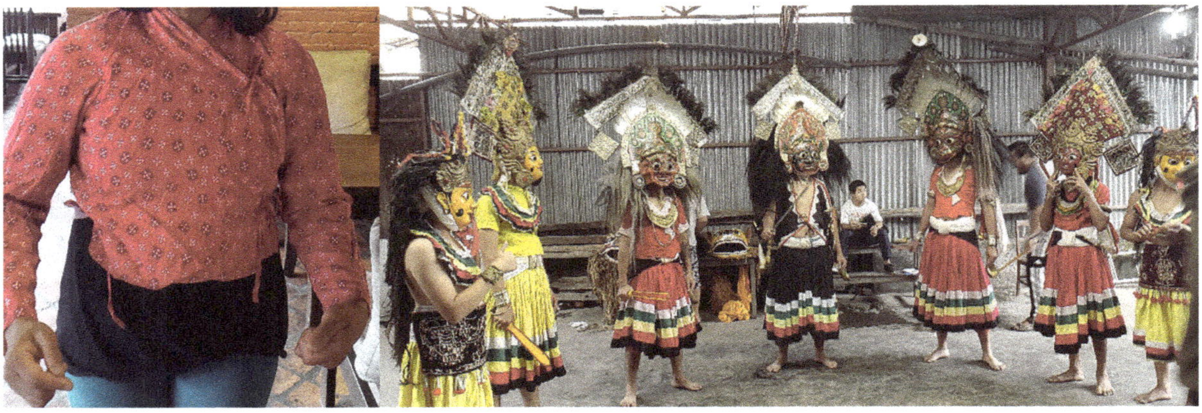

Figures 9 and 10: Performers dressed in surplice-style tied shirts and voluminous circular skirts, elements characteristic of *Bhairab Nach* ritual costume. *(Photos by the author)*

southeast is Agni, northwest is Bayubya and the southwest is Nairitya. If there are two ties (there are some characters with two), it indicates the east and west. The back of the costume includes a swastika symbol, a sign of wellness in the spiritual Tantric system. Even though the ties on the tunic maybe not align with these directions, they are indicative of directions. There was not direct explanation for the skirt style. Skirt colors typically match the blouses. However, what was apparent was that the skirt facilitated movement in its wide, circular structure. Costumes are made by local tailors—many of them women—who have knowledge of clothing construction. These tailors also understand and include the *tantric* meanings in the costumes. I interviewed Ram Pyari Banamala who shared how she sets up a workshop in her home before festival season. Depending on the numbers required she can get help with her sewing. The stitchers are from the community and are practitioners of the faith. For the acquisition of materials either she or members of the troupe purchase the textiles. For costumes, the issue of maintenance of secrecy or codified knowledge is not as important as in the case of masks.

The act of putting on the mask and costume is significant for each performer and the performance. The process of putting on the mask also reinforces the efficacy of the objects---both for the user and for the audience-viewer-devotee. The mask proper, made by the Chitrakar, is quite large, fitting a male face with length about 10-12 inches. The metal plates of the halo are about 6-8” long. The decorative peacock feather trim is 3-4”. The yak hair attached to the back is 24-40” long. When worn, the mask is 14-18” higher than the head, with the yak hair reaching down to the hip level or even to knee level in some characters. The masks are also quite heavy, weighing between 5-12 lbs. Once these items are put on, the mask is activated through vigorous movements and accompanied by loud and significant musical instruments such as gongs and drums (as seen in movement testing in Figure 8 and in the choral movement pattern in Figure 10)

In the most immediate sense, cultural capital from the ritual masked performances comes through tourism. Tourists may come from India, South Asia, and Global North countries or others with access to financial capital. This attention invariably provides income and exhibition opportunities. In addition to tourism, the artists are invited for mainstream performances in urban circuits. While this does not detach the performances from the roots, it affects the way the performances are perceived by tourists in the original locations. More visitors may know of such ritual performances and may assign more value to them. Thus, what was once a strictly efficacious or auspicious performance is now *also* understood as entertainment and a cultural product in the community. Yet there is a fine line. The community, when witnessing

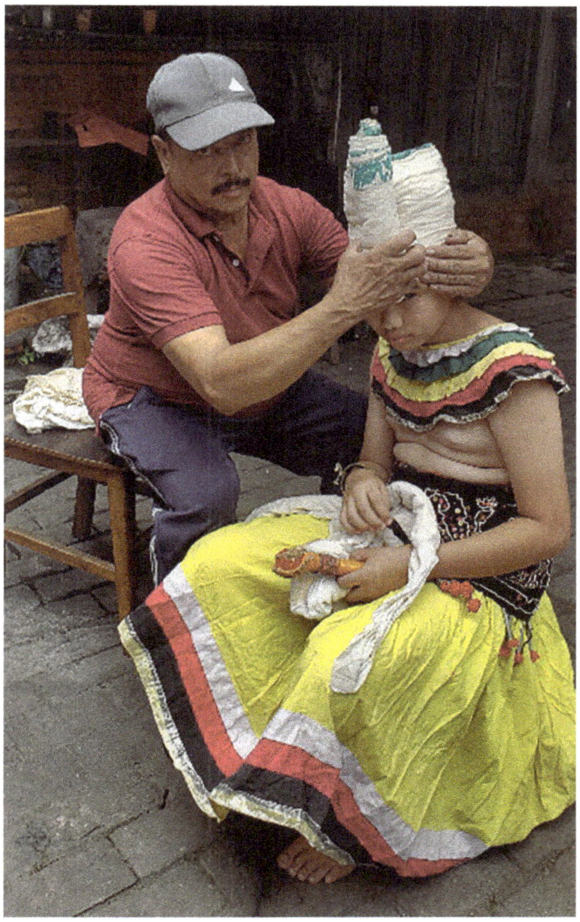

Figure 11: To ensure stability and comfort, performers wrap their heads in cotton padding before donning the mask. A padded chinstrap, tied from the chin to the crown of the head, provides additional support. This setup cushions the head, reducing bruising and allowing for vigorous movement, including jumps and twirls. *(Photo by the author)*

a *Bhairab Nach* performance in Bhaktapur, still regards it as an efficacious piece worthy of respect, yet the same is somewhat diluted if it is done in a hotel or a tourist-oriented space. Thus, the audience and the space/ location play a major role in determining where within the efficacy, entertainment, and culture triad a particular performance is placed.

Through the aforementioned systems, the larger umbrella helps sustain these genres. The artists, audience, immediate community, outsiders, and institutions all play a part in the process of continuity. They also play a role in shaping the performance in the present and in the future. The community or the audience that supports the genres today may slowly withdraw tomorrow, or because of external added attention, the community might double down in its support. In the five genres I have studied across India, Nepal and Indonesia, touched upon here, the community maintains a portion of the support because of the ritual connections. The materials associated with the genres are also one way to assess how well (or not) the genres are supported. Once again, because of the ritual value, the materials have an elevated position. Most of these genres have thriving masked performances because the artists and the community are invested in continuing the ritual forms.

Conclusion

The characteristics of the masks and costume-apparel in *Bhairab Nach* and *Navadurga* both indicate a deep allegiance to tradition. This helps maintain the efficacious nature of the performance. *Navadurga*'s annual image/mask display at the Chitrakar home furthers this belief. The genre might be on the fringe of a greater ecosystem of performances in South Asia, but by anchoring on the idea of tradition, the artists command a significant role in the community through their artistry. The materiality of the performance—whether in the features of the masks and costumes, or the way the material is activated through ritual offerings including ritual dance-contributes to the efficacy. The artists in the community are not deterred by the lack of relative visibility compared to their similar counterpart genres in India or Indonesia. They do not tour extensively or are invited to festivals outside Nepal frequently. Rather, the community backs up the performances and the artistry with support and zeal. This enthusiasm is palpable in how the community comes together on festival events such as Dasain, provide support and offerings to the performance groups and take in their rituals. In a way, the community is the glue holds together the performances and are co-creators with the artists.

Through this detailed process of ritual image-making and image use we see in the work of the Chitrakars and Prajapatis, a world rich in visual religiosity is reaffirmed. This is not a surprise for South Asian traditions. Art historian Kajri Jain, focusing on art practice and consumption in India in her book *Gods in the Bazaar: The Economies of Indian Calendar Art* (2007) describes such a world - steeped in images is self-evident. It is also a world where religion, art, and everyday life co-mingle (Jain 2007, 1-3). Jain's observation is that a plethora of popular art images is visible in the visual world of India that compete for attention (Ibid.). While Jain mostly talks about print images and is focused on India, unlike the focus here on handmade masks, both print and handmade ritual objects compete in the same visual landscape. Jain's observation can be extended to Nepal and the greater South Asian region, also noted for visually rich everyday life. Within such a space, the mask-makers discussed here, compete for as well as command artistic space. They do this by claiming their allegiance to the tradition and the genre in which they are trained. At times, they participate in the world of popular image-making. The Chitrakars make smaller *Navadurga* masks for sale. Some of these are purchased as full sets of masks, but occasionally they are purchased as singles. The Chitrakar's ritual imagery for households and portable masks for sale are such examples of popular items. By carefully pivoting from the rituals, the performances are repackaged for homes or as entertainment at hotels, stores, and tourist-facing spaces. In these settings, the dance or the mask gets detached from its original meaning, but for the artists, the intent remains the same. They repackage the genre knowing these products are appreciated, attracting a set of new devotees/appreciators. They cautiously veer from tradition only to such a degree that they can create popular demand, without disconnecting from the roots. In these instances, it is because of the rich materiality of the masks and costumes that the performances and masks continue to hold their value beyond their ritual and community-supported context. Thus, the artists have made the best use of the conditions, which on the surface may seem limiting, but have been pivoted to make them liberating.

Through this article's emphasis on artists who make one-off art pieces, within this image-laden world of South Asia, it becomes evident that such image-rich ritual worlds rendered through masked performances and decorative masks provide multisensory experiences for the devotee, connoisseur/consumer, and tourist. In *Bhairab Nach* and *Navadurga* the impetus has been on continuity, with mask makers working to sell their art products only occasionally. The community also invests in this continuity of performances. For example, in 2022 when I interviewed artists they had not performed for two years because of the pandemic. They looked forward to performing again and the community members were eager to support or sustain the ritual performances. The artists understand that the locals value these performances and artifacts for their ritual meanings. They also know outsiders and visitors value the objects and experiences as unique and culturally tethered, thereby recasting them as new audiences, consumers, and appreciators. They come to see these images, pray to these images, and consume these images. Some of this happens because of the traditional context of the genres. Yet because of continued artistic relevance, the artists can assert their place within the broader visual, performative, and artistic landscape. Within these genres, religion, art, performance, artistic tradition, and innovation converge. They help create polysensory experiences through movement, music, masks, and costumes for the devotee/audience/consumer. And despite growing popularity, knowing they shoulder the responsibility of continuing the tradition, the artists and community come together to build a rich and fulfilling experience through the performance and its rich visual imagery.

The following individuals generously shared their knowledge and experiences through interviews conducted as part of this research on *Bhairab Nach* between 2016 and 2024:

Padmodhar Prajapati (2016–2024);
Arbindra Prajapati (2020–2024);
Sthaneswar Timalsina (initial consultation, June 2022);
Saroj Shrestha (June 1–30, 2022); Amit Banamala (June 20–30, 2022);
Purna Chitrakar (June 20–30, 2022);
Rajesh Chitrakar (June 20–30, 2022);
Sandesh Chitrakar (June 20–30, 2022);
Lakshmi Sundar Prajapati (June 20–30, 2022);
Pasupati Prajapati (June 20–30, 2022);
Ram Pyari Banamala (June 20–30, 2022);
Nagendra Awal (June 20–30, 2023); Reetu Jyakhwa (June 20–30, 2023);
Prem Sundar Prajapati (June 20–30, 2022);
Kalpana Sintakalan (Kalindi Priya) (2020–2024);
Bimal Timalsina (June 20–30, 2022 and electronic);
Lakshmi Prasad Banamala (June 20–30, 2022).

Endnotes

1. Shubhash Ram Prajapati, The Masked Dances of Nepal Mandal, Madhyapur Art Council and UNESCO, Thimi, 2006; ethnography was conducted in 2022 that included over 50 interviews and 10 days of dance and artistic process observation funded through an University Grant. I have continued the research in a virtual format since then.

2. Bhaktapur is also called Thimi. Thimi is one part of Bhaktapur district.

3. For further study, I took the online course *Victory of the Goddess: Myth, Philosophy, and Ritual*, taught by religious studies scholar Sthaneswar Timalsina and offered by the Vimarsha Foundation. See Vimarsha Foundation, "Courses," accessed October 2, 2022, https://www.vimarshafoundation.org/courses.

4. Davis, Theatre of Nepal, 2-4; Davis suggests how the earliest oral storytellers were the Pyakha performers from the Gopali settlers. They may have come to the region roughly 5000 years back. They continue to perform Jhinhihri/Jhinjhari Pyakhan. The current Indra Jatra festival was established around 10th century CE by Licchavi rulers and continues to be seen in the Lakhe Pykahan now.

5. In consideration of Tantrism, Wedemyer finds its analysis deeply perplexing (Wedemeyer 2013).

6. Jyotindra Jain studying religious Indian art in circulation states the same (Jain 2007).

7. "Sakti" can also be spelled "Shakti" but I am using the spelling seen in other English texts. Similarly, Bhairab is referred to as Bhairava in some texts. Sakti worship is also seen termed as "Kula" or "Kaula" indicating ancestral worship.

8. Kinship in Nepali culture is believed to be through families but also culturally cemented around religion and wrapped around systems of care, community, and connection to land as discussed by Sienna Craig.

9. For more on tantric temples and Yogini iconography, see Vidya Dehejia's *Yogini Cult and Temples: A Tantric Tradition*.

10. UNESCO "World Heritage Convention" https://whc.unesco.org/en/list/121/, accessed 8/7/2023.

11. Gutschow and Basukala remind us of the deep religious connotation of every element of the Newar architecture that is visible in Bhaktapur.

12. Similarly, in Coburn's Devi Mahatmya's foreword, Daniel H.H. Ingalls asserts how the cult of the devi (goddess) occupies a subordinate position in South Asian religious practice. He believes the religiosity around devi enjoyed greater presence in pre-literate cultures and non-Aryan cultures.

13. On auspiciousness see Dehejia, The Body Adorned, 14.

14. Typically, the responsibility is on a male performer. Gender is discussed in detail in another section later.

15. In the unique pandemic years of 2020 and 2021, many children (and adults) also learned that the simpler and individual rituals had to be maintained rather than organizing larger congregational events. Through my interviews I learned that most of the artists looked forward to the post-pandemic life, not just because it promised grander artistic opportunities but also because it would offer a familiar repetition. In some instances, folk-ritual patachitra artists of eastern India created pandemic-centric new works.

16. Saroj Shrestha (tantric scholar), conversation with the author, June 24, 2022. According to local belief, there are ten forms of Bhairav with protective powers: Swet Bhairav (seen in performances), Aakash Bhairav (sky), Kaal Bhairav (time and death), Bagh Bhairav (menacing tiger), Pachali Bhairav (king or farmer), Unmatta Bhairav (guardian of Pashupatinath), Shaant Bhairav (protector of children), Batuk Bhairav (joyous), Kritimukh Bhairav (terrifying visage), and Hayagriva Bhairav (leader, ferocious). See also Online Khabar, "The Guardians of the Valley: 10 Bhairavs of Kathmandu Valley That Keep People Safe," Onlinekhabar (Nepal), September 23, 2024, https://english.onlinekhabar.com/different-forms-of-bhairav-kathmandu.html.

17. Birkenholtz reminds us how these spaces are a product of the locals elevating these spaces such that become significant for the community.

18. Navadurga mask making is an exception to this, in that it some parts of its making process needs to occur in secrecy, following the tenets of tantric practice. However, the masks are placed in full view during ceremonies as seen in Figure 2

19. Every youth interviewee of Bhairab Nach such as students of Lakshmi Sundar Prajapati and Pasupati Prajapati reported that they learned by observing the seniors, and then tried it themselves.

20. "Chhau Dance (India)," UNESCO Intangible Cultural Heritage Lists, https://ich.unesco.org/en/RL/chhau-dance-00337, accessed August 2, 2024; "Three Genres of Traditional Dance in Bali," UNESCO Intangible Cultural Heritage Lists, https://ich.unesco.org/en/RL/three-genres-of-traditional-dance-in-bali-00617, accessed August 2, 2024.

21. "Kathmandu Valley," https://whc.unesco.org/en/list/121/. Accessed August 21, 2023.

22. My interpreter Arbindra Prajapati and his wife both work for Nepal Airlines. He has often shared with me how Nepal Airlines creates targeted ad campaigns that feature traditional genres, such as Bhairab Nach, to gain more tourism-related visibility. My other informant, Padmodhar Prajapati, narrated the opportunities for performing ritual dance they got from hotels in Kathmandu and other tourist-facing organizations.

References

Amatya, Shaphalya. "Somes aspects of Cultural Policy in Nepal" *Studies and Documents on Cultural Policies*, UNESDOC Digital Library, 1983. https://unesdoc.unesco.org/ark:/48223/pf0000054841, accessed 3/14/2023.

Banerji, Arnab. "Performing the City: Theatrical Practices and Urbanism in India." *Contemporary Theatre Review* 30, no. 3 (2020): 366–382. https://doi.org/10.1080/10486801.2020.1770359.

Bell, Catherine M. *Ritual Theory, Ritual Practice*. New York: Oxford University Press, 1992.

Bell, Deborah. *Mask Makers and Their Craft: An Illustrated Worldwide Study*. Jefferson, North Carolina; London, McFarland and Company, 2010.

Birkenholtz, Jessica Vantine,, *Reciting the Goddess: Narratives of Place and the Making of Hinduism in Nepal*. Oxford: Oxford University Press, 2018.

Coburn, Thomas B. *Devi Mahatmya: The Crystallization of the Goddess Tradition.* Delhi: Motilal Banarasidass

Coldiron, Margaret. "Lions, Witches, and Happy Old Men: Some Parallels between

Balinese and Japanese Ritual Masks." *Asian Theatre Journal: ATJ* 22, no. 2 (2005): 227-48.

Coldiron, Margaret. *Trance and Transformation of the Actor in Japanese Noh and Balinese Masked Dance-Drama.* Lewiston, NY: Mellen, 2004.

Cordry, Donald Bush. *Mexican Masks.* Austin: University of Texas Press, 1980.

Craig, Sienna R. *The Ends of Kinship: Connecting Himalayan Lives between Nepal and New York.* Seattle: University of Washington Press, 2020.

Davis, Carol. *Theatre of Nepal and the People Who Make It.* Cambridge: Cambridge University Press, 2019.

Dehejia, Vidya, "Yogini Temples of India: A Tantric Tradition", *Art International,* Volume XXV, New Delhi, (1986), 6-29.

Dehejia, Vidya. *The Body Adorned: Dissolving Boundaries between Sacred and Profane in India's Art.* New York: Columbia University Press, 2009.

Emigh, John. *Masked Performance: The Play of the Self and Other in Ritual and Theatre.* Philadelphia: University of Pennsylvania Press, 1996.

Gellner, David. "The Guthi System Should Be Regarded As Important Intangible Cultural Heritage" *Spotlight Nepal, June 23, 2019,* https://www.spotlightnepal.com/2019/06/23/the-guthi-system-should-be-regarded-as-important-intangible-cultural-heritage-prof-david-gellner/,accessed 8/3/2024.

Grieve, Gregory P. *Retheorizing Religion in Nepal.* London: Palgrave Macmillan, 2006.

Guthisansthan.com, "Welcome to Guthisansthan," *Guthisansthan.* Accessed March 10,2023. https://guthisansthan.org.np/en/

Gutschow, Niels and Bijay Basukala. 2011. *Architecture of the Newars: A History of Building Typologies and Details in Nepal.* Chicago: Serindia Publications

Hingorani, Alka. *Making Faces: Self and Image Creation in a Himalayan Valley.* Honolulu: University of Hawaii Press, 2013.

Hüsken, Ute and Christiane Brosius, eds. *Ritual Matters Dynamic Dimensions in Practice.* London: Routledge, 2010.

Jain, Jyotindra, ed. *India's Popular Culture: Iconic Spaces and Fluid Images.* Mumbai: Marg, 2007.

Jain, Kajri. *Gods in the Bazaar: The Economies of Indian Calendar Art.* Durham: Duke University Press, 2007.

Kapferer, Bruce, and Georges Papigny. *Tovil: Exorcism and Healing Rites.* Colombo, Sri Lanka. Viator Publications. 2005.

Kohn, Richard J. *Lord of the Dance: The Mani Rimdu Festival in Tibet and Nepal.* SUNY Series in Buddhist Studies. Albany: State University of New York Press, 2001.

Koizumi, Fumio. *Dance and Music in South Asian Drama - Chhau, and Yakshagana.* Tokyo: The Japan Foundation, 1983.

Mason, David V. *Theatre and Religion on Krishna's Stage: Performing in Vrindavan.* New York: Palgrave Macmillan, 2009.

Meaden Wendy J. and Michael A Brown. *Theatre Masks Out Side in: Perspectives on Mask History Design Construction and Performance.* London: Routledge, 2023.

Online Khabar, "The guardians of the valley: 10 Bhairavs of Kathmandu valley that keep people safe" Onlinekhabar (Nepal), 9/23/2024, https://english.onlinekhabar.com/different-forms-of-bhairav-kathmandu.html

Prajapati, Shubhash Ram. *The Masked Dances of Nepal Mandal,* Thimi: Madhyapur Art Council and UNESCO, 2006.

Ross, Laurie Margot. *The Encoded Cirebon Mask: Materiality, Flow, and Meaning along Java's Islamic Northwest Coast.* Leiden: Brill, 2016.

Schechner, Richard. *Between Theater and Anthropology.* Philadelphia: University of Pennsylvania Press, 2011, 35-116.

Sponsler, Claire. *Ritual Imports: Performing Medieval Drama in America.* Ithaca: Cornell University Press, 2004.

Turner, Victor W. *From Ritual to Theatre: The Human Seriousness of Play*. New York: Performing Arts Journal Publications, 1982.

UNESCO: "Chhau Dance: India" *Inscribed in 2010 (*5.COM*) on the Representative List of the Intangible Cultural Heritage of Humanity*. 2010. https://ich.unesco.org/en/RL/chhau-dance-00337, Accessed 8/2/2024.

UNESCO "Protecting our Heritage and Fostering Creativity" https://www.unesco.org/en/culture, accessed 2/6/2023

UNESCO "World Heritage Convention: Kathmandu Valley", https://whc.unesco.org/en/list/121/, accessed 8/2/2024.

UNESCO, "Intangible Cultural Heritage" https://ich.unesco.org/en/, accessed 8/2/2024.

UNESCO, "Chau Dance", Nov 5, 2010, https://www.youtube.com/watch?v=u3YLq7CVavc, accessed 9/5/2023.

UNESCO, "Three genres of Traditional Dance in Bali," 2015, https://ich.unesco.org/en/RL/three-genres-of-traditional-dance-in-bali-00617, accessed 8/2/2024.

Vimarsha Foundation, "Victory of the Goddess: Myth, Philosophy, and Ritual: A course on the Devi Mahatmya" taught by religious studies scholar Sthaneswar Timalsina, offered under the banner of Vimarsha Foundation, "Courses" https://www.vimarshafoundation.org/courses, accessed 10/2/2022.

Wedemeyer, Christian K. *Making Sense of Tantric Buddhism: History Semiology and Transgression in the Indian Traditions*. New York: Columbia University Press 2013.

White, David Gordon *Kiss of the Yogini: "Tantric Sex" in Its South Asian Contexts*. Chicago: University of Chicago Press, 2003.

HIMALAYA
The Journal of the Association of Nepal and Himalayan Studies

Research Article

The Difficult Art of Parenting: Social Change and Parent-Child Avoidance in a Painted Account from Nepal

Paola Tiné

The University of Adelaide

DOI: https://doi.org/10.2218/himalaya.2025.10044

Abstract

Conducting fieldwork among middle-class families in Bhaktapur, Nepal in 2018-2019, I found that local parents are concerned with teaching their children the notion of 'moral measure'. At the same time, a strategy of avoidance, rather than open negotiation, is preferred to maintain harmony and preserve kinship networks. Focusing on the case study of Dor Bahadur and his children Sita and Vishnu around a contested birthday celebration, in these visual works in gouache, acrylics, and oil colors, I explore and analyze the role that parent-child interactions play in the making of moral selves among middle-class people in Nepal. Through layers of colors, I convey the sense of the conflictual processes that the protagonists of this story experience, and the concomitant 'opacity of minds' established between their existential perspectives.

Keywords

art, morality, Nepal, parenting

Recommended Citation

Tiné, Paola (2025). The Difficult Art of Parenting: Social Change and Parent-Child Avoidance in a Painted Account from Nepal. *HIMALAYA* 44(1): 29-49.

CC BY NC ND

This work is licensed under a Creative Commons Attribution-Noncommercial-No Derivative Works 4.0 License.

Introduction

On a winter day at sunrise, a man in his 40s named Dor Bahadur Bhakta was jogging in white clothes[1] around the Siddha Pokhari pond, on the outskirts of Bhaktapur's old town. After his run, when the early morning fog had been replaced by the sun, Dor Bahadur generally would go back home to get ready for work. On that day, he was off duty, and he invited me to his house for breakfast. While he was boiling some water in his kitchen, his teenage daughter passed by to grab a snack before going to school. Just before leaving, she casually said:

> Bye dad. Vishnu and I won't be at home for dinner this evening. We will go to the cinema with our friends, and we were also thinking of having a cake later on. You know, it's Vishnu's birthday tomorrow...

'What?', Dor Bahadur snapped out of surprise, 'you know that we are in a mourning period! You cannot throw parties in our house!'. The daughter rolled her eyes with impatience and replied: 'Yes, I know, but we'll go to *paju*'s [maternal uncle] house. I have also bought a present for Vishnu, with my savings, it is our birthday tradition and...'. 'Enough!', he said angrily, 'I don't want to know anything about this present, bye now!'. The girl left the house, Dor Bahadur composed himself and served us tea, commenting:

> You see, I am a modern father, and I treat my children as friends. I believe that since they are about 16, children start to be able to think with their minds and make good and wise points. So we need to listen to them, have mutual understanding, and consider each other's point of view as *pāsā-pāsā*.

When using the term *pāsā-pāsā*, Dor Bahadur performed a gesture that I had seen before when talking to local people in Bhaktapur. He first moved his hand right and then slightly left with the palm facing down, each of the two movements accompanying one of the two repeated words, *'pāsā'* and *'pāsā'*. Repeating a word two times is a common way in Newari to express the resemblance of two things. In the case of this expression, through the repetition of both words and gestures, local people stress the equality of the relationship between parents and children.'...But...', Dor Bahadur continued gravely, 'even if we are like friends, there are things that are unacceptable, such as this'.

The case of Dor Bahadur and his children sums up a recurrent theme that I encountered when researching parent-child relationships in Bhaktapur in 2018-2019 (Tiné 2020, 2021b, 2022a, 2022b, 2022c, 2025a, 2025b), that is to say, an ongoing reflection on the boundaries of acceptability within the sphere of domestic moralities and on the relational dimensions of the making of moral selves. With its recent civil war, a devastating earthquake, the increase in outmigration, and the spread of education and media following a century-long dictatorship, Nepal is the ground of accelerated social change, which can be vividly seen at the household level. I found that local parents recurrently used the notion of being 'advanced' (used in its English form by people of different ages) in opposition to the local term *lajjā* (shame). 'Advanceness' is conceptualised emically as the urge to express and realise one's own desires as an attribute of a 'modern' individual. Through the ideal of 'moral measure', parents attempt to guide their children in the delicate navigation between different goals, duties and desires and projects of the self. Akin to Liechty's (2008) findings among a middle class in Kathmandu, this sense of measure was conceptualized by my informants as a moral and relational principle. Despite these efforts, interviews with parents and young adults also revealed that a strategy of avoidance, rather than open negotiation, is preferred to maintain harmony and preserve kinship networks.

Focusing on the case study of Dor Bahadur and his children Sita and Vishnu around a contested birthday celebration, in these visual works in gouache, acrylics, and oil colors, I explore and analyze the role that parent-child interactions play in the making of moral selves among middle-class people in Nepal. Using the style of abstract expressionism that I have been developing during the last decade (Tiné 2021a, 2021b, 2022c, 2024a) and drawing on my ethnographic findings on social change and relationships in Nepali society (Tiné 2021c, 2024b, 2025a), through layers of colors, I convey the sense of the conflictual processes that the protagonists of this story experience, and the concomitant 'opacity of minds' established between their existential perspectives. The notion of 'opacity of minds', developed by Robbins & Rumsey 2008 (also Feinberg 2011), indicates that effort people employ with various levels of intensity, to mask their real thoughts and feelings. Visually, opacity here is expressed through the technique of layering, which includes different mediums with transparent bases and opaque strokes. In the following 'Gallery of images', I visualize the case study of Dor Bahadur and his children, gradually abstracting into a broader reflection on parent-child relationships in contemporary Nepal.

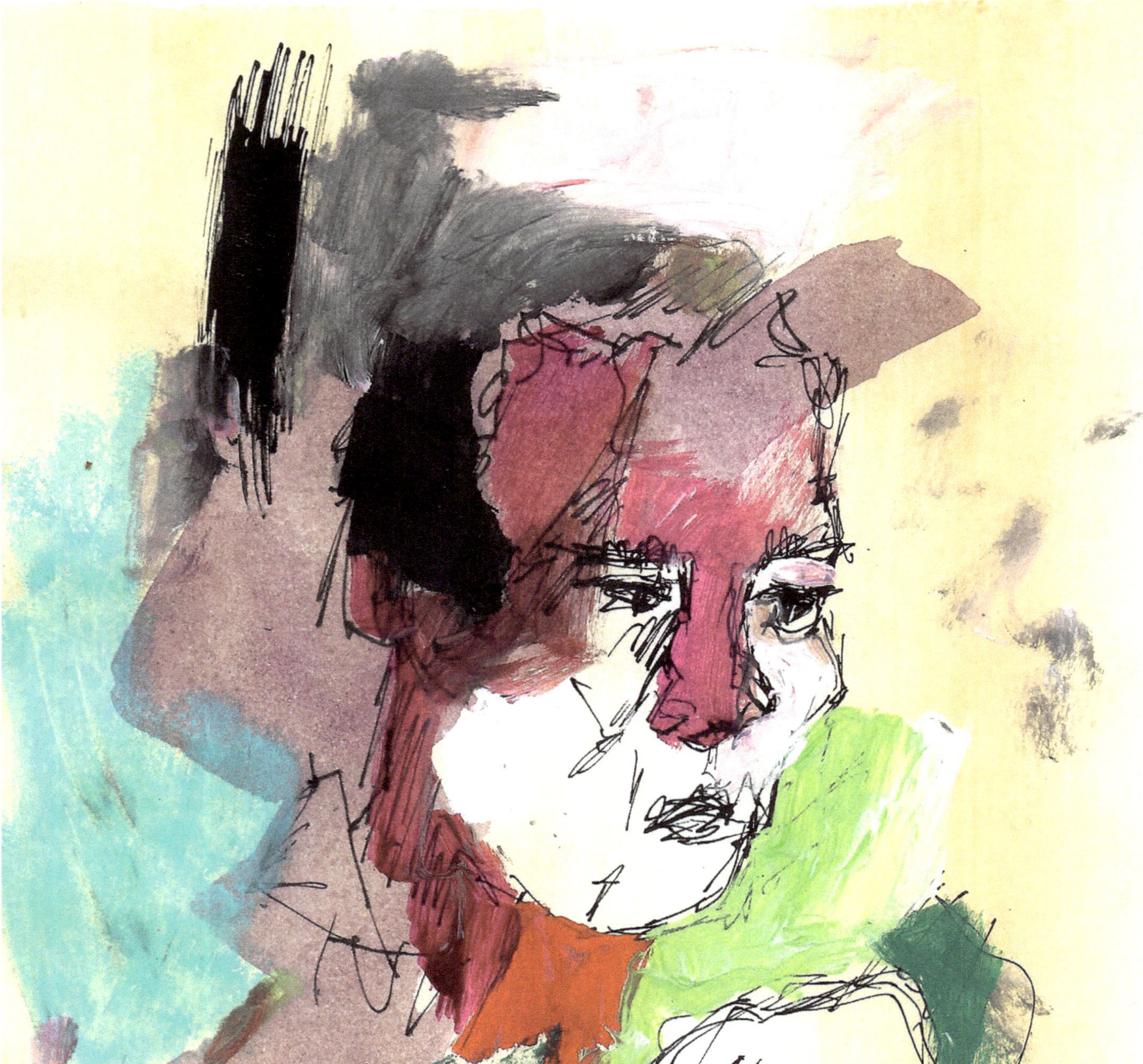
DOR BAHADUR THINKING
ES

Dor Bahadur could not accept the idea that his son Vishnu would celebrate his birthday in their house because they were in a mourning period following the death of his mother a few days before. Local people say that attending a ceremony during a mourning period is considered improper (*ucit chaina*), let alone organizing a party and sharing gifts. This event caused Dor Bahadur to keep thinking about his position in relation to his children.

Figure 1: *Dor Bahadur Thinking*. Gouache on paper. Author © 2023

For Dor Bahadur's children, celebrating the birthday mattered a great deal, enough to act against the convention. For how mundane, perhaps frivolous it might seem, celebrating his birthday was for Vishnu much more than a cake and some gifts. 'Traditions are not always right' he commented, 'my birthday was the occasion to finally have fun and relax with my friends; after so much study and stress during the year, we could finally meet up and enjoy ourselves.' Vishnu's reflection reveals a self-reflective scrutiny of what was right and wrong.

Figure 2: *Vishnu*. Gouache on paper. Author © 2023

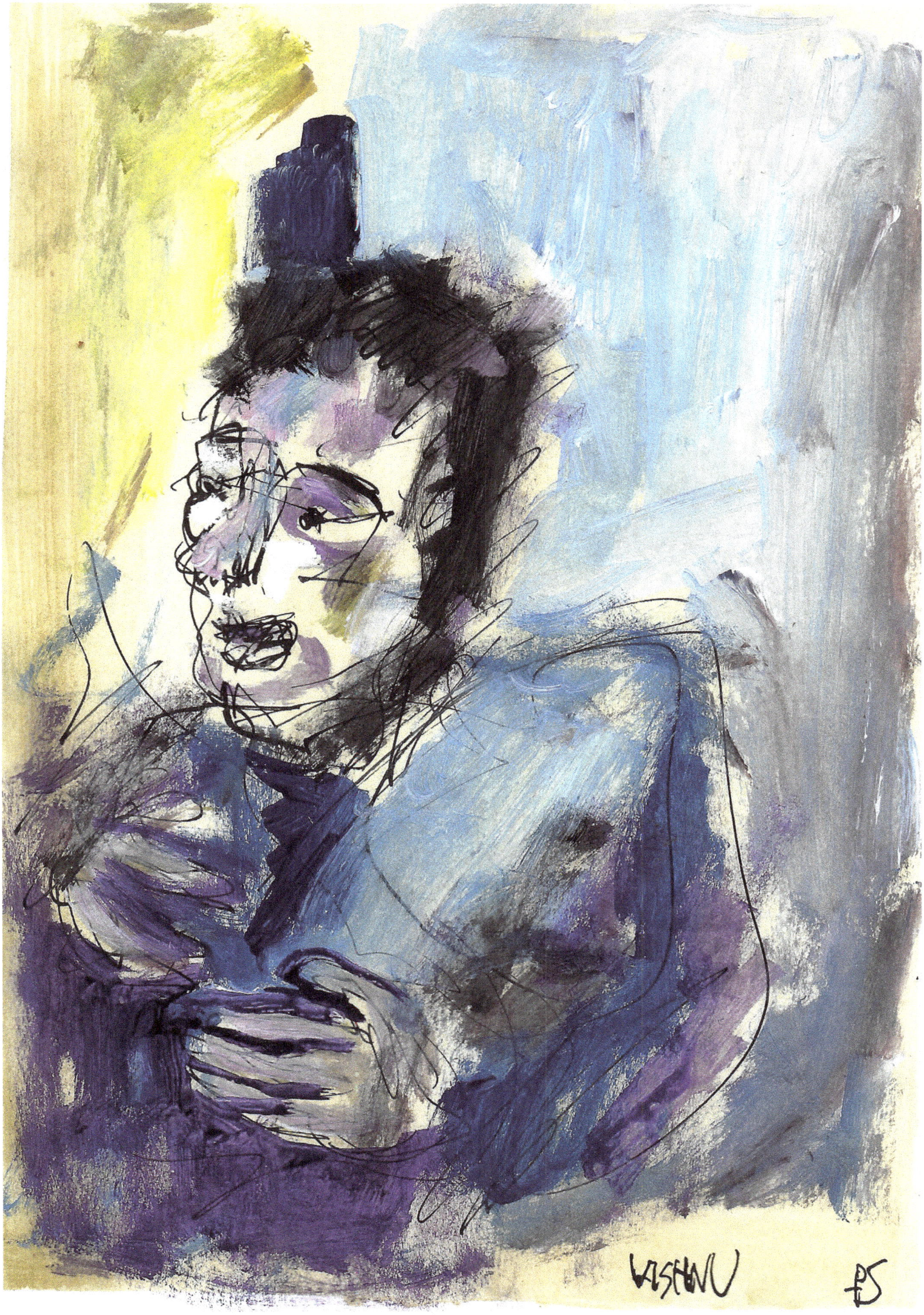
VISHNU

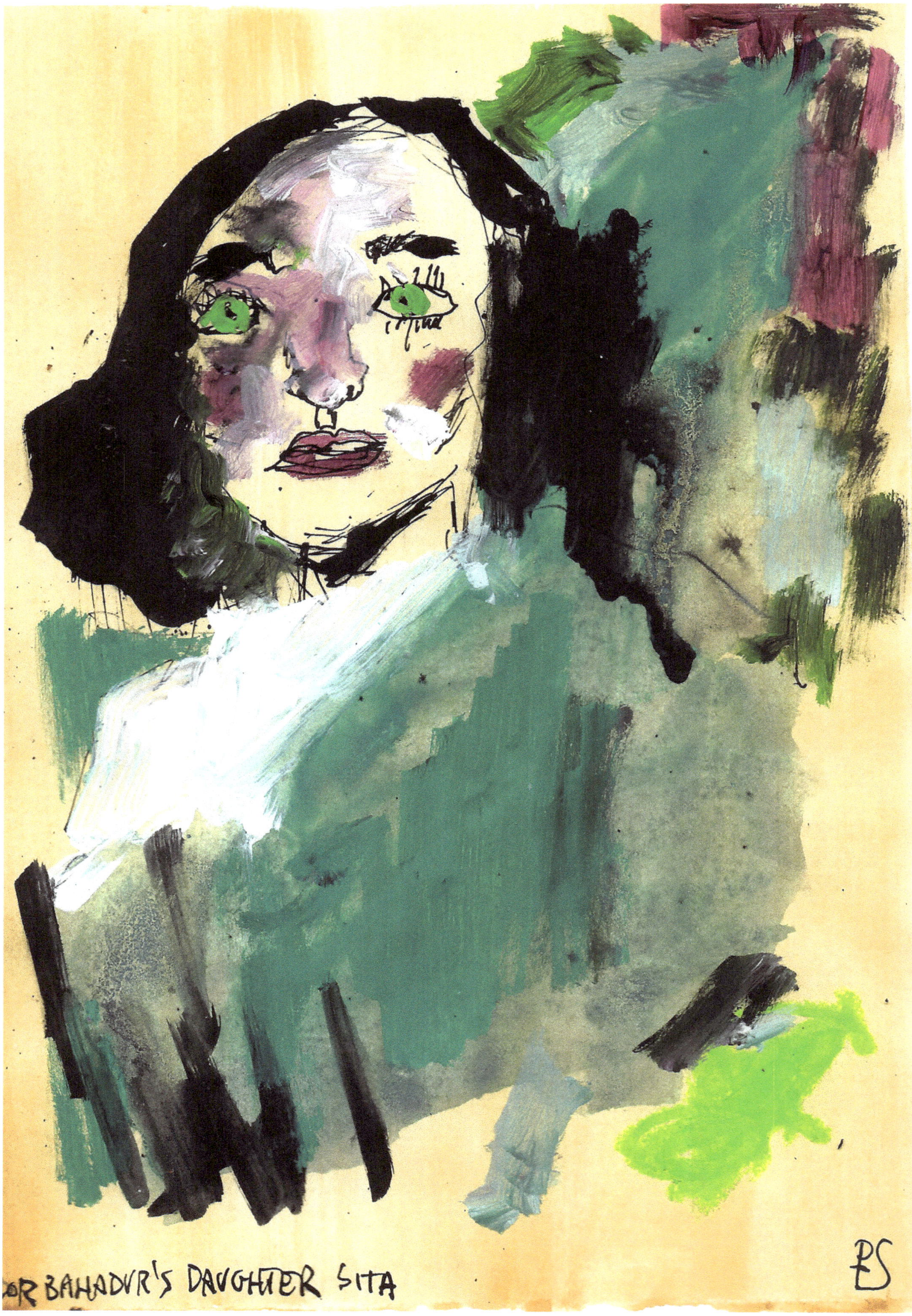
OR BAHADUR'S DAUGHTER SITA
PS

There are precise reasons why celebrations are not allowed in a mourning period. Festive occasions are considered dangerous because they can attract the spirit of the dead back to the house when they should be leaving for the after-world. While celebrating the birthday in the uncle's house in a sense overcame these issues, it was still a new behavior that created uneasiness in the father, who therefore preferred not to know anything about it. In so doing, he allowed them to follow their own preferred line of action, and to experience an alternative moral world from that of his own. This story is an example of how a dichotomy of perspectives is dealt with through strategies of avoid-ance and opacity become the preferred solutions when individual conflicting desires or needs strongly undermine the potential for an open agreement.

Figure 3: *Sita*. Gouache on paper.
Author © 2023

Parents widely believe themselves to be guides for their children in the process of seeking a moral balance between new values and pre-existing social and religious beliefs and practices. They call themselves 'friends' to their children, thus enabling them to 'open their heart' and embrace 'advanceness' rather than 'hesitate' to express themselves due to a feeling of shame. At the same time, parents are also firm in defining what they expect their children to do. This involved the achievement of socio-economic improvements for the whole household and the respect of social and religious norms. The title of this image derives from a quote from one of my informants who referred to parenting as a 'difficult art', a notion that tells of the delicate balance that parents and children have to find between old and new pressures and moralities while they pursue family wellbeing. This work visualizes more directly this ongoing 'conversation' (using a term by Schutz 1970 that connoted the ways in which people interact to establish a common moral ground) between parents and children.

Figure 4: *The Art of Parenting*. Gouache on paper. Author © 2023

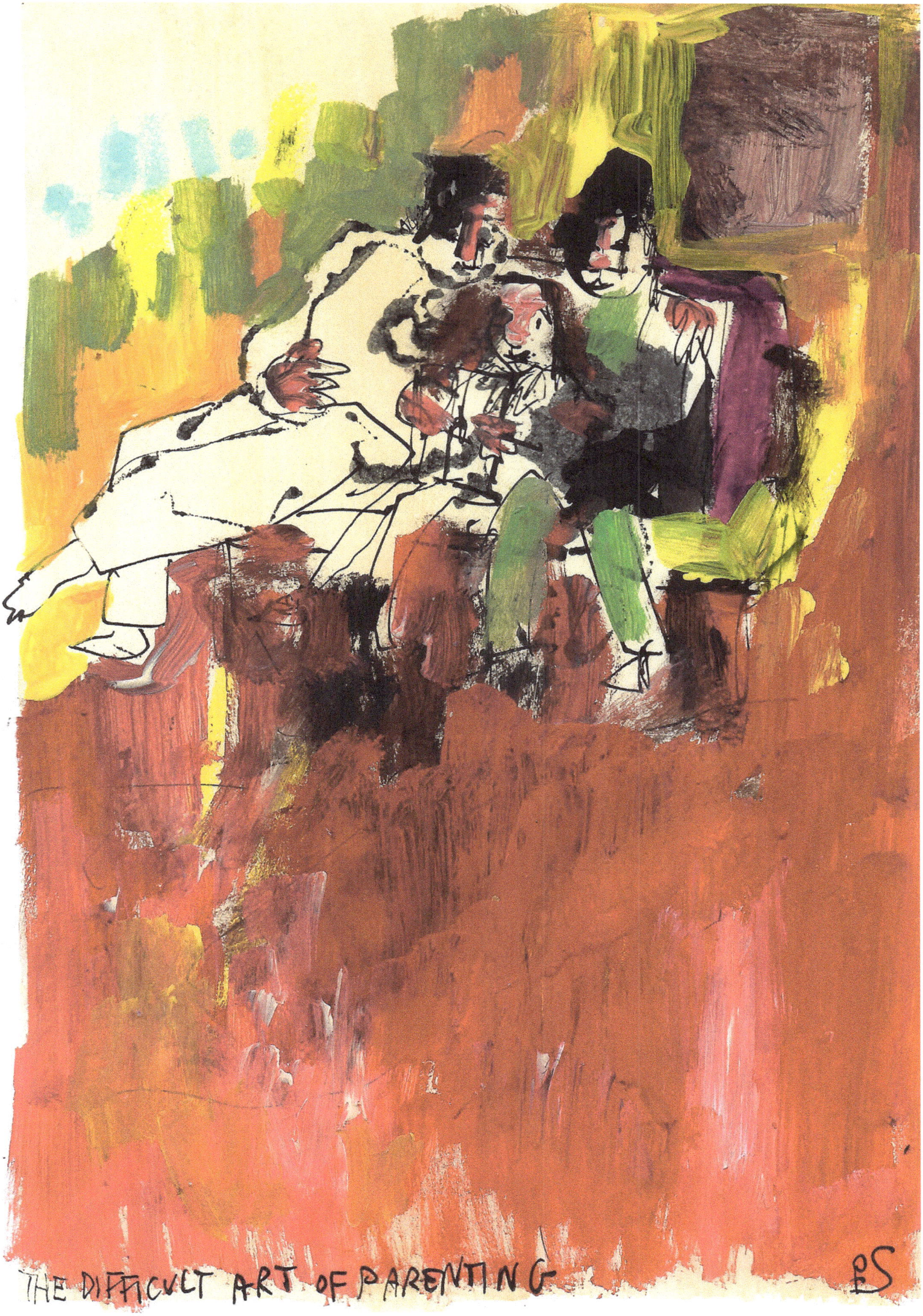
THE DIFFICULT ART OF PARENTING
ES

HIMALAYA
The Journal of the Association of Nepal and Himalayan Studies

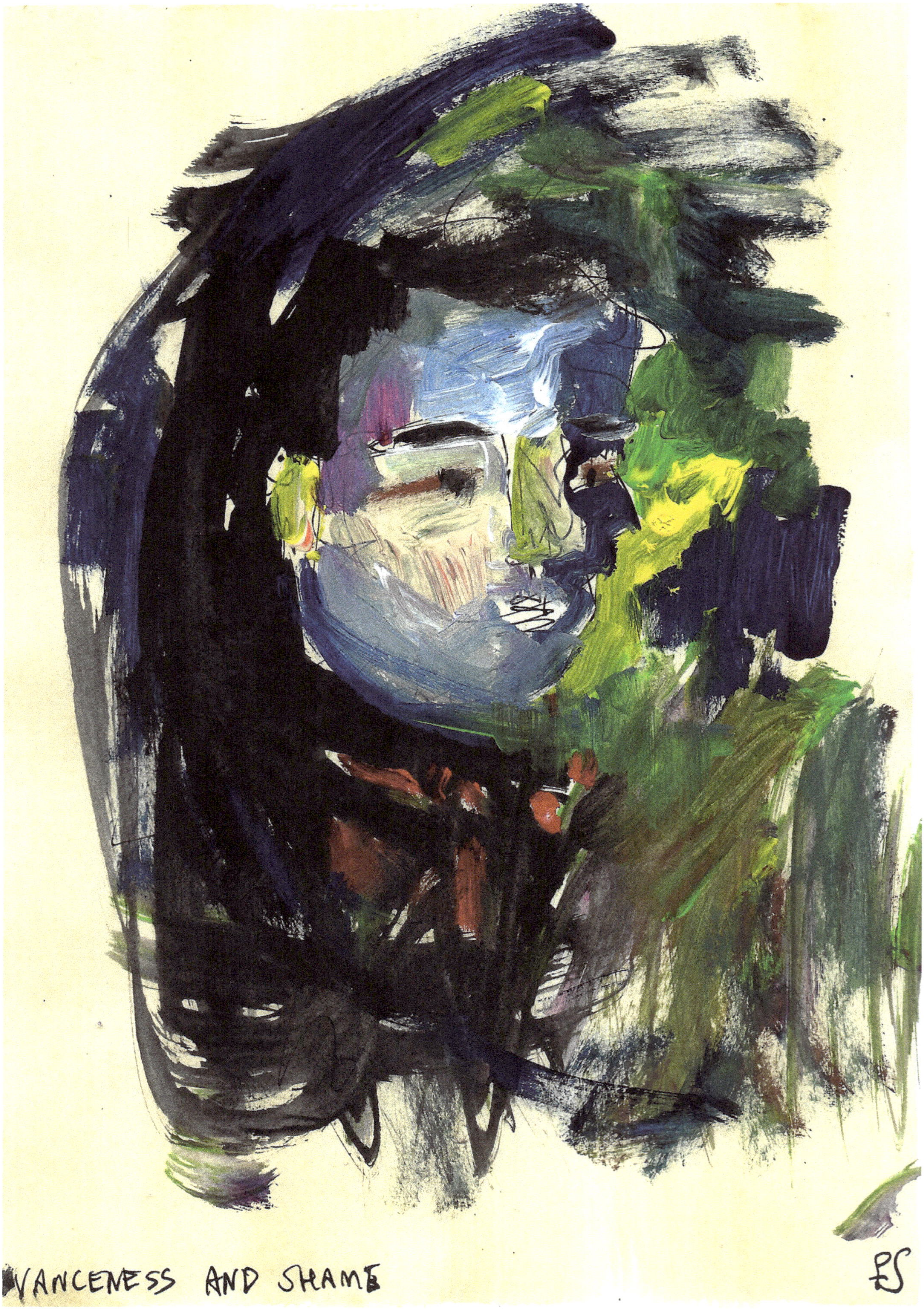

Having open conversations when there are different perspectives on how the 'moral self' should behave are experienced as painful and shameful, and therefore are generally avoided by both parents and children. Instead, both establish an 'opacity of mind' so that thoughts remain obscured, particularly when it is believed that empathy for their perspective (and as such any mediation) would not be possible (see Robbins & Rumsey 2008; also Feinberg 2011). Children then address the situation as a negotiation of their desire for 'advanceness', which is more socially acceptable and therefore mitigates shame.

Figure 5: *Advanceness and Shame*. Gouache on paper. Author © 2023

Among Newar people, Steven Parish suggested that empathy is a process of 'identification with cultured others' (1994, p. 305). That is, empathy is carefully embraced, and content is filtered and adjusted, based on what information one is willing to share and receive. This becomes particularly critical when parents and children have different existential perspectives and also diverging ideas on how 'mutual understanding' should be established.

Figure 6: *Generational Gaps*. Gouache on paper. Author © 2023

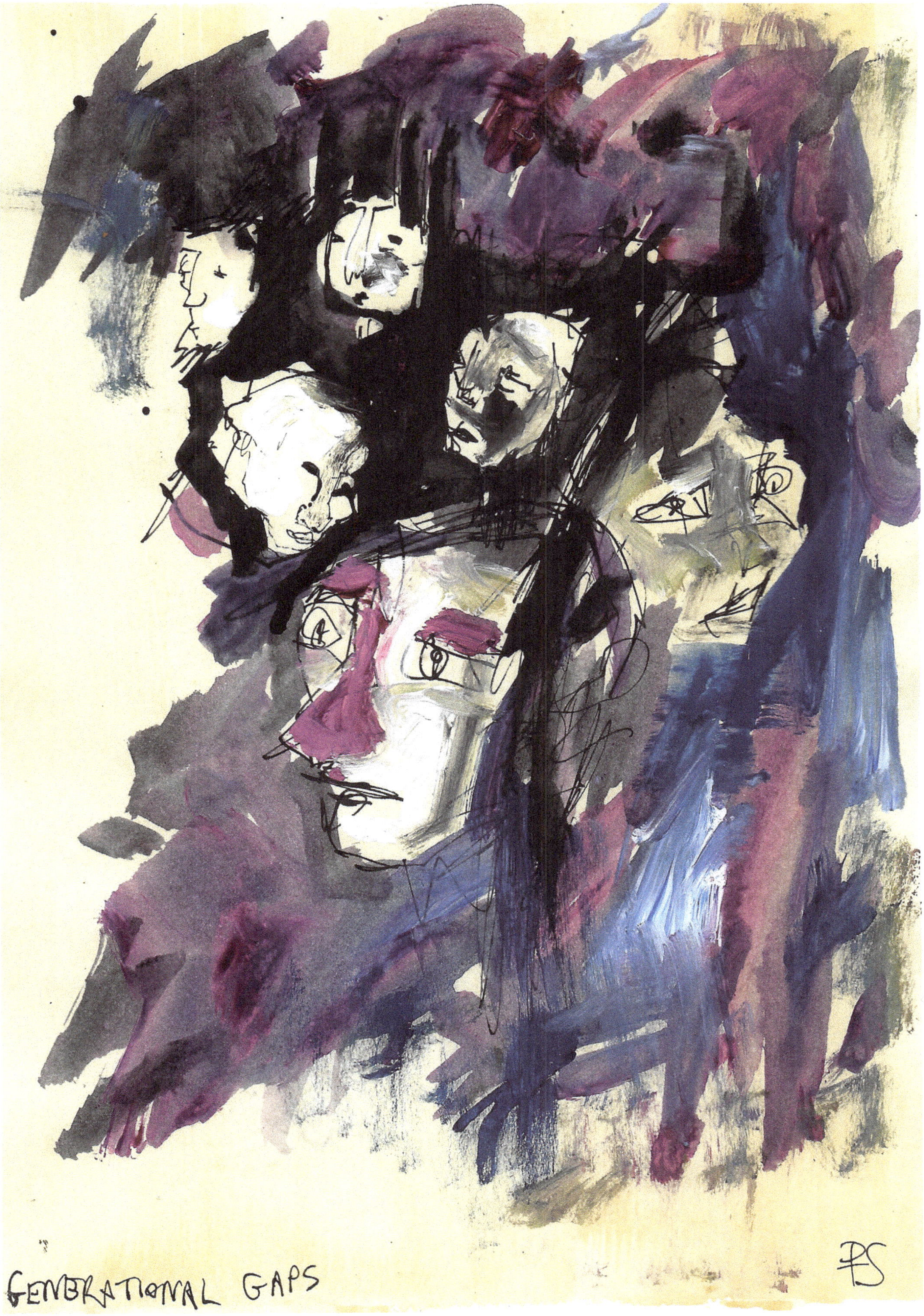
GENERATIONAL GAPS

HIMALAYA
The Journal of the Association of Nepal and Himalayan Studies

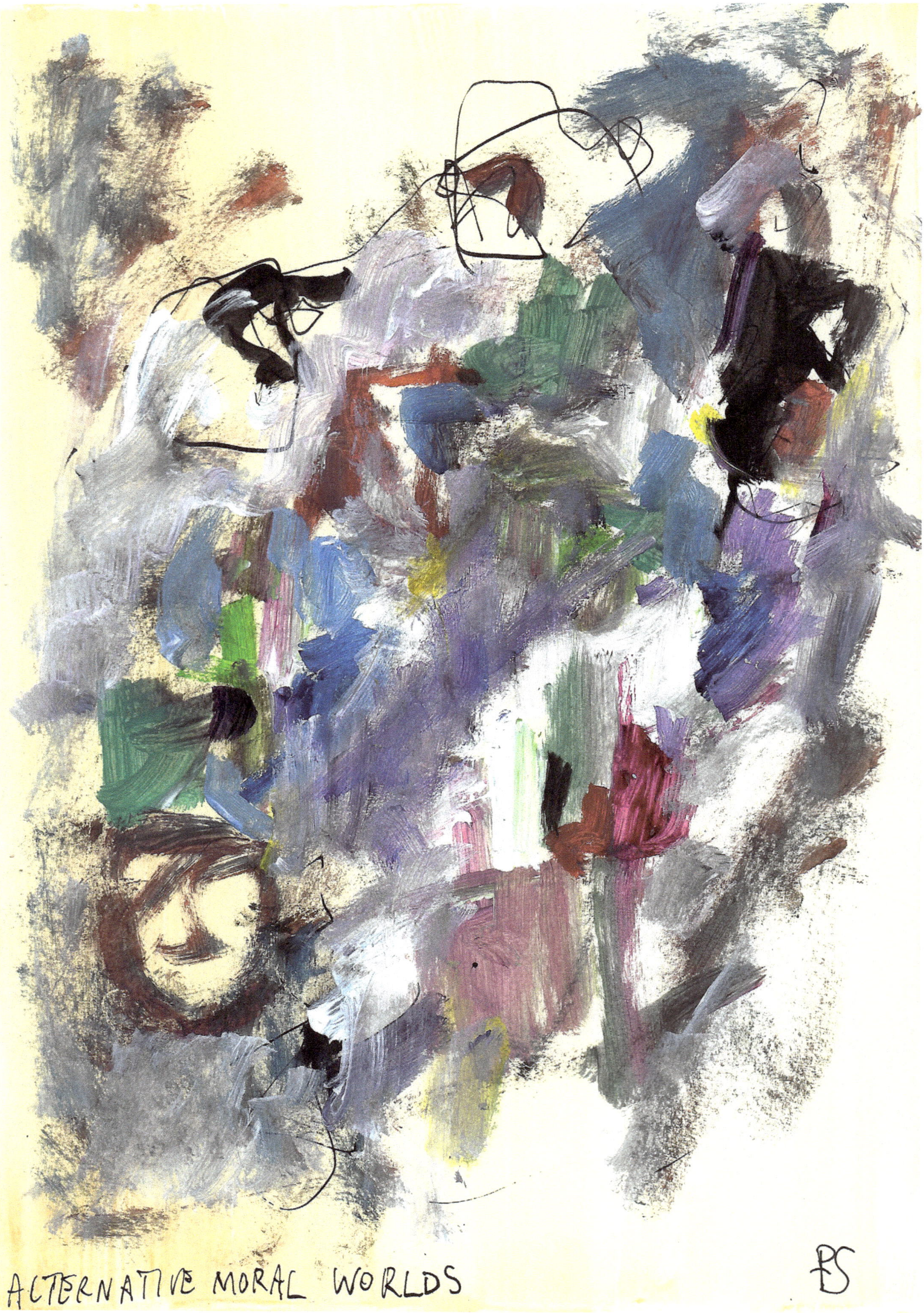

Concomitantly, younger people only open up with those that they feel closer to and in the contexts that are considered appropriate and safe (see Image 7). As a consequence, a moral state of 'advanceness' brings about the manifestation of a new dimension of the emotion of *lajjā* that differs from what was observed by Levy (1990) and Parish (1994) 30 to 50 years ago in Bhaktapur. Experienced as a 'shamelike affect' (Parish 1994, p. 208) shaping the boundaries of empathy between parents and children, *lajjā* becomes here a motive for seeking alternative venues of sociality and moral creativity rather than completely suffocating individual desires. Alternative dimensions of expression carried out through dating, socializing in public spaces and virtual engagements demonstrate the affirmation of a different shade of the moral emotion of *lajjā*, which, rather than suffocating 'unauthorized feelings', restores them in alternative contexts. This is possible due to the working of the feeling of 'advanceness', which enables a new dimension of expression outside the domestic sphere.

Figure 7: *Alternative Moral Worlds*. Gouache on paper. Author © 2023

While Images 6 and 7 zoom onto experiences of opacity and the establishment of alternative moral worlds and support networks, the work 'Dimensions of Mutual Understanding' invites reflection on the centrality of kinship networks in enabling at once the development of self-concepts and the negotiation of broader ethos systems.

Figure 8: *Dimensions of Mutual Understanding*. Gouache on paper. Author © 2023

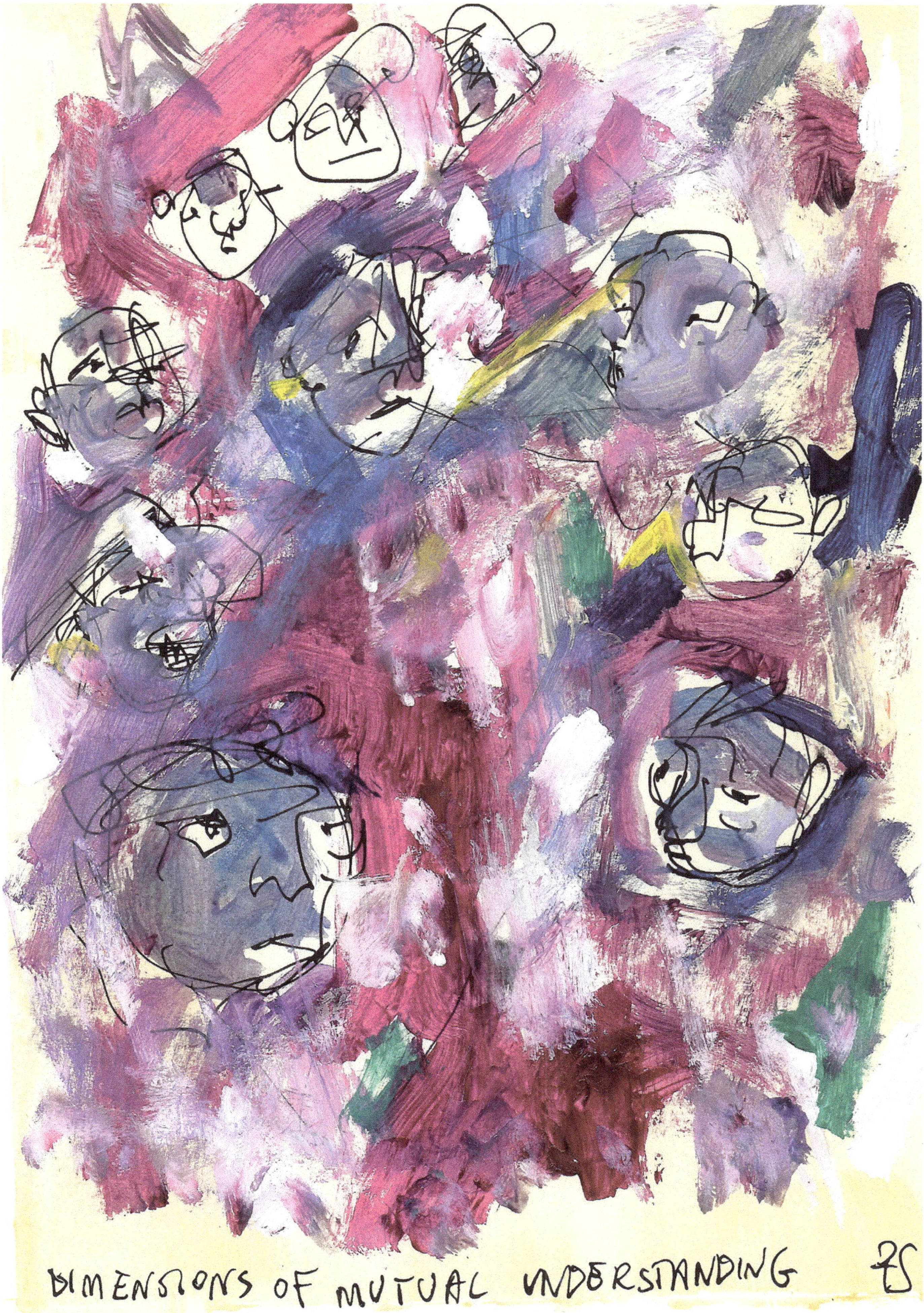
DIMENSIONS OF MUTUAL UNDERSTANDING

Conclusion

By visualizing the relational dialogue through which parents and children in Nepal navigate and contribute to social change, the drawings in this essay provide a window into domestic transformations in a climate of socio-economic uncertainty. Starting from the case study of Dor Bahadur and his children, I discussed my broader findings that in the local context strategies of avoidance and opacity rather than open confrontation are adopted as techniques to navigate interpersonal conflicts. These findings pave the way to further lines of investigation, for example, on what consequences these dynamics have in the formation of moral personhood and in the overall well-being of the social actors in question. More broadly, this work highlights the centrality of kinship networks in the development of individual selfhoods as well as in the negotiation of broader ethos systems virtually among all societies across the world.

Endnote

1. During a mourning period, all the direct men of a family have to wear white clothes.

References

Feinberg, R. 2011. 'Do Anutans empathize? Morality, compassion, and opacity of other minds', in *The Anthropology of Empathy: Experiencing the Lives of Others in Pacific Societies*, edited by DW Holland & CJ Throop, pp. 151-68. New York: Berghahn Books.

Levy, Robert I. 1990. *Mesocosm: Hinduism and the organization of a traditional Newar city in Nepal.* Berkeley: University of California Press.

Liechty, Mark. 2008[2003]. *Suitably Modern: Making middle-class culture in a new consumer society.* Kathmandu: Martin Chautari.

Paola Tiné is a Lecturer in Cultural Anthropology at Victoria University of Wellington Te Herenga Waka, New Zealand, and an Honorary Visiting Research Fellow at the University of Adelaide, South Australia. Over the last ten years, she has conducted ethnographic research in Australia, Italy, and Nepal with a focus on domestic relationships, moralities, and well-being. She is the author of *Modern Dharma: Seeking Family Well-Being in Middle-Class Nepal* (2025, The University of Pennsylvania Press) and *She Fell and Became a Horse* (2024, Dev Publishers).

I would like to thank the people of Bhaktapur; my research assistants; and Professor John Gray, Dr Dianne Rodger, Greg Donovan, Josh Smiech, Dr Jeevan Sharma, Dr Kapil Babu Dahal, Professor Todd Lewis, Professor Mark Liechty, and Professor Niels Gutschow, who all contributed, in different ways, to this essay. I also would like to extend my appreciation to the University of Adelaide and Sight and Life Foundation for their financial support to conduct the fieldwork on which this paper is based. Finally, I wish to recognises the unique role of Māori as Tangata Whenua and embraces Te Tiriti o Waitangi recognising Māori as tino rangitiratanga of Aotearoa/ New Zealand, the land where the Victoria University campus is built.

Parish, Steven M. 1994. *Moral knowing in a Hindu sacred city: An exploration of mind, emotion, and self.* New York: Columbia University Press.

Robbins, J & Rumsey, A. 2008. 'Introduction: Cultural and linguistic anthropology and the opacity of other minds'. *Anthropological Quarterly*, vol. 81, no. 2: 407-420.

Schutz, Alfred. 1970. *On phenomenology and social relations*. Chicago: The University of Chicago Press.

Tiné, Paola. 2020. 'Parenting, Food Practices and Health Conceptions in Bhaktapur'. *Dada Rivista di Antropologia Post-Globale* 2: 107-124.

Tiné, Paola. 2021a. 'Maya's Story: Spirit Possession, Gender, and the Making of the Self in a Painted Anthropological Account'. *Current Anthropology* 62 (4): 498-504. https://doi.org/10.1086/716551

Tiné, Paola. 2021b. 'Painting the Self in a Study of Modernity: Using Art in Anthropological Research'. *Re: Think – A Journal of Creative Ethnography* 3 (1): 1-14.

Tiné, Paola. 2021c. 'Seeking Heartfelt Help: The Emergence of the Friendship Guthi as a Middle-Class Practice in Contemporary Nepal'. *Studies in Nepali History and Society* 26 (2): 313-345.

Tiné, Paola. 2022a. 'The Anthropologist as Artist: "Voice" and "Positionality" When Using Art in Anthropological Research'. In *Ethnography as Art/Art as Ethnography: Art, Observation, and an Anthropology of Illustration*, edited by Max Carocci and Stephanie Pratt, 23-38. London: Bloomsbury Academic.

Tiné, Paola. 2022b. 'Two Kitchens and Other Modern Stories: Rethinking the Family in Contemporary Nepal Through Household Conflict and Fission'. *HIMALAYA: The Journal of the Association for Nepal and Himalayan Studies* 41 (2): 127-143.

Tiné, Paola. 2022c. 'What Makes a Family? A Visual Approach to Ontological and Substantial Dimensions of the Domestic in Nepal'. *HIMALAYA: The Journal of the Association for Nepal and Himalayan Studies* 41 (2): 107-126.

Tiné, Paola. 2024a. *She Fell and Became a Horse*. New Delhi: Dev Publishers and Distributors.

Tiné, Paola. 2024b. 'Feeling Social Change in the Gut: Gyāstrik and the Problematisation of Domestic Roles Among Newar Women in Contemporary Nepal'. *Anthropology & Medicine*, 31(1-2), 174-194. https://doi.org/10.1080/13648470.2024.2387502

Tiné, Paola. 2025a. *Modern Dharma: Seeking Family Well-Being in Middle-Class Nepal.* Philadelphia: University of Pennsylvania Press.

Tiné, Paola. 2025b. 'Making Moral Selves Through Comparison: Narratives of Moral Decline and the Modern Virtuous Self Among Middle-Class Older Adults in Nepal'. *Ethos* e70006:1-12. https://doi.org/10.1111/etho.70005

HIMALAYA
The Journal of the Association of Nepal and Himalayan Studies

Research Article

Upland Agriculture, Entrepreneurship, and Innovation: Performing Developmental Responsibilities in Northeast India

Sanjay Barbora
University of California, Santa Cruz

DOI: https://doi.org/10.2218/himalaya.2025.9688

Abstract

In the last two decades, different governments in India have made a concerted effort to address the plight of the marginal farmer who owns (or has access to) some private or communal land across the uplands in the northeast of the country. Various governmental schemes and subsidies have been initiated to ensure that other ways of earning a livelihood mitigate falling returns from agriculture and the increasing need for cash among farmers. Upland farmers have evoked both hope and despair from governments that look to transform subsistence-style agricultural practices into revenue-earning endeavours. They have been the source of much political posturing, as the regional political elite, scientists, and industry have taken up their cause. The same farmers have also been subjected to intense policy pressure, persuading them to think differently and pull themselves out of poverty. There is, therefore, an increasing demand for them to prepare for radical changes in their livelihoods and way of thinking. In this article, I draw from fieldwork conducted in Arunachal Pradesh, Assam, and Mizoram to examine how new discourses of entrepreneurship and innovation have become essential to understanding social and economic transformations in the uplands of Northeast India.

Keywords

agriculture, Eastern Himalayas, entrepreneur, innovators, militarisation, market

Recommended Citation

Barbora, Sanjay (2025). Upland Agriculture, Entrepreneurship, and Innovation: Performing Developmental Responsibilities in Northeast India. *HIMALAYA* 44(1): 50-65.

This work is licensed under a Creative Commons Attribution-Noncommercial-No Derivative Works 4.0 License.

Introduction

Amid India's crippling COVID-19 pandemic in 2020, farmers' organizations came out in protest against three new agricultural laws introduced by the government to reform the sector. The laws loosened regulations surrounding the sale, pricing, and storage of agricultural produce. They also permitted private corporations to hoard essential commodities for future sales—a practice previously restricted to government-authorised agents. Most controversially, the laws permitted farmers to sell directly to private buyers, thereby dismantling the government's role in procuring crops and guaranteeing a minimum support price (MSP). The protests drew scores of people, including students and farmers, primarily from northern Indian states, who marched to New Delhi. Farmers' groups from Northeast India were conspicuous by their absence in the protests, raising critical questions; for example, would the new laws impact only a certain kind of farmer, one who had already benefited from land consolidation, technological advances, and political patronage since the 1960s?

Northeast Indian states are emerging as essential areas for agriculture and marketing reforms, but in a profoundly distinct and uncritical manner. Agriculture in the upland regions serves as a source of cultural pride and a target for frequent government interventions. Most hills and plains communities have had an organic connection to seasonal rhythms, including the long cycles of swidden agriculture in the mountains and foothills.[1] On the other hand, the rent-collecting bureaucracies of national and regional governments view such agricultural practices as primitive and have constantly pushed for change among the practitioners. This approach emphasises revenue generation through innovations in upland agriculture, privileging the entrepreneur's role in a region traditionally associated with subsistence farming and violent demands for political autonomy (Barbora, 2018).

In the following sections, I examine how entrepreneurship and innovation serve as critical lenses in understanding this problem. I develop three interrelated arguments: (a) that the upland farmer or peasant has emerged as a problematic category for developmental experts and state governments; (b) the entrepreneur has ascended as the preferred agent of modern development in the region; and (c) the network of educational institutions, media and government have collectively worked to recast the peasant/farmer as an entrepreneur, with varying degrees of success. The three arguments follow a well-established line of thought in social anthropology and history focusing on upland areas ranging from northern Vietnam to western Tibet (van Schendel, 2002; Scott, 2009; Guite, 2018). They contribute to ongoing debates about the invisibility of the region in social sciences, especially after the militarisation of everyday life became highlighted in the 1960s and placed the region within the spatial history of capital expansion in the 19th century (Baruah, 2020; Kar, 2013; Ludden, 2011). Both processes—militarisation and capital expansion—are critical lenses for understanding the contemporary puzzle of the plight of the upland farmer and its emerging cousin, the entrepreneur.

I carried out immersive ethnographic fieldwork in three phases. The first phase took place in Mizoram during the winter of 2012 (January-February), where I had gone to study the New Land Use Policy (NLUP) in the state. The second phase was during the winter of 2019-2020 in two of Assam's autonomous districts, Karbi Anglong and Dima Hasao, where I studied the slow pace of the digitisation of land. The third phase of research was during the summers of 2022 and 2023 in the East Siang, Lower Dibang, and Lohit districts of Arunachal Pradesh. In addition, I studied state government budgets and analysed specific agriculture-related policies in the uplands between the years 2005 and 2014 to understand why upland farmers are often erased from policy and politics.

This article addresses reasons for this absence of upland farmers from Northeast India's agricultural discourse by invoking two interrelated realities concerning how markets and market-friendly laws have developed in the country. First, the region has long been associated with dominant rural, agriculture-based social systems that coexisted with cash crop regimes. Therefore, a complete absence of representatives from peasant or farming constituencies requires some explanation. Secondly, in Northeast India, political assertions centred around identitarian and social justice often coalesce around the image of rural, agriculture-based communities, where the upland farmer is both celebrated and denigrated simultaneously. The farmers are celebrated as custodians of tradition but are also seen as politically and economically insignificant obstacles to modern development. Hence, this absence of upland farmers at the protests marks a politically significant moment for agrarian change in India, requiring a critical analysis of agricultural interventions and political change in these uplands.

Since the 1980s, the dominant mode of governance in India's eastern Himalayan region has been characterised by political violence and the co-optation of a local elite, which has displaced many and provided for a few. Agriculture has been a primary site for transformative policy-making, where the interests of technocrats, politicians, and owners of capital converged to change the shape of the highland farmers' (and their families') farming practices. In the following sections, I look at how government policies encourage entrepreneurship to address declining agricultural returns from Northeast India's highland communities from a sociological perspective.

Following James Scott's theory about the farmer's ability to stay beyond the reach of the state, the figure of the highland farmer in the uplands across the Burma-Northeast India frontier has emerged as an imposing metaphor in the social sciences. This fact is rendered more critical as the region is seen to represent a frontier of capitalist expansion, a phenomena where subsistence indigenous farmers across the globe are pressured to shift from subsistence agriculture to commercial plantations in their uneasy coexistence with settlers and a militarised state (Baruah, 2007; Borras and Franco, 2012; Geiger, 2008; Tsing, 2003). Recent scholarship and political developments reveal how the state's capacity to nationalise space has enabled the proliferation of modernist developmental discourse and practices, without necessarily changing the material conditions of the marginalised farmer in the region, whilst making them more market-dependent (Baruah, 2017; Ledoc and Choudhury, 2012; Li, 2014a). So, while the upland farmers may not have financial security or improved access to public health and education, they are increasingly being persuaded to grow commercial crops and undertake considerable risks to their livelihoods in exchange for an unreliable, unstable future. Over the decades, the state apparatus—universities, the media, and specific industries—has adopted a more persuasive narrative aimed at changing upland farmers' land use and cropping patterns.

Since the 20th century, upland agriculture has been viewed as both a detriment to economic growth and an integral part of the cultural repertoire of the region's indigenous communities (de Maaker and Tula, 2021). Government documents and agricultural extension officers' notes attest to the difficulties encountered in attempting to change upland agriculture practices, though these attitudes are slowly shifting due to efforts by inter-governmental agencies like the International Centre for Integrated Mountain Development (ICIMOD) attesting to certain positive aspects of low-technology upland agriculture (Choudhury et al., 2021).

Since the late 1990s and early 2000s, governments in Northeast India have attempted to showcase their states' upland agricultural produce and handicrafts at various expositions and festivals. Nagaland's iconic Hornbill Festival, held in December every year, is an excellent example of such efforts, even as other regional governments attempt to follow the Nagaland model. At similar regional festivals, indigenous women sell rice, beer, skewered pork, chicken, beef, and fish sticks, while others offer bamboo handicrafts, elaborately patterned shawls and stoles, and delicately crafted jewellery. Regional state governments support some of these festivals, with departments allocating budgets to ensure their smooth operation. These events sometimes draw interest from seemingly unrelated agencies. Other festivals must rely on multiple funding sources, including public sector companies, local businesspeople, and individuals.[2]

However, festivals that celebrate the produce of upland agriculturalists are relatively new in Northeast India. While such events certainly signify the benign aspects of government interventions, there is also a history of violent intrusions in the lives of upland communities. Essential studies have shown how the Indian state often destroyed highland crops and agriculturalists. During the 1950s-1980s, the Indian army burned down granaries and corralled farmers into concentration camp-like villages during counterinsurgency operations (Kikon, 2005; Sundar, 2011). Several initiatives seek to change how policymakers and institutions, including universities and various government departments, view upland agriculture across these two polarities.

Upland Agriculture, Peasants, and Farmers in Northeast India

The terms peasant and farmer have long-standing usage in the social sciences, each denoting specific characteristics that social anthropologists have sought to clarify throughout the 20th century. While a farmer is defined by land ownership for cultivation and a single occupational concern (Wolf, 1966), Teodor Shanin (1972) identified four interlinked facets of peasantry: (a) the farm as a multi-functional unit of social organisation, (b) land farming and livestock as sources of primary livelihood, (c) distinct traditional culture linked to rural communities, and (d) multidirectional subjection to powerful outsiders. Recent Latin American scholarship and experiences have drawn parallels between peasant and entrepreneurial/industrial farmers who share key features, particularly in attempts to reduce economic risks through cost minimisation and diversification of crops and livelihood practices (Van der Ploeg, 2008).

I use these terms interchangeably because upland agriculture in Northeast India is characterised by small, community-controlled landholdings. However, much of it is becoming insidiously privatised (Fernandes and Barbora, 2009).[3] This privatisation process comes with a loss of knowledge about the intricate links between upland agriculture and hunting practices, pre-colonial tributes, and the migratory cycles of indigenous communities.[4] I wish to add that upland farmers in Northeast India are not homogeneous, often requiring disaggregation by their capacity to take risks, diversify crops, and access agricultural finances (and related livelihoods).

As previously noted, the upland farmer has been a source of paradoxical pride and embarrassment for a modernising indigenous elite in the hill states of Northeast India. Other than owning the essential tools to work the land and family labour, the farmers needed more to invest in improving the economic productivity of the land. Hence, the state has encouraged mono-cropping in the uplands, in attempts to appropriate the function of adding value to agricultural production. This contradictory response has material manifestations.

State governments in Mizoram, Nagaland, and the autonomous councils in the hill districts of Assam have constructed heritage villages to showcase the ingenuity of indigenous farming practices. Overlooking magnificent views of the hills and situated just a short drive from state capitals and district headquarters, these heritage villages represent a bureaucratic perspective on indigenous futures. Empty models of rural villages reflecting the types of bamboo and mud homes that indigenous peoples might have lived in form the core of these villages, classified as tourist resorts. Examples of such official commemoration of agriculture in the region include the Reiek village in Mizoram, where the state's tourism department has built a complex hoping to attract visitors to the state during the flower blooming season, and the Heritage Village at Kisama (near Kohima in Nagaland). The Hornbill Festival at Kisama is an attraction for those who want to experience Naga culture condensed into a few hours. In these and similar efforts, the peasant way of life, especially in the hills, is showcased as a tourist attraction. A key concern here is how deceptively cultural tropes have been used to erase discussions on relations of production for the region's upland farmers.

Much is erased in these touristic ideas of peasant life in selective efforts to memorialise culture. During fieldwork, especially in the autonomous hill districts of Assam, Meghalaya, Manipur, and Mizoram, one was always struck by the narrative of hardship shared by practising cultivators in interviews with researchers. Most older farmers cited hardship and poor returns from agriculture as reasons they do not wish their children to follow them in the backbreaking work of upland cultivation. Instead, they invoked a repertoire of alternative activities, placed on a spectrum of choices. These alternatives would range from migration on one end to acquiring specific non-agricultural skills on the other. This trend was reinforced by the work, budgets, and emphasis allocated by state governments to skill-development and entrepreneurship departments.[5]

Experiences of upland agriculturalists in Northeast India and the eastern Himalayan region differ from those of peasant life. Similar processes are at work in the highlands of Indonesia as well, where indigenous cultivators are forced to supplement their livelihoods with more than one kind of work, and where migration increasingly emerges as an inevitable consequence of the economic unsustainability of subsistence agriculture in the highlands (Li, 2014a). The mid-1990s marked a critical moment owing to the participation of large numbers of rural women, who were previously less likely to migrate. As expected, this threw upland agriculture off course, since family labour is crucial (especially women's labour) in cleaning the fields, planting, and cultivating crops. As a result, cultivators from the plains expect to see wetland agriculture in the hills today.

Added to the narrative of hardship was the constant pressure to improvise, innovate, and grow crops to yield higher prices in the market. In many ways, such pressures by most developing countries in the 20th century (including the postcolonial Indian state) are part of a broader effort to modernise agriculture (Harriss and Stewart, 2015). In the same vein, the Indian government had begun an ambitious project to provide farmers of Mizoram with a stable trade to wean them away from agriculture as part of its NLUP.[6] Much of this depended on central funding, technological support from industry, and scientists. The idea was to turn the local farmer into a surplus producer like the 1960s Green Revolution did in states across northern India. However, the upland farmer needed the kind of landholdings that plains farmers might have had. They needed individual land titles to leverage for finance from banks and passed on to their progeny. Instead of titles, upland farmers had access to complex community-controlled lands, where individual land ownership coexisted with rights of access to clan and community land (Karlsson, 2011; Ltu, 2021; Shimray, 2009). Upland farmers also lacked access to connections such as university and industry networks, primarily because of the conflict-ridden years 1960s and 1970s in the region. Several years of counterinsurgency in Mizoram had led to a brutal crackdown by the Indian army and forced relocation (by regrouping of villages) of almost 85 per cent of the population in around 5 per cent of Mizoram's current territory (Nunthara, 1981).

Such experiences highlight the vulnerabilities of Northeast India's upland agriculturalists. Unlike political patronage seen in other parts of the world, where the peasantry can mobilise for itself, upland agriculturalists in Northeast India have yet to be able to negotiate with the state. Thus, in their isolation and lack of coordination, they needed advocates on their behalf. Nonetheless, the violent period was mediated by peace-making episodes: new states like Nagaland and Mizoram were formed in 1963 and 1987, respectively, ceasefires were signed, and local assembly and council elections were held. Spanning decades, these efforts enabled the extension of governmental departments and the expansion of the state's bureaucracies into the region's uplands.

However, one must remember that in the violent decades between 1960 and the late 1980s, governments viewed the upland farmers and peasants with much apathy, even demanding an end to the harmful practice of *jhum* (swidden agriculture). In conjunction with emerging opportunities beyond the agricultural sector, this prompted numerous medium and small-scale farmers to adopt unsustainable cash crops, primarily coffee, tea, rubber, and palm oil, during the early 2000s (Barbora, 2002). The shift failed to endure as urban buyers were not used to such small-scale production. Furthermore, the various government-constituted boards for tea, coffee, and rubber were financially stretched and unable to sustainably procure from isolated upland producers (Moa and Chakraborty, 2020; Debbarma and Debbarma, 2018). Scholars highlight that peasants with access to small farms and community land often choose unsustainable alternatives, not for opportunist land grabbing but as a self-inflicted short-term risk to secure basic amenities (Li, 2014a; Sturgeon, 2007). Hence, with the political violence plateaued in the first decade of the 21st century, regional state governments prioritised essential training and entrepreneurship skills for local youth (Kikon and Karlsson, 2019).

Bureaucratic Budgets and Entrepreneurs in the Hills

Modern bureaucracies have a stabilising function to them. The governments in the hill states of Northeast India had to work with a relatively small, predominantly rural population at the beginning. Unlike Mizoram, where earlier decades of groupings had ensured that local populations got concentrated along specific semi-urban centres, most other states had a relatively dispersed population that lived far away from district centres. One of the problems they inherited was the verticality of the landscape, where distances could be optically deceptive. In his elaborate description of the impact of the resettlement of indigenous Andean communities following the 16th-century Spanish conquest, historian Jeremy Mumford threw light on the specific ways in which the verticality of landscapes is essential for understanding the kind of power relations that evolve in mountain areas (Mumford, 2012). Scott (2009) used a similar lens to explain how upland societies had different sensibilities regarding rules and social organisation.

Modern bureaucracies are meant to provide impersonal services and must be geared to incorporate such nuances. However, this Weberian idea of an impersonal bureaucracy remains integral to the exercise of increasing the state's authority in the hills, especially when various national governments in India attempted to alleviate conflicts. One of the main ways to read this expansion is by looking into how governments plan their spending in the hill states. In looking through recent budget plans for Manipur, Mizoram, Meghalaya, and Assam, as well as referring to literature on disaffection of upland communities, one is struck by the frank acknowledgement of how state governments addressed the issue of the falling returns from agriculture, especially in the hills (Kipgen and Chowdhury, 2016; Umdor and Syiem, 2017). Between 2016 and 17, the government of Assam showed a marginal increase of 0.88 per cent in farm income between 2003 and 2013, a trend that continued and adversely impacted the agrarian crisis in the state (Haque and Barua, 2021).

The situation is partially worse for upland farmers in Arunachal Pradesh, Manipur, Meghalaya, and Mizoram, partly because these states depend on central funding. Moreover, unlike Assam, where consolidated figures from the valley and hills show some agricultural surplus, there are no comparable figures in the hill states. For a bureaucrat looking at revenues and expenses, there would be very few revenue lines from agriculture in the hills. Instead, they would see costs incurred by extending central government schemes for farmers in other parts of the country. The role of state grants and loans for agriculture is an essential factor in recalibrating agricultural policies in the hill states.

Furthermore, the need for more readily available labour for shifting agriculture was often bypassed seasonally by involving landless workers from the plains, who were usually brought to the hills for road construction and other infrastructure (Mishra, 2017).

Labour scarcity in the hills is a historical fact with cultural and political ramifications. In precolonial times, valley kingdoms and societies (especially in the Brahmaputra valley) sustained reciprocal relationships where surplus and labour were shared between the hills and valleys (Kar 2016). This has changed in present times. With greater investment in labour-intensive crops and plantations in the uplands, the quest to look for surplus labour from the plains has become inevitable. Many upland farmers, including those capable of taking greater economic risks, depend on plantation workers and seasonal farmers from the plains in the river valleys. The farmers from the plains and their employers in the hills enter into highly personal contracts enforced by affective relationships, rather than the established rule of law.[7]

For the political elite, such informal arrangements between local farmers and workers were cause for concern, for they could raise ethnic tensions. However, the main worry for political representatives and bureaucrats in these states was the need to enforce some sense of discipline in the upland farmers and ensure they added economic value to the land they occupied and farmed. Hence, bureaucrats and politicians in the region often encourage the involvement of experts from outside. Professionals and development agencies with additional budgets and expertise have come in to help persuade the upland farmer to do more, do different things with the land, and change the crops they grow. More recently, such transition has been called for in the name of climate adaption, where local advocacy groups and agricultural experts in the uplands recommend a mix of plantation crops (like cardamom), as well as harness the potential of neglected and underutilised species (like buckwheat and millets) (Karlsson, 2021).[8]

While on a tour with officials from the Japanese International Development Agency (JICA) and agricultural consultants in Mizoram in 2012, I was struck by the number of times non-Mizo bureaucrats accompanying us would apologise for the lack of revenue emerging from the JICA projects. As the local sociologist called upon to explain cultural mores and traditions, I defended the seemingly extravagant farmers to the Japanese donors. The bureaucrats were keen to transfer one line of expenses from their budget, minor irrigation projects, to the Japanese. The JICA officials were curious to know how and why the government of Mizoram was spending such seemingly large sums of money on an effort that could have brought them more revenue. In the evenings, as we settled into dusty inspection bungalows and prepared for dinner, one saw a distinct division of opinion between the Mizo bureaucrats and their non-Mizo counterparts from the plains. The former thought that the state's expenses incurred in extending irrigation to the hills were a part of its duty to the Mizo farmer, an obligation of sorts. They kept reminding the group that much of the central funds for such projects were eventually funnelled back to the mainland as payment for material not produced in Mizoram and for salaries of engineers and consultants from outside the state. The non-Mizo bureaucrats seemed annoyed that the upland farmer was wasting money and attempted to convince the JICA officials that the farmers should stop growing rice and grow something that would bring revenue, like palm oil. For their part, the JICA officials were in two minds, as they, too, argued about the possible ill effects of plantations in the hills.

Over the day, they had spent as much time as anyone else attempting to understand upland agriculture's complexities. When we stopped at roadside markets, they joined me in buying fermented soya beans from women farmers. We discussed produce from the swidden fields and the beautiful forests and terraces we saw along our journey. At the same time, they savoured the view of the mountains and food; as members of JICA, they were invested in infrastructure development in Mizoram. For many in the group, the idea of a surplus-producing infrastructure utilising upland agriculture seemed like an excellent project to aspire to. For upland farmers, however, being included in this project was predicated upon accepting all the infrastructural costs added to the irrigation project. While they were seen as the beneficiaries of small minor irrigation projects, the bulk of money spent was funnelled into paying for material (like PVC pipes and motors sourced from outside the region) and salaries for skilled professionals. The individual farmer did not receive cash benefits from such projects and was supposed to reap the benefits of an infrastructural investment that they had not even asked for. Sometimes, the costs of experimentation with market-friendly cash crops like coffee and perishable ones like flowers led to huge risks that farmers had to bear as individuals and without any safety net from the industries they were supplying (or their local governments).

This vignette embodies the numerous contradictions the upland farmer faces when dealing with modern, impersonal bureaucracies. Since the late 1990s, especially with the intervention of organisations such as the International Fund for Agricultural Development (IFAD), the India-Canada Environment Facility (ICEF), and the International Centre for Integrated Mountain Development (ICIMOD), there has been a renewed attempt to rehabilitate the idea of a productive and valuable upland agriculturalist. These organisations have added new ideas for old bureaucratic budget lines that left states with the concept that upland agriculture could have been more productive and modern. They brought with them a more nuanced notion of upland agriculture, concentrating on gender roles, lack of use of chemicals and pesticides, and the possibility of leveraging such practices for the market. During this period, specifically those that began in the late 1990s, the discourse on upland farming began to transform from a highly negative one to one that was willing to see its benefits if the peasant was able to find a niche in the expanding markets.

These significant changes had other effects on the social fabric of the world of subsistence farmers in the uplands. The push towards entrepreneurship, as scholars of development and the politics of aid argue, can be a double-edged sword for the kind of aspirations they encourage. While they offer an escape from poverty for a few, they reproduce an unsustainable demand for neoliberal economies, furthering the conditions for more significant inequalities and conflicts (de Maaker, 2020; Duffield, 2002, 2017; Nilsen, 2021; Peck and Theodore, 2019).

Institutions, Innovations, and Markets

The first generation of scholars who challenged the view that upland agriculture was wasteful were geographers and social anthropologists, mainly from local universities such as North Eastern Hill University (NEHU). In the 1980s, geographers like P.S. Ramakrishnan wrote extensively on the importance of traditional knowledge in preserving the biodiversity of the Himalayas (Ramakrishnan 1992, 1996). His sociology and social anthropology counterparts, like M.N. Karna, T.B. Subba, and Virginius Xaxa, expanded on the knowledge of social structures among mountain communities (Karna, 2009; Subba, 1999; Xaxa, 2008). Some of this research contributed directly to the interventions by multilateral organisations discussed above. The links between researchers and implementation agencies (including donors) in Northeast India and its transnational neighbourhood have always been complicated, contentious, and rewarding in equal measure (Siddiqi, 2009)[9]. My point here is to underscore how educational institutions, the media, and the state have converged in describing the future of upland agriculture in Northeast India since the turn of the century. The need to balance academic approaches to learning and their application in the field has continued to animate debates around agrarian societies, especially in the uplands of Northeast India.

Hence, the emergence of innovation as a crucial means of addressing these debates and the impasse they pointed to, primarily routed through universities that were more than just dedicated to agriculture.[10] In the last decade, traditional departments in local colleges and universities have had to include concerns about sustainable development, entrepreneurship, and innovation in their curriculum. Social sciences and commerce, and technology departments have also begun to contribute to programmes that teach students about agriculture.[11] As a result, there has been a renewed debate on agricultural technology's applicability and apparent universality in the region's uplands. Additionally, the Government of India has mandated the National Innovation Foundation to extend some of its work to include small farmers in the area. This has created interfaces where social sciences, technology, and the ground realities of farmers in the field have converged to yield exciting results. There is a more critical awareness about celebrating the gains of industrialised farming, at least in the social sciences.

Furthermore, the granular details of the working lives of individual farmers and their families have been collated in creative case studies by various projects. The emphasis of these developments has been to focus on the positive contributions that agriculture can make to future livelihood strategies. More importantly, they include ways to improve access to the market, even for some of the most isolated farmers. Since 2010, the government of India has introduced several rural-based fellowships and projects that allow young social work and social sciences graduates to spend at least two years in the villages of India. In the past decade, students who have graduated from local universities in the region have found it exciting to join programmes like the National Rural Livelihoods Mission, the National Health Mission, the Prime Minister's Rural Development Fellow Scheme, and other schemes, some of which are initiated by state governments. They work long hours and are placed with district officials who are still trying to find a role for them in rural governance. Others find placement in interesting non-governmental research initiatives, encouraging rural children to express their ideas about innovation and change. These are new areas of inquiry that one needs to allow to settle before one can see their impact reflected in the government's annual balance sheets. So far, they are still in the realm of incubation. This term is borrowed from the biological sciences, and there is a growing concern that they cannot comprehend the intricacies and complexities of upland communities and their complicated pasts.

This predicament reverts to the old question—discussed in the earlier sections—about the direction of traffic in ideas. Here, too, one can see the emphasis on expanding markets, where the focus is on adding value to the traditional upland produce. One outcome of such a realisation is the investment of considerable sums of finance in marketing mountain products. The long rows of shops selling similar artefacts at the airports and state government emporiums, as well as the sustainable development forums in the mountain states of India, bring together a professional interest in upland agriculture to improve links with the market. These are interesting, new interventions in an old debate on the peasantry in upland areas. In addition, the local media in the region have begun to actively participate in encouraging entrepreneurship in farming. Local television channels and voluntary agencies have come together to celebrate the innovations of upland agriculturalists, especially women (Pinto-Rodrigues, 2020).

Such initiatives have a different view of work and labour, as they attempt to draw rural people to avail government schemes for healthcare, education, and diversification of occupations. They are also predicated on the success of additional government schemes like the public distribution system that allows farmers some leeway to plan their futures, especially if they wish to diversify. In some states of India, such as Madhya Pradesh, Rajasthan, and Chhattisgarh, these initiatives have indeed succeeded in improving the lot of individual farmers in the plains, significantly through procurement and prices that have been streamlined by local (federal state) governments (Dreze and Khera, 2019; Reddy, 2018). There is still some doubt about their effectiveness in the hills, where old doubts about upland farmers' character come into question occasionally.

I returned to my fieldwork in Mizoram for further corroboration of the need for more conversation between national planners and upland farmers whose livelihoods they seek to change. The fruit juice concentrate plant outside the town of Chhingchhip in the Serchhip district was one of the flagship projects of the Mizoram Food and Allied Industries Corporation, a company set up by the Government of Mizoram's Department of Industries. Its machines were geared to pulp oranges, pineapple, and passion fruit, all growing in abundance in the neighbouring hills. However, as it was February, the unit did not get the usual volume of fruit from neighbouring farms, so the place was relatively quiet. As the managers showed us around the sparkling new plant, they mentioned that it had no procurement procedures and farmers had to bring the fruit to the unit for processing. This, they emphasised, explained the fact that there was never enough raw material and that the unit was running at a loss. It was producing approximately 5% of its capacity. The unit had a Memorandum of Understanding with Shimla Hills Offerings Private Limited, a New Delhi-based company, that bought the passion fruit sulphite juice from the Mizoram unit. The expensive unit was set up with great hope but without much consultation about its efficacy for the district. When faced with such a monumental example of innovative imagination waiting for its potential to be realised, I asked the most obvious question: Were any local fruit growers consulted before the project was placed in Chhingchhip? The manager looked puzzled at first and then said he was unsure. Still, he knew the plan for setting up the unit was done by consultants from the Central Food Technological Research Institute in Mysore, Karnataka, located more than 3,600 kilometres away.

I took my questions to researchers at Mizoram University and journalists in Aizawl for clarity on the various activities supporting online farmers in Mizoram. In several ways, the intense pressure on upland agriculturalists to change their farming practices was incommensurate with the actual numbers of those who could access the markets, thereby making upland agriculture more viable for their children. If anything, upland farmers were more than happy to receive financial incentives from the government and use them for purposes other than intended. For instance, under NLUP, farmers were given a certain amount of money to help them move towards growing cash crops in their fields. Instead of following the script, anecdotal evidence from journalists and government functionaries suggested that farmers were spending the cash transfers on health and education. To their credit, the local government functionaries did not see the farmers' actions as transgressions or theft, as some of the consultants from Delhi seemed to suggest. They hoped, instead, that the NLUP would be able to draw in allied issues, such as retaining forest cover and ensuring regular water and electricity supply (by building dams). The views of bureaucrats, researchers, and journalists on these issues had converged on the inability of old modes of upland agriculture to sustain the requirements of a new century, where people were increasingly moving away from farming and into cities (and towns).[12]

Upland farmers in Northeast India have yet to be able to live up to the expectations thrust upon them by economic planners and politicians. This, however, has kept the performative aspects of the process from taking on new meanings. State governments (in Northeast India) continue to allocate funds, albeit increasingly modest, to showcase the cultural underpinnings of upland agriculture in the hope that it adds value to farmers' produce. Hence, efforts to introduce geographical indexing and patents for upland agriculture occasionally make it to the local news. Nevertheless, these efforts dissipate in the face of governmental inability to make markets (of the capitalist kind) more accessible for farmers in the uplands. The recent announcements by the Government of India to expand the cultivation of edible palm oil in Northeast India's uplands to make up for import shortages have been met with alarm by environmentalists and agriculturalists alike (Bhattacharya et al., 2021).[13] These efforts by the government have further erased upland farmers from narratives of economic progress. They conform to the contentious land use transition from food production to biofuels that Borras and Franco described in their global land grab typologies (ibid). The question is, will this process be relatively less violent and aggressive? The principal armed insurgencies in these uplands are on the wane, and the farmers of the region do not have as much at stake to find common ground with those protesting the new farm laws.

Conclusion

Occasionally, I follow sceptical students who had forgone good placements with government initiatives. They were not entirely convinced by the attempts by industry and government to impose the onus of development on the upland farmer. Instead, I have followed their questions with ideas of justice and the complicated futures that upland farmers see ahead of them. While innovations and entrepreneurship are being promoted, there is a need to revisit older accounts of work and labour, especially considering the historian's evidence that upland agriculture was part of the region's intricate ecological and political history. The entrepreneurial push lacks a certain authenticity for upland farmers. Their inability to comply with its demands resonates with the protesting farmers from the more agriculturally developed states, in conflict with the state on pushing them towards globalised markets (Valbona, 2021). Moreover, as Tania Murray Li and Janet Sturgeon point out, the political optics of using the most vulnerable demographic in the great developmental leap forward are closely linked to other forms of structural violence (Li, 2014b; Sturgeon, 2007). Can these narratives be circled off, like an Aristotelian tragedy with plot, character, thought, diction, song, and spectacle? Again, history provides evidence that this need not be the case.

In the middle of Diphu—the main town in Karbi Anglong hill district in Assam—there is a remarkable statue of a peasant woman bearing an axe, with her comrades and a dog following her. The statue was sculpted by Biren Singha, an artist involved in the struggle for territorial autonomy for the hills in Assam in the 1980s and 1990s. Kareng Rongpharphi was a figure plucked from late 18th-century folklore by activists and archivists of a left-leaning movement for autonomy in Assam. In her compelling story, she was a peasant incensed by the King's demand for milk from nursing mothers so that he could feed the royal tiger cub. Kareng, a nursing mother, fought off the soldiers who had come to force her to give milk. She then organised her village to build roads into the wilderness so the King's soldiers would follow them and get stranded in the forests. The demands on upland farming communities by planners, political representatives, and the local elite might seem less dramatic today. However, they are still quite significant, and observers ought to expect some pushback in the future. It is difficult to pinpoint where this resistance might germinate, as few platforms can unite upland farmers as bearers and subjects of history. Still, it could include refusing market forces in their current forms.[14]

In May 2023, the Karbi Anglong Autonomous Council representatives decided to move the iconic statue from the town centre to the interstate bus terminus along the Diphu-Manjha road. The council members claimed that a new flyover would diminish the monument's stature, so ironically, they decided to move it to an impersonal bus stop terminal, where the metaphor of resistance would be further erased. Indigenous communities and student bodies protested this move, arguing that the small town did not need a flyover.

The challenge for social scientists, historians, and those advocating for the rights of farming communities in India will be to absorb the many different trajectories that farmers have taken within the country. While the current protests by north Indian farmers on the mainland have received deserved attention from commentators and activists, this is also an opportunity to understand how the market is such an elusive and contentious object. The market demands sacrifice from farmers who were beneficiaries of state subsidies, scientific and technological advancement, and political mobilisation. Several generations of upland farmers have already forgone peace in the nation-building process in 20th-century India. Even as governments seek to integrate them into inconclusive projects for the future, it would be meaningful to ensure their pasts are not erased in the process.

I thank the Swedish Research Council for their financial support (Project no. 2020-03859). This work emerged from the ***Practicing Food Sovereignty*** project (2021-2023) conducted in Bangladesh, Bhutan, Nepal, and Northeast India. I thank my colleagues, Prof Bengt Karlsson, Prof Dolly Kikon, Dr Dixita Deka, Dr Meenal Tula, and Joel Rodrigues for sharing their work and ideas with me. Thanks to Prof Erik de Maaker, Ms Seno Tsuhah, Mr Manoram Gogoi, Mr Mohan Bora, Dr Walter Fernandes, and the two anonymous reviewers for sharing their ideas and work with me. Any errors remain mine alone.

Endnotes

1. This includes rites of passage, religious rituals, and festivals for many communities. Through the 20th century, upland communities in the region have engaged and negotiated with dominant religions like Buddhism, Christianity, Hinduism, and Islam, have retained many agriculture-based rituals from the past (Burlings 1963, van Schendel 1992, Zou 2009).

2. Funders for government-supported events like the Hornbill Festival are not without their critics. Political commentators argue that states like Nagaland should prioritize unpaid government wages over funneling funds from other development projects into the festival. See: http://morungexpress.com/hornbill-festival-the-need-to-get-it-right/ (accessed October 16, 2017).

3. People who live off the land, mainly by farming, are called Nongrep in Khasi, Kuthnathawk in Mizo, Lotamei in Mao Naga, Louuba in Meiteilon, and Loubolmi in Thadou Kuki. These terms denote someone who looks after agricultural land, especially rice cultivation. They may be economically differentiated from the small but emerging group of wealthier community member with better access to political power.

4. The state museum in Guwahati displays late-Ahom period (18th century) exhibits that allude to tributes paid by upland agriculturalists to the Ahom Kings. In exchange for hill produce such as poison and salt, they received rights to agricultural surplus and labor from the valley. Known as called posa, this system was labeled 'blackmail' by colonial British officials, who overlooked its cultural and historical significance (Kar 2016).

5. All Indian states have a skill development and entrepreneurship departments that reflect regional adaptations of the vision and mission statement articulated by the Ministry of Skill Development and Entrepreneurship, Government of India.

6. For details, see NLUP Mizoram, https://nlup.mizoram.gov.in/ (accessed October 17, 2017).

7. There is a wide range of affective relationships between lowland and upland

farmers. During fieldwork in 2012 (in Mizoram), I observed Mizo paddy farmers employing Muslim farmers, who often came with their families from Assam's Barak valley. Both groups kept to their own. The Muslim farmers, usually men who headed the family, spoke a few words of Mizo to interact with the landowners. Their families did not mingle. During fieldwork in 2017 and later in 2022 and 2023 in Arunachal Pradesh (in East Siang, Lower Dibang, and Lohit districts) and Assam (Karbi Anglong and Dima Hasao Districts), I observed markedly different relationships between Assamese and Adivasi farmers from the plains and their Adi or Galo landowners and employers. They shared language, food, festivities, and sometimes brawled with one another.

8. Such experiments have occurred in the 1990s and early 2000s as well, especially with crops like cardamom in Nagaland. The cardamom experiment ran into difficulties following the fall in prices in the early 1990s, leaving local farmers in Nagaland at a loss. Adding neglected and underutilised species like millets was an innovation popularised by women's groups in villages like Chizami (in Nagaland). In the past decade, this has expanded into small, celebratory events around the production and consumption of millets.

9. Writing about women workers in Bangladesh, Dina Siddiqi raises a point that holds true for other South Asian contexts as well. Some of the most critical scholarship that emerged from grassroots advocacy was quickly adopted into the developmental donor discourse that was being pushed by multi-lateral agencies. The traffic of ideas between the field, classrooms and donor spreadsheets was mediated by exceptionally committed teachers and their students, who worked towards translating classroom discussions into practical action-oriented work in rural settings. Donors furthering developmental goals that were supported by multiple actors, including the United Nations and other multi-lateral organisations, were keen to include such work in their portfolios.

10. Agricultural universities and colleges were created in the region following India's independence from Britain. However, efforts to conduct research on rice in the region, especially Assam, had begun in the 19th century. These efforts offered the beginnings of agricultural research and became the foundations of the Assam Agricultural University when it was established in 1969. Its earliest Vice Chancellors and professors were trained in agricultural sciences in the United States and were instrumental in providing intellectual support and research for India's green revolution in agriculture.

11. For instance, Tata Institute of Social Sciences (TISS) has a Centre for Ecology, Environment, and Sustainable Development, where concerns of abuse of public and natural resources are part of the curriculum; North Eastern Hill University (NEHU), has a department of Rural Development and Agricultural Production that focuses on promoting entrepreneurship in various agricultural fields. Similarly, the Indian Institute of Technology (IIT), Guwahati, has a Centre for Linguistic Science and Technology, where historians, linguists, and engineers come together to provide practical information to indigenous farmers in languages that they (the farmers) speak at home.

12. I hasten to add here that among the three—bureaucrats, researchers, and journalists—some were less convinced about the celebratory potential of radical land use. Some researchers, especially those who did archival work, as well as journalists, were cautious. They were not surprised that farmers were not behaving as the planners hoped they would, and they attributed this to a long history of impoverishment and neglect of upland farming. Even the inheritors of the two-decade-long guerrilla war (1966-1986) who wanted Mizos to be self-sufficient in food production, were not quite convinced that the upland farmer would be the right vehicle. They too, I was told, focused on lower-elevation paddy growing to expand grain and vegetable production in the 1980s and 1990s (when they came to power).

13. On 18 August 2021, the Government of India announced that the cabinet had approved a plan to expand the area and productivity of edible oils, especially palm oil, in Northeast India and Andaman Islands: https://www.pib.gov.in/PressReleasePage.aspx?PRID=1746942 (Accessed on October 10, 2021). Both places—the uplands of Northeast India and Andaman Islands—

fit awkwardly into the national map and imagination as peripheral places.

14. There are platforms that seek to bring them together, but as objects of history that require greater skills, more trainings, and sometimes even seek to change their occupations altogether.

References

Barbora, S. (2002). "Ethnic politics and land use: Genesis of conflicts in India's North-East", in *Economic and Political Weekly,* 37 (13), 30 March 2002. Pp. 1285–1292.

Barbora, S. (2018). *Peasant, Students, Insurgents and Popular Movements in Contemporary Assam,* Policies and Practices, 97; Kolkata: Calcutta Research Group.

Baruah, S. (2007). *Postfrontier Blues: Towards a New Policy Framework for Northeast India,* Washington, DC: East-West Center.

Baruah, S. (2017). "India and its Northeast: Another Big Push without a Take-Off." in Y. Saikia and A. R. Baishya (Eds.) *Northeast India: A Place of Relations,* New Delhi: Cambridge University Press. Pp. 45–67.

Baruah, S. (2020). *In the Name of the Nation: India and its Northeast,* Stanford: Stanford University Press.

Bhattacharya, B., G. Talukdar and N. Guha. (2021). "Mizoram's balancing act with palm oil's ecological impacts and economic benefits" in *Mongabay-India,* https://india.mongabay.com/2021/09/mizorams-balancing-act-with-palm-oils-ecological-impact-and-economic-benefits/ (13 September)

Borras Jr, S and J.C. Franco. 2012. "Global Land Grabbing and the Trajectory of Agrarian Change: A Preliminary Analysis" in *Journal of Agrarian Change* 12 (1). Pp. 34-59.

Burlings, R. (1963). *Rengsanggri: Family and Kinship in a Garo Village,* Philadelphia: University of Pennsylvania Press.

Choudhury, D. S. Bhuchar and S. Thomas. 2021. *Transitioning shifting cultivation to resilient farming systems in South and Southeast Asia: Guidelines for policymakers and development practitioners* (Resource Book), Kathmandu: ICIMOD.

Debbarma, A and A. Debbarma. 2018. "Perspective on Rubber Monoculture in Tripura, North-East India" in *International Journal of Ecology and Environmental Sciences* 44 (1). Pp. 27-31.

De Maaker, E. (2020). "Who Owns the Hills? Ownership, Inequality, and Communal Sharing in the Borderlands of Northeast India" in *Asian Ethnology* 79 (2). Pp. 357-375.

De Maaker, E and M Tula. 2021. "Introduction: Reinterpreting Customary Land Relationships" in Erik de Maaker and Meenal Tula (Eds) *Unequal Land Relations in Northeast India: Custom, Gender, and the Market,* Guwahati: North Eastern Social Research Centre. Pp. 1-30.

Dreze, J and R. Khera. 2019. "Food Security Act: An Indecent Proposal? The PDS Turnaround in Chhattisgarh" in Jean Dreze, *Sense and Solidarity: Jholawala Economics for Everyone,* New Delhi: Oxford University Press. Pp. 178-182.

Duffield, M. (2002). "Social Reconstruction and the Radicalization of Development: Aid as a Relation of Global Governance" in *Development and Change* 33 (5). Pp. 1049–1071.

Duffield, M. (2017). "Human Security and the Development-Security Nexus. A historical overview" in *Ragion practica, Rivista semestrale" 1/2017, pp. 61–76, doi: 10.1415/86437*

Fernandes, W. and S. Barbora. "Introduction" in W. Fernandes and S. Barbora (Eds) *Land, People, and Politics: Contest Over Tribal Land in Northeast India,* Guwahati and Copenhagen: North Eastern Social Research Centre and International Working Group on Indigenous Affairs. Pp. 1-15.

Harriss, J, and D. Stewart. (2015). 'Science, Politics and the Framing of Modern

Agricultural Technologies' in R.J. Herring (Ed) *The Oxford Handbook of Food, Politics and Society*, Oxford and New York: Oxford University Press. Pp. 43–64.

Haque, J and N.A. Barua. 2021. "Income Diversification as a Strategy for Agrarian Crisis Management: A Case Study of Assam" in *Asian Journal of Advances in Research* 11 (3). Pp. 1–10.

Kar, B. (2013). "Heads in the Naga Hills", in P. Chatterjee, T. Guha-Thakurta and Bodhisattva Kar (eds.), *New Cultural Histories of India: Materiality and Practices*, New Delhi: Oxford University Press. Pp. 335–370.

Kar, B. (2016). "Nomadic capital and speculative tribes: A culture of contracts in the Northeastern Frontier of British India" in *The Indian Economic and Social History Review* 53 (1). Pp. 41–67.

Karlsson, B.G. (2023). "Resource Frontier" in J. Wouters and T.B. Subba (Eds). *The Routledge Companion to Northeast India*, New York: Routledge. Pp. 382–387.

Karlsson, B.G. (2011). *Unruly Hills: A Political Ecology of India's Northeast*, New Delhi: Social Sciences Press.

Karna, M.N. (2009). "Tribal Areas of Meghalaya: Land Ownership of Women" in P. Chowdhry (Ed.) *Gender Discrimination in Land Ownership (Land Reforms in India, Vol. IX)*, New Delhi: Sage Publications. Pp. 176–195.

Kikon, D. (2005). "Engaging Naga Nationalism" in *Economic and Political Weekly* 40 (26). Pp. 2833-2837

Kikon, D and B.G. Karlsson. 2019. *Leaving the Land: Indigenous Migration and Affective Labour in India*, New Delhi: Cambridge University Press.

Kipgen, N and A Roy Chowdhury. (2016). "'Contested State-craft' on the Frontiers of the Indian Nation: 'Hills-Valley Divide' and the Genealogy of Kuki Ethnic Nationalism in Manipur" in *Studies in Ethnicity and Nationalism* 16 (2). Pp. 283–303.

Leduc, B and D. Choudhury. 2012. "Agricultural transformation in shifting cultivation areas of Northeast India: Implications for land management, gender, and institutions" in D. Nathan and V. Xaxa (Eds), *Social Exclusion and Adverse Inclusion: Development and Deprivation of Adivasis in India*, New Delhi: Oxford University Press. Pp. 237-258.

Li, T.M. (2014a). *Land's End: Capitalist Relations on an Indigenous Frontier*, Durham: Duke University Press.

Li, T.M. (2014b). "Can There Be Food Sovereignty Here?" in *Journal of Peasant Studies* 36 (3). Pp. 629–636.

Ltu, V. (2021). "Women, Property, and Angami Customary Law" in E. de Maaker and M. Tula (Eds) *Unequal Land Relations in Northeast India: Custom, Gender, and the Market*, Guwahati: North Eastern Social Research Centre. Pp. 62–86.

Ludden, D. (2011). "The process of empire: frontiers and borderlands" in P. Fibiger Bang and C.A. Bayly (Eds.) *Tributary Empires in Global History*, London: Palgrave Macmillan. Pp. 132–150.

Mishra, D.K. (2017). "Agrarian transformation in mountain economies: field insights from Arunachal Pradesh" in D.K.Mishra and V. Upadhyay (Ed) *Rethinking Economic Development in Northeast India*, London and New York: Routledge. Pp. 258–272.

Moa, L. and S. Chakraborty. (2020). "A Study on Coffee Production in Nagaland" in *International Journal of Innovations in Management, Engineering and Science* 6 (2). Pp. 44–53.

Mumford, J.R. (2012). *Vertical Empire: The General Resettlement of the Indians in the Colonial Andes*, Durham: Duke University Press.

Nilsen, A.G. (2021). "Give James Ferguson a Fish" in *Development and Change* 52 (1). Pp. 3–25.

Nunthara, C. (1981). "Groupings of Villages in Mizoram: Its Social and Economic Impact" in *Economic and Political Weekly*, 16 (30). Pp. 1237–1240.

Peck, J. and N. Theodore (2019). 'Still Neoliberalism?', *The South Atlantic Quarterly* 118(2): 245–65.

Pinto-Rodrigues, A. (2020). (February 25). Against the grain: Why millet is making a comeback in rural India. *The Guardian.* https://www.theguardian.com/global-development/2020/feb/25/against-the-grain-why-millet-is-enjoying-an-indian-revival-nagaland. (Accessed on 10 March 2021).

Ramakrishnan, P.S. (1992). *Shifting agriculture and sustainable development: an inter-disciplinary study from north-east India,* Paris: UNESCO.

Ramakrishnan, P.S. (1996). "Conserving the sacred: from species to landscapes" in *Nature and Resources* 32 (1). Pp. 11–19.

Reddy, B.S. (2018). *Patterns of Agricultural Transition in Tribal Areas of Madhya Pradesh: A Macro and Micro analysis* (Working Paper No. 142), Hyderabad: Centre for Economics and Social Studies.

Scott, J.C. (2009). *The Art of Not Being Governed: An Anarchist History of Upland Southeast Asia,* New Haven: Yale University Press.

Shanin, T. (1972). *Awkward Class: Political Sociology of Peasantry in a Developing Society, Russia, 1910-25,* Oxford: Oxford University Press.

Shimray, U.A. (2009). "Land use system in Manipur hills: A case study of the Tangkhul Naga" in W. Fernandes and S. Barbora (Eds) *Land, People and Politics: Contest over Tribal Land in Northeast India,* Guwahati, and Copenhagen: NESRC and IWGIA. Pp. 88–112.

Siddiqi, D.M. (2009). "Do Bangladeshi factory workers need saving? Sisterhood in the post-sweatshop era" in *Feminist Review* 91 (1). Pp. 154–174.

Sturgeon, J. (2007). *Border Landscapes: The Politics of Akha Land Use in China and Thailand,* Seattle: University of Washington Press.

Subba, T.B. (1999). *Politics of Culture: A Study of Three Kirata Communities in the Eastern Himalayas,* Hyderabad: Orient Longman.

Sundar, N. (2011). "Interning Insurgent Populations: The Buried Histories of Indian Democracy" in *Economic and Political Weekly* 46 (6). Pp. 47–57.

Umdor, S and B.R. Syiem. 2017. "State of Finances in the Autonomous District Councils of Meghalaya" in *Social Change and Development* 15 (July). Pp. 12-26.

Valbona, M. (2021). "Stealing the common from the goose: The emergence of Farmers' Rights and their implementation in India and Brazil" in *Journal of Agrarian Change* 21. Pp. 356–376.

Van Der Ploeg, J.D. 2008. *The New Peasantries: Struggles for Autonomy and Sustainability in the Era of Empire and Globalization,* London: Earthscan.

Van Schendel, W. (1992). "The Invention of the 'Jummas': State Formation and Ethnicity in Southeastern Bangladesh" in *Modern Asian Studies* 26 (1). Pp. 95–128.

Wolf, E. (1966). *Peasants,* Englewood-Cliffs: Prentice Hall.

Xaxa, V. (2008). *State, Society and Tribes: Issues in Post-Colonial India,* Delhi: Pearson Longman (Dorling Kindersley India).

Zou, D.V. (2009). "The Pasts of a Fringe Community: Ethno-history and Fluid Identity of the Zou in Manipur" in *Indian Historical Review* 36 (2). Pp. 209–235.

HIMALAYA
The Journal of the Association of Nepal and Himalayan Studies

Research Article

Two Decades of Conservation in Ladakh: Accessing the Achi Association (AA) and Achi Association India (AAI) Archives

Sushan Bhattarai

Achi Association India (AAI)

DOI: https://doi.org/10.2218/himalaya.2025.10112

Abstract

Ladakh's climatic conditions have preserved some of the most impressive monuments in the Himalaya. These temples trace the spread of Buddhism in the Western Himalaya and the development of artistic and architectural styles. However, they are increasingly under threat due to the introduction of modern construction materials and methods, as well as the intensification of climate change induced events. In 1999, Achi Association was formed to conserve temples belonging to the Drikung Kagyu sect of Tibetan Buddhism, one of the oldest orders in Ladakh, and one under which many of the earliest temples in the region were built. In 2010, the establishment of Achi Association India (AAI) expanded this to any Buddhist heritage in precarity throughout Ladakh, regardless of sect. With a quarter of a century of experience in the region, the two organizations collectively produced an impressive fountain of documents that chart and record all aspects of conservation work done across nine sites that date from the late 13th century to the 19th century. In this paper I scaffold an interdisciplinary approach to access these archives, which range from architectural surveys to community engagement reports, accentuating that conservation is a dialectic between stakeholders, where decisions made by conservators — shaped by their training and available technology — are interpreted by other stakeholders, namely locals and the clergy, through their own epistemic frameworks. Mapping the entirety of conservation and restoration, this paper covers multiple aspects of the process, including documentation, community engagement, technical procedures, and the ritual ramifications of decisions.

Keywords

archives, conservation, Western Himalayas, Ladakh, restoration

Recommended Citation

Bhattarai, Sushan (2025). Two Decades of Conservation in Ladakh: Accessing the Achi Association (AA) and Achi Association India (AAI) Archives. *HIMALAYA* 44(1): 66-80.

cc BY NC ND

This work is licensed under a Creative Commons Attribution-Noncommercial-No Derivative Works 4.0 License.

Introduction

In a pink folder in Palay House — AAI's office in Phey, Ladakh — are printed email correspondences between European conservators dating back to 2004. It is part of a collection of early printed documents that heed back to a time before digital archives. Over the years, Achi's archive grew, and now most of the corpus is digitized. The collective archive is a montage of documents, often either produced on site — like bills from purchases and work logs — or reports — condition assessments, surveys, and proposals. The archives on conservation oscillate between these two types of documents, providing a holistic snapshot of history, conservation technologies, and community engagement.

Despite the significance of conservation in Ladakh and the Himalaya, little has been written or discussed about how it is conducted and its significance. This is largely due to the particularities of disciplines like art history and architecture that use a frame of reference that prioritizes documentation of the past. The resulting canon is rich with academic material on Ladakh's Buddhist heritage and art, emphasizing the rarity of well-preserved sites that offer a chance to study traditions and artistic styles extinguished in other places where Buddhism once existed. Simultaneously, recent scholarship produced by anthropologists and geographers has engaged with the effects of modernization on the region, drawing attention to the erosion of cultural practices and the traditional way of life. Before proceeding, it will be helpful to understand how "traditional" is usually understood by Achi architects and conservators. "Traditional" refers to historical practices that have persisted into the present, offering a sense of continuity with the construction techniques used in Ladakh before the introduction of modern building methods. Furthermore, there are no organizations that have worked as extensively on Buddhist religious sites, and since the AAI archives have only recently been organized and accessed, there is limited scholarship on temple conservation in Ladakh.[1] Moreover, AAI's archives allow for a holistic approach because of the wide array of documents that different stakeholders involved in conservation work over the last two decades have produced. The availability of these different voices allows us to see how perceptions of conservation both converged and, at times, diverged. How these contending perceptions were negotiated is a central theme in this paper. A concerted effort was made by a coalition of participants who worked on conservation projects in the village of Wanla. The book *Against Forgetting (2021)* is a compendium of essays that contour the perspectives of project members from their respective disciplinary training. The holistic nature of this book has helped me formulate my own approach to writing this paper.

Documentation concerning community engagement and technical work serve as the foundations of this paper. The former is a process of navigating the cultural and religious matrix these sites are under, as conservation is not possible without the clergy and community support, while technical documentation covers a collection of approaches that are highly specific to the needs of traditional Ladakhi construction methods. Technical documentation has also involved a scientific approach to studying materials. For example, Achi conservators conducted tests using fragments of detached wall paintings to examine how the renders and plasters supporting the paintings at the Avalokiteshvara Temple at Wanla were created (Bläuer 2021, 72). This understanding of the composition unveiled the method through which a select set of materials had to coalesce to create a canvas and informed how conservators approached areas of abrasion and dereliction. The final type of material in the archive, and one I will not address in this essay, is a form of bureaucratic documentation. These documents, ranging from grant applications to budget allocations, highlight the institutional scaffolding required to build an international pool of partners, who, working with their Indian counterparts, have successfully delivered projects. The continuity of Achi, and the collaborations it has fostered, can be understood through these sets of administrative documents.

The purpose of this paper is threefold. One, it is a survey of almost two decades worth of material, covering a breadth of projects, and experiences accumulated by various members who were a part of these projects, offering some of the most comprehensive documentation of conservation and restoration not just in Ladakh but the entirety of the Trans-Himalaya. Two, the essay situates conservation within a much broader process of ideological shifts, encounters with clergy and community members, and its place in modern-day Ladakh. In doing this, I hope it expands the ways through which heritage is understood and how conservation is often an epistemic dialogue that architects, conservators, communities, and the clergy are constantly negotiating and converging on. Lastly, I hope this essay can function as a schematic tool for conservators and architects, introducing those interested to the multidimensional nature of conservation in the Trans-Himalaya.

Formation of Achi Association (AA) & Achi Association India (AAI)

Conservation-related research visits started as early as 1998, preceding the establishment of the Achi Association (AA) in 1999 (Roy 2021, 41). The AA was initially founded in Switzerland by a group of European conservators and scholars, with H.H. Kyabgön Chetsang Rinpoche as honorary president. The organization aimed to safeguard the outstanding but endangered heritage of the Western Himalaya by bringing together scholars specializing in the early art and architecture of the region (41). Achi Association India (AAI) was formed in 2010 to further and strengthen AA's work in India. Both organizations take their name from the Dakini Achi who is considered to be the protectress of the Drikung Kagyu order; she can be seen practically outside every Drikung monastery or temple, often over the entrance porch (Achi Association 2011). While Achi Association was mandated to work solely on Drikung heritage, Achi Association India was not, and was able to factor in other considerations regarding conservation priorities. Given that both organizations have closely worked together, have shared histories, overlapping personnel, and a collective archive, I will refer to both organizations as Achi in this paper.

Ladakh's long-standing connection with the Drikung Kagyu order, and the unique climatic conditions in the area, have made the temples there a principal cultural and visual repository for the history of Buddhism in the Himalaya. The Drikung Kagyu school was founded at Drikung in Central Tibet by Jigten Gönpo (1143-1217), with a focus on meditative practice. In the first few decades after the Drikung order was established, Jigten Gönpo sent disciples to Mount Kailash in Western Tibet for meditative practice. At the beginning of the 13th century, he began establishing hermitages throughout the Kailash–Manasarowar region, successfully gaining the support of local rulers, among them the Lhachen Ngroub, the Ladakhi king at the time (Petech 1977, 19-20). We know he embraced the Drikung sect because he sponsored the construction of a monastery near the sacred Mount Kailash in 1215, alongside the king of Guge and the Purans (Rizvi 1996, 61). The Drikung Kagyu monuments are vestiges of Ladakhi and Tibetan history that have mostly been destroyed elsewhere, offering a rare look into the circulation of Buddhism between the Western Himalaya, Indo-Gangetic plains, and the Tibetan Plateau.

Achi's projects span multiple centuries and political dynasties, which can be broadly divided into three distinct time periods. The temples at Wanla, Kanji, and Nyoma are from the late 13th to early 14th century, when political chieftains controlled large swathes of land in Ladakh and ruled their own fiefdoms. Sometime in the 14th century, this model collapsed, and Kashmiri art, which had been a major source of inspiration, also began to wane — although Buddhism in Kashmir had largely been supplanted by orthodox Brahmanical Hinduism by the middle of the 12th century (Sarao 2012, 38). The temples at Henisku and Mulbek date from the 14th to 15th century, with Photoksar also belonging to the same period, but built after the Namgyal dynasty came into power. The assembly hall ('du khang) at Ensa and the Skurbuchan Fortress (khar) are from the 19th century after the Dogra Empire took control of Ladakh. All three of these time periods contain significant artistic and architectural features that Achi's teams have tried to preserve and document. The range of dates involved provides an archive that traces how temples and artistic processes evolved in Ladakh, allowing for a unique opportunity to tell stories across time.

Contextualizing Conservation in the 21st Century

Before delving into conservation, it is imperative to understand the material elements that produce the Ladakhi architectural vernacular. Almost all the temples that Achi has worked on were built using locally sourced materials that are inherently tied to the geography. A question that looms large over all conservation and restoration projects is how new and old materials will interact and to what extent. Since Achi was one of the first organizations to carry out restoration work, there were no parameters to draw from; architects and conservators had to make decisions that were culturally, religiously, and technically sound, predicated on a scrupulous understanding of earthen construction processes in the region.

The foundations of most Ladakhi temples, like those of houses, are made up of stone, often collected from riverbanks. Ladakhi bricks, or *pagbu*, are made by putting local mud into a wooden mold and sunbaking them; sometimes, when larger bricks are made, straw is mixed in for strength (Ferrari 2021, 48). To make mortar, local soil is mixed with water, resulting in a strong and durable mixture due to the high clay content of the soil. Typically, poplar beams with wooden branches are placed in a herringbone pattern across sun-baked bricks to form the flat roof; although for temples, designs tend to deviate considerably sometimes (Norberg-Hodge 2016, 32). Temples are then plastered with a fine clay called *markalak*, or "butter mud." Many sites where *markalak* is available contain paleolake deposits — a lake that existed in the past when hydrological conditions were different. In temples, *markalak* is used to produce the smooth surface for wall paintings, while *karsti*, a white primer, is applied as the surface to be painted on (Bläuer 2021, 72). It is only during the late 20th century that materials like cement became available, radically changing how buildings were made and looked. Conservation work done by Achi had to contend with not just sourcing traditional Ladakhi construction materials but also finding individuals who were suitably trained to apply them properly. As monasteries in the region have transitioned to modern construction materials and practices, in line with the rest of the Union Territory, the conservation process presents an opportunity to study and record traditional construction methods in detail. In addition to capturing the procedures, scholars used technology to gain new insights on construction materials used as far back as 800 years ago, such as testing the *karsti* (primer) in Wanla, and apply this information to make contemporary decisions. Furthermore, the shift to modern construction materials and practices has naturally led to a decline in Ladakhi masons or artisans who are able to work with traditional materials. The decline of this knowledge, which is cited in different project reports, served as an impetus for documentation.

A point of Achi's work thus became explaining and interrogating what conservation is. John Harrison, a British architect who has extensively documented and restored buildings across the Himalaya and has been restoring with Achi since 1999, emphasizes that "we are dealing with different perceptions on heritage and its importance, and preservation...in their culture, change is an intrinsic attribute of life, and building modification[s] have been made whenever necessary or desired" (Harrison 2021, 212). Harrison's comment reveals the matrix within which time, material, and religion operate. Building and consecrating temples has long been a vital way to accrue merit (karma) for oneself or one's kin; the Avalokiteshvara Temple at Wanla offers a compelling example. Conservation in an academic and technical sense stresses a type of stillness that values preservation as a method to access the past. It is not that Ladakh and the greater Himalaya do not value history; rather, there is an epistemological shift in how it is recorded and what can count as truth. Objectivity in academia is often reached through "tangible" evidence, material that can be seen or recorded, so preservation sustains a historical portal that allows for such scholarly work. With Ladakh modernizing, an influx of new materials and cultures have penetrated the region. Alongside an embedded religious value, temples and monasteries have become sites of a secular knowledge production that derive value through being significant for scholarship. Ladakhi peoples have acquired a dual and seamless engagement of heritage — performing religious rites and simultaneously viewing heritage as access points to understand culture. The interest shown by Achi and the work done by architects and conservators further amplifies this.

Temples as Visual Repositories

Beyond acting as repositories for Ladakhi art, sites that Achi has worked on are reminders of the rich visual ecosystem that operated in the Trans-Himalayan region. The temple of Wanla, for example, is done in the Central Tibetan art style, a shift from the Kashmiri style seen at Alchi. The temple is an imposing and comprehensive piece of work in the Western Himalaya that signals a shift in the artistic milieu of Ladakh. Built by a local chieftain, Bhak Darskyabs, it houses an eleven-headed Avalokiteshvara and was commissioned by the benefactor to assure a good rebirth for his parents and himself, a common rationale for Buddhist patronage. The murals of the temple are predominantly painted in the northeastern Indian style of Sharri, while the Nepali style of Beri can be seen as a secondary style. The alternation between the two styles gives variation to the thrones of the main deities and conveys a sense of gradation from secondary Nepali deities to principally northeast Indian ones. The assembly of the deities and the teaching they represent is another site of amalgamation — the Eight Forms of Padmasambhava and the Eight Pronouncements relate to the teachings of the Ancient Nyingma tradition, while others, like the mandala of the deity of Chakrasamvara, are from the teachings of the new traditions (Sarma), obtained from India and Nepal over the 11th and 12th centuries (Martin 2023).

The Avalokiteshvara Temple at Wanla is related to two other monuments that Achi conserved and restored. Between 2016 and 2017, Achi worked on the Kankani Chorten — a gateway chorten that belongs to a group of chortens situated below the ancient settlement of Nyoma village. Nyoma was an important checkpoint on the trade road to Ladakh. It is most likely that Bhak Darskyabs — the chieftain who commissioned the Avalokiteshvara Temple at Wanla — died on the way to a military campaign or en route to Mount Kailash for pilgrimage. The presence of a mandala with the *dharani* (a sacred Sanskrit phrase used as a verbal protective talisman) of Akshobhya, a mantra believed to purify many eons of negative karma and liberate oneself and others, suggests that this was likely a funerary monument. Both the mandala and *dharani* of Akshobhya are common practices in the Drikung order of Tibetan Buddhism for funerary rituals (Vets et al. 2015, 4). Moreover, stylistic analysis by art historian Nils Martin revealed that the painter(s) of the right wall in the Avalokiteshvara Temple in Wanla also worked on the Kankani Chorten (4). They feature common iconographic subtleties in depicting protective deities or masters of the Drikung lineage and show similar quality, technique, and manner of wall paintings — execution of facial features, falls of the garment, multicolor scrollwork all over the nimbus of the Buddhas, and the same light red contour lines are some of the similarities. The local oral tradition corroborates this, recording that pigments left over after the painting of the chorten at Nyoma were brought to Wanla to paint the Avalokiteshvara Temple (5).

The 700-year-old Kanji Temple (gTsug lag khang) in Ladakh's Leh district, which was Achi's first conservation project, is also part of the same visual ecosystem. Martin suggests that the left wall of the Avalokiteshvara Temple in Wanla and the temple in Kanji were done by the same painter (Martin 2022, 292). This pioneering research further nuances the visual ecosystem from regionalities, Buddhist art styles traveling from Bengal to the Kathmandu Valley, and then via Central Tibet to Ladakh, to a further localized and intimate setting, where individual artists are exercising a hybridity of repertories by tapping into a wider circulation of Himalayan visual culture.

Community Engagement & Partnerships

Over the last two decades, Achi has worked with several communities around Ladakh who have explicitly sought collaboration and contributed to restoration and conservation projects. No Achi effort would be successful without input from local communities, who have provided services as masons, laborers, and fundraisers. In 2012, Achi began to work on the deteriorating and crumbling Skurbuchan Fortress in the village of Skurbuchan. The fortress was initially constructed to be a defensive tower and at some point in its history was converted into an Avalokiteshvara Temple. The villagers had been collecting funds for the project since 1998 and contributed en masse. A report from 2012 details these contributions:

> "Practically every single family supported the work in one way or another according to their possibilities... there were at least 40 instances where building materials such as timber elements (talu and dungma) were donated, aside from large contributions of sun-dried mud bricks (pagbu). Furthermore, there was a steady flow of contributions coming in throughout the conservation campaign. Over 50 families provided food supplies such as rice, flour, butter, milk, sugar, oil, eggs, lentils, and vegetables. Many more families made sure that the work team and volunteers had constant on-site provisions of tea, snacks, fruit, and various drinks during working hours. The complete work crew also received several breakfast, lunch, and dinner invitations to different family homes. Moreover, the conservation team could count on the daily presence of volunteers. There were over 30 volunteers, including 13 monks from the local monastery and one nun, several of them taking part in the work for several days." (Harrison 2012)

Alongside the community, Achi received funding from the tourism department of the Jammu & Kashmir state, marking the first time the organization engaged with a government entity. This project also involved working with the National Institute of Design (NID). The collaboration with NID was carried out as a part of the Education Outreach Program (EOP), an initiative aimed to "expand experience as heritage preservation and interpretation to a larger Ladakhi community for long term impact and overall sustainability of heritage preservation initiatives in the region (EOP 2019, 3)." NID students and faculty collaborated with Achi on two museum projects as a part of the EOP: a kitchen and agriculture museum.

Restoration is a process that is very dynamic, where materials and thoughts from different time periods interact, and decisions made centuries ago need to be considered. The rigid pursuit of aesthetic or historical accuracy in preservation can at times conflict with structural needs, requiring a range of carefully considered inputs to arrive at the most pragmatic solution. Like Skurbuchan, the villagers of Photoksar also requested support from Achi to preserve their old temple. Photoksar is on the way from Wanla to Zanskar, located just before the high pass of the Shinge-la. A bit above the village are two religious buildings: a Drukpa and a Drikung Monastery. The Drikung monastery was built some twenty-five years ago to replace the old one, which is situated higher up against the rock face of the mountain and protects the area from the north. The community's historical and contextual knowledge was meaningfully augmented by the technical expertise of Achi architects, enabling the preservation of an older site that held greater cultural and emotional value for local residents. Following extensive consultation with the villagers, the second floor of the temple was entirely dismantled. This upper room, constructed 120-140 years ago atop the original temple structure to accommodate a visiting Rinpoche or official, had introduced significant structural vulnerabilities (Ferrari & Sukman 2018). Achi's conservation and restoration work is shaped by an ongoing dialogue between the community and architects, grounded in regular community meetings and the cultivation of relationships with local masons and laborers.

Structural Intervention

Before embarking on technical work, conservators and architects conduct thorough condition assessments that document any prior local interventions and the nature of the damage. Local upkeep has taken place in Ladakh through a variety of means, like the annual whitewashing of monasteries and chortens. These maintenance procedures are mainly done in a religious and cultural setting, and, when done correctly, can contribute to prolonging an edifice's stability. Occasionally, clergy members will undertake conservation; at the Ensa monastery, local monks carried out amateur fillings with local earth on areas with cavities within the building (Jahan). The first part in almost every assessment involves identifying the cause of deterioration and then looking at each individual architectural element that is at risk.

At Ensa, Achi architects collected information from the locals to conceptualize how damage occurred. Older villagers spoke of a spring located under the northern part of the assembly hall, and how in winters, the ground froze, turning into layers of ice. Sporadically, the water flow from the spring also flooded the assembly hall entrance. Due to the spring being underneath the entrance wall, it resulted in a shifting of the foundations. As the entire entrance hall started to shift, columns moved thirty-three centimeters at the height of the capitals, the upper part of the entrance wall of the assembly hall tilted, beams that supported the upper layer of bricks got disconnected from each other, and big cracks became visible in the wall near the entrance. Achi architects first stabilized the entrance room, breaking down the roof from above, so the northern columns could be moved, and the windows of the assembly hall reinstalled. The roof was in bad condition, so architects checked and repaired it with new earthen layers and shaped it to make slopes for drainage pipes (Vets 2016). Since the decay of the roof accelerated damage in other parts of the building as well, architects designed a parapet with waterspouts for effective waterproofing, which would require less maintenance (Ferrari & Sukman 2018). This not only prevented water incursions temporarily but was a farsighted move that will mean less maintenance over time for the community.

The eight-chorten building at Wanla was the site of another structural intervention. The building is situated on the traditional circumambulation path of the village, built on a ridge at Zomal, the oldest inhabited part of the village, facing the castle ruins found in Wanla. It gets its name from the eight different chortens that are inside the building. The building consists of a rectangular inner room, which is then surrounded by a 'veranda' where people circumambulate the shrine, and paintings approximately 110-120 years old cover the walls of the inner shrine (Vets et al. 2014). The building had been owned by the Kharpa family but was handed to the community of Zomal to gain more support for its conservation and upkeep. Due to the complexity of the problem, the owner and community asked Achi for assistance. The first series of efforts focused on stabilizing the structural elements of the building. A structural assessment of the eight-chorten revealed several causes of instability: the rear wall of the inner structure and the large wooden screen leaned outward due to the thin supporting walls, made of single adobe, which were only twenty centimeters wide; the wooden supports of the balconies were inadequate; there was no supporting beam above the large opening of the wooden screen; the roof joints were interrupted at the rear wall; and the heavy load on the roof, with twenty to thirty centimeters of earth above it, contributed further to the structural weaknesses (Vets 2012, 82).

Prior to beginning restoration work, the chortens inside were first covered with protective layers made of soft foam and plastic sheets. All painted wall surfaces received two layers of Japanese paper in order to minimize mechanical damage during the propping procedure. Three rows of seven oblique props were positioned against the inclining wall and wooden screen. Plywood boards covered with insulation foam were attached to the props to protect the paintings. The parapets, the dirt, and the willow sticks were then removed from the roof. The roof joists were cautiously lifted out and the balcony constructions removed. As soon as the interior was exposed after the roof was removed, the painted walls and screen were covered with plastic sheets. The badly eroded walls of the outer structure were taken down while recuperating as many bricks as possible (Vets 2012, 85). This stage of the restoration process underscores the structural and historical decisions undertaken by Achi's architects, particularly in cases where interventions extend beyond cleaning and stabilization to include the sequential preservation, deconstruction, and conservation of elements. Even quotidian implications of tasks like brick removal posed a hazard to the century-old wall paintings. Thus, conservation, as much as being a linear execution of detailed planning, is also a dynamic environment where the movement of material is often an inherent risk to other elements of a building.

All the architectural restoration and conservation measures undertaken at the eight-chorten were done using traditional techniques and materials employed by local masons and craftsmen. The final report by the team explicitly identifies that the "project aimed to maintain its [the building's] authenticity of functions (Vets et al. 2014)." The epistemological gap surrounding restoration practices became evident in the misunderstandings Achi team members encountered on site. As one team member noted, "often they [locals] didn't understand why a certain part had to be preserved and others not, why we didn't use cement/concrete to reinforce the walls, why such an effort was necessary to safeguard the painted walls... they tended anyway to 'contemporary' techniques, a lot of times of 'inferior quality' (Vets 2012)." Structural stability and the religious value of the building were well understood and motivated the locals to join, but the significance traditional technique was viewed anachronistically. Architects remarked that Achi "must continue strenuously to transmit conservation strategies to the local communities and to support pride in traditional technical know-how by promoting the use of traditional building materials (Vets et al. 2014)." One way architects stressed this is, while parts of the building were being dismantled, all materials were stored for reuse, including red-painted willow twigs, and earthen bricks of the parapets, willow branches of the ceiling roof beam, flat boards in between the beams, adobe, and the wooden door (Vets 2012, 86). Building materials that might have otherwise been discarded or replaced, such as willow twigs, were preserved after conservators highlighted their historical value.

In rare instances where intervention by someone from outside of Ladakh has taken place, these measures have to be accounted for before implementing any new conservation procedures. At the Avalokiteshvara Temple in Wanla, photographer Benoy K. Behl, with some assistance from Indian army contractors, undertook repairs; he had also made similar interventions at the Phyang monastery. Although there was no documentation, the extent of the work could be gauged by comparing photos of the site before and after, revealing the reconstruction and re-leveling of roof parapets, the re-laying of the roof to create new drainage positions, and the black plastic pipes that had been fitted as rainwater spouts to replace the traditional wood channels. Although the pipes installed were intended to stop water from gathering on the roof, they were too small and blocked by loose sediment washing down from the surface of the roof, whilst the pipes installed on the lantern discharged on the main roof. Furthermore, parapet walls above the side walls and original capping stones to all the parapet walls were removed and replaced with a tin sheet and capped with dirt. Both the tin sheets and the earthen capping were already cracking with pieces breaking off, which Achi architects deemed "visually and technically unsatisfactory (Oeter and Skedzuhn-Safir 2012, 133)."

Investigation of the roof by Achi architects found that the interior height of the apse — a large semicircular or polygonal recess that is arched or has a domed roof — was one meter lower than the height of the outside roof. Another issue was the massive weight on the roof, due to the layers of dirt that locals had kept on adding in attempts to seal the roof against water infiltration, which was now causing damage to the interior of the temple. This was pressing on an already broken painted beam and the ornamented coffered ceiling. Although architects installed auxiliary support structures underneath the broken beam and the coffered ceiling to prevent the roof from collapsing entirely, this support was deemed unfit to serve as a permanent solution, since it obstructed the view of the statues and paintings inside the building. The solution Achi architects Roland Pabel and Wolfgang Heusgen presented was to clear the top layers of the roof and install two independent, triangular, three-tiered metal carriers in the cleared space. This would redirect the weight away from the broken beam on the upper floor and support the secondary beams of the wooden ceiling, as well as the carriers. The first carrier, placed in close proximity to the stone wall, distributed the pressure downwards via the supporting walls, and the second carrier, placed next to the first one, supported the restored roof structure (Pabel 2012, 143). Achi architects chose a lightweight carrier made from corrosion-resistant aluminum alloys, developed by a company that specialized in heavy-duty carriers for concert stages in the Netherlands. The aluminum carrier was lightweight, supported 560 kilograms of weight, could be easily transported, and could be assembled on site. The architects stressed that the carriers would be "completely integrated into the structure of the multi-layered roof and remain invisible...only six bolt heads with the corresponding buffer elements for the suspension of the secondary beams in the ceiling would be noticeable from the inside (144)."

For a structure like the temple, removing any elements, such as the painted beams, is a loss of heritage. Here, restoration becomes a form of continuity, preserving architectural elements, even if they do not fulfill the structural purposes they were created for. Architects recognized that the temple still needed to fulfill religious and cultural purposes that required an unaltered view of its contents. The temple derives a part of its legitimacy from the sanctity generated through visual elements that guide a devotee or a visitor through the space, a creation of habitus within its premises. The "invisibility" of such interventions constitutes not merely an effort to preserve the visual integrity of the sacred landscape, but also a strategic means of maintaining the temple's functional role in facilitating religious practices that orient and mediate inward, experiential dimensions of devotion.

In some cases, in lieu of invisibility, Achi architects choose to "overlap (Ferrari 2023)." In the most recent conservation effort, at the Nyima Temple (nyi ma lha khang) in Mulbek, the roof and its load bearing beams needed to be restored. The new wooden elements, made from pre-cut buldu wood imported from Kashmir, were used to replace deteriorated components. A customized wooden capital was crafted to integrate both the main and secondary new beam profiles with the original structure. This capital overlapped with the original beam, capital (kazhu), and pillar, creating a tailored connection (Ferrari 2023). The replication and blending into the vernacular created an effect of continuity, preserving the visual effect of the space on the devotee. The sourcing of materials from Kashmir represents a shift in conservation that is broadly representative of Ladakhi construction in general. Ladakh historically imported timber from Jammu and Kashmir, as Ladakh's environmental conditions do not lend to mass production of wood. However, the timber was fashioned in Ladakh, acquiring its vernacular form through the labor performed by a Ladakhi craftsman. As many Ladakhis move away from labor intensive work and with the injection of capital from the tourism industry, a consumerist culture of import has developed. Even today, Ladakhi architecture continues to retain elements of wood in their intricately carved windows, beams, and doors; but what was once localized, like many other things, can now be produced elsewhere. With better transportation, Ladakh is connected to a network of production that it can tap into and export ideas to. The result of this is a preservation of traditional architecture, albeit diminishing knowledge of local labor practices.

Wall Painting Conservation

Wall paintings, as mentioned earlier, are visual repositories and, alongside architectural elements, define the experience of a temple. While the passage of time is one reason wall paintings deteriorate, water incursions and soot from the burning of butter lamps indoors also accelerate the damage. Many temples and monasteries have constructed separate outdoor spaces for the burning of butter lamps; at Wanla, monks installed a vitrine outside the temple (Pfund 2012, 183). At the Nyima Temple at Mulbek, the temple interior was affected by the use of oil lamps, and by its use as a kitchen by an invading Dogra army in the 19th century, which covered large areas of the murals with soot and dust. Furthermore, in areas where water was penetrating the roof, clay slaked and formed clay runners running down the wall (Ferrari 2023). At the temples in Wanla, Ensa, Photoksar, and Mulbek, conservators encountered areas of flaking and detachment of paint layers along with cavities that had developed along the wall. It is important to consider that wall paintings may not be contemporaneous, as they were often created or retouched at different periods. At Ensa, conservators found different colors in the paintings and speculated that overpainting may have been done (Mitschke 2016).

Although the extent of damage to wall paintings varied from temple to temple, requiring site-specific interventions, the conservation reports reveal a notable consistency in approach. Here, I have selected the processes of wall painting conservation that are used in most projects. Prior to the commencement of wall painting conservation, structural stability must first be ensured. As such, the initial phase typically involves the secure consolidation of the wall paintings to prevent any damage during subsequent structural interventions. This is achieved through the temporary application of Japanese tissue paper, affixed using adhesives such as Tylose or Klucel (Ferrari 2023). Japanese tissue paper or *washi* is made from "traditional methods using materials that contain few impurities, is natural or alkaline, slow to deteriorate... and can be removed cleanly simply by adding moisture, returning the document [wall paintings] to its pre-repair state if necessary (IFLA Website)." In some cases, like at Mulbek, due to the instability caused during construction, architects may make the decision to install temporary boarding that shields the entire painting area from fall debris (Bühler 2022). Similarly, loose wall fragments are temporarily secured with cyclododecane, "a binding medium and adhesive that is fully reversible" (Rowe & Rozeik 2008). Its ability to "sublimate without residues" allowed conservators at Photoksar to speed up this process using a blow dryer and applying warm Shellsol T

— a popular, near-odorless mineral solvent — with a brush (Ferrari & Sukman 2018). Similar to the invisible structural interventions, the chemicals used in wall paintings are transitory and reversible, fully blending in and supporting the painting once applied.

Once paintings are secured, work can begin on other parts of the wall. First is the removal of portions of historic earthen fills that might cover original paint, which are mechanically removed after locally softening the areas with deionized water using a combination of blunt tools and dry cotton swabs. Because the paint is highly sensitive to water, overfilled areas are only slightly dampened and the layers of mud are then thinned or removed mechanically to the best possible extent. Better results are achieved when addressing mud deposits caused by water infiltration from roof leakages, as these layers are typically thinner and less firmly adhered to the paint surface. Cavities and voids that arise from the separation of coarse plaster are given injection grouting through the openings and cracks leading inwards. The cracks and losses are sealed with cotton, leaving a small hole for the catheter to enter before the grouting process to avoid any leakage or overflow and damage to the painted surfaces. In addition to the voids and cavities, certain areas that exhibit tenting of the paint layer are not flattened on account of inflicting further damage or loss. Such areas are consolidated by injecting grout of finer composition into the gap between the paint layer and plaster with the help of small surgical needles. Conservators also encounter fallen fragments of paintings of different sizes and set them aside for inspection. After close examination of walls, conservators can identify the area of origin of the fallen fragments and re-attach them to the walls using the coarse mortar at the base and filleting the edges with the fine mortar (Vets 2017).

In most reports, the cleaning process receives minimal documentation or discussion. However, Heike Pfund — an architect who has worked on numerous restoration projects with Achi — and Susanne Bosch devote a chapter to the process of wall painting conservation in the book *Against Forgetting* (2012). Although they write about this process in the context of the Avalokiteshvara Temple at Wanla, it can largely be extrapolated to the general procedures followed at other conservation sites. Cleaning is done in several steps:

> To begin, loose dirt was gently removed with soft paint brushes. Eraser sponges and mechanically reduced the dirt. Deposits of earthen material were also thinned mechanically, but had to be cleaned with water as a last step. This was due to the fact that earth can only be cleaned properly with water. The paintings' high-water sensitivity presented a significant challenge. These deposits had damaged the wall paintings and displayed losses varying from slight to total, affecting primer and plaster alike (181).

To deal with the soot that accumulated over almost eight centuries, conservators took the following steps:

> Thorough research and testing of cleaning agents had to be undertaken to find the appropriate agent and method to remove the black sooty layer without causing any harm to the highly water sensitive paintings. A major component of this black layer was fatty soot, which had accumulated over centuries on the ground floor walls. Fatty oil substances can be removed with organic solvents. The best results were achieved by using methyl ethyl ketone (MEK), which did not affect the paintings at all. Small cotton swabs were moistened with the solvent and softly rolled over the painting surface. This helped the dissolved soot move into the cotton, which we replaced with clean swabs repeatedly throughout the cleaning process (181).

The use of these scientifically trialed materials and methods speaks to how conservators understand the extent of their treatments. Like the "invisibility" of introduced architectural elements, applying cyclododecane and MEK, enhances to some extent the originality of the paintings but does not alter them in any way. The objective of wall painting conservation work is the safeguarding and prolongation of the extant original.

Conservation in a Ritual Context

Most of the monuments with which Achi has engaged are living heritage sites that remain ritually functional and are affiliated with the various Tibetan Buddhist sects present in Ladakh. Architects and conservators must have an added dimension to their work that accounts for how conservation decisions interface with religious understanding. Temples are often communal by design, but the "ownership" is more akin to ritual responsibility than private property rights and held by a bigger monastery that is often the headquarters of a particular sect in Ladakh. For example, the temple of Ensa falls under the care of the Diskit monastery. All temples are integral to how the community imagines itself, fulfilling a religious need that is mediated by the clergy. If the temple is not treated carefully during conservation and restoration, the community could potentially experience harmful effects. Before a project can begin, high-ranking monks who are in-charge of the sites are consulted and asked for permission. For the projects at Skurbuchan and Photoksar, H.H. Kyabgön Chetsang Rinpoche — head of the Drikung lineage to which both sites belong — stood firmly behind the project and encouraged the community to give support (Vets 2017). The clergy's support provided legitimacy, enabling Achi to proceed with the conservation work while assuring the community that appropriate care would be taken throughout the process.

Temples in Ladakh are activated, living spaces where deities possess a divine agency, and monks perform daily rites to appease them. Prior to the start of restoration work, monks temporarily pause this agency by desacralizing the site. At the eight-chorten building in Wanla, restoration entailed a considerable risk of severe damage to the painted walls and chortens inside, so two Drikung monks, Lama Tsewang Chumpa and Könchok Richen Chupipa, performed the *Agra* ceremony to request the spirits of the paintings and chorten to leave the space and reside temporarily in a ritual mirror (me long). The ritual mirror, covered with cloth, was then stored in the house shrine (mchod khang) of the Kharpa family, the previous owners of the building. Furthermore, after this ceremony, all portable religious items were evacuated — hundreds of small sculptural votive offerings (tsha tsha), butter lamps, and other relics (Vets et al. 2014). The physical consolidation of wall paintings is cognate with the ritual intermission of the space; thus, conservation depends on the controlled creation of a vacated, secular environment. It is perhaps important to note that this does not equate to a deactivation of space; rather, it is the ceremonial transfer of the deities' agency, briefly, into another space.

However, even after acquiring permission from the religious clergy, differences in perception about conservation work can appear. During the cleaning of the Avalokitesvara temple in Wanla, a Rinpoche approached Achi conservators and explained that "removing soot also meant removing traces of prayers that have been left by monks for generations, as each person who had donated a butter lamp left traces of worship in the form of soot on the wall paintings... and it is very important to preserve the wall paintings, because with their age they had increased their powers (Pfund 2012, 185)." The insights provided by the monk added a chance to further expand how conservation should be handled in the Himalayan context. Conservators decided to consult high-ranking teachers within the order to develop an approach that integrated the technical process of cleaning wall paintings with their religious significance. The opportunity for discussions materialized during preparations for the Dalai Lama's Kalachakra teachings that were going to take place in Leh, the district capital. Concurrently, a one-week ceremony was held in Wanla with monks and ceremonial masters from Lamayuru, giving conservators an opportunity to interview high-ranking teachers of the order and seek advice. Drupön Dawa Norbu, a meditation master and a high-ranking teacher from Lamayuru, engaged with the team, explaining “that the soot is powerfully charged in two ways: it represents numerous prayers of generations of believers, and is spiritually enhanced through direct contact with painted mandalas and deities...and the small cotton swabs used for cleaning should then be regarded as sacred and should not mix with ordinary waste. Here, conservators, even if they are not part of the religion, are directly in contact with how belief is constructed in the spaces they are working in. When asked how to proceed with the spiritually charged cotton swabs, Drupön Dawa Norbu identified two possibilities: “one appropriate action would be to bring the soot-saturated swabs to a secret place in the mountains, where the winds could take them in all directions...[or] hand over the swabs to the river, as the sacred cotton swabs had the power to pacify water deities.” He also clarified that “wall paintings would not be less sacred or powerful after cleaning and consented that this activity should continue (186).” This allowed conservators to proceed while fulfilling religious obligations. Furthermore, following the completion of work and the handover of the site to the clergy, a ritual act may be conducted to mark the transition. In Nyoma, for instance, once the restoration of the vase or *bumpa* of the Kankani chorten was completed, Gen Könchok Motup whitewashed restored parts of the façade (Vets 2017).

Conclusion

The Achi archives contain an abundance of material that situates conservation in a complex and multifaceted range of perspectives. At its center, conservation is a negotiation of how a building is understood, retaining its ritual function rooted in long-standing tradition, while simultaneously imbuing a historicity through its material and architecture. Documents reveal that architects and conservators, working with lay devotees and the clergy, engaged in the epistemic co-creation of a space that allowed for both functions to be realized.

From the beginning of a project, community engagement is sought, starting from consultations on expectations to contributions in the forms of material and labor. In the conservation process, architects and conservators stress the use of traditional materials and methodologies, creating a value for techniques that have fallen out of favor in modern construction. In the materials that architects and conservators did import or add, care was given to structurally alter the building and apply chemicals that were easily reversible or indiscernible, so monks and devotees would return to using the space in the same ritual way as before. Architects and conservators had to be attuned to the multifaceted nature of their decisions, which, in addition to being technical, encompassed spiritual considerations and their broader implications. Recognizing the repercussions of the spiritual dimension often required consultations with local monks, devotees, and occasionally, higher-ranking monastic figures.

The multiple stakeholders and their respective perspectives are an entangled yet interconnected web of ideas that have to be contended with. Operating within this, Achi team members have engaged in conscientious research, producing voluminous amounts of data to inform their decision making. However, given the interdisciplinary nature of these archives and the siloed nature of research, their fullness and multidimensionality have not yet been explored. As climate change increasingly threatens heritage sites across the Himalaya and local expertise in traditional construction techniques diminishes, it is crucial to encourage interdisciplinary research. By examining successful conservation efforts, scholars and conservators can glean valuable insights that can guide future practices and foster resilience in preserving cultural heritage in the region.

Sushan Bhattarai is an early-career researcher from the Kathmandu Valley. He holds a B.A. in History and Environmental Studies from Amherst College and has previously worked at the Smithsonian's National Museum of Asian Art (NMAA) in Washington, D.C. His research focuses on the circulation of Trans-Himalayan artistic and architecture styles. He is currently documenting sites in the Central Himalayas associated with the Khas-Malla kingdom in Nepal and India, supported by a grant from the Rubin Museum of Himalayan Art.

A special thanks to Abeer Gupta, Director of Achi Association India (AAI), for facilitating my time in Ladakh and providing generous insights throughout the research and writing process.

Endnote

1. Conservation efforts in Ladakh go beyond religious sites and include a wide range of historic buildings. A notable example is the Achi Association India's restoration of Choskor House, once owned by a prominent trading family that played a key role in the Leh-to-Lhasa caravan trade. Today, this building serves as the region's first conservation laboratory. Similarly, the Palay House, a traditional Ladakhi residence, has been transformed into a vibrant space for exhibitions, research, and education. Additionally, organizations like the Tibetan Heritage Fund (THF) have contributed significantly to restoration efforts, particularly in Leh's old quarter. In partnership with the Leh Old Town Initiative (LOTI), THF has restored several important buildings, including the Balay House, West Stupa Gate, Sankar Labrang, and the Rigsum Gonpo shrine.

References

Bühler, Björn. 2022. Tech. Project Mulbek 2023. Leh, Ladakh: Achi Association India.

Ferrari, Edoardo Paolo. 2021b. Khangpa: A Ladakhi Vernacular Architecture's Glossary. Roma: Scienze e lettere.

Ferrari, Edoardo Paolo. 2023. Rep. Nyima Lhakhang - Mulbek: Restoration Proposal - 2023. Leh, Ladakh: Achi Association India.

Ferrari, Edoardo Paolo, and Tsering Motup Snyemo Sukman. 2018. Rep. Ensa's Dukhang Yoka Detailed Project Report: Advanced Architectural Analysis and Protective Measures for the Restoration Project. Leh, Ladakh: Achi Association India.

Harrison, John. 2012. Rep. Conservation of the Skurbuchan Khar – A Community-Based Conservation Initiative. Leh, Ladakh: Achi Association India.

Jahan, Noor. n.d. Rep. A Preliminary Survey of the Temple and Its Surroundings. Leh, Ladakh: Achi Association India.

Martin, Nils. 2023. "The Temple of Wanla." Project Himalayan Art. 2023. https://projecthimalayanart.rubinmuseum.org/essays/the-temple-of-wanla/.

Martin, Nils. 2022. "The Wanla Group of Monuments: 14th -Century Tibetan Buddhist Murals in Ladakh." Dissertation. Préparée à l'École Pratique des Hautes Études.

Mitschke, Angela. 2016. Rep. Short Report of the Survey on the Wall Paintings and the Wooden Elements (Ensa). Leh, Ladakh: Achi Association India.

Norberg-Hodge, Helena. 2016. Ancient Futures. East Hardwick, Vermont: Local Futures.

"Paper Conservation by Using Japanese Paper, Washi – IFLA." n.d. International Federation of Library Associations and Institutions (IFLA). Accessed October 17, 2024. https://www.ifla.org/paper-conservation-by-using-japanese-paper-washi/.

Petech, Luciano. 1977. The Kingdom of Ladakh: C. 950-1842 A.D. Roma: Istituto italiano per il Medio ed Estremo Oriente.

Rizvi, Janet. 2012. Ladakh: Crossroads of High Asia. New Delhi: Oxford University Press.

Rep. 2019. Education Outreach Project. Achi Association.

Rowe, Sophie, and Christina Rozeik. 2008. "The Uses of Cyclododecane in Conservation."

Studies in Conservation 53 (sup2): 17-31. https://doi.org/10.1179/sic.2008.53.supplement-2.17.

Sarao, Karam Tej Singh. 2012. The Decline of Buddhism in India: A Fresh Perspective. New Delhi: Munshirm Manoharlal Publishers.

Skedzuhn-Safir, Alexandra, Martina Oeter, Hilde Vets, and Heike Pfund, eds. 2021. Against Forgetting: Investigating and Preserving Historic Buildings in a Himalayan Village. Cottbus: Brandenburgische Technische Universität Cottbus-Senftenberg.

"The Name Achi." n.d. Achi Association. Accessed October 17, 2024. https://www.achiassociation.org/association/name-and-organization/the-name-achi/.

Vets, Hilde, Elektra Castsoulis, Quentin Devers, and Nils Martin. 2015. Rep. The Kankani Chörten of Nyoma: Report on the Survey of Architectural Structure. Leh, Ladakh: Achi Association India.

Vets, Hilde, Heike Pfund, Anne Voll, and Susanne Bosch. 2014. Rep. Restoration of the 8 Chörten Building. Leh, Ladakh: Achi Association India.

Vets, Hilde. 2016. Rep. Report on Short the Survey of the Architectural Structure. Leh, Ladakh: Achi Association India.

Vets, Hilde. 2017. Rep. The Old Drigung Temple at Photoksar — Report of the Survey of the Architectural Structure. Leh, Ladakh: Achi Association India

HIMALAYA
The Journal of the Association of Nepal and Himalayan Studies

Research Article

Tibet through a Native Lens: Charles Alfred Bell's Image-Archive and the Roles of his Photographic Interlocutors

Parjanya Sen

University of Calcutta, Deshbandhu College for Girls

DOI: https://doi.org/10.2218/himalaya.2025.10021

Abstract

This essay attempts to foreground the question of native agency in the making of the photographic archive of Charles Alfred Bell, British Political Officer for Sikkim, Bhutan and Tibet. It seeks to approach a new hermeneutics of British imperial archive-making vis-á-vis Tibet by assessing not only how native agency variously informed the sacerdotal, epistemic and technical content of most of Bell's photographic archive, but also how such agency was central to its very process of visual production. By examining the roles of Rabden Lepcha, Sonam Wangyal or Palhese and Kartick Chandra Pyne, apropos their contribution to Bell's visual archive, the essay shows how British imperial knowledge-construction on Tibet deployed native agency, thereafter relegating them (mostly) to archival silence. In the process, the essay demonstrates how these silences were not merely accidental, but fundamental to the process of knowledge-production on Tibet.

Keywords

photography, Charles Bell, native agency, Kartick Chandra Pyne, Rabden Lepcha, Tibet, British Raj

Recommended Citation

Sen, Parjanya (2025). Tibet through a Native Lens: Charles Alfred Bell's Image-Archive and the Roles of his Photographic Interlocutors. *HIMALAYA* 44(1): 81-106.

cc BY NC ND

This work is licensed under a Creative Commons Attribution-Noncommercial-No Derivative Works 4.0 License.

Introduction

> Another man comes out of the same building and walks towards the postern-gate... He is an oddly proportioned man, tall, with a small head and a pronounced nose... He enters a bookseller like others—leather-bound volumes behind the display windows... Mount and Page are maritime publishers, *the* maritime publishers of the town. James Cook is comfortable... He does not own more than a dozen of these books and charts but he has at one time or another studied more than he can recall. He is in a library of his own accomplishment.
>
> — Nicholas Thomas (*Discoveries: The Voyages of Captain Cook*)

Nicholas Thomas begins his fascinating biography of the eighteenth-century English explorer Captain James Cook (1728-1779) through a fictionalized reconstruction of a December afternoon in 1767 at Tower Hill, London, with Cook walking into an archive of his own making. Thomas conjectures how Cook's encounter with his printer, Mount, would have likely occurred 'around this time' and Cook 'would surely have browsed Mount's stock' that, besides his own books, would have included 'a formidable number of other works' (Thomas 2018: 34).

Thomas's fictionalized positioning of Cook 'in a library of his own accomplishment' speaks to me of a different colonial setting, a different actor and a different archive, albeit with continuities within their modes of making. This other colonial archive is represented by two photographs, part of the robust visual archive on Tibet produced by Charles Alfred Bell (1870 -1945), British Political Officer for Sikkim, Bhutan and Tibet from 1908-1918. The photographs were taken at Kong-kar or Gongkar in September, 1934, during Bell's trip to eastern Tibet. The images position Bell (seated at the centre in both illustrations) within an archive 'of his own making'. The first photograph [**Figure 1**] shows two figures with Bell, Sonam Wangyal or Palhese (1870-1936), Bell's Tibetan interlocutor, standing behind him, and Lt. Colonel Harnett, who accompanied him on this trip, standing on Bell's right. The second photograph [**Figure 2**], shows another figure, a brown man, standing on Bell's left. From Bell's curating of his own photographs, we know that this person is Kartick Chandra Pyne, the professional photographer Bell had recruited from Kalimpong for his 1934 trip.[1] Bell carried two cameras with him during this trip, the Zeiss Ikon Universal Jewel Camera (model number 275, with 9 into 12 cm plates)[2] and a 6 into 6 cm German-made Franke & Heidecke (later Rollei GmbH) Twin Lens Reflex/ TLR Rolleiflex camera. Bell curated the photos from each of these cameras individually, into two sets, the J-Series and the R-Series, with occasional overlaps in content. During the 1934 trip, K.C. Pyne was Bell's professional photographer handling both his cameras, and the one responsible for producing almost the entire corpus of Bell's photographs.

The two photographs with which I begin this essay, one with Pyne, and the other without him, suggest the processes of archival erasure which remain key to its structural formulation. Bell's central position within the image bears verisimilitude to his locus as the 'maker' of this photographic archive on Tibet. However, as we shall examine in the course of this essay, Bell was merely the facilitator of this archival production, even as the archive itself became a bricolage brought together through the efforts of several other native actors and agents. In this sense, Bell placing himself centrally within 'an archive of his own making' (in this case the two photographs above) often tends to obfuscate the processes and agents behind its production.

Theorizing Indigenous Agency: Configuring Absences within the Tibet archive

Before proceeding to a fuller assessment of the roles played by the various interlocutors and agents employed in the production of Charles Bell's photographic archive, let us dwell on some of the important concerns vis-á-vis the notions of indigenous agency and archival absence that underpin this study. In questioning 'the principles and

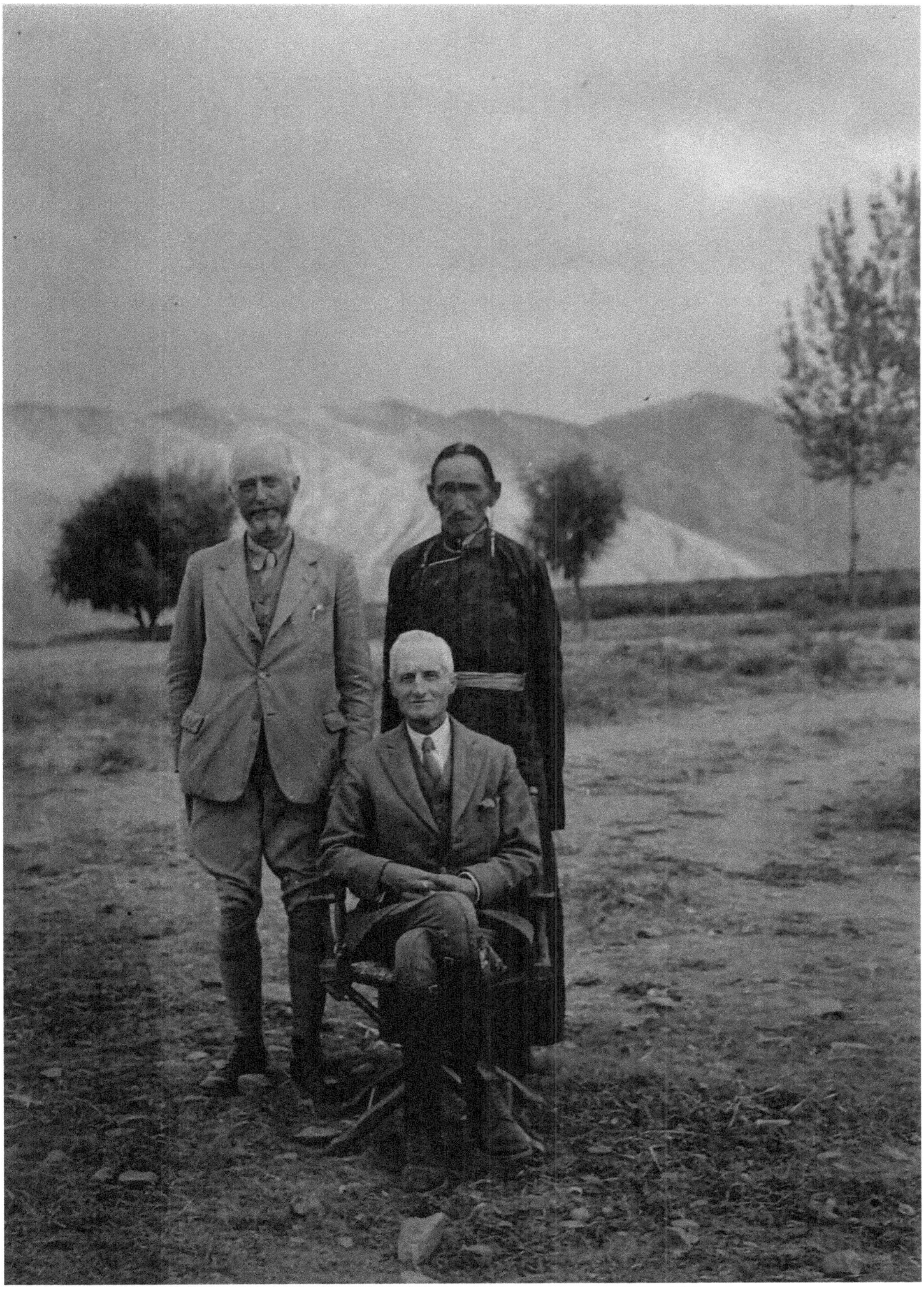

Figure 1: Charles Bell, seated, with Sonam Wangyal (Palhese) standing behind him and Captain Lt. Harnett standing on his right, Gongkar, September 1934, photographed by Kartick Chandra Pyne. From the British Library Collection: [Photo 1112/5 (488)].

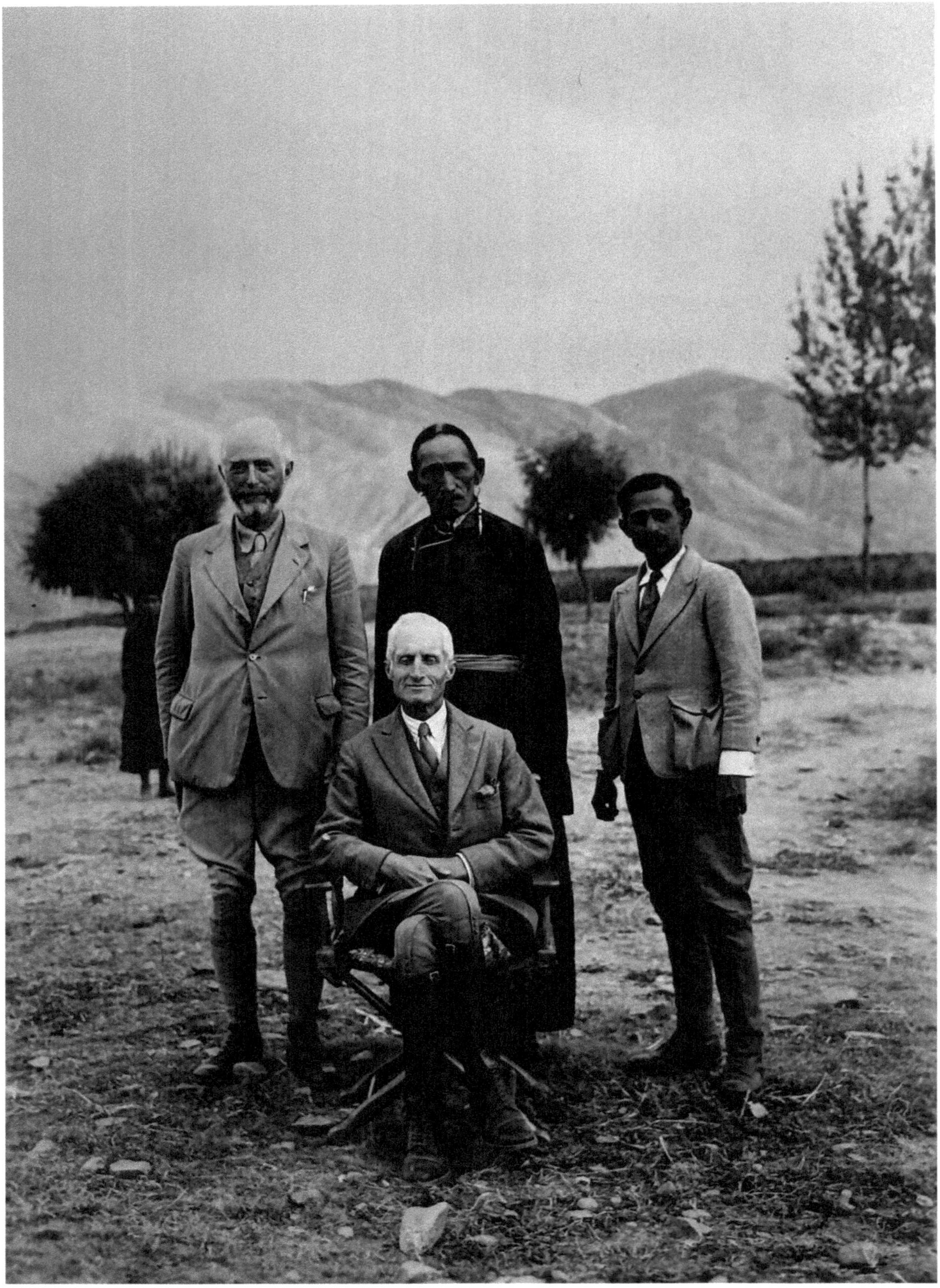

Figure 2: Charles Bell, seated, with Sonam Wangyal (Palhese) standing behind him, Captain Lt. Harnett standing on his right and Kartick Chandra Pyne on his left, Gongkar, September 1934, photographed by Kartick Chandra Pyne. From the British Library Collection: [Photo 1112/5 (489)].

practices of governance lodged in particular archival forms' with regard to the Dutch colonial archive in the Netherland Indies and its discursive construction of racial taxonomies, Ann Laura Stoler looks at imperial archives themselves as 'condensed sites of epistemological and political anxiety..., both transparencies on which power relations were inscribed and intricate technologies of rule in themselves' (Stoler 2009: 20).

Stoler's examination of the processes of epistemic ordering within the colonial archive can be used to study a different set of archival processes from the British empire in India with regard to Tibet. The careers of some of Charles Bell's chief interlocutors and collaborators, such as Sonam Wangyal or Palhese, Rabden Lepcha and Kartick Chandra Pyne[3] reveal the complex interplays of British colonial power and indigenous agency. These figures, as we shall interrogate through the course of this essay, were important agents in the process of orchestrating and producing Charles Bell's photographic archive of Tibet, even as their own contributions were often not adequately credited or acknowledged.

How do we begin to approach this question of agency? In her study on the histories of nineteenth-century explorations in Africa and the Himalayas that were carried out under the aegis of the Royal Geographical Society with the Institute of British Geographers (RGS-IBG), Lowri Madeleine Jones highlights how these were 'a collective experience, in which work and knowledge was shared and exchanged' across different loci of power (Jones 2010: 14). Jones, in her appraisal of non-Western participation in these explorations, does not seek to substitute a Western archive premised on a 'celebration of a canon of European and American explorers' with a 'heroic indigene'; instead she unravels 'the more mundane ways in which 'local' circumstances, knowledge and inhabitants affected the course of exploration and its associated field sciences' (Jones 2010: 18). Taking this cue from Jones, it is important to foreground the idea that this study of Bell's visual archive is not merely a recursive exercise of uncovering indigenous agency. Rather, it aims to offer an understanding of how forms of local knowledge became constituent parts of the visual archive itself, in turn shaping and determining its epistemic form and content.

Jones describes that only a few non-European individuals are actually named in the expedition reports and maps that she examines, while 'traces of innumerable others survive in various guises', their roles 'circumscribed by their representation' (Jones 2010: 19). Bell mentioned many of his interlocutors by name, on various occasions, in his diaries, notebooks, curated lists and, sometimes, in his published books. However, such acknowledgements by Bell are not uniform (figures credited in the diaries and indexes are left out from published books), nor do they fully acknowledge the contributions of these native agents as equal (if not greater) collaborators in the process of making of his photographic collection. Further, even where they are mentioned, these figures remain delineated by their roles as Charles Bell's orderlies, informants and inferiors, locked within unequal relations of power apropos the archival production process.

Filtering out the white dialectical noise within this visual collection then becomes the crucial first step into assessing the roles and agencies of the photographers who were the main producers of Bell's images on Tibet. If these photographs can be read as colonial texts loaded with ethno-historical potential, they begin to serve then, in Bronwen Douglas's words, as 'ethnographic palimpsests', their 'language, content and silences registering traces of indigenous actions, relationships and settings'[4] (Douglas 1999: 70). Mining the archives to reconfigure these absences becomes a key step towards framing a new hermeneutics of Tibet Studies that spotlights the contribution of these non-white agents. With regard to Tibet, native agency, 'far from being exterior to the archive' (Arondekar 2009: 16-17)[5] was central to its process of making, and its sacerdotal and epistemological content was mediated through the knowledge of these figures.

One also needs to interrogate the efficacy of terms such as 'local' and 'native' when attempting to reconfigure the role of indigenous agency within this visual collection on Tibet. Emma Martin has discussed how some of the men whom 'Bell considered pure in their *local knowledge*...were valued differently because of their separateness,... were in fact highly mobile men who travelled vast distances [and] were open to far greater external influences and networks than Bell himself was' (Martin 2014: 69-70).

Building on Martin's idea, an important concern in highlighting the agency of these figures is to contest the ascription of the term 'local', that became a hermeneutic prerequisite of the process of British imperial knowledge making on Tibet through the late-nineteenth and early-twentieth centuries. The delineation of certain forms of knowledge as 'local' by Western scholars, all the while retaining the sole custody over authorship (of the knowledge archive), was central to the very process of its making. Martin's conjecture that 'the objective style of the much-constrained reporting system' meant that the 'source of the information' had to be silenced (Martin 2014: 70) may be expanded into an understanding of how this silencing was not merely coincidental to or required by the objectivity demanded of British official reports; rather, it was fundamental to the dialectical foundation of knowledge produced on Tibet through this period.

To return to the two photographs with which we began this essay, the second one is among the few images within Bell's copious visual archive where K.C. Pyne actually makes an appearance.[6] His presence becomes 'inadvertently registered' in the second photograph, taken at the exact same location as the first image, at Gongkar. Pyne had forgotten to set the shutter button with the delayed action in the first photograph,[7] and thus becomes 'absent', only to make an appearance in the second. The first registers his trace through his 'silence'. One has to position these the two images palimpsestically in order to recover the photographer's trace.

Revisiting Bell's Photographic Collection: The Contributions of Rabden Lepcha[8]

I came across an image in the Print Room in the British Library. Part of Bell's curated Postcard/P-Series, the photograph shows a bare-footed middle-aged man **[Figure 3]**. At the back of photograph, scribbled in pencil in Bell's handwriting is the first name of the person 'Rabden (orderly)' along with the date the photograph was taken— November, 1921 and the location— outside Major Carey-Evans's house in Delhi.[9] Some more biographical details about this person become available from Bell's curated index for his Postcard/P, Quarter-Plate/Q and Half-Plate/H Series. Here, Bell gives us his full name 'Rabden Lepcha', his orderly, 'who was with me for 18 years and took many of my photos for me'.[10] Within Bell's copious visual collection, the few images of this person, who was responsible for producing many of Bell's photographs during his 1920-21 official mission to Lhasa, are perhaps, the only material traces that remain of this man. Very little exists in terms of biographical information about Rabden Lepcha. The possibilities of 'knowing' remain dependent on Bell's written texts (his diaries, books and notes). In the absence of ethnographic material, unlike in the case of Pyne (about whom I discuss in a subsequent section of this essay), one needs to begin the process of recovering Rabden Lepcha's contributions through a process of semantic dismantling of Bell's photographic archive.[11]

In early 1904, when Francis Younghusband's mission was halted by the Tibetan resistance,[12] at the head of the Chumbi Valley, Bell was given the task of leading a small party of men to evaluate the viability of a road from India to Tibet through Bhutan, avoiding the high mountain passes (Bell 1946: 26). Between September, 1904 and November, 1905, Bell became the person in-charge in Chumbi Valley, standing in for John Claude White (1853-1919), who was posted as Chief Political Officer for Sikkim, Bhutan and Tibet between 1889 and 1908 (Bell 1924: 73). Earlier too, from May to

October, 1904, Bell had stood in for Claude White as Political Officer, filling in for the latter's absence during the Younghusband Mission, which had basically been a proxy invasion of Tibet (Bell 1924: 2). The shift from Younghusband to Bell also marked a shift from an attempted armed invasion of Tibet, towards the possibility of establishing more diplomatic ties. Bell was in favour of what he describes as a 'liberal policy' towards Tibet,[13] even going as far as to acknowledge that the Younghusband invasion of 1904 was what led to imperial Chinese aggression and a tussle over Tibet between imperial Britain and China.[14]

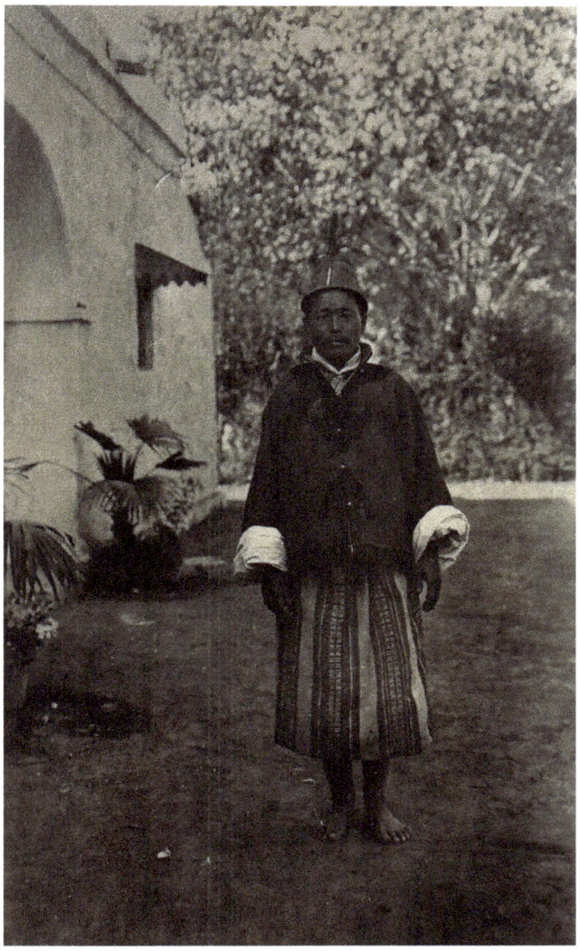

Figure 3: Photograph of Rabden Lepcha outside Major Carey-Evans's house in Delhi, taken by Charles Alfred Bell in November, 1921. From the British Library Collection: [Photo 1112/3 (1a)].

Between 1910-12, when the Thirteenth Dalai Lama, Ngawang Lobsang Thupten Gyatso (1876-1933) was in exile in India, Bell had successfully cultivated friendly diplomatic ties with him.[15] It was with a view to effectuating this 'liberal policy' that involved 'gaining the confidence of the people, both lay and ecclesiastical',[16] that Bell would finally head an official mission to Lhasa in 1920 at the invitation of Thupten Gyatso, accompanied by a retinue of his Tibetan and Sikkimese collaborators (Bell 1946: 219) which included Sonam Wangyal/ Palhese, Rabden Lepcha, Sonam Wangfel Laden La (1876-1936)[17] and Rai Bahadur Norbu Dhondup (1904-1947).[18]

For Bell, photographs were a way of elucidating his observations with regard to the volumes he was preparing for European readership in England, and Bell required very specific kinds of illustrations. Bell got this opportunity for collating the visual archive necessary for substantiating his volumes during his year-long stint in Lhasa, between November, 1920 and October, 1921.[19] Prior to this, Bell had collected various photographs of Tibet and Tibetans, many of these taken by John Claude White.[20] Bell's photographs, like those of his predecessor Laurence Austine Waddell (1854-1938), were intended to serve the dual purpose of ethnographic scientism and populist seduction (of a white European readership).[21] However, unlike Waddell's visual archive, Bell's comes across as more nuanced, primarily through the ethnic semiotic imprints of his collaborator figures such as Rabden Lepcha and Palhese.

Clare E. Harris elucidates the specific nature of the Rabden Lepcha- Charles Bell collaborative relationship, through an incident when Bell required a specific image of a Nyingma priest for his book, *The Religion of Tibet* (1931). Harris writes how Bell sought out Rabden Lepcha's active cooperation in coercing the monk, 'overturning the priest's scruples and his acceptance of a photographic gift'. Harris's observations on the extent of Rabden Lepcha's role in the making of Bell's images, deserves to be quoted here:

> Charles Bell thus had the linguistic and diplomatic skills of an ethnographer and the close personal relations with

> individuals from all levels of Tibetan society that could enhance the range and nature of his photographs. The collection of images he accumulated has a more empathetic quality than those of previous British photographers, but that tone could not have been achieved without the skill and character of Rabden Lepcha. (Harris 2016: 76)

Expanding on Harris's reflection on the nature of this partnership, it becomes necessary to dwell on some of the ways in which Rabden Lepcha aided and collaborated on the production of Bell's photographs. Right from the outset of the mission, Rabden Lepcha had been appointed as the unofficial photographer of the group.[22] However, a more specific need of Rabden Lepcha's services arose whenever any particular Tibetan religious figure was the subject to be photographed.

Bell, during his later visit to Tibet in 1934, would attribute the Tibetans' unwillingness to be photographed (as told to him by Sera Drupdi, the husband of Palhese's sister) to a belief by Tibetans in the image's ability to be used as a destructive tool upon which detrimental incantations could be performed by one's enemies.[23] The assistance of his Tibetan and Tibetan-speaking collaborators was thus necessitated in order to bridge this barrier with regard to the different cultural significations of the photographic image, and obtain the consent of his photographic subjects.

In his diary entry for 11 November, 1920, Bell describes his encounter with one of the most prominent religious figures of Tibet, the eleventh reincarnation of the woman mystic Dorje Phagmo. At the time she was a twenty-five-year-old woman, whose seat was the Samding monastery.[24] Within Tibetan political and spiritual hierarchy, Dorje Phagmo's status was next only to the Dalai Lama and the Panchen Lama. Enthused by Waddell's ethnographic descriptions of her in *The Buddhism of Tibet, or Lamaism* (Waddell 1895: 245),[25] the opportunity of taking the first-ever photograph of this high-ranking female religious figure from Tibet [**Figure 4**] was irresistible for Bell. Both Palhese and Rabden Lepcha were tasked with arranging this photograph. Bell writes:

> At the beginning of our reception our clerks and servants, as well as Palhese bowed down before her, made their offerings to her and took her blessing, she touching each on the head with her hand.
> After I had left, she allowed Rabden with whom I had left Palhese— very willingly— to take a photo of her, asking for five copies of the result, if it turned out well.[26]

Rabden Lepcha had taken both portrait as well as landscape shots of Dorje Phagmo. Unfortunately, the photograph 'was much too under-exposed to be of any use'.[27] Nonetheless, the portrait shot became part of Bell's *The People of Tibet* (1928) where Bell describes his meeting with the 'The Thunderbolt Sow', 'the holiest woman in Tibet' whom he had the 'privilege to visit' *en route* to Lhasa accompanied by Mr. Dyer, 'our doctor from Sikkim' (Bell 1928: 165-167). Bell enthusiastically depicts himself and Dyer as 'the first white men to be received by her, indeed the first she had seen' (Bell 1928: 166). Although Bell mentions, transcribing from his diary, his clerks and servants being present on the occasion and Palhese receiving a blessing from Dorje Phagmo, he omits any reference to the photographer, Rabden Lepcha (Bell 1928: 167).

Both Palhese and Rabden Lepcha were not only agential in the production of the image, but may have also influenced its sacerdotal staging. Dorje Phagmo is photographed as sitting on an elevated religious platform, adorned by Tibetan regalia. Both Bell's collaborators were Tibetan Buddhists, and the shots were taken after both Europeans, Bell and Dyer, had departed the scene.[28] Things were assisted further by the fact that Dorje Phagmo herself desired to be photographed, an earlier attempt by Tibetans under the instructions of the Thirteenth Dalai Lama having resulted in failure.[29] The transcription, from Bell's diary to his book was accompanied by the omission of

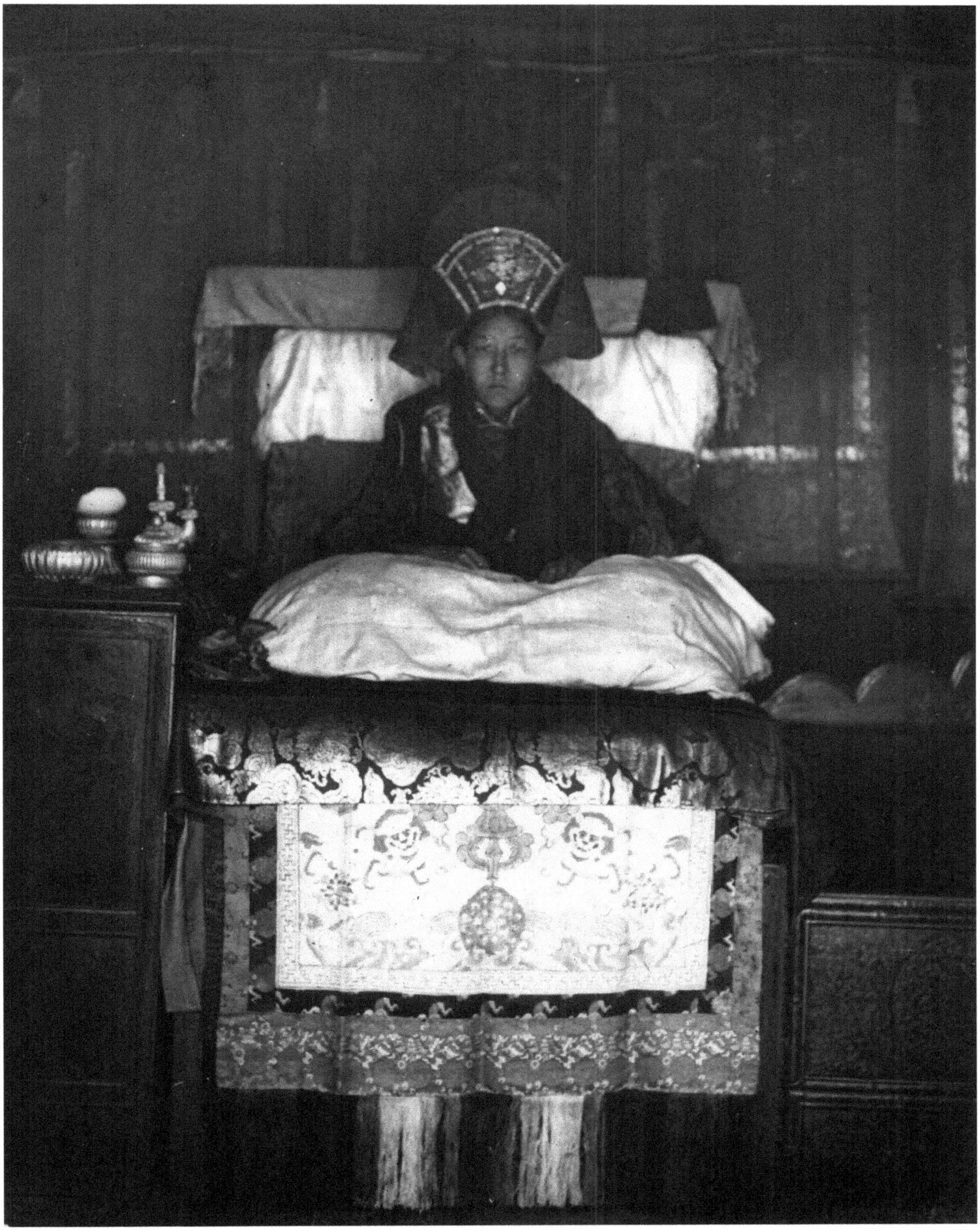

Figure 4: Dorje Phagmo on her seat at Samding Monastery, Tibet, photographed in November, 1920 by Rabden Lepcha. [Accession number 1998.285.137.2], Copyright Pitt Rivers Museum, University of Oxford.

Rabden Lepcha. Within the hierarchy of his interlocutors, Rabden Lepcha was an orderly, unlike Palhese, who was a Tibetan aristocrat,[30] whom Bell often mentions in his books and whom he credits as 'an old friend' in the Preface to *Tibet— Past & Present* (Bell 1924: i).

This decision, to acknowledge Palhese while overlooking Rabden Lepcha's role as photographer, may have also had to do with the kind of readership that Bell was targeting for his books in England. Published from the Clarendon Press and the Oxford University Press, Bell's books were meant for circulation among an elite coterie of (mostly) academic readers comprising British and European Orientalists and Indologists. His omitting of the names of his collaborators from his published books, while crediting them in his personal diaries, lists and notebooks, perhaps had much to do with the complacent class attitudes prevalent among the privileged public-school Oxbridge men, who comprised his primary target readers.

The internal hierarchy that remained operative amongst Bell's collaborators, accentuated as it was by the hierarchies within British colonial bureaucracy, becomes symbolically iterated through a photograph of the Lhasa Mission group of 1920-21 [**Figure 5**], showing most of Bell's interlocutors. The photograph, part of Bell's Half-Plate/H-Series, was later published in *Tibet— Past & Present* (Bell 1924: 196). It shows Bell seated at the centre, with Lieutenant Colonel R.S. Kennedy, who replaced Dyer as the mission's chief medical officer, on his right,[31] S.W. Laden La, who is on Kennedy's right,[32] and Palhese seated on Bell's extreme right. On Bell's left are seated Tibetans deputed for the mission by the Thirteenth Dalai Lama— Kusho Lötro, one of the Dalai Lama's secretaries,[33] Netö or Tsewang Namse, who accompanied Bell as his guide from Gyantse to Lhasa[34] (on Kusho Lötro's left) and an assistant secretary. Standing immediately behind Bell, to his right, between Kennedy and him, is Rai Bahadur Norbu Dhondup. While Bell remains at the centre of the image, positioned centrally as 'author' of his own archive, both his orderlies, Purbu Lepcha (on Bell's right) and Rabden Lepcha (on his left) remain seated on the ground below him.

The same photograph of the Lhasa Mission group was also taken on a full-plate camera, on the same occasion, from a slightly different angle. This 6" by 8" photo [**Figure 6**], which is part of the private collection of Charles Bell's great-grandson, confirms that the photographer was indeed Rabden Lepcha, a zoomed-in view showing Rabden Lepcha holding the cable to the automatic shutter of a plate camera.[35]

Rabden Lepcha, in addition to numerous photographs that he produced for Bell,[36] was responsible for taking one of the most important images for Bell's book, that of the Thirteenth Dalai Lama himself. In early-1921, by which time Bell was increasingly assigning Rabden Lepcha to take his photographs (Harris 2016: 76), on 7 March, Bell instructed him to take a shot of the Dalai Lama as his procession travelled from Potala to Norbulingka, the Dalai Lama's summer palace. Light conditions being unfavourable at 7 a.m. in the morning, the enterprise was unsuccessful.[37] Bell would make another attempt to photograph the Dalai Lama, this time in his throne-room in Norbulingka, on 14 October, 1921. Bell writes in his diary entry of the day 'Rabden and I photographed the Dalai Lama on the throne in his throne-room, as he would sit when blessing pilgrims. The photos on the whole turned out well'.[38] The photograph would appear in Bell's *The Portrait of the Dalai Lama* (Bell 1946: 233) and Bell mentions that this was 'the first time that anybody has photographed him in the Holy City' (Bell 1946: 336).

The illustration was meant to evoke among Bell's readers a sense of religiosity associated with Tibet and the Dalai Lama. The photograph [**Figure 7**] thus shows Tibet's supreme leader within a sacerdotal setting, seated on his throne, 'four feet high, a seat without back or arms', the 'nine silk scrolls, representing Buddha in the Earth-pressing attitude...placed on the wall behind and

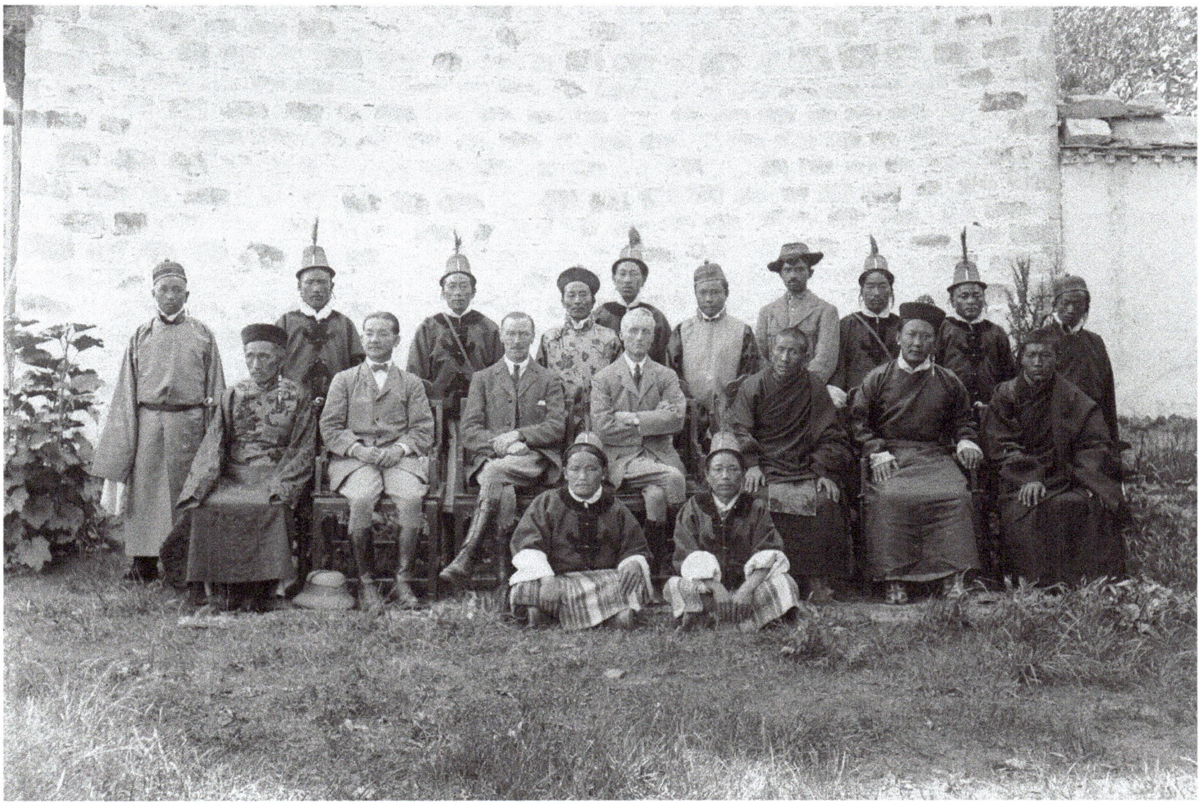

Figure 5: Lhasa Mission group, photographed sometime between end-December, 1920 and early-January, 1921.[39] [Accession number 1998.285.339.1], Copyright Pitt Rivers Museum, University of Oxford.

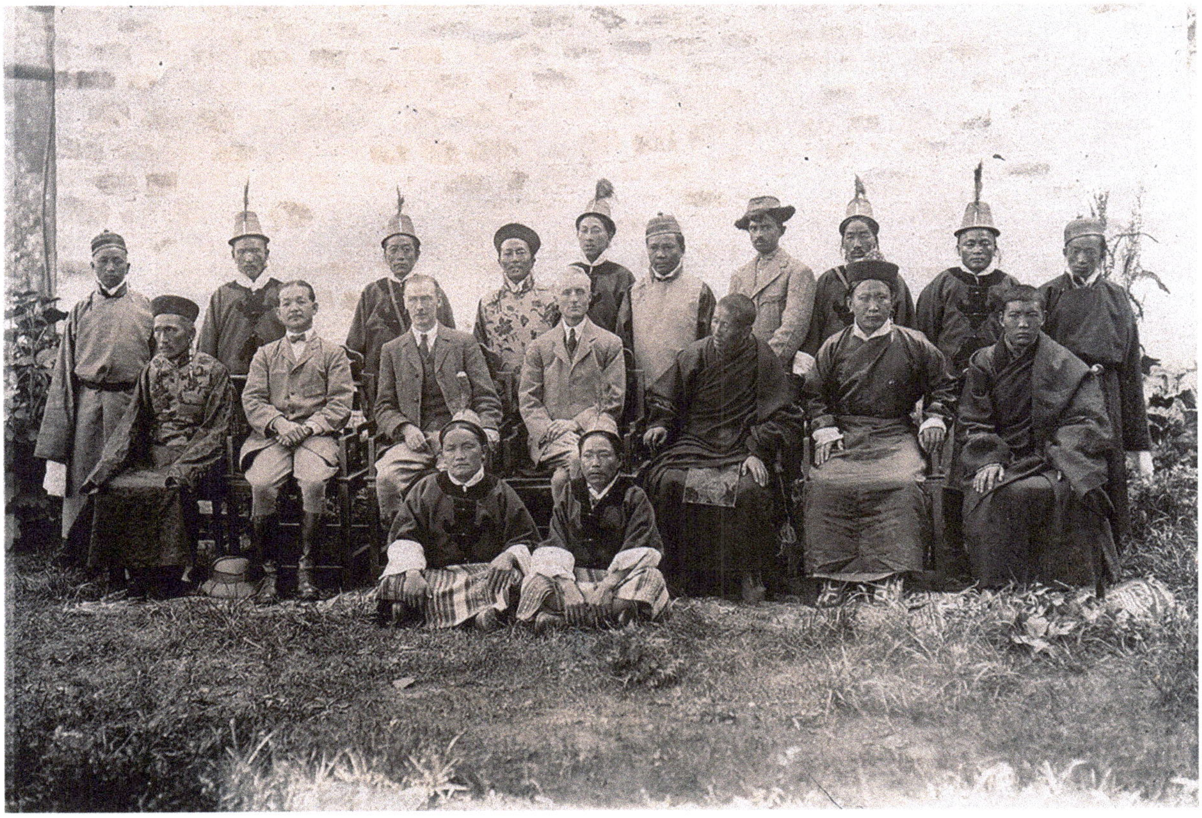

Figure 6: Lhasa Mission group, photographed by Rabden Lepcha. From the private collection of Jonathan Bracken.

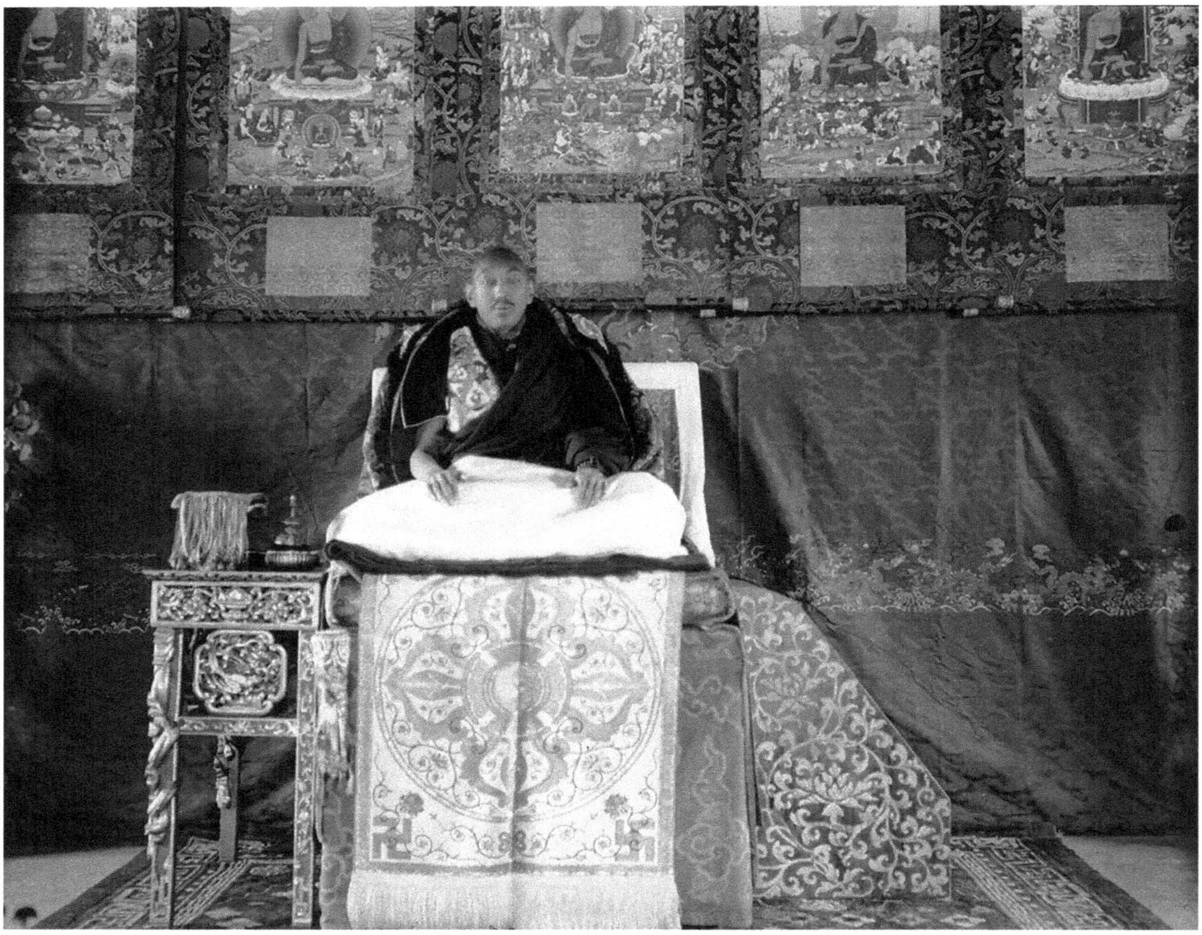

Figure 7: Ngawang Lobsang Thupten Gyatso, the Thirteenth Dalai Lama seated on his throne at Norbulingka, photographed on 14 October, 1921 by Rabden Lepcha. [Accession number 1998.285.91.1], Copyright Pitt Rivers Museum, University of Oxford.

above the throne', the red silk brocade covering the wall, the 'eighteen-inch high' dais 'with a low balustrade of well-covered woodwork' on which the throne stood and 'a cloth of rich white silk, handsomely embroidered in gold with crossed dorjes (thunderbolts) hanging down in front of the throne'.[40] As in the case of the Dorje Phagmo image, the making of this photograph was not of Bell's orchestration. Instead, it was guided by the Dalai Lama himself, familiar as he was with Bell from the long hours spent with him in Darjeeling. The Dalai Lama personally supervised the arrangement of the throne-room in which the photograph was to be taken,[41] orchestrating and structuring its content and determining the way in which he wanted to be represented. We see here a veritable trace of an 'indigenous countersign' (Douglas 1999: 70) where Tibetan agency and desire begin to determine the epistemic language of the photograph, with the Thirteenth Dalai Lama directly influencing its hieratic content.

The photograph itself was likely taken by Rabden Lepcha, under Bell's instructions, although in the book, unlike the corresponding entry in his diary, Bell clearly designates himself as the photographer.[42] The hierarchical nature of their collaboration, entrenched within a colonial hegemonic machinery of power,[43] resulted in the elision of Rabden Lepcha's name as photographer from Bell's books, unlike the diaries where the name occurs often. In the absence of local commemoration, the restoration of Rabden Lepcha's agency[44] relies almost entirely on the archival clues available through Bell's diaries.

The Move to a Professional Cameraman: Kartick Chandra Pyne and Bell's 1934 Photographic Archive

In 1934, Bell once again returned to Tibet. The Thirteenth Dalai Lama, however, had died in December, 1933, and Bell would not visit Lhasa this time, travelling instead in Eastern Tibet for five months, between 12 June and 12 November, 1934,[45] before returning to Kalimpong. On this trip, Bell would hire a professional cameraman, Kartick Chandra Pyne, 'the Bengali photographer who lives at Kalimpong',[46] to accompany him.

Kartick Chandra was the middle among three brothers, the eldest, Ganesh Chandra and the youngest, Durga Chandra. Their father, B.N. Pyne had been brought from Calcutta to Kalimpong to work as an accountant for John Anderson Graham, the Scottish missionary, who, in 1900, established the school and orphanage, Dr. Graham's Homes, at Deolo Hill, Kalimpong, on hundred acres of land leased by the British India government. The three boys studied at Dr. Graham's newly established school, and later, became entrepreneurs. In the early 1900s, they established the multipurpose Kalimpong Stores [**Figure 8**] in the main bazaar area of the town. By 1912, the eldest brother, Ganesh Chandra, had acquired the license for starting the regional branch of Kodak Studios, and the Kalimpong stores began to supply Kodak film, cameras and camera equipment as well as specialize in photographic productions. Kartick Chandra, who was good in developing traditional darkroom prints from film negatives, became the main professional photographer of Kalimpong town.[47]

We may note here that at a time when photographic studios by Europeans were proliferating in Darjeeling, producing picture postcards and studio photographs,[48] K.C. Pyne was the only non-European professional photographer operating in the Eastern Himalayas.[49] Bell recruited K.C. Pyne from Kalimpong and accompanied by a Tibetan interpreter [**Figure 9**], Pyne travelled to Tibet in 1934 as Bell's professional cameraman.

Bell, in his curated index, mentions that the photographs with serial numbers 1-35 in his Jewel/J-Series, taken mostly at Kalimpong, are by Phipraj, whereas the rest, from serial number 36-570 are all by Pyne.[50] Pyne, however, kept a log book with date-wise entries of the photographs taken by him on the Rolleiflex camera (12 images per roll of film) [**Figure 11**] While the ordering, as well as the descriptions, of the images are somewhat different, this log-book, now part of a private collection,[51] may have been the likely source for Bell's curated index of his R (Rolleiflex)-Series photographs, which are now housed in the collection of the British Library. The log-book also indicates that Pyne was the primary photographer who handled both cameras.

Pyne's log-book entry for 19 September, 1934, for instance, lists photographs taken during Bell's visit to Mindröling monastery on 19 and 20 September, 1934. Palhese had reached the monastery earlier, for a prior exchange of pleasantries and also to announce the arrival of Bell and Harnett.[52] A set of photographs in Bell's R-series (R-184 and R-185) corresponds to Entries 5 and 6 in Pyne's log-book for Film Roll 33, and shows Palhese and a monk of Mindröling monastery about to receive Bell and Harnett (approaching on horseback), with a white *kh-btags* or ceremonial scarf. Bell's own curated index has the caption— 'Arrival at Min-drö-ling Monastery. D.B. Palhese has dismounted from his pony to present the usual scarf (ka-ta) to the priest at Min-drö-ling, who has come out to welcome us. He is telling the priest that I am just riding up, both are looking in my direction'—for R-184, and— 'Palhese getting the scarf ready'— for R-185[53] [**Figure 10**]. Pyne's log-book entries for these photographs read as follows— 'Dewan bahadur talking to the lama. His khadha is hanging in his hand' and 'Sir Charles Bell arriving at Mindroling Gum-pa with Col. Harnett— on horseback—Dewan bahadur with Lama— going to receive him'. [**Figure 11**].

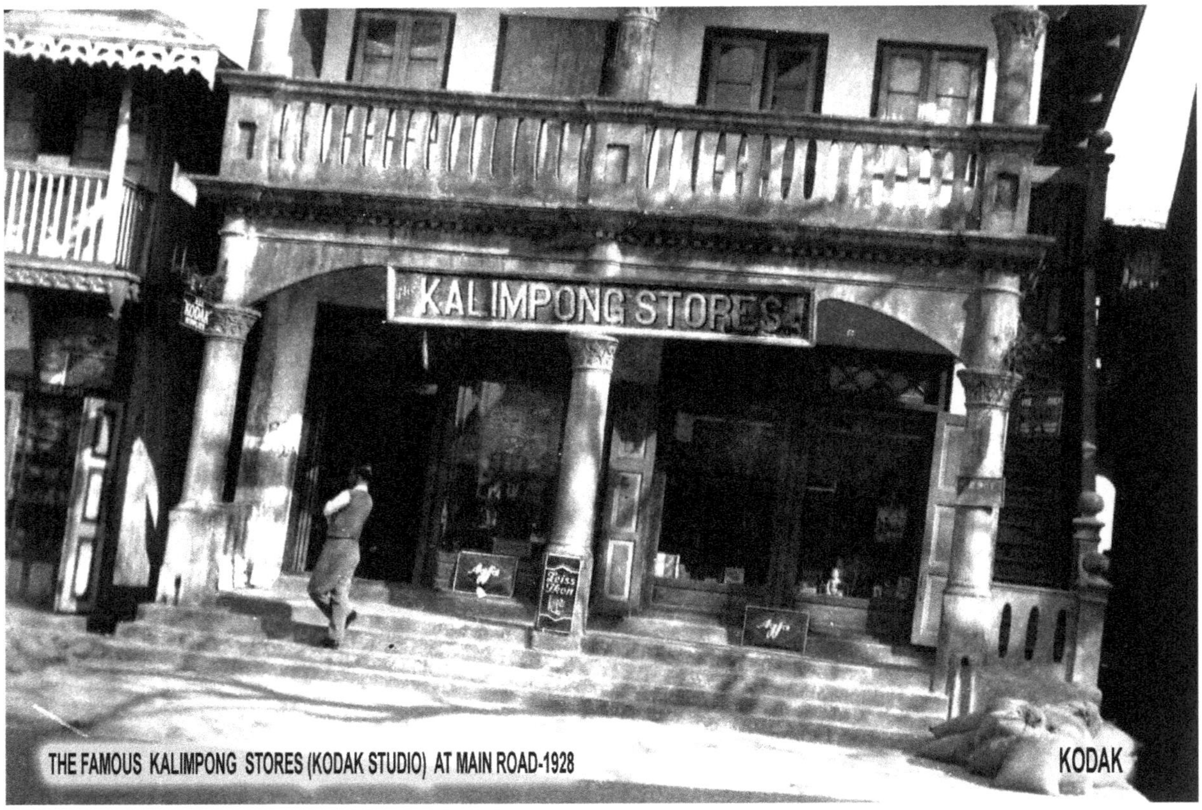

Figure 8: Kalimpong Stores run by the Pyne brothers, Kalimpong bazaar, 1928.
From the private collection of the author.

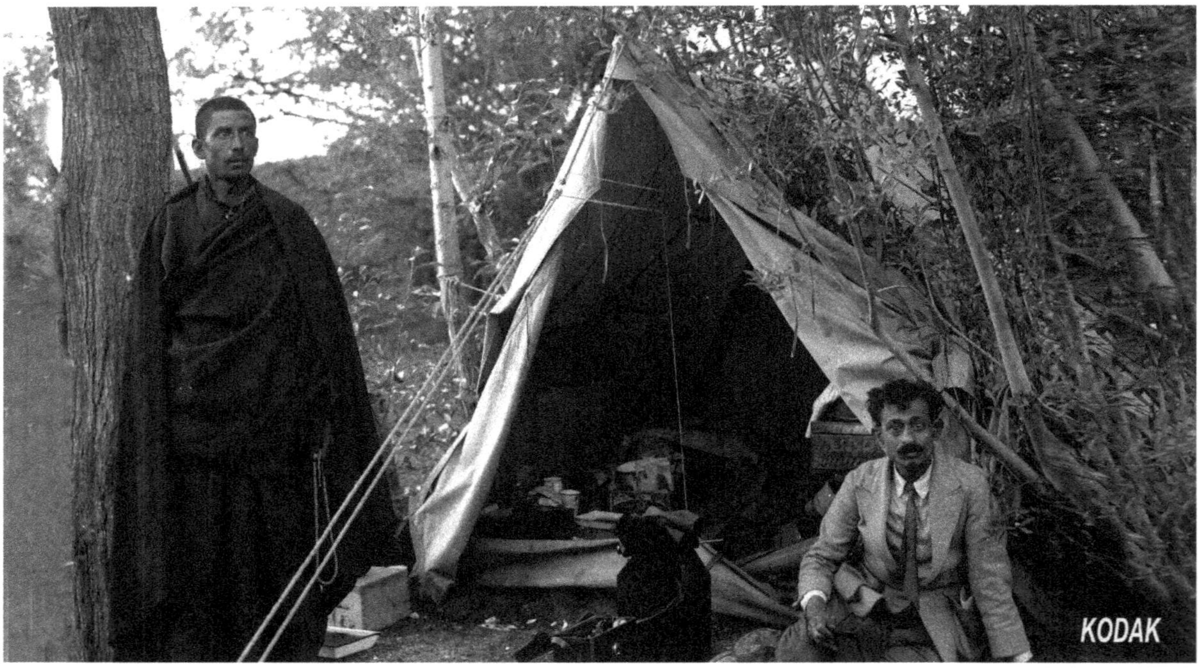

Figure 9: Kartick Chandra Pyne (right, seated) in front of a tent with his camera equipment, and his Tibetan interpreter (left, standing) *en route* Tibet, 1934.
From the private collection of the author.

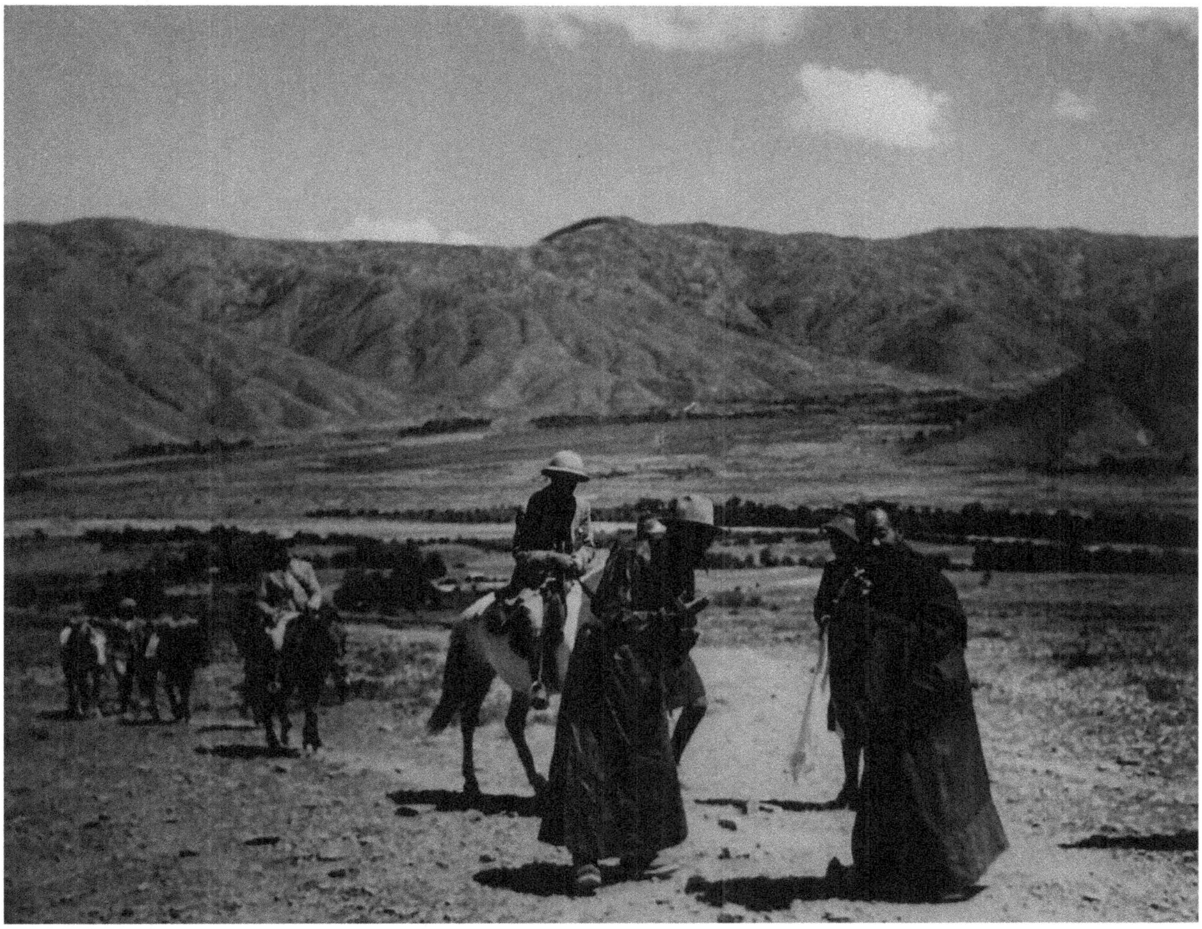

Figure 10: Palhese (left standing) and a monk of Mindröling monastery (right) receiving Charles Bell and Harnett arriving on horseback, photographed in September, 1934 by Kartick Chandra Pyne. From the British Library Collection: [Photo 1112/6 (184)].

Here, the log-book entries act as ciphers indicating how the image archive was produced. The transition, from log-book (Pyne's) to curated index (Bell's), details the processes through which these photographs were produced, catalogued and entered into collection and circulation. Interestingly, neither Bell nor Pyne, in their respective entries, use the actual Tibetan term for ceremonial scarf— *kha-btags*. While Pyne transcribes the term as 'khadha',[54] Bell uses the phonetic equivalent in English, 'ka-ta.'

What may also be noted here are how the several actors involved within the making of Bell's collections become shadowy interlopers lurking around the archival margins, outlines upon which colonial knowledge is superimposed. This is reinstated by the fact that the various collections, across the different archival and museum sites in England today, carry the name of Charles Bell.[55] The newer acts of recovery (for instance, of Pyne's log-book from Kalimpong) call for an amendment of these processes of archival ordering and cataloguing.

Bell's 1934 trip to Tibet, unlike that of 1920-21, was not part of an official mission. It was impelled by Bell's desire for more photographs as illustrations for his next and last book, *Portrait of the Dalai Lama* (1946), which would be published posthumously, after his death, on 8 March, 1945.[56] Perhaps, this was the reason that drove Bell to hire a professional photographer on this trip.

The transition, from amateur cameraman (Rabden Lepcha) to a professional (Pyne), is marked through the shifting representation of a photographic subject, who recurs in both sets of visual archives. A second photograph (catalogued J-400 by Bell[57]) taken by Pyne of Dorje Phagmo

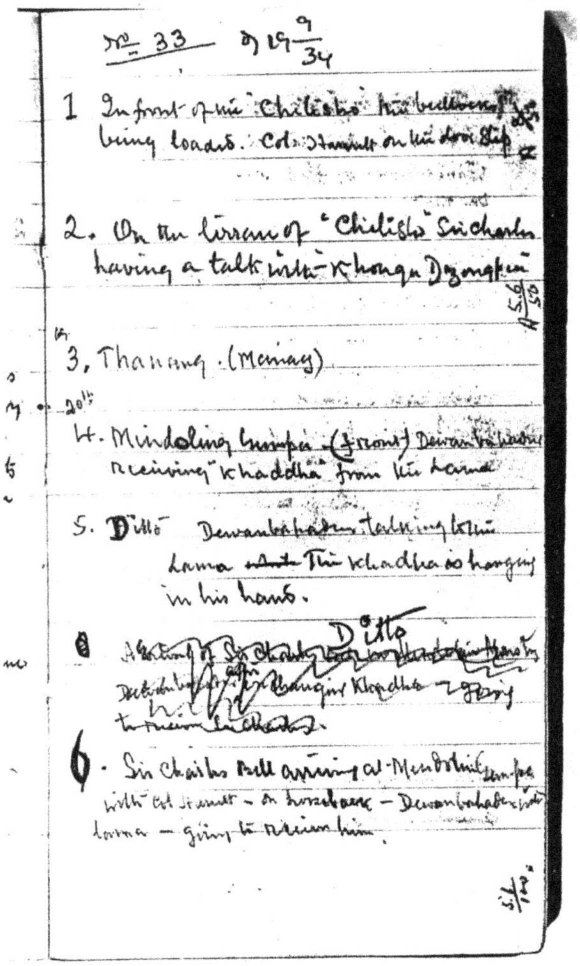
No 33 d/ 19-9-34
1 In front of the "Chilisto" the bullocks being loaded.
2. On the terrace of "Chilisto" Sir Charles having a talk with Khangsa Dzongpen
3, Thanang (Menang)
4. Mindoling Gompa (front) Dewanbahadur receiving "khaddha" from the Lama
5. Ditto Dewanbahadur talking to the Lama The khadha is hanging in his hands.
6 · Sir Charles Bell arriving at Mindoling Gompa with Col. Stewart on horseback – Dewanbahadur with lama – going to receive him.

Figure 11: A page from Pyne's personal log-book of the 1934 expedition. From the private collection of the author.

[**Figure 12**], now a thirty-eight-year-old woman, becomes a part of Bell's last book (Bell 1946: 129). Unsatisfied with the previous photo of her that had been taken by Rabden Lepcha in 1921 (Bell mentioned it as being under-exposed[58] owing to Rabden Lepcha's inexperience, though he nonetheless used the photograph in his 1928 publication *The People of Tibet*), Bell wanted a better illustration this time around, by a professional cameraman. Bell met Dorje Phagmo again on 10 September, 1934. The only person who was present with Bell on both occasions, in 1921 as well as in 1934, was Palhese, all archival traces of Rabden Lepcha having disappeared after 1921. Bell describes the meeting in his diary:

> The girlish face and form of my last visit have of course disappeared. She is now thirty-eight years of age (Tibetan reckoning), of stout build, and heavily pockmarked... She moves like an old woman. Her cramped life, without proper exercise, has, no doubt, led to this condition... One may easily infer from her whole attitude and demeanour that she would long ago have gladly exchanged her position as the holiest and highest woman in Tibet for that of the wife of a simple peasant with her own family and home. She seems bored, and weary of all the fine trappings.[59]

Bell's personal reflections on Dorje Phagmo's changed appearance, between 1921 and 1934, are accompanied by a visual recording of the same. Pyne, either working independently or under Bell's direction, photographed Dorje Phagmo within a regular quotidian setting, unlike the hieratic framing of Rabden Lepcha's earlier 1928 image. Bell's own altered perception of Dorje Phagmo, as a woman who now seemed 'bored' of her religious position, and whose 'girlish face' showed signs of premature ageing, was a noticeable shift from the enthusiasm that had characterized his earlier encounter with Tibet's highest female ecclesiast. Additionally, Pyne was a Bengali who neither knew Tibetan, nor was he a practicing Buddhist. For him (unlike for Palhese or Rabden Lepcha), Dorje Phagmo was not a revered figure. The photographic image, besides the obvious tent-like setting where it was taken, becomes devoid of any sacred trace that had characterized the 1921 image. Reading the two photographs of Dorje Phagmo, the 1921 and the 1934 image, side by side, also complicates any simplistic white/non-white binary division of agents responsible for producing Bell's images. Instead, it demonstrates how different sensibilities— white European to native Tibetan to Bengali— differently inflected the production of Bell's visual archive.

Pyne was especially good with panoramic/cinematic shots. Bell writes about taking his 'first cinema exposure' on the Rolleiflex camera, under Pyne's instructions.[60] The shot being talked about is a panoramic

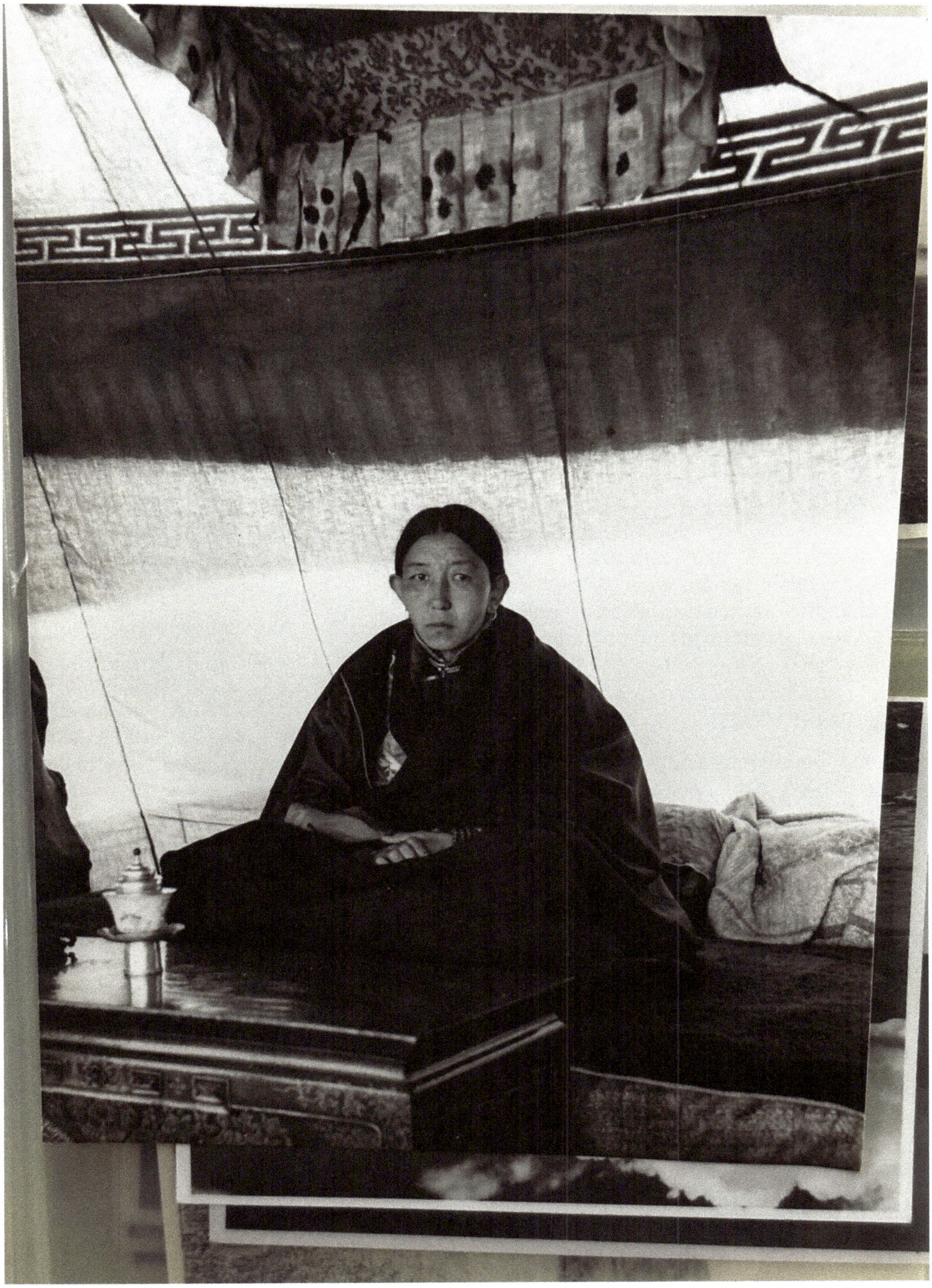

Figure 12: Dorje Phagmo, photographed in September, 1934 by Kartick Chandra Pyne. From the British Library Collection: [Photo 1112/5 (400)].

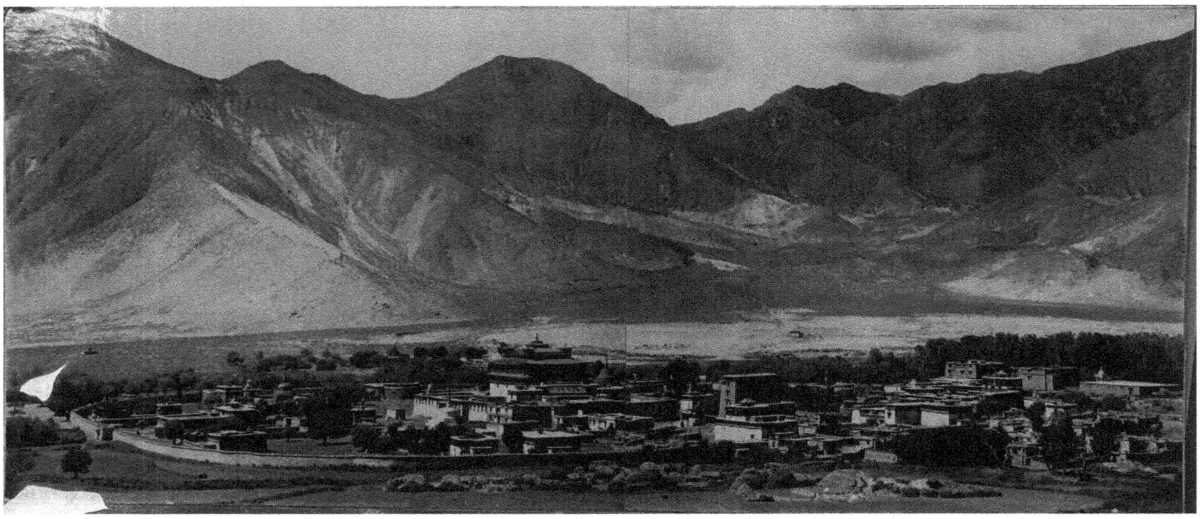

Figure 13: Panorama (cinematic) shot of the Samyé Monastery, photographed in September, 1934 by Kartick Chandra Pyne. From the British Library Collection: [Photo 1112/5 (447a) and 1112/5 (447b)].

photo (resulting from a combination of two or more shots) of the Samyé monastery that Bell visited at the end of September, 1934.[61] Pyne, too, took his own photograph of Samyé and the image (J-447)[62] **[Figure 13]** would also end up in *Portrait of the Dalai Lama* (Bell 1946: 129).

One of the more interesting illustrations that would make it to the book from Bell's 1934 trip is a photograph of a boy monk, Lhogön Kyibuk (translated by Bell as 'Inmost Happiness'), the head lama of a monastery near Penam. In Bell's book, the figure is unnamed, described only as the 'Head lama of a Monastery, aged fourteen' (Bell 1946: 373). From Bell's diary entry of 20 August, 1934, we find out that Lhogön Kyibuk was the brother of Wangdu Norbu Kyibuk,[63] one of four boys who had been sent to England in 1913 accompanied by a Tibetan plenipotentiary, Dorje Tsegyal (or Kusho Lungshar) and S.W. Laden La, to become the first-ever beneficiaries of a modern English education in England proper.[64]

In his diary, Bell also gives us the biographical details of the boy, whose ancestors, victims of the Bhutanese civil war, had fled from Bhutan to Tibet, along with Palhese's own ancestors, eight generations before, during the time of the Fifth Dalai Lama.[65] Lhogön Kyibuk's photograph **[Figure 14]** was taken by Pyne on 21 August,[66] which is the illustration that appears in Bell's book.

In a move quite uncharacteristic of Bell (the depiction of Tibetans in his books is usually more nuanced[67]), the biographical details of Kyibuk, including his name, are omitted from the published book, and he becomes reduced to a trope of Tibetan religiosity portrayed by the photograph. Pyne's name, too, is entirely left out of the book. In the case of Kyibuk's image, the archival prompts available through Bell's diaries and photograph catalogues, enable the recuperation of both the name of the photographer as well as the biography of the subject. This recursive remaking also points towards the nature of Bell's photographic archive, as a multi-agential one assembled by his Tibetan and Sikkimese collaborators such as Palhese and Rabden Lepcha, and aided by the technical expertise of his Bengali cameraman, K.C. Pyne.

Pyne would also take various photographs in and around Kalimpong town for Bell, sometimes paying the subjects for posing for the camera. A bill, signed by Pyne, to Bell, dated January, 1935, mentions paying five Rupees to the monks of Kalimpong monastery for a photograph. **[Figure 15]**. The image appears towards the end of Bell's J-Series (J-567)[68] **[Figure 16]**. Pyne's bill also mentions taking video ('cine') footage of the monks.[69]

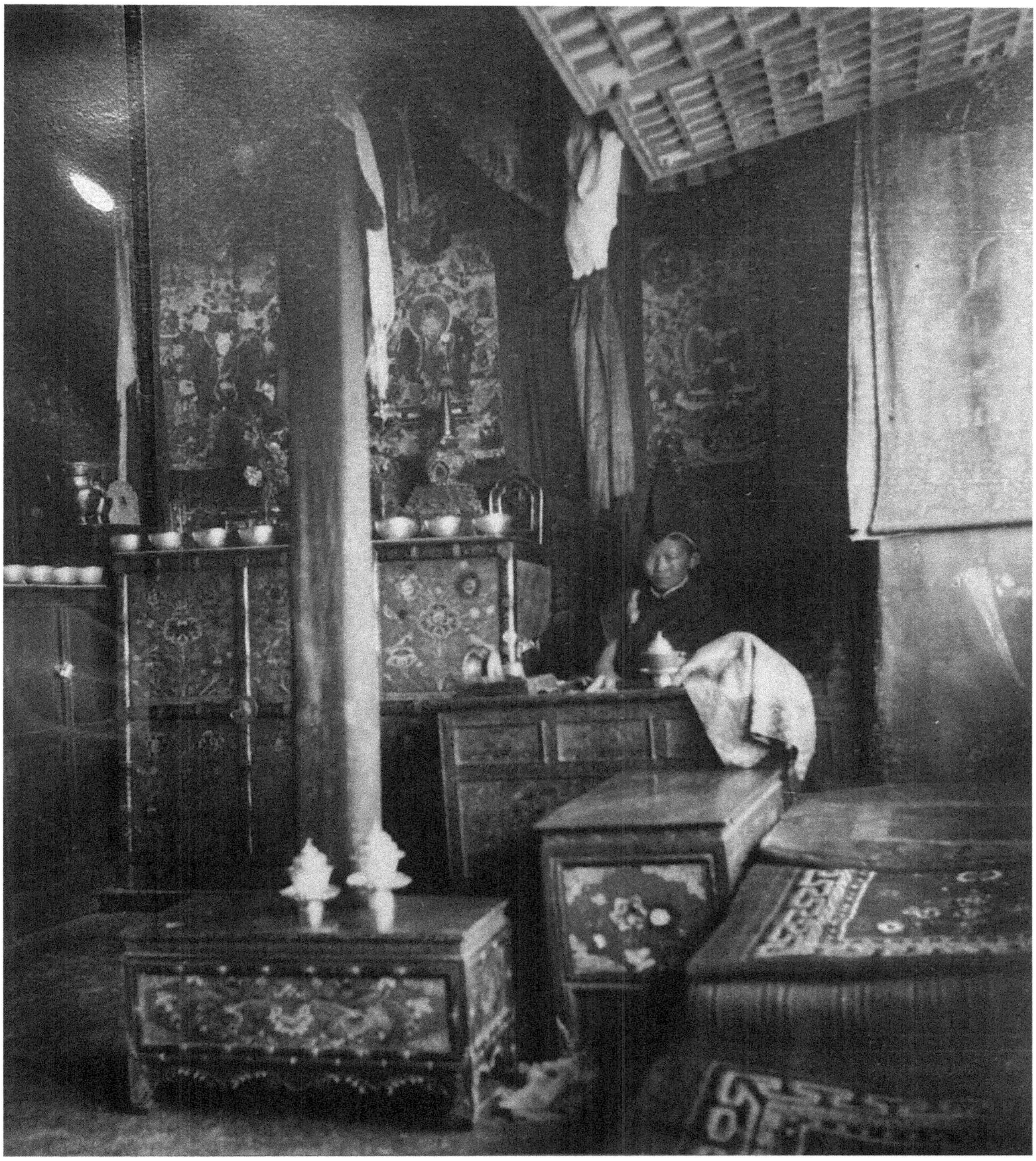

Figure 14: Lhogön Kyibuk, photographed in August, 1934 by Kartick Chandra Pyne. From the British Library Collection: [Photo 1112/6 (81)].

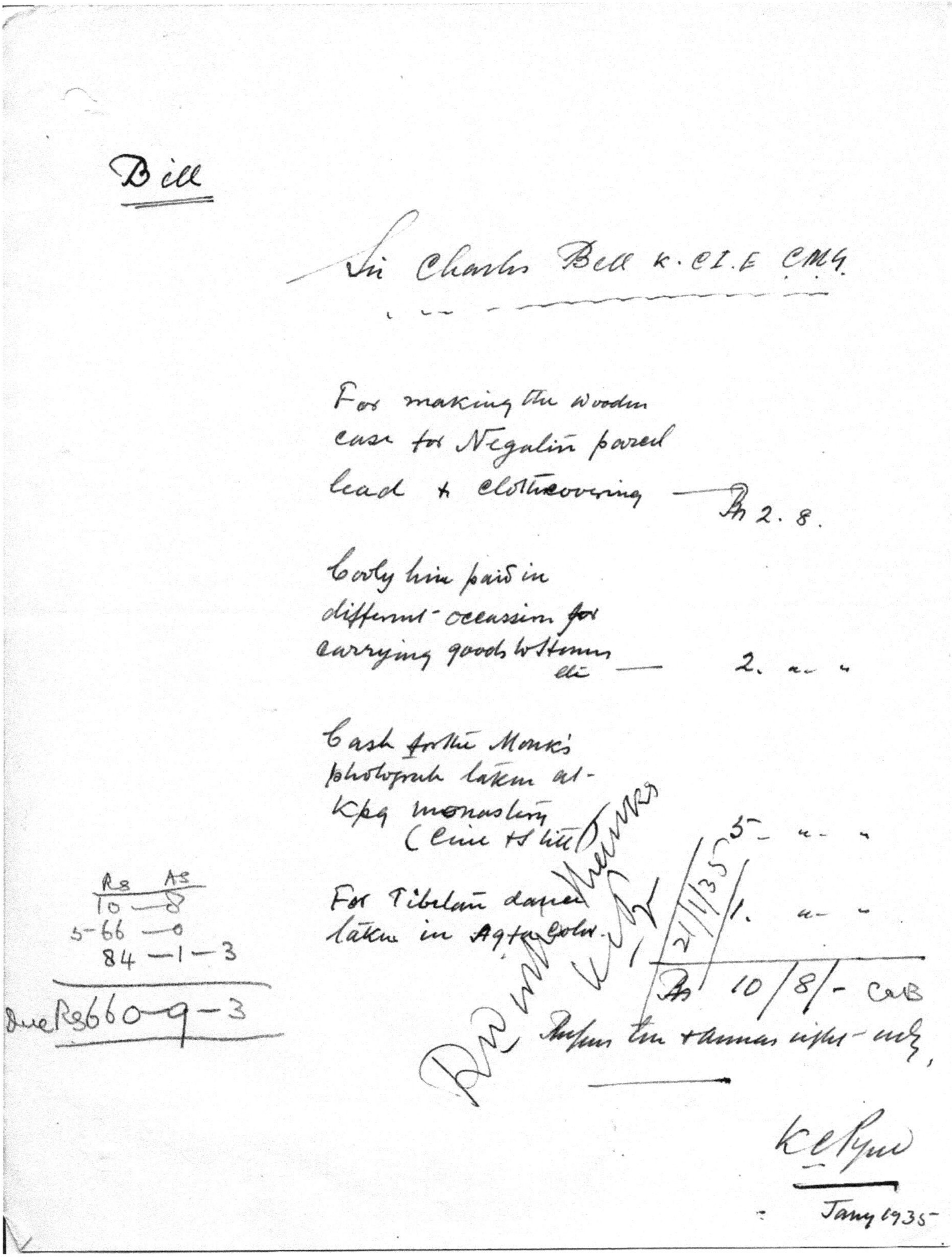
Bill

Sir Charles Bell K.C.I.E. C.M.G.

For making the wooden case for Negalin parcel lead + cloth covering — Rs 2.8.

Cooly hire paid in different occasions for carrying goods to steamer etc — 2. " "

Cash for the Monk's photograph taken at Kpg monastery (Cine + still) 5 " "

For Tibetan diaries taken in Agfacolor. 1. " "

2/1/35

Rs 10/8/- CAB

Rupees ten + annas eight only,

K C Pyne

Jany 1935

Rs As
10 — 8
5-66 — 0
84 — 1 — 3
Due Rs 660 — 9 — 3

Figure 15: Bill from Pyne to Bell dated January, 1935.From the private collection of Jonathan Bracken.

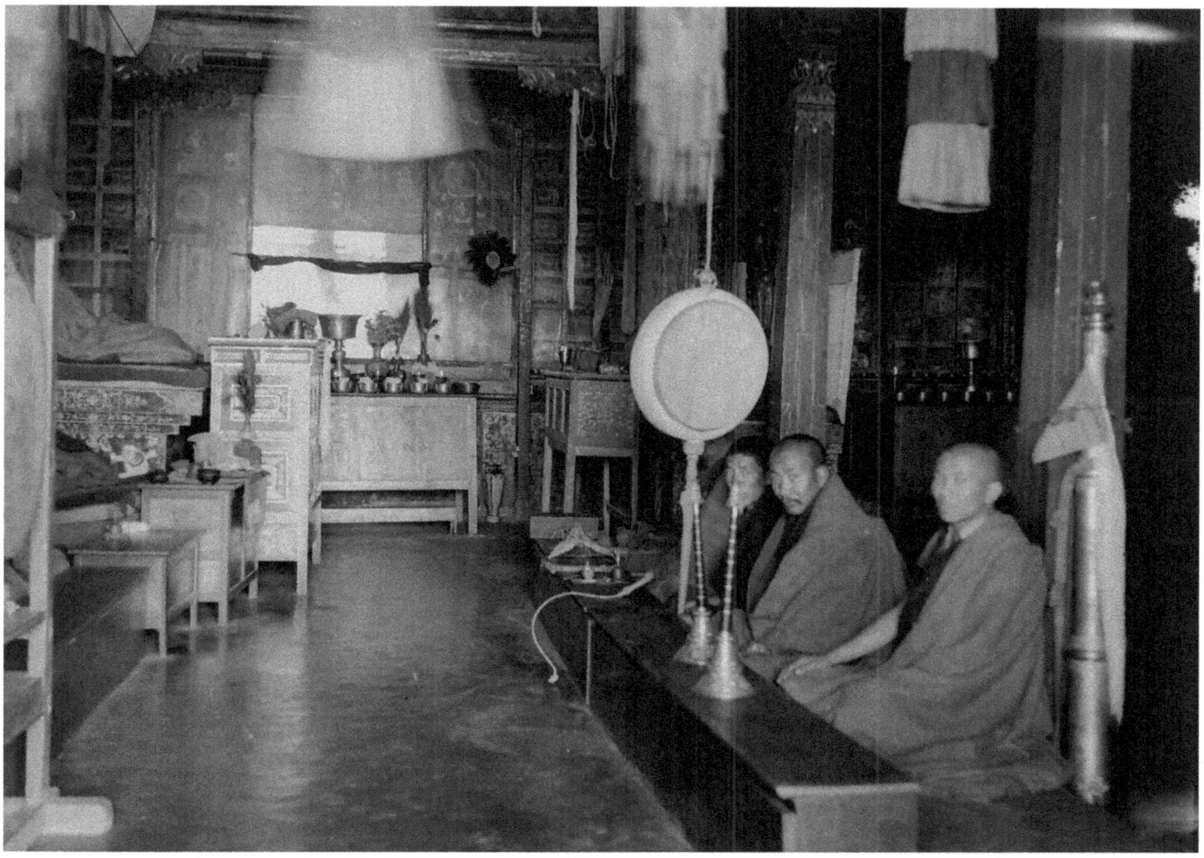

Figure 16: Monks photographed at Kalimpong monastery by Pyne in 1934. From the British Library Collection: [Photo 1112/5 (567a)].

Conclusion: Unravelling the Palimpsest

If Bell's photographic collection is read as an assemblage of several kinds of native knowledges, sacerdotal and technical, then each of his collaborator figures seems to play a crucial role in shaping the content, form and associated meanings therein. The epistemic content and religious setting of some of the P, Q and H-Series images were facilitated through the presence of, and inputs from, Bell's collaborators such as Palhese and Rabden Lepcha. The latter group of images (J and R-Series) relied entirely on the technical expertise of Pyne.

A transcription of some of the photographs (from Bell's substantial visual collection) from archive to book, ideologically oriented towards Bell's elite white readers, also reoriented the hermeneutic structure of the archive. It resulted in the archive's encompassment within and filtration through colonial hegemonies of power, in the process flattening out and compressing the roles of the multiple agents involved within its making, naming one sole white author and silencing all the other non-white collaborators. The process of 'recuperating' these lost voices does not merely seek to reinstate lost agency, but question the very nature of British colonial knowledge production, that not only repudiated the roles of its non-white producers and contributors, but remained hermeneutically premised on those very forms of disavowal. The rich assortment of visual material attributed to Bell is a layered archive. Its epistemic unpacking unveils these layers, and showcases instead several kinds of knowledges and expertise that Bell's collaborators brought to his photographic collection.

Abbreviations

AAS: Asia and Africa Studies
BL: British Library
NAI: National Archives of India
PRM: Pitt Rivers Museum

Parjanya Sen is a historian and anthropologist working in the field of Himalayan Buddhism. He is a 2023 ACLS 'Early-Career Research Fellow' funded by The Robert H. N. Ho Family Foundation Program in Buddhist Studies, and was a Postdoctoral Visiting Scholar at the School of Anthropology and Museum Ethnography, University of Oxford from January to October, 2024. He is working as Assistant Professor in English at Deshbandhu College for Girls, University of Calcutta. He has edited a book Death and Dying in Northeast India: Indigeneity and Afterlife (Routledge, 2022). His upcoming monograph, from Palgrave Macmillan, is on Sarat Chandra Das, and examines his role and agency in the production of knowledge on Tibet from colonial Bengal, through the late-nineteenth and early-twentieth centuries.

I thank the American Council of Learned Societies (ACLS) and The Robert H. N. Ho Family Foundation Program in Buddhist Studies for the 2023 Early-Career Research Fellowship, which provided me the time and resources to conduct archival research for this essay. I also thank the School of Anthropology & Museum Ethnography, University of Oxford, for affiliating me as a Postdoctoral Visiting Fellow during the nine-month tenure of my ACLS Fellowship.

Endnotes

1. 'Typescript index for Sir Charles Bell's Photographs J and R Series,' 1933-34, Box 2, PRM, Oxford, 56.

2. I thank Charles Bell's great grandson, Jonathan Bracken, for the exact model number and specifications.

3. I have been unable to ascertain the years of birth and death, from archival records, of Rabden Lepcha, Kartick Chandra Pyne as well as of some of the other figures discussed in this essay. Where unknown, these have not been mentioned.

4. Bronwen Douglas studies ethnographic images emerging out of late-eighteenth and early-nineteenth century maritime explorations in Oceania, by James Cook (during 1772-75), Bruni d'Entrecasteaux (during 1791-93) and d'Urville (between 1826-29), for their 'indigenous countersigns' bearing the 'oblique stamp of indigenous actions, desires and agencies on recorded imperial imaginings.' (Douglas 1999: 70)

5. My methodology of 'recuperative hermeneutics' with regard to British imperial knowledge-production on Tibet, draws on Arondekar's work on the hermeneutics of archival absences that characterized British colonial discourses on sexuality (Arondekar 2009: 1-10).

6. For instance, there is a particularly striking image of him (R-302) under a set of ice-stalactites between Gyantse and Sangang, taken on 31 October, 1934. See 'Typescript index for Sir Charles Bell's Photographs J and R Series,' 96. I thank Jonathan Bracken for bringing this to my notice. Jonathan also identified Pyne in another photograph, while looking through the negatives, from Bell's J Series (J-392). The corresponding entry by Bell in his index does not mention Pyne, and Bell only notes that the two photographs (J-391 and J-392) were taken 'in the narrow valley going up towards Karo La [pass]'. See 'Typescript index for Sir Charles Bell's Photographs J and R Series,' 43-44. The reason for Pyne's infrequent trace may be owing to the fact that on most occasions, he was the one handling both the Jewel and Rolleiflex cameras, and not among the subjects being photographed.

7. 'Typescript index for Sir Charles Bell's Photographs J and R Series,' 56.

8. I have used his full name throughout the essay, instead of referring to him only by his surname, as Tibetans or Lepchas do not have the concept of a surname.

9. Photo 1112/3(1a), Bell, Charles. 'Bell Collection: 'Photographs of Tibet and Sikkim ('P' Series)' c. 1910-1920, AAS, BL.

10. 'Typescript index for Sir Charles Bell's Photographs P, Q and H Series,' 1. To be noted here, Bell has two sets of curated indexes for his photographs. There is one index for the Postcard/P, Half-Plate/H and Quarter-Plate/Q series, which are ordered following an ethnographic typology, where the photographs are arranged under 'subject' headings, such as 'the people', 'the religion', 'arts and craft' etc. These do not

follow a numerical sequence. The other index, for the Jewel/J and Rolleiflex/R series, comprising photographs from 1933-34, is curated numerically and chronologically, based on when an image was taken.

11. This process has been one of the many impetuses of *The Tibet Album* project of the PRM, Oxford. *The Tibet Album*, <https://tibet.prm.ox.ac.uk>.

12. The mission was basically an armed invasion of Tibet. Headed by Lieutenant Colonel Francis Edward Younghusband (1863-1942), it was despatched in August, 1904, by Lieutenant-governor, George Nathaniel Curzon (1859-1925) under the auspices of the British Frontier Commission. Its purpose was to forcefully open three British trade marts at Gyantse, Yatung and Lhasa, under the terms of Anglo-Chinese Trade Regulations of 1893, agreed upon between Britain and Qing China, which considered Tibet its protectorate. Tibet itself had never been a party to this, and Younghusband's mission, which turned into an invasion, compelled Lhasa into signing the Convention in 1904 (McKay 2009: 13).

13. Telegram from Bell to Foreign Office, Simla, dated 9 May, 1921, IOR NEG F80/5e/22, AAS, BL.

14. Letter from Bell dated 21 February, 1921 to the Secretary to the Government of India, IOR NEG F80/5e/21, AAS, BL.

15. The long period of exile of the Thirteenth Dalai Lama in India from 1910-12 was a result of the hostilities between China and Tibet and the Chinese invasion of Tibet in 1910, that has been read as a direct consequence of Francis Younghusband's 1904 invasion of Tibet (Bell 1946: 61-130).

16. Bell's Final (Confidential) Report dated 29 November, 1921 of the Lhasa Mission, November 1920 to October, 1921, IOR NEG F80/5f, AAS, BL.

17. The biography of S.W. Laden La was compiled by his daughter, Deki Laden La nee Rhodes and her husband Nicholas Rhodes (Rhodes and Rhodes 2006).

18. For a brief biographical sketch of Norbu Dhondup, see McKay (McKay 2009: 126-129).

19. Bell would also use his photographs to vindicate his lectures such as the lantern-slide lecture given at the Royal Geographical Society in 1924 (Harris 2016: 74).

20. The albums attributed to Charles Bell and containing photographs by other British officers remain in the collection of the National Museums, Liverpool.

21. Clare E. Harris has, in her evaluation of the photographic career of Waddell in Darjeeling, and his unpublished *Types of Natives of Nepal, Sikhim and Tibet photographed by Messrs Johnston & Hoffman, Calcutta, with Notes*, remarked how photography, for Waddell, served a two-fold purpose— an evidentiary one, as a handmaiden to what was construed as ethnographic scientism, and a more popular one that catered to a European Orientalist fantasy of Tibet and the Himalayas (Harris 2012: 104). Harris also investigates how within Waddell's *The Buddhism of Tibet, or Lamaism*, published in 1895, primarily for his 'Christian British readers', photography not only served as 'the handmaiden to artistic invention' but also to Waddell's 'ideologically charged interventions'. Such interventions continued to be used to generate many myths about Tibetans and Tibetan Buddhism throughout the nineteenth century as objects simultaneously exotic and disdainful. In fact, it was through the efforts of those like Waddell that images of Tibetans and Tibetan Buddhism began to mutate from the purely anthropological specimens to 'something altogether more alluring', eventually becoming a very popular subject within 'colonial print culture, catering to the fantasies of British consumers.' (Harris 2012: 89)

22. Bell, Charles, Handwritten Diary Vol. VII, 17 November, 1920, private collection of Jonathan Bracken.

23. Bell writes that Tibetans would, for this reason, hide photographs (the few that they possessed) under their beds. Bell, Charles, Typescript Diary Vol. XVIII, 19 July, 1934, AAS, BL, 29-31.

24. In Tibet, Dorje Phagmo is considered as the highest female reincarnation, an emanation of Vajravārāhī. Chökyi Drönma (1422-1455), the consort of Thangtong Gyalpo or Chakzampa, was venerated as the first reincarnation.

25. Bell correctly alters Waddell's English translation of the Tibetan meaning of her

name, drawing upon the corresponding Sanskrit name *Vajra-Varāhī*, from 'the diamond sow' to the 'thunderbolt sow'.

26. Bell, Handwritten Diary Vol. VII, 11 November, 1920.

27. Bell, Handwritten Diary Vol. VII, 11 November, 1920.

28. Whether Palhese and Rabden Lepcha played any direct role in the actual 'staging' of the image can, at best, be only conjecture. What is certain is that both Bell and Dyer had already left the scene, leaving the work of photography to be carried out by the two interlocutors.

29. Bell, Handwritten Diary Vol. VII, 11 November, 1920. Harris studies at length how increasingly Tibetans themselves began to work as photographers (Harris 2016: 113-53).

30. For a biographical sketch of Palhese, see Martin. (Martin 2014: 84-93)

31. Kennedy was an old friend of Bell's, and had been the former medical officer and acting Trade Agent at Yatung. (McKay 2009: 68)

32. The figure is wrongly identified as David Macdonald in *The Tibet Album*, 'Lhasa Mission Group, 5 December, 2006. The PRM, <http://tibet.prm.ox.ac.uk/photo_1998.285.339.1.html>.
S. W. Laden La had replaced Achuk Tsering as Bell's personal assistant on the mission. Achuk Tsering (1877-1920) was one of Bell's most crucial cultural interlocutors. A Sikkimese Buddhist, he served as Bell's confidential clerk and worked with him for fourteen years prior to accompanying him on the 1920-21 Lhasa Mission. Tsering, unfortunately died in Lhasa on 11 December, 1920, succumbing to an attack of influenza and gout, a few weeks after the mission had reached Lhasa. He was replaced by Laden La. Bell, Handwritten Diary Vol. VII, 11 December, 1920. For a reconstruction of the biography of Achuk Tsering, see Martin. (Martin 2014: 74-84)

33. Bell, Handwritten Diary Vol. VII, 20 November, 1920.

34. 'Sikkim, Bhutan and Tibet: List of Chiefs and Leading Families', IOR L/P&S/20/D216, AAS, BL, 19.

35. I thank Jonathan Bracken for sharing the photograph with me, as well as for pointing out the hidden cable held by Rabden Lepcha through a zoomed-in view.

36. The process of identification and re-attribution of Rabden Lepcha's photographic oeuvre was a detailed one and involved several methodological approaches. See Mandy Sadan's notes on methodology, *The Tibet Album*, https://tibet.prm.ox.ac.uk/tibet_methodology_Bell.html.

37. Charles Bell, Handwritten Diary Vol. IX, 7 March, 1921, private collection of Jonathan Bracken.

38. Charles Bell, Handwritten Diary Vol. XIII, 14 October, 1921, private collection of Jonathan Bracken.

39. Laden La had joined the mission, taking over as Bell's clerk, almost immediately following Achuk Tsering's death, on 11 December, 1920. Bell, through a letter dispatched from Lhasa to the Foreign Office, on 12 December, 1920, had specifically asked for the services of Laden La. See Telegram No. 48-S from Charles Bell to the Foreign and Political Department, Delhi, 12 December, 1920, in 'Appointment of Sardar Bahadur S.W. Laden La, Deputy Superintendent of Police, Darjeeling, as Personal Assistant to Mr. C.A. Bell, C.I.E. Political Officer on Special Duty in Tibet', Foreign Department Proceedings, 291-306, June, 1921, NAI. This would indicate that the photograph featuring Laden La was likely taken sometime between end-December and early-January, 1921.

40. Bell, Handwritten Diary Vol. XIII, 14 October, 1921; Bell 1946: 336.

41. Bell, Handwritten Diary Vol. XIII, 14 October, 1921; *Portrait of the Dalai Lama*, 336-37.

42. In the book, although Bell mentions that Rabden was with him at the time, he writes that he took the photograph (Bell 1946: 336). The entry in the diary— 'Rabden and I'— leaves the question of authorship (of the photograph) unclear.

43. By the mid-nineteenth century, Sikkim had been reduced to a British protectorate. As Rabden Lepcha was from Sikkim and not Tibet, he was very much a colonized subject

locked within an unequal hegemonic relation of power with his English overlords.

44. This has been done through *The Tibet Album* project of the PRM, Oxford.

45. Bell, Typescript Diary Vol. XVIII, 17 November, 1934, 127. From Kalimpong, Bell would proceed to Mongolia, Manchuria and Siberia. Unfortunately, Cashie Bell, his wife, who accompanied him on these trips, died of meningitis in Beijing on 20 September, 1935. Bell, Typescript Diary Vol. XXI, 20 September, 1935 AAS, BL, 27.

46. Bell, Typescript Diary Vol. XVIII, 24 October, 1934, 113.

47. I interviewed Sanjay Diyali, grandson (adopted) of K.C. Pyne on 7 June, 2024. None of the brothers had married and they adopted a local Nepali boy from Kalimpong.

48. For a discussion of the photographic studios of Thomas Paar and Johnston and Hoffman in Darjeeling, see Harris. (Harris 2012: 90-98; Harris 2016: 38-43)

49. The Das Studio was established by Thakur Das Pradhan more than a decade later, in Darjeeling, in 1927.

50. Bell, Typescript index for Sir Charles Bell's Photographs J and R Series, 5. Unfortunately, the name of Phipraj occurs just once in Bell's catalogue and no local memory of the person survives in Kalimpong.

51. I thank Sanjay Diyali, proprietor and owner of Kodak Studios, Kalimpong, for sharing the images of Pyne's log-book with me.

52. Bell, Typescript Diary Vol. XVIII, 19 and 20 September, 1934, 40-49.

53. Bell, Typescript index for Sir Charles Bell's Photographs J and R Series, 84-85.

54. Pyne's transcription derives from the local Nepali usage of the term (Nepali, over time, has become the main language spoken in Kalimpong and Darjeeling, with Tibetan reserved mainly for monastic rituals, a fuller exploration of which is outside the scope of this present essay). Pyne's spelling of 'gum-pa' (from the Tibetan *dgon-pa*) is also borrowed from local Nepali usage.

55. In the archives of libraries and museums where I conducted research in the UK through 2023-24, including the BL, the collections (of objects, photographs, papers and notes) are all assigned to Bell. Despite recent anthropological efforts by various institutions such as the *Tibet Album Project* at the PRM, Oxford, and the Liverpool Museums, most archives in the UK have not yet adopted a 'corrective' appellative to refer to these collections.

56. Bell had intended to undertake his second trip to Tibet earlier, during the writing of his book *The Religion of Tibet*. This he indicated to Palhese during the latter's year-long visit to England in 1927-28. Bell, Charles, Handwritten Diary Vol. XIV, 3 February, 1928. He would, however, only be able to make the journey in 1934, after the publication of *The Religion of Tibet* (1931).

57. Bell, Typescript index for Sir Charles Bell's Photographs J and R Series, 44.

58. Bell, Handwritten Diary Vol. VII, 11 November, 1920.

59. Bell, Typescript Diary Vol. XVIII, 10 September, 1934, 17.

60. Bell writes that hitherto Pyne had been taking these shots. Bell, Typescript Diary Vol. XVIII, 26 September, 1934, 58-59. Although the images in the R-Series are not credited to Pyne within Bell's curating of his own visual material, it may be evidenced from Bell's diaries that Pyne had, in fact, been handling both the Rolleiflex as well as the Jewel cameras.

61. The Samyé monastery is believed to be the oldest in Tibet, established by king Tri Songdétsen/ Khri-srong-lde-btsan in the mid-eighth century.

62. Bell, Typescript index for Sir Charles Bell's Photographs J and R Series, 49.

63. Bell, Typescript Diary Vol. XVIII, 20 August, 1934, 90-91.

64. As part of a modernizing drive initiated by Bell and the Thirteenth Dalai Lama, Bell arranged for four boys to be sent to England to receive an 'English' education. The teenagers, Wangdu Norbu Kyipup/Kyibuk, Khenrab Kunzang Mondong, Sonam Gompo Gongkar and Rigzin Dorje Rinchengang were sent to England in 1913, accompanied by a Tibetan plenipotentiary named Dorje Tsegyal of Kusho Lungshar (Lung Sharwa) (P.1968, IOR L/P&S/10/400, AAS, BL). The British

colonial incentive behind this 'experiment' was, to strengthen British influence on Lhasa, making use of these four boys, who would be sent back to Tibet after being adequately Anglicised and indoctrinated. This was also designed to ward off Russian influence over Tibet and woo the Dalai Lama in favour of the British, using the boys as pro-Raj emissaries. Dhondup 1984: 38-58.

65. Bell, Charles, Typescript Diary Vol. XVII, 20 August, 1934, AAS, BL, 90-91.

66. Bell, Typescript Diary Vol. XVII, 21 August, 1934, 93.

67. Harris has remarked that Bell's linguistic abilities as well as the close relationship he cultivated with many of the subjects in his photographs brought about a more ethnographic perspective to his images, in contrast to the photographs produced by many of his predecessors such as Waddell (see Harris 2016: 76).

68. Bell, Typescript index for Sir Charles Bell's Photographs J and R Series, 64.

69. Video footage was also taken during the 1934 trip to Tibet, once again, possibly by Pyne. Unfortunately, I wasn't able to look at these. The footage remains housed, under Bell's name, in the collection of the British Film Institute. <https://collections-search.bfi.org.uk/web/Details/ChoiceFilmWorks/150064496>. I thank Jonathan Bracken for drawing my attention to this information.

References

Arondekar, Anjali. 2009. *For the Record: On Sexuality and the Colonial Archive in India* Durham and London: Duke University Press, 16-17.

Bell, Charles Alfred. 1924. *Tibet— Past & Present.* London: Oxford University Press.

Bell, Charles Alfred. 1928. *The People of Tibet.* Oxford: Clarendon Press.

Bell, Charles Alfred. 1946. *Portrait of the Dalai Lama.* London: Collins.

Dhondup, K. 'The Thirteenth Dalai Lama's Experiment in Modern Education.' In *The Tibet Journal* 9.3, Autumn 1984. Dharamsala: Library of Tibetan Works and Archives. 38-58. Accessed 12 May, 2024 <https://www.jstor.org/stable/43302190.>

Douglas, Bronwen. 1999. 'Art as Ethno-historical Text: Science, Representation and Indigenous Presence in Eighteenth and Nineteenth Century Oceanic Voyage Literature'. In *Double Vision: Art Histories and Colonial Histories in the Pacific*, edited by Nicholas Thomas and Diane Losche, 65-99. Cambridge: Cambridge University Press.

Harris, Clare E. 2012. *The Museum on the Roof of the World: Art, Politics and Representations of Tibet.* London: University of Chicago Press.

Harris, Clare E. 2016. *Photography and Tibet.* London: Reaktion Books.

Jones, Lowri Madeleine. 2010. 'Local Knowledge and Indigenous Agency in the History of Exploration: Studies from the RGS-IBG Collection'. Unpublished Ph.D. Thesis. Department of Geography, Royal Holloway University of London. K232557. Royal Geographical Society, London.

Martin, Emma. 2014. 'Charles Bell's collection of 'curios': negotiating Tibetan material culture on the Anglo-Tibetan borderlands (1900-1945)'. Unpublished PhD thesis. SOAS, University of London.

McKay, Alex. 2009. *Tibet and the British Raj: The Frontier Cadre 1904-1947.* New Delhi: Indraprastha Press.

Rhodes, Nicholas and Deki Rhodes. 2006. *A Man of the Frontier S.W. Laden-La (1876-1936): His Life & Times in Darjeeling and Tibet.* Kolkata: Library of Numismatic Studies.

Stoler, Laura Ann. 2009. *Along the Archival Grain: Thinking Through Colonial Ontologies* Princeton and Oxford: Princeton University Press.

Thomas, Nicholas. 2018. *Discoveries: The Voyages of Captain Cook.* London: Penguin Books.

Waddell, Laurence Austine. 1896. *The Buddhism of Tibet or Lamaism, with its Mystic Cults, Symbolism and Mythology, and in its Relation to Indian Buddhism.* Cambridge: W. Heffer & Sons Ltd.

HIMALAYA
The Journal of the Association of Nepal and Himalayan Studies

Research Article

Vkur Nukuj (Let Us Return): Taking Ancestral Photographs Home

Menia Taba
University of Oxford

DOI: https://doi.org/10.2218/himalaya.2025.10118

Abstract

This article explores the complexities of colonial photography, archival ownership, and visual repatriation within the context of Arunachal Pradesh, India, focusing on historic Nyishi photographs from the Pitt Rivers Museum. By reconnecting the families of Nyishi interpreters Bath Heli and Kop Temi with photographs taken by colonial administrators Ursula Graham Bower and Charles Robert Stonor, the study examines the power dynamics embedded in the archival process. Using an autoethnographic approach, the research situates visual repatriation as a medium for restoring Nyishi cultural memory and examining tribal identity. The findings reveal how photographs, once decontextualized in the colonial archive, carry distinct meanings when reintegrated into their communities—challenging colonial narratives locked within museum spaces and enabling cultural resurgence.

Keywords

visual repatriation, colonial photography, Arunachal Pradesh, Nyishi, indigenous memory, autoethnography, archival decolonization

Recommended Citation

Taba, Menia (2025). Vkur Nukuj (Let Us Return): Taking Ancestral Photographs Home. *HIMALAYA* 44(1): 107-126.

CC BY NC ND

This work is licensed under a Creative Commons Attribution-Noncommercial-No Derivative Works 4.0 License.

Introduction

This work delves into the intricate relationship between institutions, colonial history, visual documentation, and local memory in Arunachal Pradesh, a remote frontier region of India. The study develops a provenance-research and visual-repatriation approach by uncovering the "present" of Pitt Rivers Museum–archived photographs of Bath Heli and Kop Temi, taken by Ursula Graham Bower and Charles Robert Stonor, among Temi's and Heli's direct kin in Arunachal Pradesh.

As stated by Mooren et al. (2022), provenance research sheds light on the "microhistory" of photo collections housed in institutions such as the Pitt Rivers Museum, providing insight not only into their successive ownerships but, above all, into the entanglement of Nyishi history within the larger colonial history of India. This approach emphasizes critical analysis of the acquisition, appropriation, colonial intention, and ongoing ownership of the photo collections depicting Nyishi individuals. It aims to uncover the significance of these photographs within their original context, as Peers and Brown (2009) put it: "We seldom know much about their other realities, about the quite different sets of meanings attached to them within their source communities, about who the people in such photographs are to their relatives."

Visual repatriation—fundamental to this study—focuses specifically on viewing colonial photographs through an Indigenous lens. As Edwards (2003) notes, visual repatriation entails a conscious shifting of photographs from "public," "outsider" spaces to "private" and "appropriate" ones. These photographs, once considered colonial documents or "ethnographic" records, through their entanglement with specific institutional structures, become family history, clan history, and tribal history. This shift in photographic narrative is activated through the repatriation of images—a process described by Dudding (2005) as the return of photographic copies held in museum or institutional collections to their original communities or sites.

With the return and photograph's meaning-making, this study seeks to revitalize the photo life[1] by deconstructing the archive of Pitt Rivers Museum and visually repatriating the archived photographs from Ursula Graham Bower and Charles Robert Stonor collections. It will be navigated through my experience as a native Nyishi, taking a narrative auto-ethnographical framework in the words of Linda Smith (1999) from "the vantage point of the colonized". I put my experience at the center of this research on visual repatriation, and situate myself as a "key informant", a "consummate insider" (Houstan, 2007), transforming my experience as both an insider and outsider of the Nyishi community throughout the process of repatriating the photographs of community elders and oscillating to and fro within the scientific and Nyishi social realm.

A Note on Methodologies

I worked with a set of 24 photographs of Kop Temi and 9 photographs of Bath Heli taken by Ursula Graham Bower and Charles Robert Stonor. The photographs were primarily selected and identified through a keyword search for "Kop Temi" and "Bath Heli" in the Pitt Rivers Museum's online photo collection. These were enlarged to A4 size and printed directly from the laser scanner in both TIF and JPG formats to make the image content more visible for group viewing. Two clear files contained the photographs of Bath Heli and Kop Temi, respectively. Each photograph was marked with its PRM accession number in pencil on the back, to allow cross-referencing with the PRM dataset.

These printed photographs did not carry any captions. Instead, PRM data—including the year the photo was taken, location, photographer, year of accession, and caption—were printed on A4 sheets and compiled in a clear file alongside the photographic prints. As distributing hard copies to every kin member was not feasible, digital copies in both JPG and TIF formats, along with an Excel sheet containing metadata from the Pitt Rivers Museum, were placed on two external drives—one for Bath

Heli and one for Kop Temi—and handed over to their kin. The digital files were also shared via WhatsApp and email with other family members.

Understanding the position of these photographs within the frameworks of anthropology, colonial power, and the archive was guided by a provenance research approach. The journey began within the colonial context of touring governance in the Subansiri Hills of Arunachal Pradesh and proceeded with a critical analysis of the photographs' current archival domicile in the Pitt Rivers Museum. This entailed a deconstruction of the archive as an imperial epistemic institution and an effort to untangle the layered meanings of the photographs.

The return of these images to the kin of Kop Temi and Bath Heli in Papumpare and Keyi Panyor districts, Arunachal Pradesh, aimed to understand the process of engagement and recontextualization of these visual documents, including their sensorial and corporeal impact. "Observant Participation" was employed as a method to grasp the phenomenology of visual repatriation. Unlike the traditional participant-observer role, I adopted a more active and embodied stance, aligning with Wacquant's (2002, 2006) notion of *habitus*, immersing myself in the Nyishi social world and the lived reality attached to these photographs through an inward gaze.

Situating in the Archive

Following the notion of the contested presence of photographs in museum space by Edwards (2005)[2], the archived photographs of Kop Temi and Bath Heli in the Pitt Rivers Museum, with their "knotted" colonial history, have formed as a site of intersecting histories, a visual legacy, and colonial historical deposits. These photographs by Bower and Stonor of Bath Heli and Kop Temi now stand as a mnemonic of the 'colonial gaze' of the British colonial infiltration in the Nyishi settlements in the Subansiri region. The photographs currently housed in the Museum, as stated by Edwards (2000), also closed the space between the site of observation of the colonial periphery in the frontier hills and the site of metropolitan interpretation in the United Kingdom. In their current domiciliation in the archive, the photographs have thus turned into a representational machine, a mnemonic, and a contested space that is spatially and contextually divorced from the hills of Subansiri and the Nyishi social interpretation. To closely examine the current position of the photographs in the Pitt Rivers Museum archive, it is necessary, as suggested by Derrida, to deconstruct the archive. In deconstructing the archive, as argued by Clifford (1997), it is needed to critically understand and consider the circuits and the practices within the archive and not only the place. This understanding requires the exploration of the structuring of forms of accession, the processes of collecting and description, the context of collecting and use, and the range of social practices associated with them.

An Imperial Reality Woven Within the Archive

The ethnographic photographs of the Subansiri region that Haimendorf, Bower, and Stonor took were brought back to the United Kingdom and decontextualized from their original setting. The photographs were donated to different institutions and became part of archival collections. Bower donated the films and photographs from the Subansiri region to the Pitt Rivers Museum, and Charles Robert Stonor donated his photograph collection of the Nyishi to the same institution. With varied micro-intentions, the photographs arriving in the archives were transformed into public photographs. The public reading of the photographs, as in the traditional constitution of 'The Archive,' is open to different meanings about the culture while also operating within a disciplinary paradigm that reifies and objectifies the subject matter as both 'data' and archetype (Edwards, 2005). In this case, Bath Heli and Kop Temi as photo referents turned into scientific data, open to different interpretations for public reading. Within Western colonial scholarly modes of thought and institutional settings,

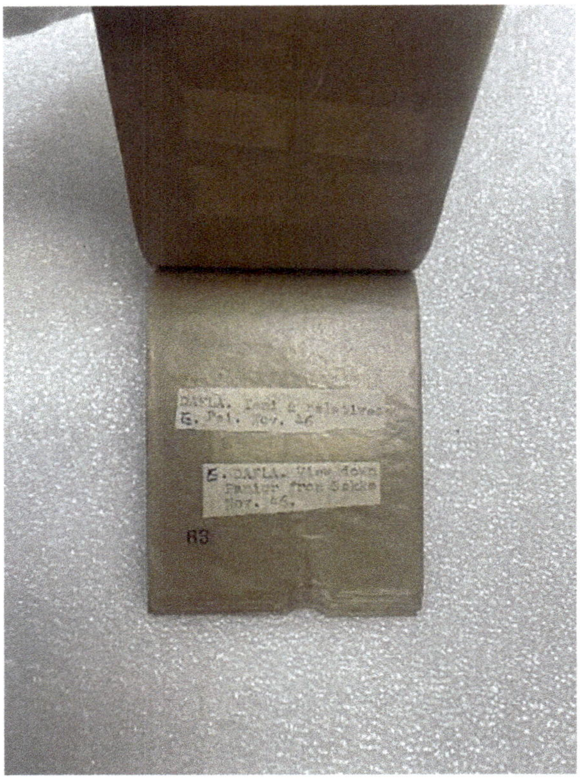

Figure 1: Charles Robert Stonor's album containing nitrate film negatives, stored in Stonor's file at the Pitt Rivers Museum. (Photo by the author)

the visual appropriation of the Nyishi included distorted identities of Bath Heli and Kop Temi, who now became Bower's or Stonor's photographs—or currently, the Pitt Rivers Museum's.

To examine more deeply the displacement of the original context and the silencing of the Nyishi interpretation of the photographs, I borrow the framework of visual economy by Poole of the thirty-three photographs, confined within the Western epistemic sphere and the imperial institution of the Archive. The production of the photographs of Kop Temi and Bath Heli could be understood in the colonial administrative and scientific context of looking at these photographs as documents of Frederick Nicholson (Tim) Betts, Ursula Graham Bower, and Stonor's activities in the periphery of the colonized territory. In this context, both Stonor and Bower took an interest in the ethnographic context of the Nyishi and its society by categorizing them in the late Neolithic phase.[3] The circulation and accessibility of these photographs within colonial institutions remained restricted and isolated from the source community. Under ongoing institutional ownership, the photographs continued to remain locked. The photographs dwelled permanently in the Pitt Rivers Museum archive and, as maintained by Derrida, this marked the institutional passage from the private to the public. The photographs travelled from the private collection of Stonor and Bower, which was donated to the Pitt Rivers Museum by Stonor in 1969 and by Bower in 1985. The Bower collection of Kop Temi and Bath Heli photographs in Agfa negative film was later digitized in November 2010, and the Stonor collection of Kop Temi photographs in nitrate negative film was recently digitized in January 2023.[4] The archive, although a dead space for the photographs, is an active space within the imperial context; in the words of Linda Smith (1999), it represents and perpetuates the imperialist collective experience. A similar position and the imperial narrative and representation can be observed in Bower's and Stonor's photograph collections in the archive of the Pitt Rivers Museum.

The Politics of Representation in the Archive and Captioning

As Edwards argued, understanding the archive requires not only a conceptualization of the ideological meta-levels but also critical engagement with the content of the images themselves. Following this notion, the theme of the images sheds light on the critical representation of the Nyishi by Bower and Stonor. Many of the photographs of Kop Temi and Bath Heli were taken as snapshots of engaging or performing traditional activities now in the museum archive, stirring the knowledge creation of the Nyishi and salvaging the 'tribal-like' activities through colonial imagination. It depicts Bath Heli with the bow and arrow and Kop Temi's active engagement in traditional peace treaty meetings called *Mel* and the rites of installing *Dapo*, mainly symbolizing the settlement of inter-tribal and inter-clan disputes among the Nyishi and Apatani of the Subansiri region.

The themes of the images shed light on the colonial and the possible intentions of the photographer more than the subjects that were photographed. The indexical truth in this sense has been an open space in the archive narrated through the experience and eyes of the colonial authorities. These archived photographs, circulated and exchanged within the colonial institutional setting, have transformed with free-floating meaning and context construction. With the free interpretation of the photographs within the archive, they are also heavily recontextualized through text attached to their indexicality.

As Edkins Jenny (2013) argues, usually a photograph comes with a context. Often this is a caption: words that frame the location, name the individual—signifying signs. The image does not often stand alone. The caption pins the photograph down, limiting or coloring our interpretation of its meaning—"taming it." It inserts the image into a textual milieu and demands it be understood in those terms.

Stating Edwards' (2005) emphasis on anthropological photographs in the museological setting creating parallel realities, an imperial reality with the continued colonial gaze walled within colonial domiciliation is woven in the Pitt Rivers Museum. Besides the dominant colonial narrative of the photograph collection, what other parallel reality subsists outside the museum—particularly a reality woven by the source community? This reality is explored through visual repatriation in returning the photographs back to kin of Bath Heli and Kop Temi in Arunachal Pradesh, India.

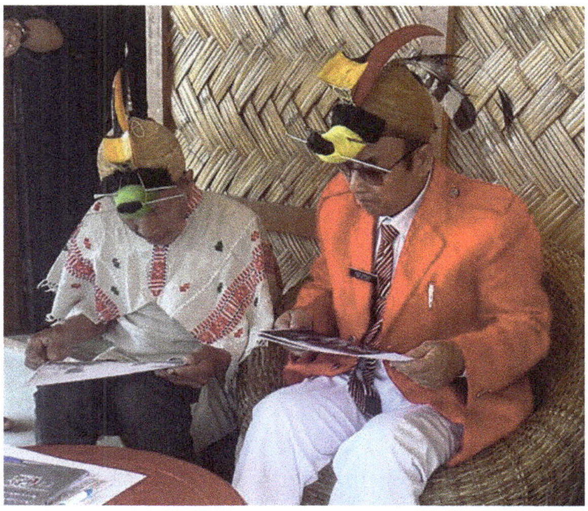

Figure 2: Bath Dopum (left) and Bath Khilling (right) viewing a photograph of Bath Heli. (Photo by the author)

Vkur Nam (The Return)

Growing up in the Subansiri hills, modernity and modern amenities were more of a recent arrival—much like they are often associated with the present young generation. With the abrupt introduction of technological development and modernity, the culture of oral knowledge-keeping has diminished in recent decades. This disappearing tradition is also partly due to the endangerment of the Nyishi language and, overall, the Nyishi identity, which has come to be regarded as a pressing issue. In this social scene, the images recorded of Bath Heli and Kop Temi from the 1940s were unique in Nyishi history. These individuals are also regarded with utmost respect within their native locality, lineage, and clan communities. They held the socially respected position of the first local *Kotoki* (political interpreter), a role generally held by influential individuals believed to be gifted with intellect and diplomatic skill among the clan and village communities.

Taking this cultural context, the experience of visual repatriation will be understood. The photographs of Bath Heli and Kop Temi that were held in the Pitt Rivers Museum archive were brought back to the insiders and into the private sphere. The photographs returned home, and another reality was formed. In a society where oral storytelling and the passing down of keepsakes have dwindled across generations due to time and societal changes, I couldn't help but deliberate on the significance of these photographs as a memoryscape, a repository of history, and a foreign tradition—entering the Nyishi cultural realm of remembering the ancestors and storytelling, and an eventual way of restoring the endangered past. In returning the photographs to the family, I let the research unfold its journey where the photographs anchored me. The interaction with the photographs was empirically observed and audio recorded. No questionnaires or interview schedules were utilized during the interaction, and strict adherence to photo-elicitation was not observed.

The Stories Within

Sontag (2004) states, "All photographs are memento mori. To take a photograph is to participate in another person's (or thing's) mortality, vulnerability, mutability." Such mutability is apparent in the archival domiciliation of the photographs, and the silencing of alternate narration is brought out in the language of the Indigenous. In the words of Linda Smith (1999), it is an alternative story: the history of Western research through the eyes of the colonized. The repatriated photographs in this scenario became a window to the hushed history and the past of the Nyishi. Drawing on the experiences of the Nyishi interpreters Bath Heli and Kop Temi for the foreign officials took on a different resonance through their eyes and the camera lens. This perspective was notably distinct from the inscribed captions and representations found in the archival records. The photographs led to the opening of stories of the past, which were narrated through the memories and traditional oral narrations passed down across generations—on social geography, identity and lineage, clan, and interpersonal relations.

In Papumpare district, Kop Saul, son of Kop Temi, carefully examined the photographs taken of Kop Temi. Despite having a print of PRM data along with descriptions of the photographs, he took his time to study and recognize the faces in the images—touching the subjects' faces, bringing the images closer for clearer vision, or requesting me to zoom in on the faces of every individual on the laptop screen, while sometimes pausing and trying to remember the time, place, and identification of the people in the photographic images. The identification extended for hours as our tea got cold. Upon finding a photograph of his father standing with Rajani Kale, he exclaimed, "Oh! This is Rajani, an Ahom from North Lakhimpur.

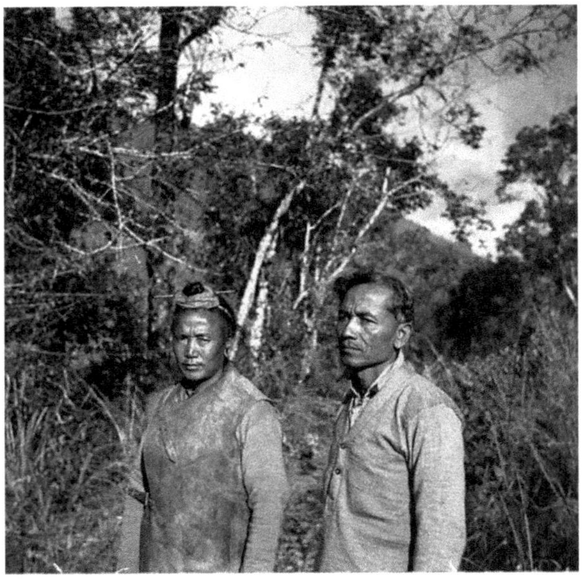

Figure 3: Kop Temi with Rajani Kale. Photograph by Charles Robert Stonor. Pitt Rivers Museum Collections Online. © Pitt Rivers Museum.

I met him before he fell gravely ill, and he shed tears when he saw me. It was years after my father passed away, and they had a very good relationship. I believe this is one of those occasions when they worked together—they appear healthy and young here." It has been over fifty years since Kop Temi passed away, and it remained a distant memory for Saul to see his father healthy and young. He said, "Aab (father) was very sick and struggled in his final days. Looking at him healthy and as a Yapa (young adult male) here, I feel very happy."

The reading of the photographs was not only confined to the image content; it went beyond what was in the photograph. The images prompted stories that navigated clan and lineage migration—fundamental elements of Nyishi oral culture within the context of a semi-nomadic, traditionally sustainable lifestyle and social memory.

Kop Saul, while looking at the photographs of Kop Temi, reminisced about a story often narrated by Kop Temi to his children:

> "The village where my father lived has a long story. Before the Mai and Kop were separated, they were one clan—KopMai—and inhabited parts of present-day Yachuli. There was once

an epidemic of Iss Dolyi (dysentery), and many people died in the village. With the growing deaths, both the Kop and Mai blamed each other for the epidemic, which resulted in a bloody clash. Some Kop migrated north, and the other group south, toward present-day Itanagar, while some settled farther south in the plains around Ranghajan seeking refuge... The Mai stayed in Yachuli. My father used to tell us about the vibrant community of Kop people living together in our village when it was part of the North East Frontier Agency. Later, the village became part of Assam, our neighboring state. My father was born in that village and was the first in our family and the Kop clan to attend school. He was smart and studious, so he got himself into an American Baptist School in Jorhat, Assam. Fluent in the languages of the plains people, Assamese, Nyishi, and Apatani, my father was appointed as a P.I. (Political Interpreter) under the Sarkar (government) and used to move around with the Sahabs (officials)."

Every photograph was examined for identification, tracing remnants of their existence in Nyishi society today through lineage and village affiliations. Beyond the faces, attention was paid to the locations where the photographs were taken—was it in the neighboring Apatani region, or the forests and steep hills of the Nyishi? These reflections indirectly shed light on the administration of the region through the practice of touring from one tribal territory to another, by both the photographer and the photographed.

While Kop Temi and Bath Heli worked together with Bower, both families also maintained friendly relations. Looking at the photographs of Bath Heli, Bath Dopum (Heli's oldest son) mentioned that Kop Temi was regarded as the first local interpreter from Arunachal Pradesh, who assisted as a translator for the Helyi ("outsiders," here referring to the British administrators). He said, "Kop Temi was the first to work as an interpreter with the Helyi. He was from Ranghajan and later got appointed as Head Interpreter, while my father was also working with him as an interpreter."

With such reference to the past, there was a similar approach in engaging with photographs and lineage and clan history, as retold by Bath Dopum, now close to 80, while viewing Bath Heli's photographs on the front porch of their house. While looking for their old village and their old house, he narrated:

"We came to Tago village from Selsemchi. I was about 15 years old. My father had two to three wives by then, and there was my younger brother, and my mother was pregnant with my other brother. I remember my father told us that we had to leave Selsemchi because there was a Dolyi (epidemic) and many people died. It was a village where the Bath lived. We started moving with my father, grandfather, and my paternal uncle to a nearby settlement called Sel. By the time we reached there, we heard the news that the Dolyi had wiped out Selsemchi, and after a few days, my paternal uncle and my grandfather also passed away with the same illness in Sel village. So we had to look for another place and we eventually settled on this hill. We were the first ones to arrive here at Tago. It was a dense forest—and look now, we also have a primary school here!"

This memory, narrated by the oldest member in the lineage, was a story that will be passed down. With Bath Heli's family being the only remaining family of the clan, it was a story of heroic survival. Bath Heli is often remembered as an influential individual, known for his impressive oratory skills and for being one of the prominent Nyishi men who married seventeen wives from different clans.[5]

The ontological status of the photographs here is more than visual imagery—they are repositories of traditional knowledge. Here, photographs functioned, as stated by

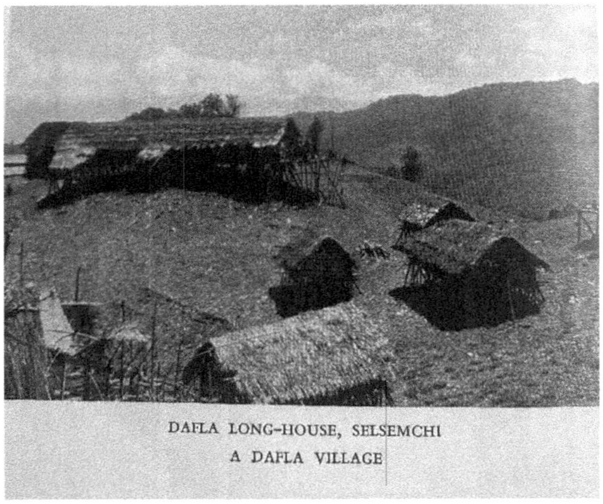

Figure 4: The longhouse in the background was identified by Bath Heli's children as their family home. Image from *The Hidden Land* by Ursula Graham Bower.

Edwards (2003), as memory-salvaging tools. The photographs, in this sense, worked as interlocutors in the process of telling histories. The photograph becomes a vessel filled with meanings, narrations, and networks, consequently embedding social roles and equated with surviving heirlooms—passed-down heritage from the ancestor's existence.

The story of clan migration and the placement of each lineage within this context is a common medium of revisiting ancestral history. Village settlements are often based on clan affiliation. Commonly, such narration is observed to understand the people and their affiliation to a village settlement and community. It is a fundamental part of social geography that connects a Nyishi to their land and to their origin as an identity marker within the tribe. The photographs were examined and embraced within the ontological setting of traditional oral culture.

As stated by Edwards (2001), the visual performativity of the photographs here had an affective tone, creating a phenomenological relationship with the viewer—not of content as such, but as active social objects. These photographs, as noted by Bell (2005), acted like ancestral heirlooms—as proof of the past—supplementing and stimulating oral narratives.

The story not only included clan migration but also changes in the spelling of clan names, as noted when family members read the captions of the photographs. Bath Khilling (Bath Heli's second son) remarked, "It should have been 'Baat', but the Helyi (outsiders, referring here to Stonor and Bower) started writing 'Bat', and that was the first time our clan names were written on paper and recorded. Eventually, we changed it by putting 'H' at the end after years of writing 'Bat'." In a similar tone, Kop Saul also commented while looking at the captions, "They wrote my father's name as 'Kop Temi', whereas it should have been 'Kup' if we pronounce it correctly. But we had to accept this written record given by the Sarkar, and our clan people still use the same spelling—'Kop'—now."

These captions and the letters provided by colonial officers had a lasting impact on clan identity and have contributed to ongoing confusion over standardized clan spellings. In the multi-clan Nyishi context—one of the largest tribes in Arunachal Pradesh—clan population and history are central to personal identity and harmonious relations with neighboring clans. In contemporary society, formal affiliation to a clan often requires adherence to officially recognized spellings using consistent English alphabetic letters. This formalization, introduced through the colonial recording of clan names, has sparked enduring discussion and confusion among members regarding the correct or unified form of their clan identities.

The photographs sparked conversations about the survival of the two clans and the migration narratives of two different lineages—narratives that remain central to identity in Nyishi society.

The image content, along with the captions, was carefully and repeatedly examined by the kin. The locations depicted in the photographs also became a common theme of active discussion. Images were socially read before captions were consulted; captions were typically only referenced to determine the identity of the subjects or the location. While the photographs opened up a dialogue on tribal and clan historical experiences, the arrival of British authorities was not the main focus of discussion. Many family members were unclear about the identity of the Sahab—whether they were British, Indian, or even American—as expressed during conversations in Tago Village. They also did not know why these individuals had come, or why they had enlisted the services of Kop Temi and Bath Heli.

On the Elements and the Materiality of the Photographs

The major emphasis in the photographic interaction and the phenomenological relationship of the viewers with the photographs was centrally laid on the image content. This also included the performativity and materiality of the photographs. Following Edwards' (2012) notion of the materiality of photographs, this can be understood through what people do with photographs.

While looking at the images, many dialogues focused on their content—particularly on the clarity and color. Requests were frequently made for clearer photographs, and there was a desire for colored versions. Viewers expressed that seeing the clothes in color would make the photographs appear more authentic and easier to interpret. Although the primary interest lay in the image content and a visual reading of the photographs, this often overlooked other sensorial and embodied engagements.

The photographs were not merely visual; they were sensorially experienced. They were passed from one person to another and handled with care. Individuals brought the images close to their faces, inspecting the facial details of the subjects attentively, touching the laptop screen or the printed A4 sheets for a closer look. Rather than remaining static, two-dimensional image content, the photographs became active social objects.

The printed images were passed down from the oldest member of the family to the grandchildren. While the oldest members were seated at the center, the younger family members stood around and read the images through vision and touch. They often remarked how happy they were to see the youthful appearance of their grandfather, as he was very sick and old in his final days, which was what remained in many of their last memories of Bath Heli. To zoom in on the image and see the details, I used the digital images on a laptop, which were viewed in smaller groups of two to five individuals. As they saw the photos of Bath Heli with other people, they requested me to enlarge the faces of the other people photographed. We looked through the photographs; Bath Dopum looked at the photograph of Bath Heli sitting with his friends and asked me to zoom in on the face of an individual. He said, "This person looks like Jorum Kulu. He was from Pei village. I was young when I saw him, but I remember his face if I see it close enough."

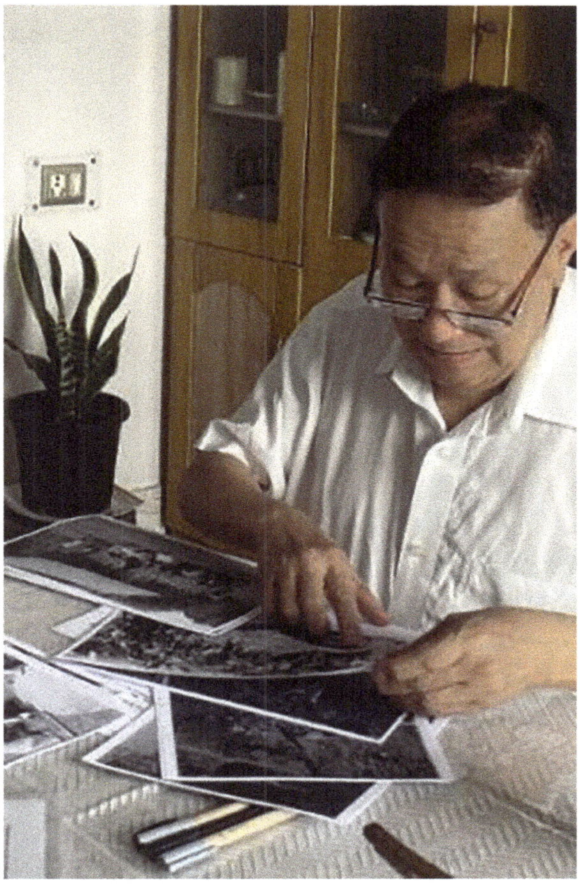

Figure 5: Kop Saul studying the faces of individuals photographed with Kop Temi by Ursula Graham Bower. (Photo by the author)

In this visual performativity, the photograph of Bath Heli was also enlarged on a laptop screen in the digital format. The faces of the individuals were closely inspected by every elder of the family as they were trying to find the missing identity of the person. The photograph was corporeally engaged, as stated by Pinney (2020), on the sensorial and physical engagement with images. As Edwards (2004) states, these material characteristics have a profound impact on the way images are "read." The image content was examined via vision and by touching the screen and the prints. After the face of the subjects, other themes such as their draped traditional clothing, hair styled in topknots and how they were tied, and how the traditional way of clothing and styling hair has massively changed, were constantly discussed.

Kop Temi's twenty-four photographs, along with the pen drive, were handed over to Kop Saul, who is the only surviving direct kin of Kop Temi. The keeping of Bath Heli's nine photographs, both in printed and digital formats, was decided among the family members and handed over to Bath Vicky, grandson of Bath Heli. Some members also photographed the printed photographs and shared them with different family members through WhatsApp groups. Although the images were shared in another digital format, the focus lay on the image content of the photographs. The photographs were shared and posted on WhatsApp without the Pitt Rivers Museum accession number and were separated from the inscribed captions. These photographs were now set into different narratives with different life stages outside the archive. The photographs of Bath Heli weren't only confined to their representation or indexicality, but to how they were getting phenomenologically enmeshed within the Nyishi social world. Here, I take forth the argument of Brietbach (2011:39), noting the material elements of digital images, as they went through similar stages as analogue photographs: they are cut, pasted, cropped, zoomed, and physically handled through the screens of modern devices. These material elements of the photographs became an inherent part of the visual experiences.

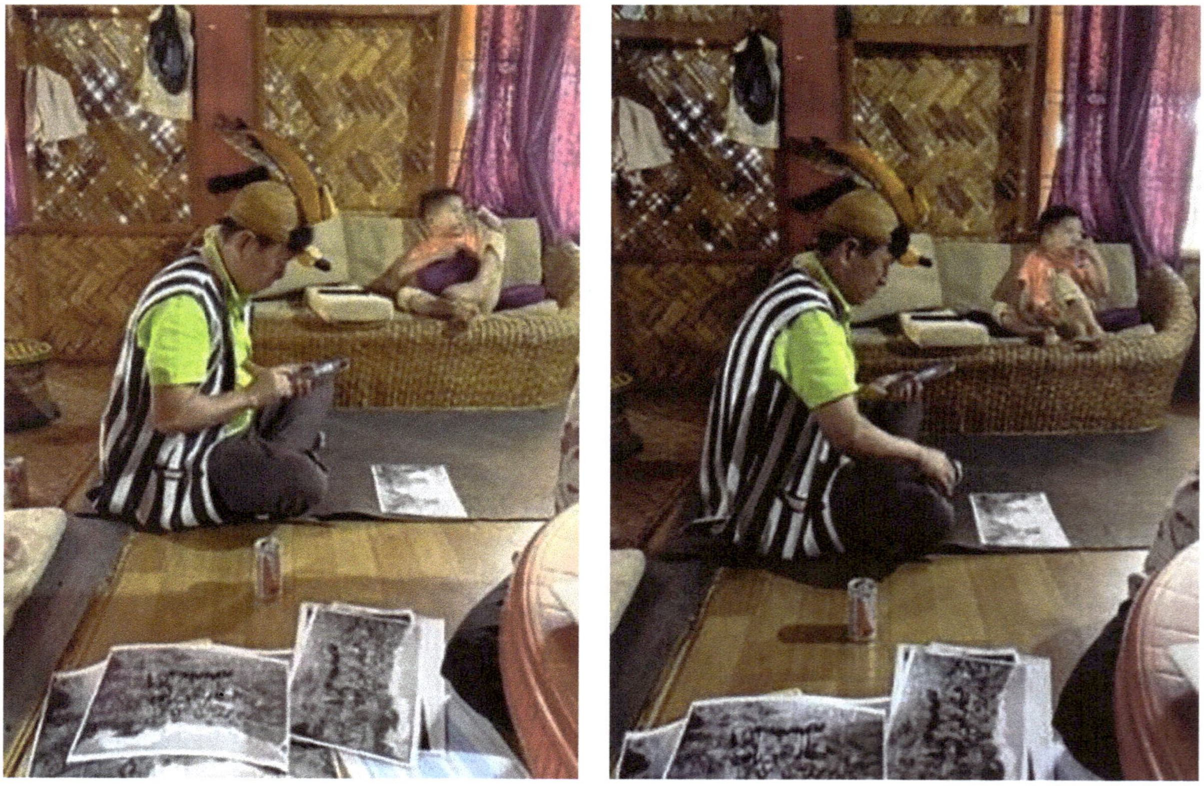

Figure 6: Bath Tadh taking photographs of the archival prints to share with family members via WhatsApp. (Photo by the author)

The Invisible and Absent Subjects of the Photographs

Barthes (1982) refers to the photograph's relationship to its subject matter as indissoluble: "A specific photograph, in effect, is never distinguished from its referent." Apart from the common interest in Bath Heli among the Bath kin in Tago village and Kop Temi with Kop Saul, a recurrent question was often directed at me—the person who had brought the photographs—about the absence of identity of those who were also photographed with Bath Heli and Kop Temi. These questions were persistent: "Who are they? Why are their names not recorded?"

Standing in the farthest corner, Bath Heli's great-granddaughter, who was busy serving us tea and standing behind the seated elders, remarked while looking at the photographs of Bath Heli standing with a group of women: "Who must have been these people, whose wife, daughter, or mother?"

In the discussion, the identity and the village affiliation even the surviving members of the subjects that became part of the photograph with their involvement with Bath Heli and Kop Temi were greatly discussed in detail. Such discussions of tracing members of a lineage was a common practice is a community set up of Nyishi society, throwing light on the inter-personal relationships maintained inter generationally.

Another subject that was greatly discussed among the elders of the Bath family was the particular image of Bath Heli seated in the center, and the identity of the person seated facing Heli on the extreme right of the image (figure 8). Bath Dopum exclaimed, while pointing to the unidentified subject, "This looks like Taba Tath; he is Tedir's and Yedir's father."

Bath Khilling joined in, "Yes, look at his eyes — they do look like Tedir's father."

When I asked who Tedir was, Bath Tadh answered, "He is the current minister of our constituency; he is known by many people."

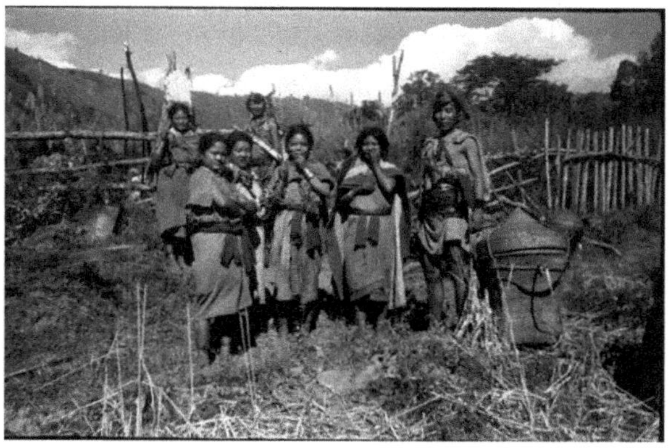

Figure 7: Bath Heli standing with women, photographed by Ursula Violet Graham Bower. Pitt Rivers Museum Collections Online. © Pitt Rivers Museum.

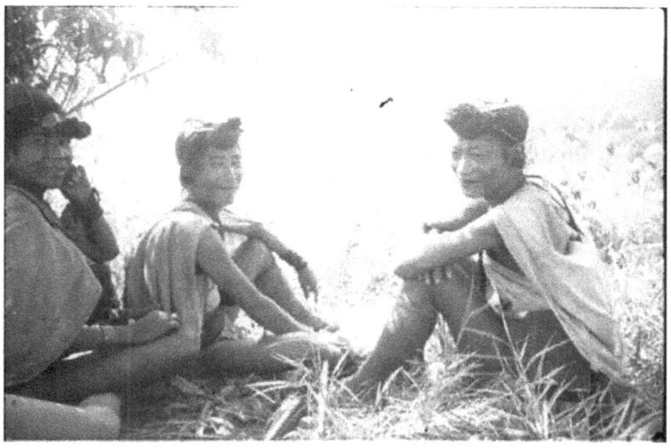

Figure 8: Bath Heli (left) with companion. Photograph by Ursula Violet Graham. Pitt Rivers Museum Collections Online. © Pitt Rivers Museum.

Bath Tadh also added to their discussion, "He does look like Tedir. I have never seen him myself, but he was our father's friend from the neighbouring village."

To this, Dopum further responded, "This photo also looks like it was taken when they had to carry around luggage and loads for the Sahabs (officers of high status, referring here to Betts and Haimendorfs), together with Father. And when they were resting, they must have been photographed... but they should have added their names with the photos."

Many nodded with frustration and agreed that the individuals in the photographs should have been identified by name, which would make it easier to trace the ancestors of people even from different villages. These individuals, although photographed alongside Kop Temi and Bath Heli, remain invisible subjects—unnamed, often unrecognized by the camera of Bower and Stonor.

There was also a general observation made by both families about the absence of Bower or Stonor within the image frame. Many had never seen their faces until I showed them through a quick Google search. While Bower was still known among the local population by her localised name of Yapar, the same wasn't true for Stonor, who stayed only briefly and did not build a close relationship with the locals.

Their absence can be termed a punctum, borrowing from Barthes' conception, which centres on the subject of the photograph. The absence of Bower, F.N. (Tim) Betts, and Charles Robert Stonor in any photographs was a repeated question posed to me—often in the hope that some images might exist which included both the photographed and the photographer. These absences could be sensed ocularly.

With the constant search for photographs depicting Bower and Stonor alongside Kop Temi and Bath Heli, I was asked to search for any such images that may exist in archives—even beyond the Pitt Rivers Museum, anywhere in the United Kingdom. Additionally, there were requests to look for photographs not only of the Nyishi but also of neighbouring tribes such as the Adi and Apatani. These requests continued even after I returned to the University of Oxford, through calls and texts.

Although many of the photographs in the archives are already digitised and available for public access—especially following the digital turn of the museum in the spirit of Malraux's dream of "museums without walls"—museums in the West, including the Pitt Rivers Museum, have not fully considered the technological gap and the persistence of the digital divide. This pertains both to the availability of photographs and the technical literacy required to use a web browser—still a challenge for many individuals hoping I might help locate photographs of their ancestors.

Consequently, the digitised archival photographs remain effectively inaccessible. For many Indigenous communities from remote corners of the world, access to heritage materials locked away in Western archives remains a distant dream. As I was leaving, family members asked me to write down the steps for searching the archived photographs in PRM in bold letters on a sheet of paper, which they carefully folded and kept alongside the photographs in a clear file.

Colonial Historiography of the Photographs

Having hours of discussion on the photograph collections in Arunachal Pradesh with Bath Heli and Kop Temi's kin, the question of why the photographs were taken by Stonor and Bower, their nationalities, and what was the motive of their tour were greatly absent, and this complex yet simple question is entangled in the web of active political history between China and colonized India in the mid-twentieth century. Taken at the end of the colonial regime in India in the 1940s, the photographs were colonial products and artefacts of imperial science. To understand the colonial entanglement, a narrative context of Bower and Stonor's photographic collection is situated through the temporal narration setting, shedding light on the creation of Barthes's *studium*[6] of Kop Temi and Bath Heli's archived photographs. Within this narrative context of the photographs of Bath Heli and Kop Temi, I examine the spatio-temporal history of the Subansiri region in Arunachal Pradesh, where the indexicality lies. Taking Barthes's (1982) notion of the camera as an instrument of evidence and an assertion of the overwhelming truth, this stance of the "evidential force" of the Bower's and Stonor's photograph collection can be traced as the colonial historical outcome.

Arunachal Pradesh is located in the Eastern Himalayas, bordered by the Assam plains to the south, the Chinese Tibetan Autonomous Region to the north, Bhutan to the west, and Burma to the east. Owing to its strategic

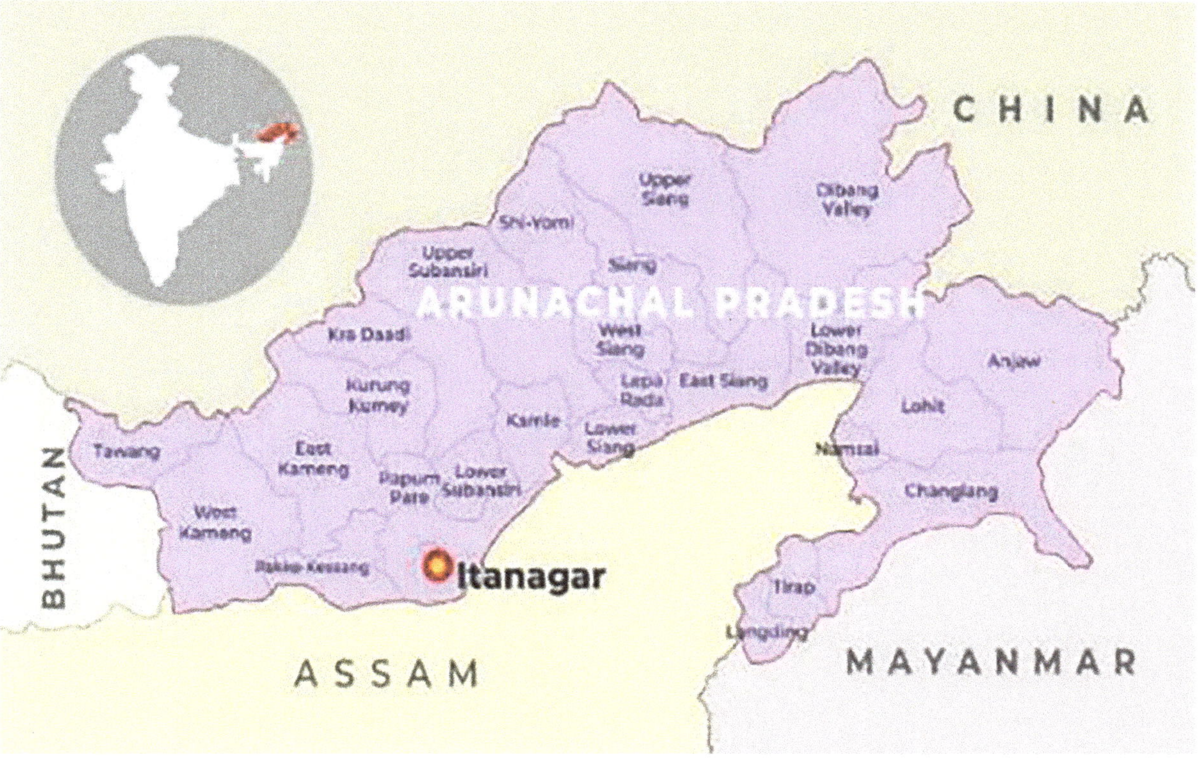

Figure 9: Map indicating the location of Arunachal Pradesh in India. Source: https:// arunachal-pradesh-district-map. Retrieved July 2024.

geographical location, the state remained relatively historically insulated from extensive external control, both from the Indian empires and beyond. According to Scott (2009), Arunachal Pradesh is under the "shatter zone" and a part of "Zomia," which is the largest region of the world across seven different countries whose people have not yet been fully incorporated into nation-states. With its prolonged historical isolation and political confusion, the state consequently became part of greater India with the later involvement of British colonial rule in the early 19th century and the administrator-anthropologists penetrating to take control of the hills.

When the British assumed control of the Assam Valley from the Ahom kingdom in the early 19th century, they inadvertently gained control of the surrounding hill areas. In 1909, Arunachal Pradesh—then part of Assam—was subjected to the British Raj's policy of "non-interference." During the early phase of British control over Arunachal Pradesh, the region was marked by continuous raids and tensions between the colonial government and the tribes of the Northeast Indian hills, including those residing in what is now Arunachal Pradesh.[7]

The Second World War catalyzed a revival of British colonial interest in expanding administrative control over the hill regions of Northeast India. Arunachal Pradesh, owing to its strategic location along the Tibetan frontier, assumed renewed geopolitical significance. This shift in strategic priorities—particularly in light of emerging Sino-Indian tensions—prompted a reassessment of earlier colonial governance models. Consequently, the previously upheld policy of non-interference in tribal affairs was progressively dismantled during the latter half of the 20th century, paving the way for more direct political intervention and territorial integration in the frontier region.

The practice of touring and exploration expanded significantly following the establishment of new administrative positions. The bureaucratic practice of touring became an activity associated with the frontier—as a space of state expansion and uneven rule. Many tours in the initial decades of colonial rule had a punitive element; some were "pacification campaigns," others flag-carrying "promenades" intended to impress and intimidate (Guyot, 2017). Tours were thus essential to the incipient information order that Raj officials strove to establish on their northeastern frontier (Bayly, 1996; Misra, 1998).

Arunachal Pradesh, lying on the frontiers, became a space for intensive touring under colonial governance. The tours of British administrative officers, accompanied by Assam Rifles regiments, produced tour diaries recording ethnographic data on the tribal population. This documentation was aided by photographs and films taken of tribal inhabitants, serving as visual data and records of colonial subjects. This touring government paved the way for Bower and Stonor to enter the Subansiri hills. The touring governance in Subansiri aimed to ascertain the Chinese threat in 1943 concerning the delineation of Tibetan frontiers, which ran hundreds of miles south of the McMahon Line—thus claiming parts of British Indian territory.

Ursula Graham Bower, in her 1953 book *The Hidden Land*, noted the urgency of establishing colonial governance in Subansiri:

> "The invasion of Burma and the Naga Hills by the Japanese had taught the Indian Government that undeveloped territory, however difficult the terrain, could no longer be reckoned on as a defence and the Chinese threat made it desirable that a firm claim to the Subansiri region be established."

The implementation of touring administration was to be accompanied by closer observation of cultural aspects, primarily the political sphere of the tribal communities of Arunachal Pradesh, particularly the frontier tribes. This observation was to be carried out in an anthropological manner through participant observation during extended stays with the tribal communities, with particular emphasis on building rapport in the context of the Subansiri with the Nyishis and the Apatani.

Alongside the administrative intent, there was a parallel shift in Indian social anthropology. Although countering the direct colonial administrative utility employed by the administrator-anthropologists, there was growing interest in studying small-scale tribal societies in India, rather than focusing on anthropometric details of the amorphous caste society, with an emphasis on a strict fieldwork tradition. Fieldwork, as the sine qua non in anthropology, shifted toward the "quick and the living" as opposed to the "still and silent" (Tayler, 1992).

The method of intensive fieldwork with extended stays was carried out by Von Fürer-Haimendorf, an Austrian anthropologist on his administrative tour in the Subansiri hills in 1944-45, appointed as the first Special Officer of the region. This approach was later adopted by Political Officer Major Frederick Nicholson Betts and his wife Ursula Graham Bower from 1946 to 1948.

According to Tarr and Blackburn (2008), such extended stays in the hills allowed an officer with a camera to observe local culture and record a wide range of activities in depth. This opportunity enabled the capturing of aspects of life that others—such as the leader of a military expedition or a tea estate manager in the plains—could not. For instance, for the first time, a ritual was captured unfolding over a sequence of six or eight shots. Alongside this, depictions of year-round agricultural practices and other everyday activities were recorded—details that could only be discerned by a long-term visitor. Notably, these long-term visitors were often the touring administrators.

The transformation in colonial touring and the surge in visual documentation were accompanied by advancements in camera technology. Heavy tripods were replaced by smaller, more portable cameras, resulting in increased visual documentation during tours. This shift also sparked changes in scholarly discussions in anthropology by emphasizing the study of culture beyond physical categorization. Together, these factors ushered in a new era of ethnographic photography in Northeast India.

The change in visual data collection during tours extended from the Naga Hills to the hills of Arunachal Pradesh, capturing the diverse and rich cultural heritage.

As Sbriccoli (2016) notes, photography has been one of the primary tools through which objective knowledge about Indigenous subjects was produced. In such a way, within this scholarly and bureaucratic environment of ethnographic photography and colonial touring, Nyishi interpreters Kop Temi and Bath Heli were captured and subjected through the lens of Bower and Stonor's cameras.

The arrival of the new wave of ethnographic photography was paved by James Philip Mills in Arunachal Pradesh, particularly among the Nyishi and Apatani of the Subansiri region. According to Tarr and Blackburn (2008), "Mills, when he took charge of the entire Northeast, sent anthropologist Fürer-Haimendorf to the Subansiri region to investigate the extent of Tibetan influence and establish friendly relations with the tribes." During his eight-month tenure administering the Subansiri region between 1944 and 1945, Christoph von Fürer-Haimendorf collected over 1,600 photographs. His work was later extended by another anthropologist who continued the photographic documentation he had begun.

Ursula Graham Bower, like Fürer-Haimendorf, began her ethnographic work among the Nagas in the 1930s. She arrived in the Apatani Valley in 1946, accompanying her husband, Major Frederick Nicholson Betts, who was appointed Political Officer of the Subansiri area (ibid.).

These administrative anthropological tours also gave way to an expedition of cryptozoologists. Haimendorf shared his notes on the legendary reptile in the Subansiri region, called *Buru*, with English anthropologist and naturalist Charles Robert Stonor and J.P. Mills. Stonor, who was also appointed as the Agricultural Officer, visited the territory with Mills in late 1945 and again with Ralph Izzard, a *Daily Mail* journalist, in 1946 to find out more about the Buru. The

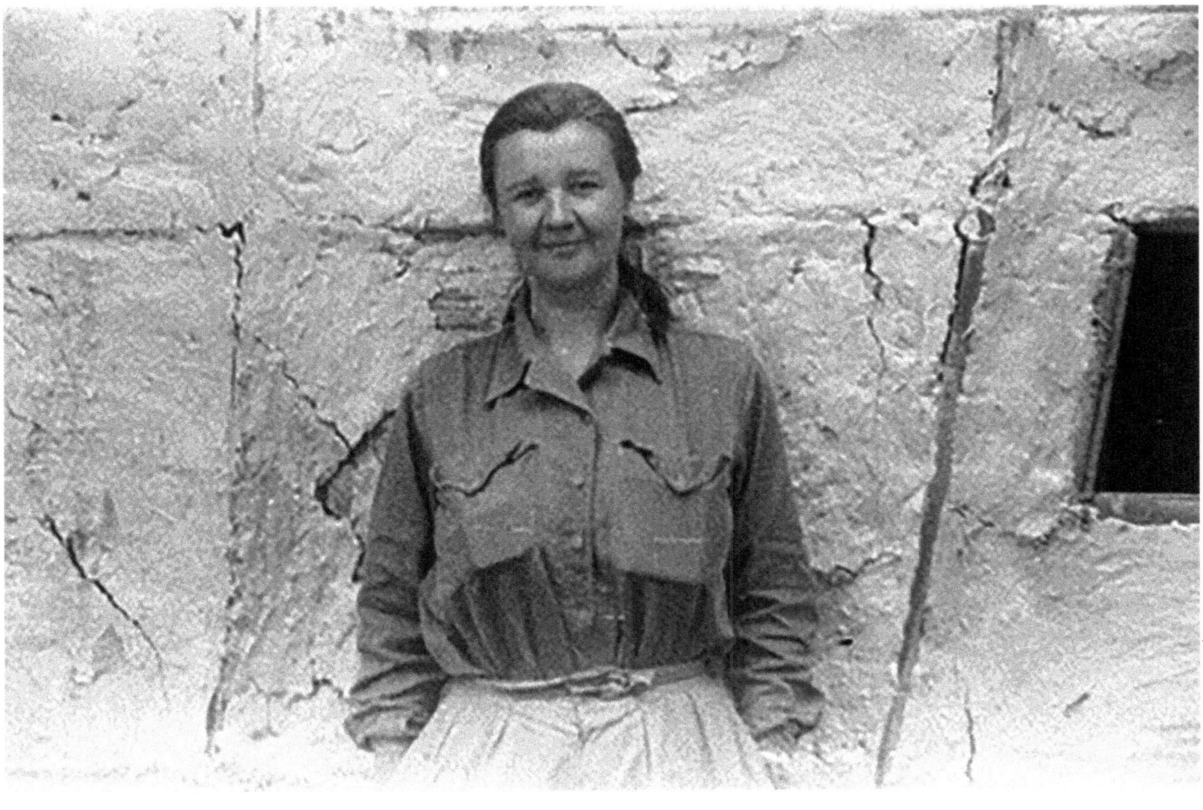

Figure 10: Ursula Violet Graham Betts (née Bower). Pitt Rivers Museum Collections Online. © Pitt Rivers Museum.

expedition was supported with adequate funding and equipped with optical instruments and cameras (Beggiora, 2018).

The combined photographic collections of Haimendorf, Betts, and Stonor—comprising over 3,000 images—offer a comprehensive view of life in the Subansiri region, particularly of the Apatanis, Nyishis, and Hill Miris, just prior to the imposition of a new political order (Tarr and Blackburn, 2008). Dealing with local Nyishi and Apatani interpreters and porters presented a significant challenge during these tours. It was common for the same tribal individuals to be recommended by tour officials. Prominent Apatani interpreters included Chiging Nime and Kago Bida, while Nyishi interpreters Kop Temi and Bath Heli were actively sought by colonial officers upon their arrival in the Subansiri hills. These notable Nyishi and Apatani individuals accompanied the Haimendorfs, the Betts, and Stonor in their expeditions, including the exploration of Buru.

The long-term stays of Haimendorf and the Betts in the 1940s in the Subansiri region among the Nyishi and the Apatani formed a significant chapter in local regional history.[8] Their extended interactions with the British *Sahab* (officer) during prolonged tours led to the publication of ethnographies as well as the creation of extensive collections of photographs and films.[9] Kop Temi and Bath Heli were notable individuals who spoke Assamese, the language of the neighbouring plains. As Nyishi, they were often pursued for their assistance in dealing with the supposedly 'unruly' Nyishi of the hills, known for their sustained resistance to governance.

While Heli was living in Selsemchi village in the Subansiri region during their visit, Temi travelled from a distant region to the south. His village, Rangajan, lay between the hills and the intersection of the Assam plains. Temi and Heli accompanied the colonial officers on their tours and expeditions.[10] During the tour with the Betts and Stonor from 1946 to 1948, they provided extensive services in resolving inter-tribal conflicts—mostly between the Nyishi and the neighbouring Apatani—as well as interclan clashes, while also leading the touring team to other tribal settlements. During this period of colonial tours and scientific expeditions in the search for the legendary Buru, Kop Temi and Bath Heli were themselves drawn into the colonial lens. They became subjects of ethnographic visual documentation by Ursula Graham Bower and Stonor.

By observing the image content of the photographs taken by both Bower and Stonor, the friendly smiling faces and poses for the camera establish the interpersonal relations between the photographers and Kop Temi and Bath Heli. As they spent days working and hiking the hills together, it was apparent that the friendly relationship — which was a prerequisite for prolonged administrative touring with local interpreters, as per the instruction on rapport-building with locals — was efficiently executed by both Bower and Stonor.

These ethnographic tour photographs, including Bath Heli and Kop Temi, were a form of, as stated by Edwards (2000), "virtual witness," translating "what I saw, you too will see" by attesting the truth value of observation during their touring experience. These photographs by Stonor and Bower, as Edwards (2001) also argues, functioned as a way of amassing raw data on Nyishi society and the Nyishi people in analogical or metonymic form, and re-presenting material for interpretation in visual form.

As amalgamated into the practice of administrative touring, and taking the words of Sontag (1978), photography in this form of documentation—of administrative touring and scientific engagement—became one of the principal devices for experiencing something, while giving an appearance of participation for both Stonor and Bower. Within this supposedly secondary experience, the two Nyishi interpreters were also included as part of the administrative record.

Although the intentions behind taking the photographs were nuanced with "micro intentions," as termed by Edwards (2001),

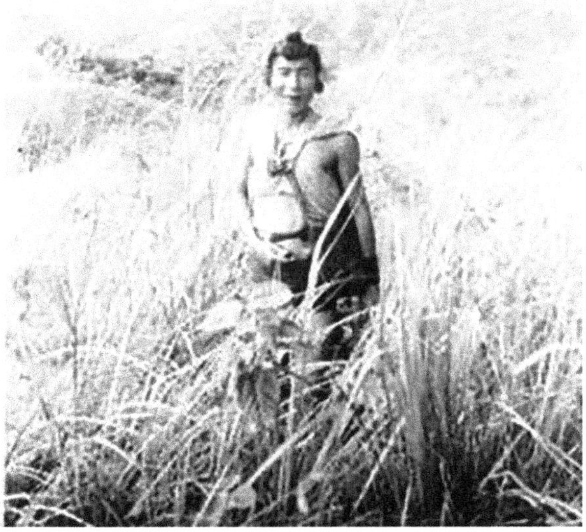

Figure 11: Bat Heli, interpreter. Photograph by Ursula Graham Bower. Pitt Rivers Museum Collections Online. © Pitt Rivers Museum.

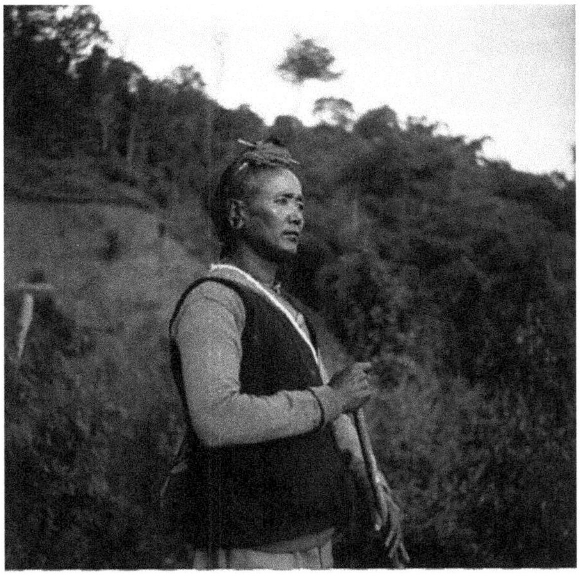

Figure 12: Temi. Photograph by Charles Robert Stonor. Pitt Rivers Museum Collections Online. © Pitt Rivers Museum.

these were later collectively transferred to the spatial setting of the archive at the Pitt Rivers Museum. These photographs by Stonor and Bower, taken as part of touring documentation, functioned as colonial epistemic tools aimed at salvaging the "savage." When freed from their frozen state in the archive and returned to the source community, they were revived with plural frames of history, recuperating historical knowledge and Nyishi identity. Visual repatriation, in a way, assisted in weaving a Nyishi reality in the present society; these photographs now circulate among tribal community members, gaining new narration by every reader of the image, separated from colonial representations.

Conclusion

These photographs are dual-natured: they function both as instruments of colonial documentation, locked within the institutional archive, and as living cultural artifacts for the Nyishi, re-engaged through their original context. Upon their return, these images transcended their colonial origins, invoking narratives that resonate deeply with the Nyishi people. The return of these photographs reconnects them with the Nyishi community's collective memory and family histories. As families engaged with these images, they recalled ancestral memories and cultural practices that were often at risk of fading, re-weaving local memory. This interaction enriches both personal and communal identities, demonstrating how photographs serve as "memoryscapes" that bridge contemporary Nyishi individuals with their heritage. The colonial archives fail to capture the full significance of Indigenous artifacts, necessitating community-driven interpretations.

Originally, these photographs supported colonial narratives of exoticism and "otherness," as intended by Ursula Graham Bower and Charles Robert Stonor—narratives stripped of cultural context. By returning these images, new narratives emerge that reflect Nyishi perspectives and cultural values, transforming them from mere representations of Indigenous subjects into meaningful family mementos. Visual repatriation, in this process, stands as an act of empowerment for the Nyishi people, rekindling connections to the past and allowing them to shape their own histories through oral tradition. The photographs become agents of cultural renewal, facilitating the recovery of ancestral identities and reaffirming the importance of Indigenous storytelling.

Ultimately, this study highlights the collaborative potential of visual repatriation in reshaping the roles of museums and archives. Institutions are urged to respect the connections source communities have with their cultural artifacts, viewing themselves as custodians of heritage rather than owners of material culture. By fostering ongoing dialogue with Indigenous communities, archives and museums of imperial origin can create a living relationship with cultural objects, ensuring they remain rooted in the traditions of the people they represent.

In this way, visual repatriation encourages a reimagination of the archive, promoting collaboration and valuing Indigenous voices. As the Nyishi people reclaim their cultural images, they exemplify the transformative potential of repatriation in redefining historical narratives, restoring cultural identity, and advancing decolonization efforts.

The author would like to express heartfelt respect and gratitude to the late Mr. Bath Heli, the late Mr. Kop Temi, the late Mrs. Ursula Graham Betts, and the late Mr. Charles Robert Stonor for allowing her to engage with their photographs and collections, which have been instrumental to this research. She extends her sincere appreciation to the School of Anthropology and Museum Ethnography, University of Oxford, for the travel grant, and to the Pitt Rivers Museum for their support throughout this project. Deep gratitude is also owed to Professor Clare Harris, whose encouragement and guidance have been invaluable. She further acknowledges the support of Taba Apo, Taba Ashu, and the many community elders of the Keyi Panyor administrative district—too numerous to name—for their invaluable assistance in locating the families of Bath Heli and Kop Temi. Finally, the author expresses her profound gratitude to the family of Bath Heli in Tago village and to Kop Saul for their generosity, time, and willingness to share their experiences.

Taba Menia hails from Arunachal Pradesh and is currently pursuing an MSc in Visual, Material, and Museum Anthropology at the University of Oxford (2024). She is also serving as a Guest Lecturer in Social Anthropology at Rajiv Gandhi University in Itanagar, Arunachal Pradesh. She previously completed her MPhil and MA in Anthropology at Rajiv Gandhi University. Her recent work includes a co-authored book titled ***Mind Matters: Unveiling Mental Health Among the Youth of Arunachal Pradesh***, published by Himalayan Publisher in 2024. She has also contributed articles to ***The Arunachal Times*** and written blog essays exploring themes of religion, indigeneity, and museum collections.

Endnotes

1. Here I take the idea of Appadurai, 1986; Gosden and Marshall 1999 and Edwards, 2001/2002, Photographs as active entities in social relations created through the web of production, exchange, consumption and meaning-making that shapes the biography of photographs.

2. Edwards (2005) describes public photographs when the subject matter of the image is removed from its context and the meaning turns free floating within the free interpretation of symbol and metaphor.

3. Ursula Graham Bower made reference to the civilization stage of the Nyishi from Haimendorf's reports and works, mentioned in 'The Hidden Land' as late Neolithic stage in pg. xv. Charles Robert Stonor also positioned the Nyishi and the overall inhabitants of the hills in the Neolithic stage of culture in pg.2

of 'Notes on Religion and Ritual among the Dafla Tribes of the Assam Himalayas'.

4. As per the database of Pitt Rivers Museum.

5. In the Nyishi polygynous setting number of wives determines the social influence and wealth owned by the individual.

6. Here I borrow the notion of Studium of Roland Barthes (1982) as a contextual intent of the photographers in the production of the photographs of Kop Temi and Bath Heli.

7. Chakravarty (1995) writes about the continuous raids in the Assam Valley by the tribal hill inhabitants.

8. "Their arrival was a point for us to be governed later by the Indian Government and eventually becoming part of India", Interview with Kop Saul, Papumpare, March 2024.

9. Haimendorf published 'Himalayan Barbary' in 1955, 'The Apatanis and their Neighbors' 1962, 'A Himalayan tribe from cattle to cash' 1980, Bower published 'The Hidden Land' 1953.

10. In Ursula Graham Bower's tour diary "The Hidden Land",1953, Bath Heli and Kop Temi were mentioned as a part of the tour group along with Assam rifle regiment. The same was repeated by Bath Heli and Kop Temi's family during the photograph viewing session.

References

Appadurai, Arjun, ed. *The Social Life of Things: Commodities in Cultural Perspective*. Cambridge: Cambridge University Press, 1986.

Barthes, Roland, and Richard Howard. *Camera Lucida: Reflections on Photography*. New York: Hill and Wang, 1982.

Bayly, C. A. *Empire and Information: Intelligence Gathering and Social Communication in India, 1780-1870*. Cambridge: Cambridge University Press, 1996.

Beggiora, Stefano. "The Mystery of the Buru: From Indigenous Ontology to Post-modern Fairy Tale." *International Quarterly for Asian Studies* 49, no. 3-4 (2018): 33-62.

Bell, Joshua A. "Looking to See: Reflections on Visual Repatriation in the Purari Delta, Gulf Province, Papua New Guinea." In *Museums and Source Communities*, edited by Alison K. Brown and Laura Peers, 111-122. London: Routledge, 2005.

Breitbach, Julia. "The Photo-as-Thing: Photography and Thing Theory." *European Journal of English Studies* 15, no. 1 (2011): 31-43.

Chakravarty, L. N. *Glimpses of the Early History of Arunachal*. 3rd ed. Itanagar: Directorate of Research, 1995.

Clifford, James. "On Collecting." In *The Predicament of Culture*, 215-251. Cambridge: Harvard University Press, 1997.

Dudding, Jenny. "Visual Repatriation and Photo-Elicitation: Recommendations on Principles and Practices for the Museum Worker." *Journal of Museum Ethnography* 17 (2005): 218-231.

Edkins, Jenny. "Politics and Personhood: Reflections on the Portrait Photograph." *Alternatives: Global, Local, Political* 38, no. 2 (2013): 139-154.

Edwards, Elizabeth. "Exchanging Photographs: Preliminary Thoughts on the Currency of Photography in Collecting Anthropology." *Journal des Anthropologues* 80-81 (2000): 21-46.

———. *Raw Histories: Photographs, Anthropology and Museums*. Oxford and New York: Berg, 2001.

———. "Objects of Affect: Photography beyond the Image." *Annual Review of Anthropology* 41, no. 1 (2012): 221-234.

———. "Introduction Section 2." In *Museums and Source Communities: A Routledge Reader*, edited by Alison K. Brown and Laura Peers, 83-99. London: Routledge, 2005.

———. "Talking Visual Histories: Introduction." In *Museums and Source Communities*, edited by Alison K. Brown and

Laura Peers, 83-99. New York: Routledge, 2003.

Edwards, Elizabeth, and Janice Hart, eds. *Photographs, Objects, Histories: On the Materiality of Images*. London: Routledge, 2004.

Gosden, Chris, and Yvonne Marshall. "The Cultural Biography of Objects." *World Archaeology* 31, no. 2 (1999): 169-178.

Guyot-Réchard, Bérénice. "Tour Diaries and Itinerant Governance in the Eastern Himalayas, 1909-1962." *The Historical Journal* 60, no. 4 (2017): 1023-1046.

Houston, Jennifer. "Indigenous Autoethnography: Formulating Our Knowledge, Our Way." *The Australian Journal of Indigenous Education* 36, no. S1 (2007): 45-50.

Malraux, André. *Le Musée Imaginaire*. Paris: Gallimard, 1965 [1947].

Misra, Sanghamitra. "The Nature of Colonial Intervention in the Naga Hills, 1840-80." *Economic and Political Weekly* 33, no. 50 (1998): 3273-3279.

Mooren, Joep, Klaas Stutje, and Frank van Vree. *Clues: Research into Provenance History and Significance of Cultural Objects and Collections Acquired in Colonial Situations*. Amsterdam: NIOD, 2022.

Peers, Laura, and Alison K. Brown. "Just by Bringing These Photographs...: On the Other Meanings of Anthropological Images." In *Photography, Anthropology and History*, 265-280. London: Routledge, 2016.

Pinney, Christopher, and Nicholas Thomas, eds. *Beyond Aesthetics: Art and the Technologies of Enchantment*. London: Routledge, 2020.

Poole, Deborah. *Vision, Race and Modernity: A Visual Economy of the Andean Image World*. Princeton: Princeton University Press, 1997.

Sbriccoli, Tommaso. "Between the Archive and the Village: The Lives of Photographs in Time and Space." *Visual Studies* 31, no. 4 (2016): 295-309.

Scott, James C. *The Art of Not Being Governed: An Anarchist History of Upland Southeast Asia*. New Haven: Yale University Press, 2009.

Smith, Linda Tuhiwai. *Decolonizing Methodologies: Research and Indigenous Peoples*. London and New York: Zed Books, 1999.

Tarr, Michael A., and Stuart H. Blackburn. *Through the Eye of Time: Photographs of Arunachal Pradesh, 1859-2006: Tribal Cultures in the Eastern Himalayas*, Vol. 1. Leiden: Brill, 2008.

Tayler, David, and Elizabeth Edwards. "Very Lovable Human Beings: The Photography of Everard im Thurn." New Haven: Yale University Press, 1992.

Wacquant, Loïc. *Body & Soul: Notebooks of an Apprentice Boxer*. Oxford: Oxford University Press, 2006.

———. "Scrutinizing the Street: Poverty, Morality, and the Pitfalls of Urban Ethnography." *American Journal of Sociology* 107, no. 6 (2002): 1468-1532.

HIMALAYA
The Journal of the Association of Nepal and Himalayan Studies

Research Article

Landscape Aesthetics of Remoteness in the Indian Himalayas

Bhoomika Joshi
National University of Singapore

DOI: https://doi.org/10.2218/himalaya.2025.9589

Abstract

This paper examines the pictorial practices of landscape painting in colonial British art and the textual practice of colonial travel writing to examine the landscape aesthetics of remoteness in the Indian Himalayas. It argues that neither the 'picturesque' nor the 'sublime' genre of colonial landscape paintings can describe the representation of the marginalised geographies of the Indian Himalayas and the colonial impetus to engineer them. By offering a paradigm of the landscape aesthetics of remoteness, this paper demonstrates how remoteness is aesthetically reproduced in the colonial visual imagination, which informs the mapping, engineering and transformation of the Himalayan landscape. It examines the landscape aesthetics in the travelogue and its accompanying illustrations of aquatints in the works of James B. Fraser (1820a, b) and of the lithographs and accompanying text in the work of Thomas Daniell (c.1800) for the North-Western Himalayan region in India. The paper situates these representations of colonial landscape paintings in a broader study of 'landscape and power' (Mitchell 1994). It analyses the pictorial and textual practices through the dialectic of the 'interior' and the 'frontier' that produces the landscape aesthetic of remoteness and provides a new paradigm for studying landscapes and their representation.

Keywords

remoteness, Himalayas, landscape painting, landscape aesthetics, travel writing

Recommended Citation

Joshi, Bhoomika (2025). Landscape Aesthetics of Remoteness in the Indian Himalayas. *HIMALAYA* 44(1): 127-145.

This work is licensed under a Creative Commons Attribution-Noncommercial-No Derivative Works 4.0 License.

Introduction

The Himalayan landscape has been an abiding subject of travel writing and production of art including the travel of spies, administrators, reconnaissance agents for mapping and surveillance, mountaineers and trekkers, saints, mendicants, pilgrims and vagabonds – folding together a myriad of people and their relationships with the Himalayas in addition to those who live and work here. Prominent among them is the genre of colonial landscape paintings. The Indian Himalayan landscape paintings were mostly produced and circulated in early nineteenth-century India and Britain as part of the broader genre of Indian landscapes, particularly through the works of artists like Thomas and William Daniell, Samuel Davis and Edward Lear. The proliferation of the 'landscape aesthetic' (Mitchell 1994) of terra incognita in colonial landscape paintings, and 'remoteness' in travel writing (administrative and vernacular) from the early nineteenth century lend themselves to modes of 'engineering' the mountainous landscape that shaped the emergence of new routes and modes of travel. In his account of 'communication' in colonial Bihar, Sinha (2014) urges us to braid the discursive representations of space (in travelogues, administrative gazetteers) with material representations (maps and construction of transport systems) in order to see how they both inform each other especially in the genre of 'office tours', 'inspection' and 'opening up the interior'. My study draws from such approaches to examine the pictorial practices of landscape painting and the textual practices of travel writing embedded in the landscape and its transformations (Mitchell 1994, Cosgrove and Daniels 1988).

The Indian Himalayan landscape paintings in early nineteenth-century India and Britain circulated as part of the broader genre of Indian landscapes. Whereas colonial hill stations were usually the sites for renderings of 'picturesque' India (Pradhan 2017, Banerjee 2014, Ray 2013, Kennedy 1996), the 'wilderness', vastness and non-urban-ness of the rest of the Indian Himalayas were characterized as 'sublime'. My study of colonial landscape paintings shifts our attention to those sites in the Indian Himalayas that emerge out of a 'remote aesthetic' (neither picturesque nor sublime), and the impetus to transform it through ' a vast program of public works, reorganizing the spatial frame of the social and economic life' (Pradhan 2017: 133) crucially embedded in the interplay between material transformation, 'civil' engineering, forced labor and resource extraction. The genre of colonial landscape paintings and its interplay with the genre of colonial travel writing is a crucial way to understand how remoteness is produced as a category. The aesthetic of remoteness produced in such visual and textual records is reflective of how the gaze of travel writing and artistic reproduction can fix people and places in space and time (Arnold 2006, Pratt 1992) along with the impetus to 'improve' them. The cartographic rendering of such landscapes and their administration also relies on earlier records and thereby reproduces their gaze. By centering on the aesthetic of remoteness, this paper provides a paradigm for examining such records, especially concerning the Himalayas. The aesthetics of remoteness are the political field on which the colonization and transformation of Himalayan territory is based, and therefore crucial to examine.

The 'frontier' geography of the Himalayan region, along with the 'interior' gaze of travellers and administrators (re)produces the landscape aesthetic of remoteness, which is reinscribed in the routes and networks of the 'imperial eyes' (Pratt 1992). In his definitive essay on remoteness, Ardener suggests that 'distance lends enhancement if not enchantment to the anthropological vision' (1987, 2012: 89). The remoteness that characterizes the Himalayan landscapes produces both enhancement and enchantment throughout the colonial, nationalist and postcolonial histories of the region. Remoteness in this sense is not merely topographical but also topological such that the relationships of identity and mobility that it characterizes are also rendered remote. In his study of remoteness in the

Gilgit-Baltistan region of Northern Pakistan, Hussain (2015) describes the persistence of remoteness as a category for the Shimshalis of the Hunza Valley despite their many encounters with the world and connections with various socio-spatial domains including nationalism, transhumance migration, international tourism and environmentalism. Remoteness, Hussain argues, like modernity, is an unfinished project. The construction of remoteness therefore entails the contradictions of making something, that can be easily worked into the nationalized territorial imagination, 'remote', and also provides the ground for integration into broader geographies (Mathur 2015, Harms et al 2014).

By offering a paradigm of the landscape aesthetics of remoteness, this paper demonstrates how remoteness is aesthetically reproduced in the colonial visual imagination, which informs the mapping, engineering and transformation of the Himalayan landscape. Remoteness transcends the pictorial conventions of 'picturesque' and 'sublime' through which the dominant analysis of colonial landscape art history has been undertaken and also interlinks both of them when seen through the lens of remoteness. This paper examines the landscape aesthetics in the work of two colonial figures and landscape painters – James B. Fraser's travelogue *Journal of a Tour through the Himala Mountains* (1820a) and its accompanying illustrations in a set of twenty aquatints – *A View in the Himala Mountains* (1820b) and Thomas Daniell's *Oriental Scenery IV* (1807), one of a collection of six volumes of lithographs and its accompanying text. The paper situates both of these, which together constitute one of the earliest representations of the North-west Indian Himalayas in Company Painting, in a broader study of 'landscape and power' which considers landscape as an instrument of cultural force and not merely as an object to be seen or a text to be read (Mitchell 1994).

However, and rather than viewing the repertoire of the Company Paintings of the Indian landscape, and particularly that of the Himalayas as the 'dreamwork of imperialism' (Mitchell 1994), and a process of colonization fully realized, this paper argues that the landscape aesthetics of remoteness should be situated in the dialectical relationship between the interior and the frontier. It also argues for a study of the enactment of the incomplete project of colonialism in the 'middle ground' (White 1991) of its events and actors rather than only from the vantage of either the metropolis or the periphery. In doing so, this paper shifts our attention towards the sites of representation, production and circulation of Indian landscape paintings in general and of the Indian Himalayas in particular that are not limited either by colonial urban development or by the impressions of wilderness. Whereas sites like Delhi, Calcutta and Madras are usually the sites for colonial picturesque renderings of the Indian landscape, colonial hill stations like Shimla, Darjeeling and Ooty constitute the sites of such representation as far as the Indian Himalayas are concerned. On the other hand, most of the Indian mountainscapes have been studied as representations of the sublime. The sheer landform of the Indian Himalayas and the scale of human effort required to navigate and surround it renders itself very well to the demands of 'sublime' representation especially when it could not be tamed or domesticated by the picturesque vantage of colonial hill stations. This paper offers a paradigm of the landscape aesthetics of remoteness characterized by the articulation of the frontier-interior dialectic through a study of colonial landscape paintings.

I. Landscape Painting and the Indian Himalayas in the early nineteenth century: James Fraser and *The Ridge and fort at Jytock*

The names of the earliest British landscape painters in India from the eighteenth century onwards can be recalled in the same tradition as the landscape painters in Britain, in order of influence and by the genres of paintings they produced.[1] James Baillie Fraser, acknowledged for providing one of the earliest representations of the Indian Himalayan landscape, especially the source of the sacred rivers of Ganga and Yamuna, and for also being the 'first' European to visit Gangotri and Jamnotri, is one of such artists. So are Thomas Daniell, uncle and William Daniell, nephew who went on to produce a large corpus of work on India over ten years from their first visit in 1786 (Sutton 1954; Archer 1969, 1980; Shellim 1979). Among the two sets of aquatints of Indian landscapes produced by Fraser as an amateur painter during his nearly ten years stay in India[2] this paper looks at one of his landmark pieces of painting and travel writing. Titled *Journal of a Tour through the Himala Mountains,* Fraser's travel journal was published in 1820 by Rodwell and Martin in London, the same year that they also published a set of twenty aquatints by Fraser titled *A View in the Himala Mountains* as illustrations for this journal. The other set of landscape paintings and accompanying text it examines is Thomas Daniell's *Oriental Scenery IV* (1807) which has lithographs of some of the earliest landscape paintings by the British of the North-western Himalayas from this region. According to Archer and Falk (1989), James Fraser may have seen the aquatint rendering of Thomas and William Daniell's landscape paintings of the Himalayas, which were published as part of Oriental Scenery IV in 1804. The Fraser brothers travelled through routes similar to and close on the heels of the Daniells. The Daniells themselves were determined to emulate and surpass William Hodges, a pupil of the British painter Richard Wilson, and his *Select Views in India* (1785-88) (Tillotson 1990). During their journey towards the north, the Daniells had stayed with Samuel Davis, the draftsman and surveyor of Samuel Turner's mission to Bhutan and Tibet in 1783, and it was Davis who had encouraged the Daniells to go up to the Himalayan mountains. Therefore, not only the 'landscape aesthetics' (Mitchell 1994) of the Indian Himalayas but even the circuits of itineraries through which it was articulated and represented were reproduced in the late eighteenth and early nineteenth-century Company painting.[3]

The aquatint through which I examine the landscape aesthetics of remoteness in the work of James Fraser is plate number 4 titled *The Ridge and fort at Jytock.* The fort at Jytock (Jaithak) in the North-western Himalayas in India was sieged by the British forces at the end of the Anglo-Gurkha war, which culminated in 1816. Beginning with the East India Company's activities in India, and especially during the late eighteenth century, the question of state formation in the British Empire was vested with the question of expanding and settling frontiers, the legacy of which survives in the postcolonial politics of borderlands and nationalism across South Asia. James Fraser hadn't arrived at Fort Jytock entirely by either chance or design. His younger brother William Fraser, who had risen in the ranks as a Company official had been appointed first, as the Political Agent of the Nepal War in 1814 and then as the Commander for the Affairs of Garhwal in 1815 to oversee the new land settlement after the war. The Anglo-Nepalese War, also known as the Gurkha War or the Anglo-Gurkha War, was fought between the East India Company and the Nepalese Gurkhas between 1814 and 1816, in one of the Company's first bids to expand its territorial control beyond India. It was a war in which the Company troops had to reckon with the Gurkha troops on many fronts before securing a difficult victory in 1816. The Anglo-Gurkha war was itself a culmination of the 'territorial disputes that emerged along the common frontiers of the Gurkha kingdom (present-day Nepal) and the English East India Company' (Michael 2014: 2). The 'spatial anxiety' (ibid) of the Company and its officials in settling the frontier was further complicated by the processes in such non-state spaces – of local power and influence which they had to contest with while they surveyed and re-ordered the frontier to settle it. More specially, British interest in Nepal centred on its significance as a conduit of trade with Tibet and China and that Nepal itself also could be a lucrative source of timber, spices and other commodities. As a function of his position, William Fraser had been tasked to recruit local people to

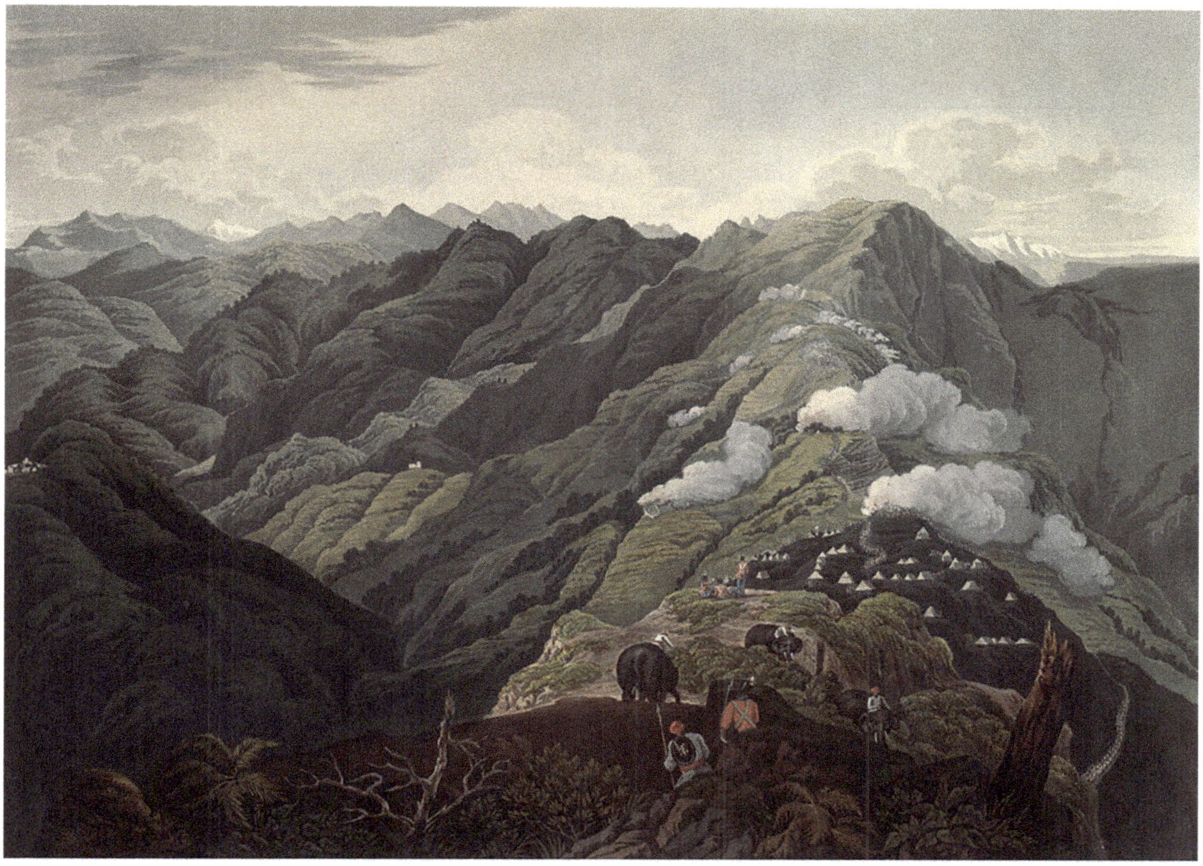

Figure 1: James B. Fraser's 'The ridge and fort of Jytock' from Views in the Himala Mountains (Robert Havell and Son), Plate 4, Aquatint, 59 x 43 cm. The British Library, London

serve in the irregular force in support of the Company's troops and to settle claims to land and land revenue amongst the local kings and chieftains as well as between the Company and such local elites. During this period, the Company had decided to draw towards their side the expelled chiefs and subjects of the hill principalities reduced by the Gurkhas (Alavi 1995). It is important to note that while recruiting local people as irregular support, William Fraser ended up recruiting a few Gurkha soldiers who were first enlisted in the British Army during this time and went on to become one of the oldest serving battalions in the British Army as well as the army of independent India.

At first view, the painting appears land-locked, almost gridlocked by the mountains. The mountain line or the horizon imposes an elevation that doesn't seem to become a vantage point; it limits and blocks the view. The gradient of the rising mountains, from the vision of the viewer, is also pronounced, like a topographical sketch of the mountain where the eye of the viewer can trace the contours of elevation in the painting. Fraser, while painting for the illustrations to accompany the journal was keen that the aquatint illustrations be an exercise in a 'tolerably accurate survey of the country' for amassing the 'materials for a map', being of the view that a geographer was comparable to a statesman (Fraser 1820a: vii). He had arrived at Jytock (Jaithak, the site of the fort) in March 1815 from Delhi, accompanying General Martindell's troops.[4] Stationed at Blackhill, the campsite for the British troops, Fraser described the 'face of the country around Jytock' to be 'peculiarly rugged' (Fraser 1820a: 61). For Fraser, the 'wild and singular sharp ridges' scarcely 'afford room for footing' (ibid: 61) and the 'ravines that separate these hills have a no less savage character' (ibid: 62). Such a representation of the landscape is not merely a physical description but also aims to convey the implicit heroic value in being able to traverse and conquer such terrain and capturing the sublime. It also lends itself to the strategic military value that the region held for the advancing British troops and their efforts to move the influence and control of the Nepali kingdom out of the region. It is therefore at once an introduction of the region, as well as its evaluation. The association of the travelling artist with the mobilization and the movement of the Company troops is clearly represented throughout the journal and is best represented in this aquatint.[5]

A closer look at the painting suggests that the landscape as represented doesn't intend to reveal – rather, it appears to be conceived as a landscape that conceals – it conceals the view, it conceals the inhabitants of the region and most importantly, it even seems to conceal the possibilities in and of the landscape as represented in its remoteness. In his account of the travelling to Fort Jytock and beyond, James Fraser provides vivid and repetitive descriptions of 'a steep and rugged ascent' and the fatigue of 'a march of nearly forty miles' (1820a: 58-59) that suggests the scale and volume of the military movement that Fraser was a part of even if not directly involved with. He describes the territory that he is moving through as 'rugged' and 'savage' as including the villages in the region, which, according to Fraser 'depopulated by the severity of the conquerors, do not excite disgust, at least not interest' (ibid: 65). In his part geographic and part ethnographic venture, quickly collapsing into one, Fraser goes ahead to lend the metaphors for the landscape to the people associated with it:

> The inhabitants of the country surrounding the capital, and the districts in its vicinity, are not calculated to excite much interest either from character or appearance. Generally speaking, they are contemptible in size, mean in aspect, cringing in address; their intellect appears degraded, and their ignorance almost brutal. (1820a: 66-67)

In lending the quality of land to the quality of its inhabitants, Fraser reproduces the landscape aesthetics of remoteness into ethnographic aesthetics of remoteness – the natives are degraded, uninteresting and gross, a people whose origin forms a 'curious subject of inquiry' (1820a: 71) – the subject of the 'remote history of an aboriginal people' (ibid: 72). Thus, the ravines are as rugged and as savage as its inhabitants which together cannot be considered either as picturesque or sublime but must be characterized in terms of their remoteness not only from the British troops, travellers and administrators but also from their counterparts in the lowlands who can be more easily classified, understood and explained without being rendered 'remote'.[6]

Whereas the inhabitants of the villages in the region occupied a frontier that the Company wanted to settle, they were characterized by the kind of remoteness attributed to the 'interior' – closed off by the rugged mountains and savage ravines, which according to Fraser characterized them as people preoccupied with the 'subsistence of the everyday' (1820a: 62). Fraser considers that even though the tracts in some of these areas may have been rich and populous, they were 'insulated and small in proportion to the vast space that is incapable of cultivation, mountainous and wild' (ibid: 73), and for which the 'revenue could have never been large'. The steep terrain of the mountains, rising from the foreground onwards as represented in Fraser's painting, makes it difficult to imagine the agricultural prospects of the landscape. It appears heavily forested, the cover of which cannot be penetrated even to determine the kinds of trees and other growth that may be beneath it, marked by a conspicuous absence of detail. Even though the expanse of the landscape spreads out, the entire scene appears automatically enclosed by the contours of the rising terrain, rendered 'interior' to its topography.

Given how the view of *Fort Jytock* is blocked and locked, it only promises to reveal something or hold out a possibility if one were to follow the march of the soldiers through it. The landlocked appearance of the painting with a rather restricted horizon makes it

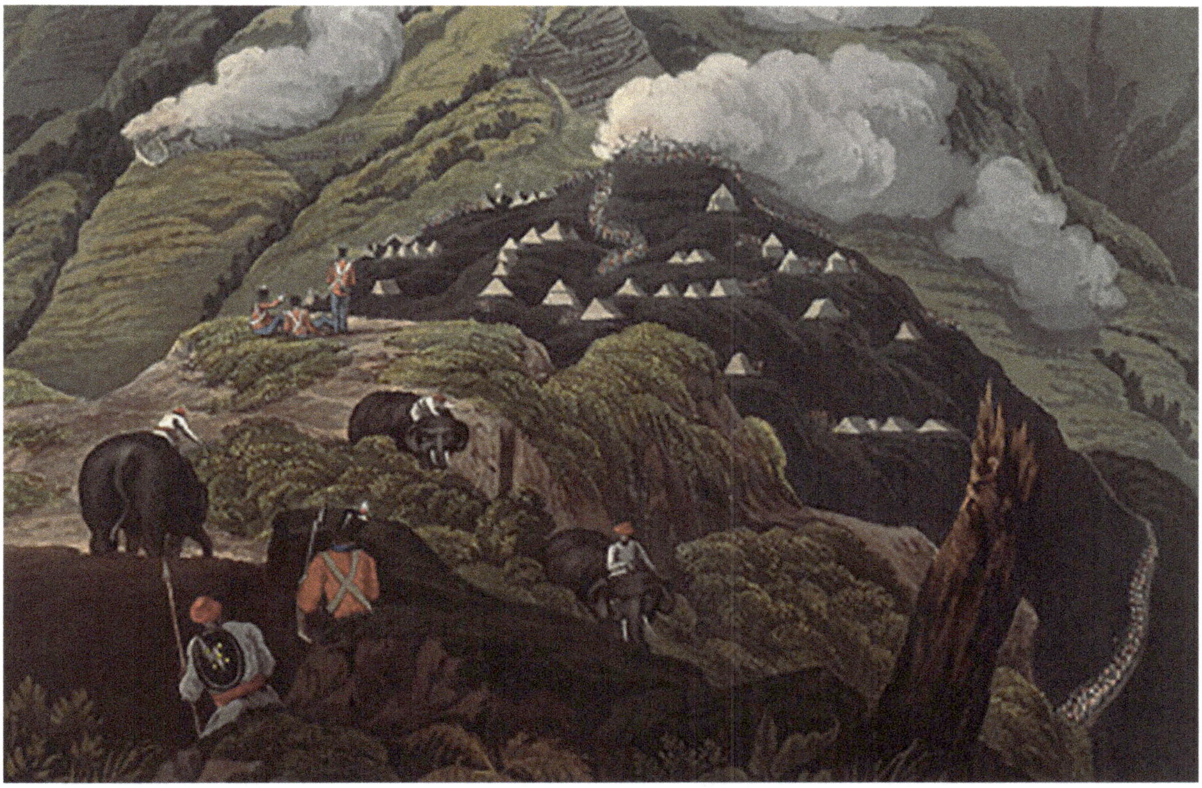

Figure 2: Details of the 'middle ground', Fraser (1820b).

difficult to distinguish between the classic background, foreground and middle ground planes in the aquatint since the painting seems to rise from the foreground upwards rather than lend itself to distinct planes of vision. However, upon a still closer look, it is easier to locate distinct planes of vision, which are related to and shaped by the movement of the troop of soldiers upwards on the hill. It is in this upward movement of the troops that the landscape seems to reveal itself and its affordances. Some of these clues can be found in the representation of the camping site of the troops in what appears as the middle ground of the painting.

While following the movement of the troops upwards in the hills, we can notice the figure of a soldier discernibly dressed in a British uniform followed by another soldier in a native uniform and preceded by native soldiers atop elephants, describing to the viewer that these marching troops consist native soldiers as they do British soldiers. James Fraser had accompanied his brother William Fraser who was commissioned to recruit locals for irregular support for the British troops during the war. In this painting, James Fraser depicts both British and local troops, who may have been recruited by William.

The success of the British troops in the region was significantly dependent upon the success in recruiting soldiers from the 'highlanders' of these districts as well as the old soldiers and dependents of the ex-hill chiefs, who were now under Gurkha rule. Unless such support could be successfully enlisted, soldiers from different groups and regions of India had to be enlisted, among them – Marathas, Sikhs, and Pathans who became the face of the Company Sepoys in the regiments of the East India Company Army. The Company's intervention in Nepal did not begin with the Anglo-Nepalese war in 1814; it had first sent an expedition to Kathmandu in 1767 at the request of the then King of Nepal who was under siege by the Gurkha army. The expedition failed and the troops were forced to retreat. Even though the Company had managed to sign a treaty of friendship with Nepal by 1801, primarily to gain access to the Nepal valley as an entrepot for trans-Himalayan trade, by 1804, the anti-company sentiment in Kathmandu had undermined the terms of the treaty and the Company resident was forced to withdraw from there. The Gurkha kingdom continued to expand during the next few years and began to encroach upon the company's territory in the North Indian plains, and the Company eventually declared war in 1814 as the Gurkhas became a military threat to the recently acquired territories, the concerns of a 'fledgling empire' (Das Chene 1991).

The British troops therefore needed the enlistment and support of the natives and the Gurkhas who, according to James Fraser were more accustomed to the 'irregular and rough ground' of the battlefield and could 'keep their footing when others lost theirs or were out breathed' (1820a: - others being the Marathas, the Sikhs and the Pathans who were not from the highlands). William Fraser had been successful in recruiting Gurkhas for policing and foraging before the Anglo-Nepalese War of 1815 and their success had increased the Company's admiration for the Gurkhas. According to Alavi (1995), the Company, unable to win over the personnel that constituted the military base of the Nepal kingdom even as it made overtures to the Gurkhas to desert from their army, had begun to invent its model of a Gurkha soldier – recruiting from among the men from Kumaon, Garhwal and Sirmour (adjoining hill territories) in the image of the 'Company Gurkha'.

According to Montogomery (1998) as boundary disputes between the Company and Nepal increased, there was a need to gather more information about the frontier and its settlement. However, the mountains presented a formidable barrier to gathering such information and operations. Bayly in his work on *Empire and Information* states that the British were confronted with a 'virtual information famine' about the India-Nepal border before the Anglo-Gurkha war (1996). The mountain terrain of warfare was expected to cause some difficulties, although it wasn't known; the military ability of the Gurkhas too could not be anticipated. According to Montogomery, much of the intelligence the Company relied on was 'based on earlier traveller's accounts of Nepal and the Himalayas, reports by naturalists, ethnographers and ichthyologists, and surveys and statistical sketches which were collected in a somewhat ad hoc manner' that characterized the frontier as rugged and wild, especially due to the 'impregnable positions' of the mountains (1998: 36). The system and principle of revenue collection that the British built upon from the Mughal administration was based upon fixed and determinate boundaries which was also different from the Gurkha view of the rights to revenue collection.[8]

The elaborate and sophisticated movement of the troops upwards on the hill in *Fort Jytock*, and towards the campsite represents the recruitment and coordination efforts of William Fraser as far as it depicts both Company troops in British Uniform and both the Company Gurkha and the irregular forces of a few Gurkhas who could be enlisted, in native uniform. According to James Fraser, the severity of the Gurkha rule had made people 'reckless, broken spirited, bowed to the dust and subdued in mind and body' (1820a: 75). However, farther north and 'the farther removed from the seat of government, the more did the latent symptoms of anxiety to throw off the yoke evince themselves'. Given the understanding that enlistment into the Company troops was a 'welcome refuge' to those Kumaonis, Garhwalis and Sirmouris who had been 'dispossessed of their high political and military status by the Gurkha' (Alavi 1995: 275), William Fraser did not have much difficulty in recruiting from among these groups, unlike when he tried from among the Gurkhas.

Even as one can notice how the British troops seem to lead the charge up the hill in the painting, marked by their visible presence at the campsite and in the figure leading in the foreground, one cannot miss the native soldiers commanding and manoeuvring the elephants ahead of the British uniformed soldier. One is, therefore also left to wonder about the

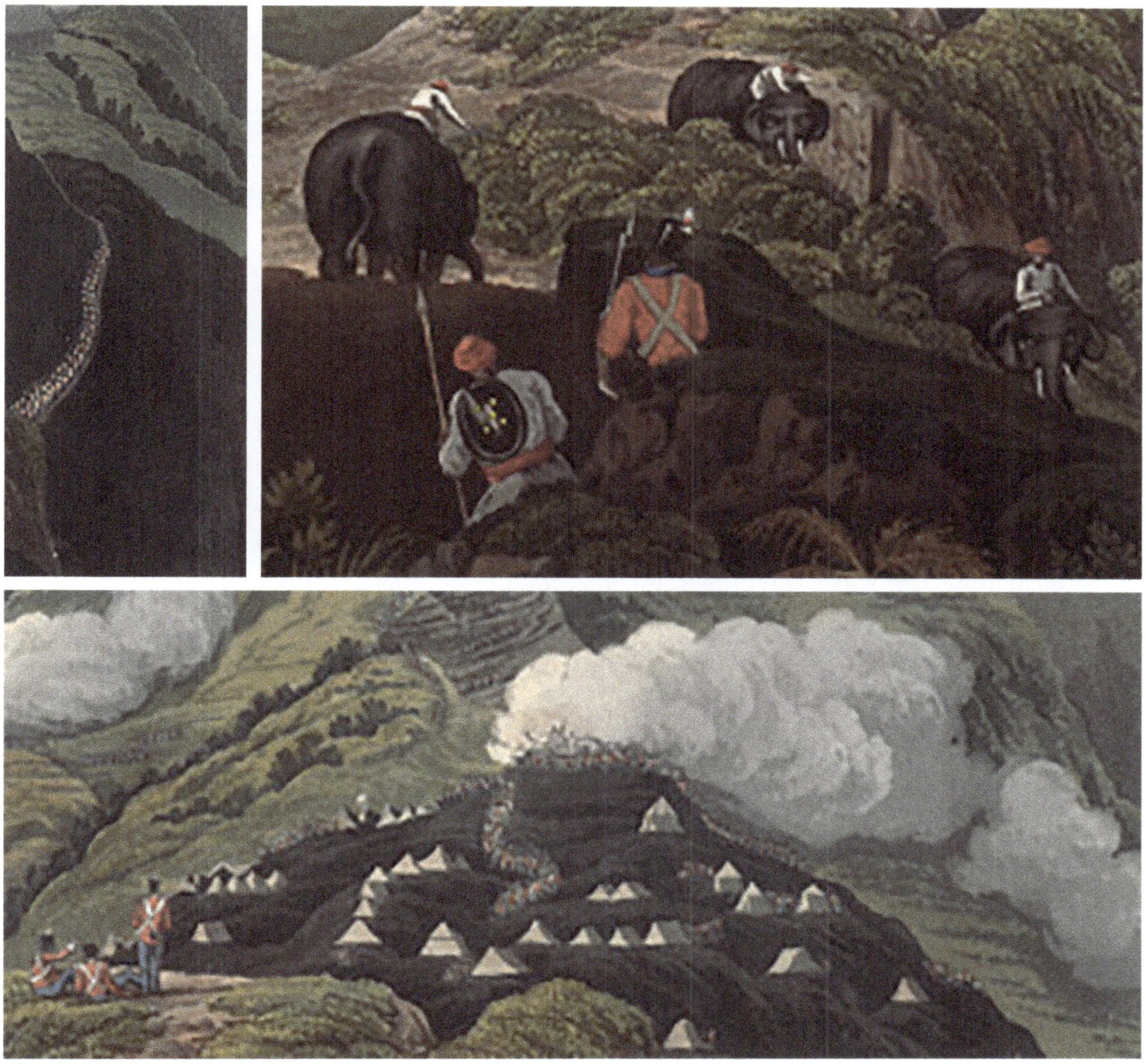

Figures 3,4,5: Details of the movement of the troop and the campsite. Fraser (1820b)

campsite itself – which may serve both as a site of strategic planning among the British soldiers for the next offensive as well as a site for the potential recruitment of irregulars. However, in order to navigate through this terrain, the British troops would have to trust the locals, natives and highlanders, especially those whom Fraser considered 'anxious to rise and assist the British to dispossess their late conquerors' (82) and therefore much 'information' was to be gained 'respecting the roads that lead from east to west' (82). But instances of even those who had 'evinced favorable sentiments towards us' (85) going over to the enemy repeatedly highlight the ambivalence of this collaboration between the British troops and the native troops.

The middle ground of the campsite that reveals the mountainscape as situated in the broader strategic pragmatic of settling the frontier is at once also representative of the tensions of trust and reliance between the British and the natives from the 'insulated interior'. The stereotypical accounts of the barbarous nature of the Gurkha rule that the Company was accustomed to were especially reliant on the accounts of Father Giuseppe, a Roman Catholic missionary who claimed to have travelled in Nepal between 1768 and 1789, which furthered the view of Nepal as a country waiting to be liberated from the 'barbaric' Gurkha rule. However, as the Company was to find out, even the British rhetoric of liberation from the oppressive rule of the Gurkhas in its correspondence to hill chiefs was not successful in bringing the hill chiefs over to their side. Such a context of misrepresented interaction between the Company, the Gurkhas and the Company Gurkhas assumes an interesting dimension in understanding the construction of the 'Gurkha' identity as well as that of the 'remoteness' of the landscape in which it articulates itself.

While talking about the 'creative misunderstandings' between Europeans and Indians in the region around the Great Lakes on what we now know as the US-Canada border, White (1991) frames his argument in terms of the problematique of the 'middle ground' – the place in between – between cultures, peoples, Empires and non-state world of villages from where arise shared meanings and practices of the middle ground (1991: xxvi). The campsite in the middle ground in this aquatint appears to function both as the literal and the metaphorical middle ground, where the itinerant political agency, army commander, travelling artist, company troops, native soldiers and the Gurkhas interact, and attribute meanings attached to the landscape and its inhabitants. While the company aimed to settle the frontier, it became hard for it to contend with the lack of knowledge about the region along with the ambivalence of depending upon the natives for navigating and occupying this territory. Much like how the members of the Iruquois confederacy in Upper Missouri were cast in the image of the Republican Indians by the portrait paintings by the Washington officials (Truettner 2010), as distinguished from the Noble Savage, the Gurkhas presented to the Company a curious case of a native representation that they were ambivalent about – characterized as barbaric and insolent in an unknown landscape while displaying the sophistication and resilience of an organized army. Such an ambivalence is also curiously represented in James Fraser's sketches of the Gurkhas where sometimes they are uniformed in a European manner which the then Gurkha king had already cast them in and sometimes, more enigmatically, in their native attire bearing traditional weapons.[9] Therefore, when the Company cast the other native soldiers in the image of the Company Gurkha, they also aimed to counter the ambivalence of the Gurkha identity by making them into Noble Savages. However, unlike the Noble Savages, the Gurkhas were not deemed expendable – rather they had to become allies of British colonialism and Nepal's crypto-colonialism, especially after the defeat of Nepal in the Anglo Gurkha war of 1815.

II. Landscape Painting and the Indian Himalayas in the early nineteenth century: Thomas Daniell and *The Rope Bridge at Serinagur*

'This bridge, which is 240 feet in length, is an ingenious contrivance, and so simple, that it may soon be erected and soon removed', Thomas Daniell wrote for the painting aptly titled *The Rope Bridge at Serinagur* (Oriental Scenery IV, 1807). Apparently the 'first' Europeans to get to the northern region of Garhwal in the Indian Himalayas, the Daniells had started on their upward trek to the region in August 1788 to arrive at Srinagar on 28 April, 1789, when they made the first sketch of the rope bridge. *The Rope Bridge* is one of the few paintings of the Indian Himalayas in the early nineteenth century, and certainly the first of the North-Western Himalayan region by British landscape painters.

The work was first exhibited at the Royal Academy in 1800 with the accompanying text -'The Rope Bridge at Serinagur, in the Sevalic mountains, taken in the year 1789 during the evacuation of the city in consequence of the approach of a large army from Almorah, East Indies' (Shellim 1979). Nothing in the painting itself however conveys the significance and volatility of the 'the evacuation of the city' or 'the approach of a large army' (ibid). On the other hand, the illuminated and near translucent mountains fading into the horizon as if they are still further away from us seem to remind us of the 'remoteness' that the Daniells wanted to highlight, how the 'wrecked state of society under these petty chieftains, whose views of government are little better

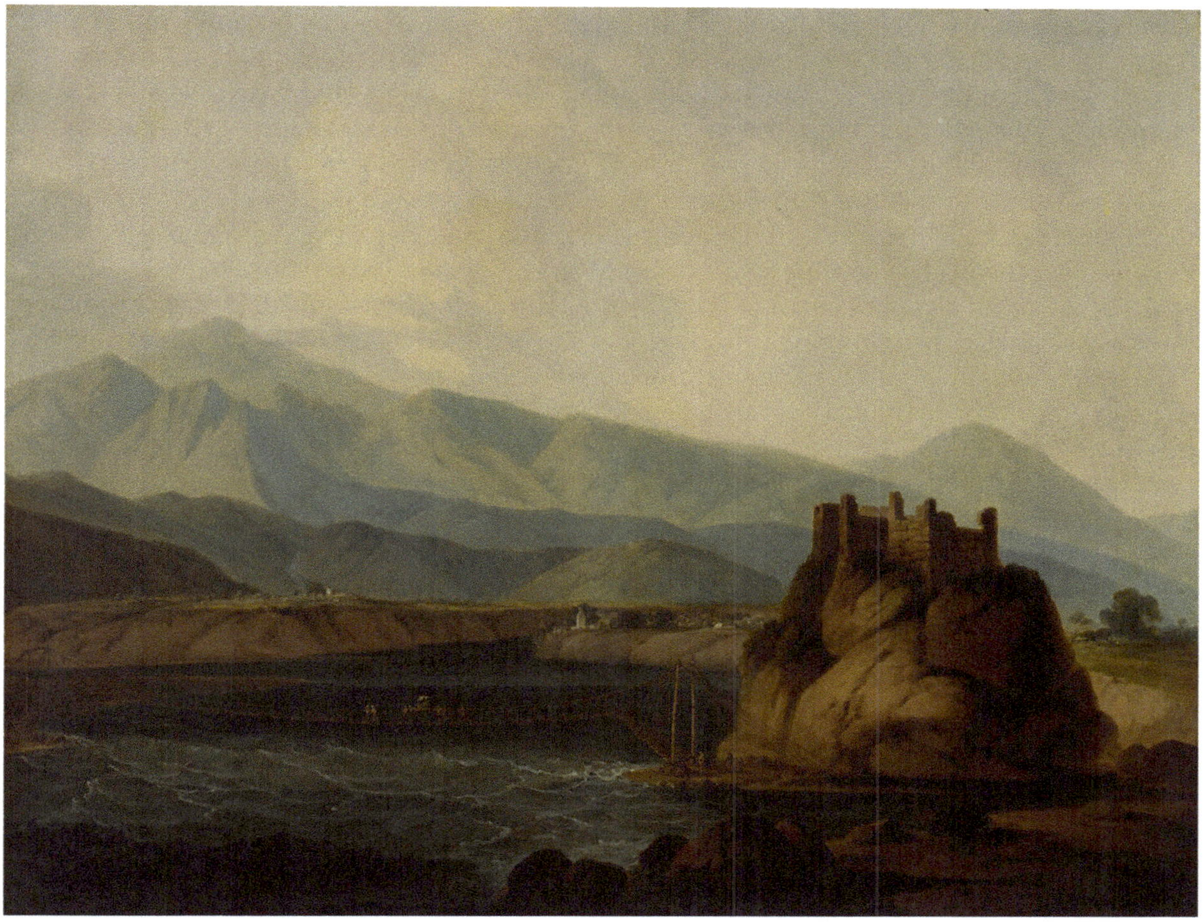

Figure 6: The Rope Bridge at Serinagur c. 1800, Oil on canvas (relined). 32.25 x 40.75 (82 x 103.5). Yale Centre for British Art, Paul Mellon Collection. New Haven

than those of savages; and with whom all questions of justice and right are, as with duelists, referred to arms; considering, like them, no decision so correct, and so honourable, as those which have been recorded in the letters of blood' (Oriental Sceneries IV, 1807). The cityscape of Srinagar, the seat of the king of Garhwal, appears south from another settlement on the top of the hill, which forms the near center of the painting. The expanse of Srinagar is notable – on the bank of the river Alakhnanda behind the fort and the village of Ranihat on the opposite bank. The illuminated and near translucent mountainscape fading into the horizon as if they are still further away from the viewer and the dim view of the cityscape at the foothills seem to remind us of the eternal 'remoteness' that the Daniells wanted to highlight given how far they had gotten themselves, especially as the 'first' set of Europeans. The combination of the sublime mountainscape on the horizon, the turbulent waters of the river in the foreground and the seemingly impregnable fort which functions to render the view 'remote' however is at once confronted by the expanse of Srinagar, Ranihat and habitation atop the hill.

It is the 'rope bridge' in the middle ground of the painting that operates as a switch between the represented 'remoteness' and the expanse of the settlement as well as the political volatility of the landscape; it is at once the medium and representation of this tension. More than the mountains on the horizon and the turbulent waters of the river in the foreground, the rope bridge emerges as the most sublime. Painted with a light stroke of the brush and a touch of paint that nearly merges into the river itself, it is only the rope bridge that can help the viewer cross the river to go further up, into the city of Srinagar and beyond. The unsteadiness of a 240 feet long bridge that 'may soon be erected and soon removed' in a composition that is half land and half water only seems to pronounce the 'remoteness' of this view and suggests the painter's conundrum in being unable to resolve the tension between the fragility and temporariness of the 'rope bridge' and the significance of the presence of a capital city, a seat of power, 'Serinagur' beyond it. It is also the rope bridge, which imparts itself to the title of the painting, that connects Srinagar to the world even if tentatively so and is the medium of movement during a siege that the Daniells describe.

Going by the text that accompanied the painting at the Royal Academy, the seemingly impregnable fort is about to be breached and the fragile and temporary bridge is the only escape route from the city. And even though Thomas Daniell describes it as an 'an affecting scene' and 'a most melancholy example of the wrecked state of society' (Oriental Scenery IV, 1807), it is hard to see how the rather small caravan of the king in the palanquin accompanied by a handful of soldiers and servants on the rope bridge represents the 'evacuation of a city' or a political coup. The course of the procession and the rope bridge, tethered on one side to the base of the fort on a strip of land and to a half-visible promontory on the other side, is abruptly cut off to deepen the effect of the 'remoteness' of the view, the fragility and unreliability of the bridge and the undecidedness of not just the course of the king and his men, but of the city and the kingdom.

By the time the Daniells exhibited this painting at the Royal Academy in 1800, the Garhwal region had only become more volatile. The Gurkhas from the bordering kingdom of Nepal wrested it from the King of Kumaun by 1803 and after the culmination of the Anglo-Gurkha war in 1815, it came under the rule of the British. The landscape paintings of the Indian Himalayas convey the tension between the perceived 'remoteness' of the region and the unfolding political and social dynamism that the Company painters confronted. This couldn't be said more clearly, even if one were to just glance at the watercolour for *The Rope Bridge at Serinagur* by Thomas Daniell (c. 1800), which records a different view. Unlike the oil painting, the fort is neither as high an obstruction to the view nor as seemingly impregnable, the waves in the river rise closer to the bridge and not merely in the foreground. The most striking contrast is, however, the course of the rope bridge to the other bank and the number of people on the bridge - men, women and children 'evacuating the city' with their possessions in tow with the royal entourage conspicuously missing. The rope bridge however appears similarly fragile and especially weighed under by the number of people using it. In the oil rendition to be exhibited at the Royal Academy, the large number of people is replaced by the royal entourage and the vision of the bridge cut off abruptly to render it more 'remote'. The middle ground of the painting represented by the rope bridge is the site of action and movement during a situation of conflict which is improved through the landscape aesthetics of remoteness in the finally exhibited lithograph at the Royal Academy.

Previously titled 'Suspension Bridge over the Ganges' and attributed to Samuel Davis, the confusion around the authorship of the watercolour is telling of the circulation of the landscape aesthetics of remoteness. Whether it was the north-west region of Garwhal (Daniells 1789, Fraser 1815) or north-eastern highlands of Bhutan and Tibet (1783), the Indian landscape, in general, but the Indian Himalayan landscape in particular, that was being represented and reproduced, was circumscribed by the same aesthetics – that of remoteness. Such a depiction was also characterized by the tensions it faced in its very reproduction and representation – of pre-colonial history, of settlement and strife that neither the 'picturesque' nor the 'sublime' could contend with and could be better understood when rendered 'remote'. *The Rope Bridge at Serinagur* is a fine representation of the landscape aesthetics of remoteness in Company painting that significantly shaped the Indian Himalayas as terra incognita for a long time.

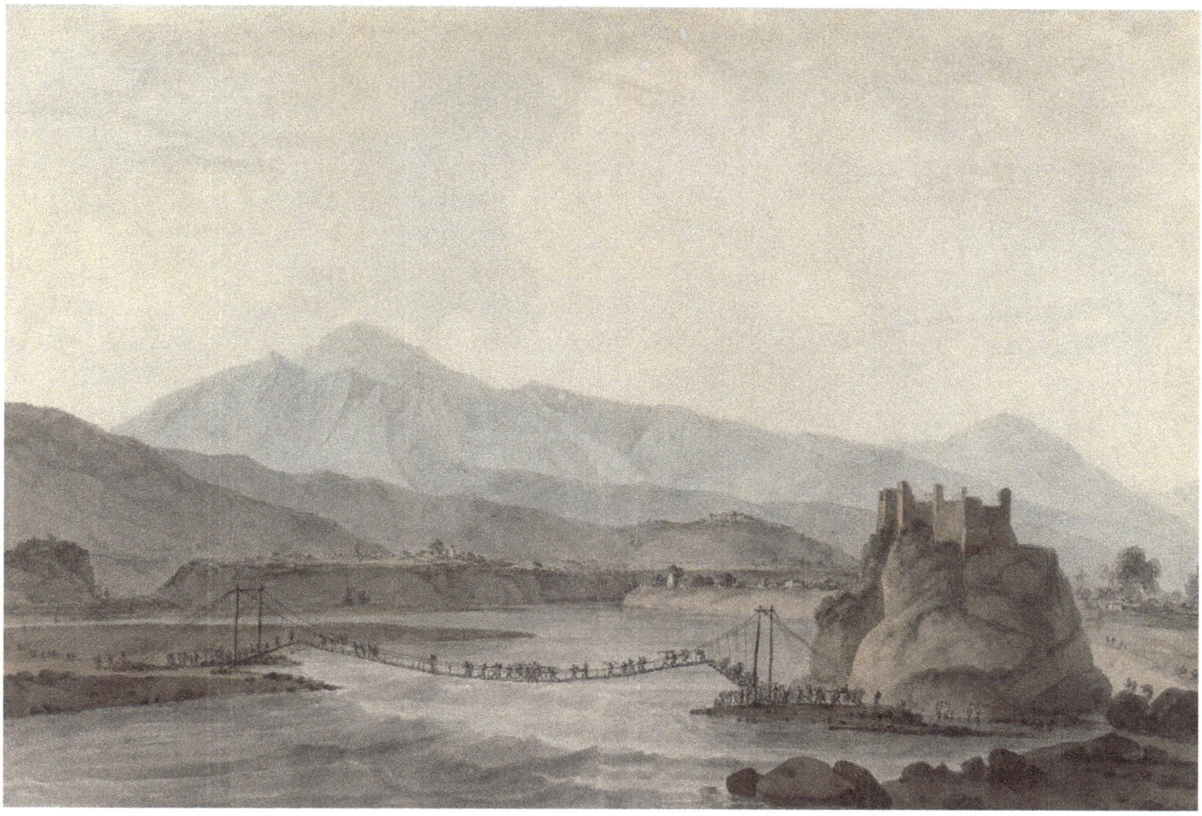

Figure 7: Watercolour of 'The Rope Bridge at Serinagur' c. 1800 by Thomas Daniell. Watercolor, with pen and brown ink and graphite on medium, moderately textured, cream-laid paper. Mount: 20 1/4 × 30 inches (51.4 × 76.2 cm), Sheet: 19 15/16 × 29 5/8 inches (50.6 × 75.2 cm). Yale Centre for British Art, Paul Mellon Collection, New Haven.

III: Landscape aesthetics and the dialectics of remoteness

What Fraser and Daniell set up is a representation of the complex processes of exchange and action between the natives/ locals and the Company troops in the middle ground of the dialectical relationship between the 'interior' and the 'frontier' as attributes of the landscape as well as those who inhabit it. Whether it is the 'interior' or the 'frontier', the power of the narrative action of the story told about them (in maps, surveys, travelogues, administrative accounts of tours and land settlements) or the landscape aesthetics of remoteness lies in setting 'a legitimate theatre for practical actions' (De Certeau 1984: 125). The Company's expansionist geopolitics and its claim to the territories on the India-Nepal border set up the 'theatre' for its counter-expansionist politics towards the Gurkha rule in Nepal to settle the frontier.

The classification of Gurkhas as a 'martial race'[10] according to British military historians and administrators developed as a discourse on the Gurkha masculinity in the aftermath of the Anglo-Nepalese war (1814-1816). Prior constructions of the Gurkha as 'barbaric' and 'insolent' shifted to them being martial and warlike; this shift marked the 'discovery' of the Gurkhas by the British. Until the war, the British hadn't come in direct contact with them, and the relationship of the Company with the Nepalese kingdom was characterized by a volatile diplomatic equation. The Gurkhas were seen as both formidable opponents and potential allies, and the Company's insistence on recruiting the Gurkhas into its troops to occupy, settle and even expand the India-Nepal frontier only became stronger after the war.

Most studies of martial races and the recruitment of the Gurkhas into the Indian Army have focused on the latter half of the nineteenth century when the idea appeared in its most recognizable form, especially after the 1857 rebellion (Barua 1995, Caplan 1995, Das Chene 1999). According to such a perspective, it was the part played by a limited battalion at Delhi during the rebellion by the soldiers that established the Gurkhas as being exceedingly brave and loyal and ensured that the British conferred martial race status upon them. However, the attempts of the Company to recruit Gurkhas even before the Anglo-Nepalese war in 1814, as we have noted, suggests that these conceptions of 'martial race' had emerged much earlier. In the history of the characterization of the Gurkhas as a 'martial race' before and certainly after the Anglo-Nepalese war in 1815, and formally institutionalised after 1857, we can chart a history of the changing British impressions of the Gurkha in the middle ground of their interactions.

The campsite and the bridge as the site of the interaction at both the metaphorical and literal middle ground of the landscapes present a question of the 'problem of authority'. By rendering such a landscape *remote*, Fraser and Daniell represent the ambivalence of what must be revealed and what must be concealed. Unlike the landscape paintings of the picturesque views of the colony, especially of the plantation colonial economies (Quilley 2003) that centre the political economy of the plantation, these paintings depict a military-pragmatic or geo-political view of the landscape.[11] Unlike the creolized landscapes of the West Indian plantations where the creolized white plantation owner could seemingly aspire to be the 'real' West Indian (Quilley 2003), the remote landscapes of the territory around Fort Jytock are outside the moral geography of the Empire, where neither the landscape nor an identity can be cultivated. Unlike the likeliness of the pastoral and imperial georgic genres in which the creolized landscapes could be reproduced and represented, there is (and ought to be) no correspondence between the frontier/interior and the metropolis. It is, therefore, remote in another sense too – this is neither the picturesque vantage of a hill town retreat nor the sublime experience of an expedition, it is the ambivalence of remoteness that conceals more than it reveals. Such a landscape can also be distinguished from the experience and representation of American colonization and the Westward expansion of the frontier (Truettner 1991). Because of its crypto-colonial nature, Fort Jytock and its surrounding territory can neither emulate nor represent the geography of moral improvement like the creolized landscape or the 'settled West' does. Rather than the articulation of 'Manifest Destiny' assured in the images of the *West as America* (Truettner 1991), the representation of such ambivalent landscapes like *Fort Jytock* swings between the desire for control and the anxiety of the unknown, which is best represented through the landscape aesthetics of remoteness.[12] The representation of *Fort Jytock*, therefore, continuously contends with the tension of limiting and expanding territory which appears remote, not only in the sense of the rhetoric of distance that the expansion of the Empire into the colonies produces (i.e. the discourse on distance in time and 'civilization') but also the friction of distance (i.e. the distance in terms of physical speed and time), which is evident in most of the landscape paintings of the Indian Himalayas.

In his seminal study on *Communication and Colonialism in Eastern India*, Sinha (2012) suggests that the term 'interior' signified the commercial attributes, politico-administrative purposes and the sociological context (Sinha 2012: 22) of the spaces it enclosed – resource-rich sites that were neither materially nor morally developed. He is equally apt in pointing out that such a mobilization of the term 'interior' only became sharply focused by building upon the gaze of the 'general travellers and sojourning administrators' of the late eighteenth century. The journeys of such travellers and administrators were materially charted out on the same routes and through the same networks as the ones before them, thereby disciplining the gaze of the 'imperial eyes' (Pratt 1992). Therefore, places that could not be reached into or accessed through such a gaze continued to be characterized and conditioned as *remote*.

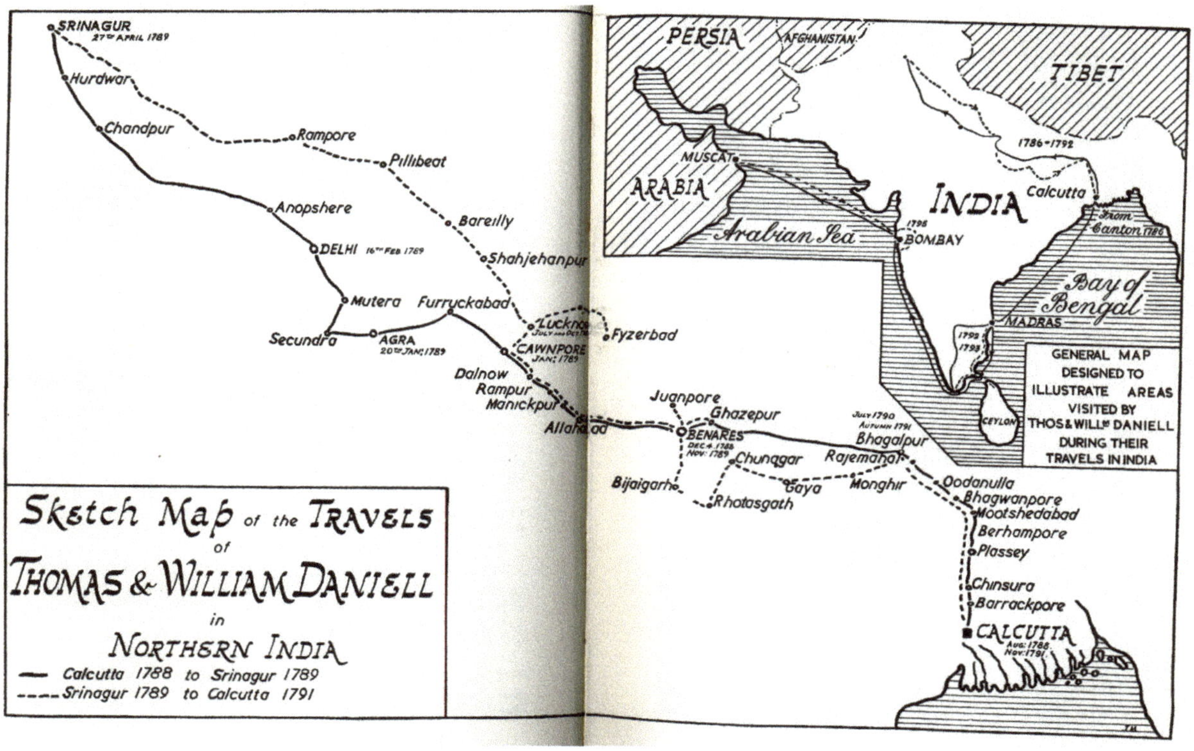

Figure 8: Route map of the travels of Thomas and William Daniell, 1789-1791 (Sutton 1954).

Most of such general travellers and sojourning administrators, including James Fraser and the Daniells arrived in India at the coast to one of the ports. Taking the coastal settlements and presidency capitals as the 'centre', the act of travelling inwards and upwards to the mainland, became an act of going into the 'interiors' (Sinha 2012: 33). Travelling to such interiors also lent credibility to the account of the 'imperial gaze', especially if one presented oneself as the 'first one' to arrive and describe the interior, constructing it to evoke the truth about the place itself. Fraser's admission of 'being recognized as the first European who had *penetrated* to several of the scenes described' (v: emphasis mine) especially 'respecting a tract of country so very little known' (v) provides us with a sense of how Fraser's travel into and upwards the country was framed by him as a travel into the unknown 'interior' of which –

> The physical difficulties are so great, and the obstacles to making such results available to the public so numerous, that a very long time will, in all probability, elapse before any description of it can appear, and till then, even so unsatisfactory an attempt as the present may be received with indulgence. (vii)

Thus, Fraser's account and representation of landscape was not only meant to discipline the native landscape but also the gaze of the subsequent travellers especially if Fraser was to continue being considered as the 'first' European to most of these sites in the North-western Indian Himalayas. However, given the cause of settling the frontiers, which was the primary aim of the troops and administrative officers that Fraser was travelling and touring with, it is interesting to note how the frontier could be rendered as the interior and the interior as the frontier. A characterization of the landscape and of the natives of the landscape as synonymous with each other constitutes an interesting dialectic of characterizing it as far out on the frontier while also attributing to it the kind of insular nature usually associated with the interior.

The aesthetics of remoteness exemplified in the Company landscape paintings which I have described here also become the premise for their incorporation into the nationalized geography of India, akin to the analysis of Harms et al which describe remoteness as 'a category subject to transformation by state agendas, majority politics, economic interests, and contested identities' (2014). In the nationalised geography of India, the Himalayas are evaluated through the remoteness of frontiers and sacrality which are also the grounds for their integration into the nationalized cartography of India – as the guards of the Indian territory and also the source of its Hinduized sacred geography. The landscape aesthetic of remoteness and travel writing makes the distance malleable to the project of postcolonial nationalism such that remote areas become most crucial to the nationalist cartographic imagination.

The landscape aesthetic of remoteness doesn't translate only as a genre but as a political aesthetic that informs the colonial view of the territory and its transformation as well as the postcolonial making of the nation-state. As Harms et al rightly point out, geographical distance is no longer the mainstay of remoteness in anthropology and 'may be present in any site of anthropological inquiry' (2014: 361). However, an aesthetic of remoteness that I have established through the study of Company landscape paintings and travel writing makes the distance malleable to the project of postcolonial nationalism such that remote areas become most crucial to the nationalist cartographic imagination. In her study of the mapping of 'Mother India' across media, Ramaswamy (2010) demonstrates how images do not merely represent history but also produce it. The landscape aesthetic of remoteness produced through the colonial paintings of the Himalayan region reifies remoteness and is also a cartographic exercise in the transformation of the landscape. Remoteness is a crucial historical characterization of the region and its landscape which is continually reproduced despite the material transformations in connectivity and mobility. The frontier geography of the Himalayas impart it a significant geopolitical value, yet one that is characterised predominantly by its mountainous terrain and unease of accessibility. The construction of remoteness therefore entails the contradictions of making something, that can be easily worked into the nationalized territorial imagination, 'remote'. Remoteness, ironically, also provides the ground for integration into broader geographies.

Bhoomika Joshi is Assistant Professor at the South Asian Studies Programme (SASP), National University of Singapore (NUS). bjoshi@nus.edu.sg

I would like to acknowledge the guidance, comments and suggestions I received from Timothy Barringer, Jennifer Raab, Holly Shaffer and Tiraana Bains on the earlier versions of this paper and the support from the staff at the Yale Centre for British Art, with much gratitude. I would also like to thank the reviewer for *Himalaya* for their feedback and engagement with the paper.

Endnotes

1. William Hodges is credited as the earliest landscape painter followed by Francis Swain Ward, Thomas and William Daniell, Samuel Davis, George Chinnery, William Carpenter and Edward Lear among others (Tillotson 1990). James Fraser, while working on his drawings of the Himalayas in 1817 and sending them to London from Calcutta benefited from the friendship and guidance of William Havell, a professional artist who had accompanied Lord Amherst's embassy to China in 1815-17 as the official draughtsman. Upon his return to England, Havell was employed by his uncle, Rodwell and Martin to engrave the paintings for Fraser's Views in the Himala Mountains, which was published in 1820. James Fraser credited Havell in the preface of his journal without naming him – 'the author enjoyed the advice of an eminent artist of this country during the period he was engaged in many of the later ones' (1820a: 3). After Havell's departure from Calcutta, James

Fraser took lessons from George Chinnery. For further information on James Fraser's time in India, please see Archer and Falk (1989). It is clear that even as an amateur landscape painter, Fraser was embedded in the network of British landscape painters who guided, encouraged and helped publish his work in the early nineteenth century.

2. James B. Fraser also produced another set of paintings on the views of the city of Calcutta published as Views of Calcutta and its Environs by Rodwell and Martin in London, 1824-6.

3. Rodwell and Martin, who published Fraser's travel journal advertised the aquatint plates as being uniform with Daniell's Oriental Scenery (1795-1808). According to Archer and Falk, 'the publishers can have had little doubt that the journal and its attendant plates of the foothills of the Himalayas which Thomas Daniell had included in part IV of the Oriental Scenery, of which no views of the area had hitherto been published' (1989: 49).

4. The Anglo-Gurkha war was fought on many fronts and Major General Martindell led the charge at Jaithak (Jytock). Martindell was appointed in place of General Gillespie after his death in December 1814 at Kalanga. The other fronts of the war were Makwanpur Gadhi, Jitgadh, Hariharpur Gadhi and Nalapani. The war ended with the signing of the Treaty of Sugauli in March 1816 by the arrangement of which the territories of Kumaun, Garhwal and Sikkim were ceded to the Company, and Nepal accepted the appointment of a British Resident in Kathmandu.

5. William and James Fraser set off on a long tour through the lower Himalayas in May 1815 while the siege of Jytock stagnated under General Martindell (Archer and Falk 1989)

6. The reproduction of the picturesque landscape of Indian cities like Delhi, Calcutta, Bombay and Madras and of the architectural heritage of Mughal and Deccan architecture (among others) across such spaces can be achieved since it can be rendered historical for it is shaped by the Company's colonial encounter with these sites in India along with the systems of administration and governance they inherited and built upon. However, the pre-colonial history of areas like the India-Nepal frontier did not constitute history in the same sense and therefore could be best explained as remote and too remote to be history.

7. See Raab (2015) for the 'aesthetics of detail' in nineteenth century American landscape painting and its significance to the contemporary scientific discourse.

8. For further information on land revenue systems and disputes between the Company and Nepal, please see Michael (2013)

9. Such an account also helps us situate the construction of the Gurkha identity prior to and after the Anglo-Nepalese war (1814-16). The term Gurkha itself has a history of inventive efforts by Prithvi Narayan Shah, the king of Nepal (1762-74) who consolidated the Gurkha identity and rule over Nepal in the late eighteenth century. Prithvi Narayan Shah recruited from various 'hill tribes' to constitute the Gurkha army and assimilated various traditions in their training, disciplining and naming – among them being the influence of the European and Mughal military practices such as drills, colours and firelocks like the English army and a payment in the form of jagir like the Mughal army. Therefore, the Gurkhas that the English naturalized as a 'martial race' were themselves the product of a historical moment in Nepal.

10. The term 'martial race' ostensibly gained currency among the British administrators and military strategists after the 1857 rebellion when large numbers of British trained soldiers rebelled against the Company. Some groups that had remained loyal to the company were classified as 'martial' whereas the rest as non-martial.

11. The distinction between a political-economic view and a military-pragmatic or geo-political view is neither exhaustive nor exclusive. While the aim and efforts of the Company troops to settle the India-Nepal frontier in the run-up to the Anglo-Nepalese war to contain the growing influence of the Russian Empire towards Central Asia may be seen as a geo-political tactic, it was also an important manoeuvre to gain a foothold in Nepal to establish trade prospects into Tibet and further, a political-economic aspect. However, by pointing out these distinctions, this section wants to take into account the differences in the emphasis of the view

and representation of the landscape and not necessarily the modus operandi of mercantile-imperialism itself.

12. For a study of colonialism and landscape paintings, it is extremely important to distinguish between the experience of settler colonialism, non-settler colonialism (or franchise colonialism) and crypto-colonialism, rather than paint them with a broad-brush understanding of colonized landscapes. Such a distinction not only takes into account the historical specificity of the colonial experience in regions as different as North America and Australia (settler colonialism), India and Israel-Palestine (non-settler colonialism) and Nepal and Greece (crypto-colonialism) but also the diversity of their contemporaneous experience informed by such histories. For further discussion, please see Patrick Wolfe (2006).

References

Archer, M. 1980. *Early views of India: the picturesque journeys of Thomas and William Daniell 1786-1794*. London: Thames and Hudson

Archer, M. 1969. *British drawings in the India Office Library*. (Commonwealth Office.) 2 vols London: H.M.S.O.

Archer, M. & Falk, T. 1989. *India Revealed: The Art and Adventures of James and William Fraser 1801-35*. London, New York: Cassell.

Ardener, E. 1987, 2012. "Remote areas" Some theoretical considerations. *HAU: Journal of Ethnographic Theory, 2*(1): 519-533.

Arnold, D. 2006. *The tropics and the traveling gaze: India, landscape, and science, 1800 1856*. Seattle: University of Washington Press.

Alavi, S. 1995. *The Sepoys and the Company: Tradition and Transition in Northern India, 1770-1830*. Delhi: Oxford University Press.

Banerjee, S. 2014. "Not altogether unpicturesque: Samuel Bourne and the landscaping of the Victorian Himalaya", *Victorian Literature and Culture, 42*(03): 351-368.

Barua, P. 1995. Inventing Race: The British and India's Martial Races. *The Historian, 58*(1): 107-116.

Bayly, C.A. 1996. *Empire and information: intelligence gathering and social communication in India, 1780-1870*. Cambridge: Cambridge University Press.

Besky, S. 2013. *The Darjeeling distinction: Labor and justice on fair-trade tea plantations in India*. Berkeley: University of California Press.

Caplan, L. 1995. *Warrior gentlemen: 'Gurkhas' in the western imagination*. Oxford: Berghahn Books.

Colley, A. C. 2010. *Victorians in the mountains: Sinking the Sublime*. Farnham and Burlington: Ashgate.

Cosgrove, D. and Daniels, S. eds. 1988. *The iconography of landscape: essays on the symbolic representation, design and use of past environments*. Cambridge: Cambridge University Press.

Daniell, T. and Daniell, W. 1807. *Oriental scenery. Twenty-four views in Hindoostan, taken in the years 1789 and 1790*. London: Robert Bowyer.

Des Chene, M.K. 1999. Military Ethnology in British India. *South Asia Research, 19*(2): 121-135.

Das Chene, M.K. 1991. *Relics of Empire: A cultural history of Gurkhas 1815-1987*. Doctoral Dissertation: Stanford University.

De Certeau, Michel. 1984. *The Practice of Everyday Life*, Berkeley and Los Angeles: University of California Press.

Fraser, J.B. 1820a. *Journal of a Tour Through Part of the Snowy Range of the Himala Mountains, and to the Sources of the Rivers Jumna and Ganges*. London: Rodwell and Martin.

Fraser, J.B. 1820b. *Views in the Himala Mountains*. London: Rodwell and Martin.

Harms, E., Hussain, S., Newell, S., Piot, C., Schein, L., Shneiderman, S., Turner, T. and Zhang, J. 2014. Remote and edgy: New takes on old anthropological themes. *HAU:*

Journal of Ethnographic Theory, *4*(1): 361-381.

Herzfeld, M. 2002. The absence presence: Discourses of crypto-colonialism. *The South Atlantic Quarterly*, *101*(4): 899-926.

Kanwar, P. 1999. *Essays on Urban Patterns in Nineteenth Century Himachal Pradesh*. Shimla: Indian Institute of Advanced Study.

Kennedy, D. K. 1996. *The magic mountains: Hill stations and the British Raj*. Berkeley and Los Angeles: University ofCalifornia Press.

King, A. D. 1976. *Colonial urban development: Culture, social power and environment*. London: Routledge & Paul.

Mathur, N., 2015. A 'remote 'town in the Indian Himalaya. *Modern Asian Studies*, *49*(2): 365-392.

Michael, B. A. 2012. *Statemaking and Territory in South Asia: Lessons from the Anglo-Gorkha War (1814-1816)*. London and New York: Anthem Press.

Mitchell, W. J. T. 1994. *Landscape and power*. Chicago: University of Chicago Press.

Montogomery, C.A. 1998. *The Gurkhas and Colonial Knowledge: Habitat. Masculinity and the Making of a 'Martial Race', c. 1760-1830*. Graduate Dissertation: University of Calgary.

Pradhan, Q. 2007. 'Empire in the Hills The Making of Hill Stations in Colonial India'. *Studies in History*, *23*(1): 33-91.

Pratt, M. L. 1992. *Imperial eyes: Travel writing and transculturation*. London: Routledge.

Quilley, G., 2003. 'Pastoral plantations: the slave trade and the representation of British colonial landscape in the late eighteenth century'. In *An Economy of Colour: Visual Culture and the Atlantic World, 1660-1830*, edited by G. Quilley and K.D. Kriz, pp.106-128. Manchester and New York: Manchester University Press.

Ray, R. 2013. *Under the Banyan Tree: Relocating the Picturesque in British India*. New Haven: YaleUniversity Press.

Raab, J., 2015. *Frederic Church: The Art and Science of Detail*. New Haven: Yale University Press.

Shellim, M. 1979. *Oil paintings of India and the east by Thomas Daniell 1749-1840 and William Daniell 1769-1837*. London: Inchcape & Co.

Sinha, N. 2012. *Communication and colonialism in eastern India: Bihar, 1760s-1880s*. London and New York: Anthem Press.

Sutton, 1954. *The Daniells; artists and travellers*. London: Bodley Head.

Tillotson, G.H.R. 1990. 'The Indian Picturesque: Images of India in British Landscape Painting, 1780-1880'. In *Raj: India and the British, 1600-1947*, edited by C. Bayly, pp. 141-151 National Portrait Gallery: London.

Truettner, W. H. 2010. *Painting Indians and Building Empires in North America, 1710-1840*. Berkeley: University of California Press.

Truettner, William H. 1991. *'The West as America: Reinterpreting images of the frontier 1820-1920*. Washington: Smithsonian Press.

White, R. 1991. *The middle ground: Indians, empires, and republics in the Great Lakes region, 1650-1815*. Cambridge: Cambridge University Press.

Wolfe, P., 2006. Settler Colonialism and the Elimination of the Native. *Journal of genocide research*, *8*(4): 387-409.

HIMALAYA
The Journal of the Association of Nepal and Himalayan Studies

Research Article

Buddhist and Shia Identity in Ladakh

Patrick Kaplanian
kaplanianpatrick@hotmail.com

DOI: https://doi.org/10.2218/himalaya.2025.10173

Abstract

There are many ways to define Ladakh: geographically (as an area between the Himalayas and the Karakoram), historically (as a kingdom from the 10th century until the Dogra conquest in 1834), or linguistically (as a region sharing a common language—a Tibetan dialect). However, most of these definitions have been put forward by foreigners or officials. Do the inhabitants of these areas feel that they belong to the same community? The author's answer is "no." He concludes that Shi'as in Kargil and Buddhists in Leh consider themselves to constitute separate communities. The survey draws on sociology, ethnology, and some history, extending back to 1931.

Keywords

Ladakh, Buddhism, Islam, Purig, Baltistan, Shiism

Recommended Citation

Kaplanian, Patrick (2025). Buddhist and Shia Identity in Ladakh. *HIMALAYA* 44(1): 146-163.

This work is licensed under a Creative Commons Attribution-Noncommercial-No Derivative Works 4.0 License.

Introduction

Ladakh lies between the Himalayas and the Karakorum, and its people speak a Tibetan dialect. Before its conquest by the Hindu maharaja of Jammu (1834), it was an independent kingdom. The maharaja then acquired Kashmir, a region with a Muslim majority, from the British, forming the state of Jammu and Kashmir (J&K). In 1947, part of J&K was conquered by Pakistan, and the remaining part was attached to India.

From 1947 to 1979, Ladakh was a single district; then, from 1979 to 2019, it was divided into two districts, Kargil and Leh. While the majority of Kargilis (or Purigis—their region is also called Purig) are Twelver Shi'as, the district of Leh is dominated by Buddhists of the Tibetan type (Vajrayana or Lamaism). There is also a Sunni minority in both districts; in Leh, they are known as the Argon.

The question considered in this paper is whether Shi'as and Buddhists feel that they belong to a single community. One can take as a reference Renan's famous phrase (1997 [1882]) when he states that nations are formed through the voluntary association of individuals with a common past who "have done great things together and want to do more" ("avoir fait de grandes choses ensemble, vouloir en faire encore"). Do Ladakhi Buddhists and Shi'as want to do things together?

The question is *a priori* a matter for sociology and takes as its model studies such as those of Hobsbawm (1992), Detienne (2010), Anderson (1996)[1], and especially Thiesse (2001). But it is also a matter of ethnology, as we shall see in relation to the definition of identity through myths of origin and rituals, as well as histories. In attempting to answer the question, I will have to go back to 1931.

History

In 1931, riots broke out between Hindus and Muslims in Kashmir. A commission headed by Sir B. J. Glancy was charged with finding the causes and remedies (Lamb 1993; Bertelsen 1996: 118). Since the Buddhist Ladakhis had no organization of their own to represent them before the Glancy Commission, the Kashmir Raj Boddhi Maha Sabha (KRBMS) did so. The KRBMS was a handful of non-Ladakhi modernist Buddhist intellectuals who mainly made demands concerning education (Bertelsen 1996: 119).

In 1933, the Ladakhi Buddhists established their own association, the Ladakh Buddhist Educational Society (LBES). The vice-president was a member of the family of the Leh *kalhon* (*bka'blon*).[2] There was also an executive of the Hemis monastery, the most important one in Ladakh. The LBES once again made demands about education. They were again rejected.

In 1934 Maharaja Hari Singh established a consultative assembly. Two seats were given to the Buddhists of Ladakh. One of them was none other than the "king," heir to the crown, whose ancestors had not reigned since 1834.

After the LBES, the Young Men's Buddhist Association (YMBA) was created. The "king" was the president, and the *kalhon* of Leh was the vice president (Bertelsen 1996: 146-147).

In 1947, after the integration of J&K into the Indian Union, the Muslim Kashmiris, the most numerous, became the majority through universal suffrage. They were represented by the National Conference (NC) led by Sheikh Abdullah. The YMBA presented a memorandum in which it expressed its rejection of Kashmir as well as Pakistan. In other words: anything but integration into a Muslim state (Bertelsen 1996: 164). But Nehru, the Indian Prime Minister, had made a deal with Sheikh Abdullah: Kashmir accepted absorption by India in exchange for strong autonomy and the integrity of the Indian part of J&K. If he wanted *pax cashmirica*, Nehru had no choice but to accept the conditions of the Sheikh. And a few tens of thousands of Ladakhis weighed little in this deal. This agreement implied the maintenance of Article 370 of the Constitution negotiated by the maharaja at the time of the attachment of J&K to India, according to which only a resident of J&K could buy land, set up a business, or become a civil servant in the state.

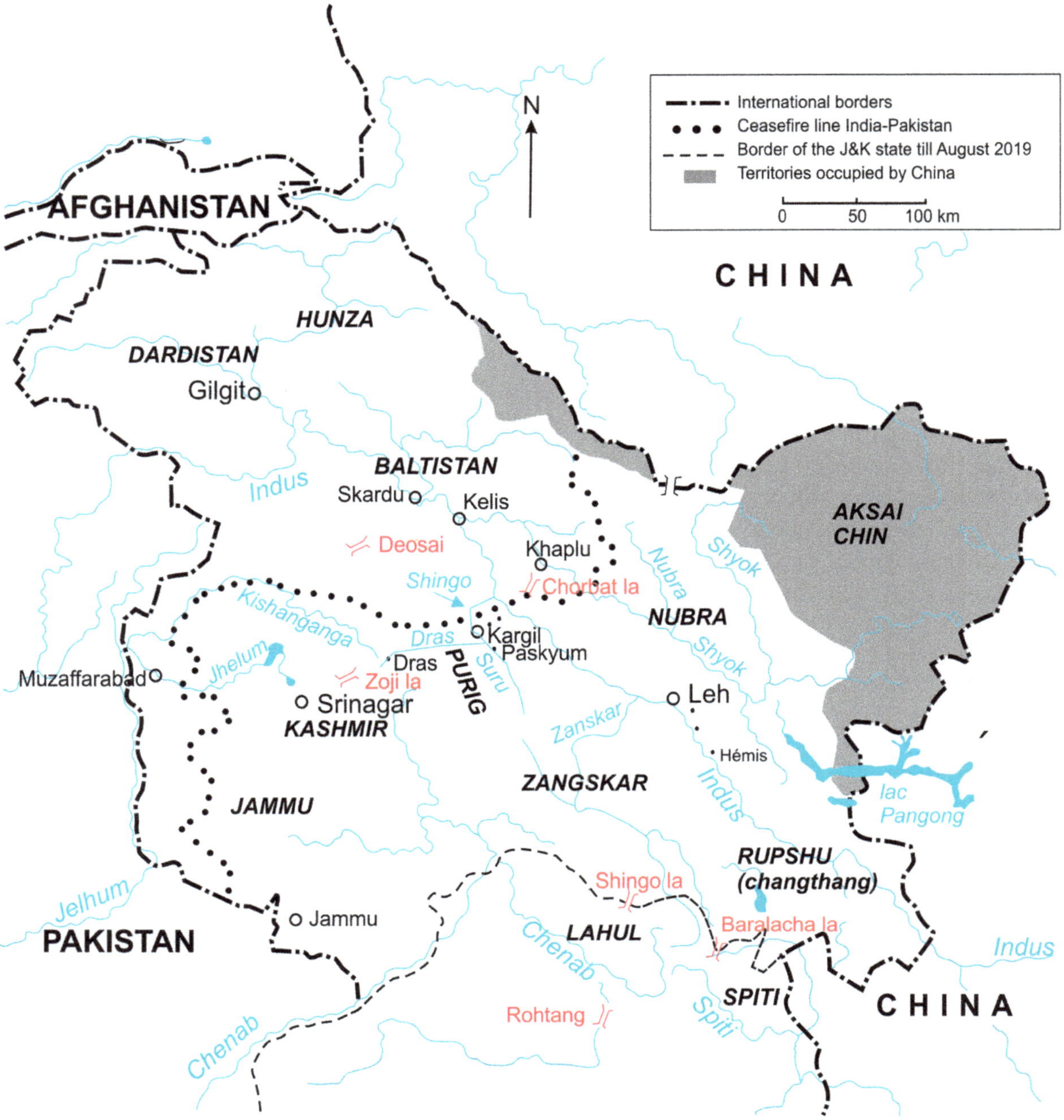

Figure 1: J&K from 1947 untill August 5, 2019

In May 1949, a Ladakhi delegation led by Bakula Rinpoche[3] went to Nehru in Delhi with a memorandum that stated, "We are a separate nation by all the tests—race, language, religion, culture—determining nationality" (Bertelsen 1996: 165-166). He added, "The right to self-determination claimed by us cannot be claimed with equal force by the people [of districts] predominantly peopled by Muslims (...)." Clearly, religion took precedence over other criteria.

In 1952, Bakula proposed to separate the Buddhists and the Muslims into two separate administrative units. And, prophetically, he added, "The past attitude of the Baltis [Ladakhi Shi'as] people, however, renders it quite likely that they may have no desire for internal autonomy, and they may even prefer to be administratively aligned with the adjoining district of Kashmir" (Bertelsen 1996: 177).

In 1967, Bakula won the Ladakh MP[4] seat in the New Delhi parliament. His right-hand man, Sonam Wangyal, won the MLA[5] seat in the Srinagar parliament. The LBA, successor of the YMBA, had become the main

Buddhist association. In 1977, the "queen" became an MP.

In 1979, Leh district was divided to form two districts: Leh and Kargil. Leh was 80 percent Buddhist, and Kargil, the second largest city in Ladakh, was 80 percent Muslim, mainly Shi'a.

In 1980, an *All-Ladakh Action Committee for Declaring Ladakh as a Scheduled Tribe*[6] (LAC) was formed. It was a true pan-Ladakh movement in terms of its composition. There were Buddhists, Sunnis, Shi'as, people from Leh, and Kargilis. During the years 1980-1982, the LAC unceasingly demanded "Scheduled Tribe (ST) Status."

In 1986-87, a "mini-census" was conducted. For Ladakhis to obtain scheduled tribe status, they must be divided into "tribes."[7]

The LAC was soon overtaken by the *Ladakh Buddhist Association* (LBA), which created a youth branch, established itself in the villages, and entered the professional unions, such as vehicle owners, travel agents, and hoteliers (van Beek 1996: 303). On 18 July 1989, the LBA held a meeting and passed a resolution. It read "Realizing that Ladakh has always been treated as a colony and Ladakhis as a third-rate citizens of J&K State {sic] and, accordingly, Ladakh having been neglected in every sphere of life socially, politically and economically, we firmly resolve to launch a movement for an alternative administrative setup wherein the ethnic cultural and traditional identity of Ladakhis is safeguarded and that alternative is in declaring Ladakh as a Union Territory" (van Beek 1996: 310).

At the same time, a *Ladakh People's Movement for Union Territory Status* (LPMUT) was formed. At a press conference in Delhi, LPMUT leaders declared that they excluded Sunnis from their movement but welcomed Shi'as, especially from Kargil. The argument was that the Shi'as are true natives, who have been there for centuries, while the Sunnis, the Argons, are outsiders.

On 30 July, a *Kargil Action Committee* was formed. It soon made known its reluctance to accept the LBA's claims. Clearly, the two main religious communities were becoming organized, each with its own representative association (van Beek 1996: 312). Again, religion seemed to take precedence over all other criteria.

From August 7, 1989 onwards, constant demonstrations were orchestrated by the LBA. Convoys of trucks, buses, and taxis were attacked. On August 27, the local police (mainly Kashmiri) opened fire, killing three people and injuring 80 others. The next day, Thupstan Chhewang (LBA president) was arrested. Security was taken away from the J&K police and handed over to the central government. The army was put on alert. The LBA called for a strike and civil disobedience. A boycott was imposed on Muslims. It was forbidden for any Buddhist to buy or sell or have any dealings with a Muslim.

On October 8, ST status was finally granted. Thus, the eight "tribes" of Ladakh were declared ST. Sunnis were excluded from this status. Thupstan Chhewang was released. However, the central government announced that UT status was absolutely excluded. The LBA continued to press for Union Territory (UT) status (including the Shi'as of Kargil). On October 27, it organized a huge rally of 10,000 people.

On October 29, negotiations took place between the Center, the State, and the LBA. Instead of UT status, the central government proposed Hill Council (HC) status. This would provide strong autonomy within the framework of J&K, whereas the UT status would have meant reporting to New Delhi. The principle of the HC was agreed upon. In exchange, the LBA consented to lift the boycott. Since the Shi'as in Kargil had refused the hand extended by the Buddhists in Leh, the HC status remained limited to the Leh district.

The Muslim perspective

Until 1989, the Muslim community around Kargil had hardly manifested itself as such. Before 1989, there were no texts, pamphlets, or similar materials. Nor have there been any groups comparable to the YMBA. Instead, Muslims organized themselves into foundations (*anjuman*) creating schools, orphanages, and dispensaries. Two are found in Kargil: the *Jamia Ulama Isna Asharia*, better known as the *Islamiya School*, founded in 1953, and the *Imam Khomeini Memorial Trust* (IKMT), founded in 1989 (Gupta 2014: 380).

In 1989, the Muslim view was expressed in a pamphlet entitled *History repeated in Ladakh*.[8] The text rebuts the accusation that Muslims are carrying out forced conversions. It says that the percentage of Buddhists is decreasing due to polyandry and monasticism and that the hand extended to the Shi'as is intended to divide the Muslims (p. 6). This assertion is followed by a long list of attacks and molestations of Muslims in recent months. In this text, the Muslim community defends itself as such. There is not a single mention of Ladakhis as such, Buddhists and Muslims combined.

The text is followed by a memorandum that begins by presenting Ladakhis as, "a people who profess Islam and Buddhism in equal numeral strength and yet speak the same language in different phonetic forms, share the same cultural roots and lifestyle despite the difference in faith. The text goes on to accuse extremist Buddhists of having "severely damaged the cohesive traditions."

Then comes a third text entitled *Leh-Kargil and Zanskari*[9] *Action Committee for Scheduled Tribe*. It is dated October 16, 1989. Here again, the text begins by stating that the two religions were living in harmony and adds, against all evidence, that "the language, the dress and the general life-style of Buddhists and Muslims are identical." (p. 29). This is followed by a long list of attacks on Muslims in recent years.

As we can see, after the formal concessions regarding the existence of a Ladakhi community across the divide between the two religions, these texts are grievances against the Buddhist community and *pro domo* pleas from the Muslim community.

Birth of the Hill Council (HC)

At the end of 1991, the boycott had been going on for two years. Negotiations began between the LBA and the governor. At the end of 1992, the LBA finally lifted the boycott.

The *Ladakh Autonomous Hill Development Council Act* was finally published on May 9, 1995. This was for the Leh district only, but it was intended that the Kargil district would be able to obtain HC status whenever it wanted (van Beek 1996: 360).[10]

The powers vested in this council were considerable. They included the disposition, reclamation, and distribution of all virgin lands; the drafting of a budget and a development plan; and the promotion of languages and cultures. The council could levy taxes and recruit civil servants, except for those of very high rank and those of the judiciary and the police (van Beek 1999: 440-441). However, the J&K government also had considerable restraining powers. The plan, the budget, and other matters had to be accepted by the state government.

First comments

Many thoughts come to mind after this first purely chronological overview.

1. The first point is the clear dominance of the nobility and high clergy. After an initial attempt by the neo-Buddhists to take their affairs into their own hands, the representation of the Ladakhis was soon controlled by the high clergy and the nobility. It was the *rinpoche* of Hemis who gave his endorsement to the KRBMS. He was the most important figure in the Buddhist clergy at that time. When the LBES was created, the "king" presided over it, assisted by a member of the family of the *kalhon*.[11] This was then the case with the YMBA, of which the king was the president. When the king was appointed to the J&K assembly, he was succeeded by the *kalhon*.

After the *rinpoche* of Hemis, the king and the *kalhon*, Bakula *rinpoche* became the main political leader of the Buddhist Ladakhis. It was always a *rinpoche* who had the upper hand in Ladakhi politics. Bakula was related to the younger branch of the royal family, that of Matho (Kaplanian 2020a). The last on this list of Ladakhi leaders is Thupstan Chhewang, president of the LBA and later president of the HC. Chhewang encapsulates the whole high religious and noble hierarchy. He is a *rinpoche*, and the reincarnation of a *rinpoche* from the village of Nyoma. His mother was the sister of Bakula Rinpoche. Moreover, he belongs to the family of the *lhonpo*[12] of Shey, and he married the daughter of the "king". But, at the same time, he marks the transition to a more modern elite. He was educated first in Benares, then in Delhi, before practicing law in Jammu (Bertelsen 1996: 190).

Thus, traditional mentalities are manifested by the attachment not only to the person of a king who, for many years, has not reigned, but also to a whole hierarchy, including the *kalhon, lhonpo*, and *rinpoche*s, which is archaic, medieval, and even feudal. The persistence of these mentalities is an aspect that struck most of the ethnologists who started working in Ladakh in the 1970s. Listening to the Ladakhis, one sometimes had the impression that the king still reigned.[13]

2. This traditional society is predominantly Buddhist, and the Buddhist identity constantly resurfaces. Let us look again at the events. When the Glancy Commission asked each religious community to come forward, the KRBMS answered "present" in the name of the Buddhists. The *rinpoche* of Hemis replied on behalf of the Buddhist Ladakhis.

Then came the war with Pakistan. Absorption by Pakistan was the Buddhists' greatest fear. Close behind was the fear of being in a J&K in which Muslim Kashmiris were in the majority. It was expressed in the YMBA memorandum of 1947, which I have already summarized as follows: "anything but Pakistan or Kashmir." Then, in 1949, the Bakula Rinpoche delegation said, "We are a separate nation..."

Bakula's position hardened after the 1969 agitation. In his letter to the PM co-signed by 20 other MPs he wrote, "The local Buddhist population has completely lost faith in the local administration, which is exclusively composed of Muslim officials who (...) not only connived but encouraged violence and atrocities committed by the local Muslim population against the Buddhists" (van Beek 1996: 229).

How the Communities Represent Themselves

The various texts, pamphlets, and memoranda published by the religious or political organizations or their leaders are insufficient to fully assess the communities' views. Only in-depth studies can determine whether the inhabitants of each region feel they belong to the same community. We have such access to such studies, namely, the origin myth of the Buddhist Ladakhis and the thesis of Nicola Grist (1998).

Origin myth of the Buddhist Ladakhis

The myth (Kaplanian 1981, 1983, and 1991) tells that three Shina[14] came from present-day North Pakistan to hunt. In their hats, they had some barley grains, which they dropped. When they returned the following year, the barley had grown in abundance. Amazed, they decided to settle here. More men came from all over. It was a golden age of abundance. They lived in the company of the *lha*, the minor deities. But soon the situation degenerated. After the golden age came the fall. Men became evil, and the deities left them. Misery and famine followed.

It was then that human civilization developed, accompanied by work and technology. An arrow was shot, and the first irrigation canal was built at the spot where it landed. Spontaneous abundance was over. From now on, the land would have to be worked.

The conversion to Buddhism and the establishment of the social hierarchy were accomplished in two stages. First, a *lhonpo* unified the country under his control. Second, the son of the king of Western Tibet inherited Ladakh and introduced Buddhism and monarchy.

The key points emerging from this myth can be summarized as follows:

1. That, according to the Buddhist perspective, Ladakhi identity is the result of a fusion between two peoples: those who came from northern Pakistan and the Tibetans who brought Buddhism and kingship. Ladakhi Buddhists do not consider their country to be a simple extension of Tibet.
2. That Buddhism is inseparable from the monarchy and both are inseparable from the Ladakhi identity.

Grist's study of the Suru Valley and Kargil

Thanks to the work of Grist (1998), we can now examine the Shi'a viewpoint. Grist's study mainly covers the Suru Valley, home to 25 percent of the population of Kargil district. She also made incursions into the "city" of Kargil, about which she gives us quite a bit of information.

The tone is set from the beginning: the Muslims of Kargil and the Suru define themselves as being in "*contradistinction*" with other peoples of the region, especially the Buddhists (p. 54). Grist notes that the main question a foreigner is asked is, "Do you burn or bury your dead?" which means, "Are you Buddhist or Muslim?"

The conclusion is very clear: "Kargili Muslims see themselves as forming a community that is separate even from Muslims from other areas" (p. 267). The Kargil Muslims have no sense of community with the Buddhists of Leh and even consider the Muslims of the latter region and the Kashmiris as outsiders. On the other hand, the Sunnis and Shi'as in Kargil seem to form a close community. We shall see that this was indeed the case until recently.

How can the Kargili identity be defined? And how can its evolution be gauged? Grist gives us three criteria: a) history as told by the informants themselves, and culture b) social organization c) language, or rather languages, of which I will speak a little later.

History and culture

It is clear that most Kargilis (Purigis) consider that they were Buddhists at one time before converting to Islam (p. 54, cf. also Sagaster, 1989: 21). Today, all traditions, epics, music, and songs, are rejected. This rejection of the Buddhist past and the mythology linked to it is recent.[15] According to the clerics, these traditions are non-Muslim customs and therefore sins (*nyespa; nyes pa*) (p. 100)[16]. This has resulted in the disappearance of professional musicians (p. 100, and Rizvi 1981: 228). Writing fifteen years later, Gupta confirms that music and dance are *haram* (forbidden). And she adds, "activists lament, for instance, the loss of a repertoire of Purigi folk songs" (2013: 46).

Social (and kinship) organization of the Shi'as

In Suru, the most important social units are the village, the neighborhood (*khor* or *mohalla*) (p. 58), the *pa*, and the *phaspun* (*pha spun*). The importance of the village and the neighborhood is now well understood (Grist 1976-77 & 1979 and Kaplanian 1981). The *phaspun* of the Shi'as closely resembles the *khangpa* of the Buddhists, the undivided household in which three generation usually live. And the *pa* of the Shi'as is very similar to the *phaspun* of the Buddhists, i.e., a clan, united in certain circumstances. But a new institution appeared around the 1950s: the faction (p. 77). Each faction is headed by *sayyid* (descendants of the prophet) who bear the title of *rehbar*. The main *rehbar* lineages seem to have arrived from Kashmir during the twentieth century (p. 101). The ancestry of the *rehbar*s who lead a faction is carefully recorded in notebooks. Thus, the *rehbar*s of the Yokmapa faction claim descent from the Prophet via the eighth Shi'a Imam. They claim to have arrived in the Suru Valley eight generations ago (p. 101).[17]

The point here is that the faction has become the most important institution (p. 268). Not that the other institutions have disappeared; "a sense of history seems to have been relocated from the *pa* to the faction, and consequently the *pa* has ceased to be of any importance."

However, it can be argued that the rest of the Shi'a population at least recognizes the fact of their Buddhist ancestry. The *sayyid*, descendants of the prophet from the Middle East, are therefore foreigners? "Yes" and "no." Primarily "no". We know how traditions can "cheat" with history, even if it is mythical. As Grist writes, "The faction is the main kinship group for its members now, and it also acts as their lineage and history. Through their ties to the *rehbar*s, the faction members share their lineage back to the Prophet" (p. 268). "The leader of the faction is descended from the Prophet, and since we are part of this faction, it is kind of like we are descended from the Prophet; at least we are related to him enough to identify with that ancestry." (page 268).

Thus, not only do the *rehbar* carefully keep a record of the genealogy that traces them back to the Prophet, but it is read on some occasions: "The history of the line of Imams and their sufferings has become the history of faction members and of Suru to some extent" (p. 268). History has been rewritten.

It is now easy to understand why the Shi'as of Kargil finally refused the alliance with the LBA. In every respect, they see themselves as completely different from the Buddhists of Leh. The argument presented by the LBA (Shi'as are indigenous converts to Islam, unlike the Sunnis who came from elsewhere) might have been convincing at the time when Shi'as accepted their earlier Buddhist origin, were not divided into factions, and sang traditional Ladakhi songs at weddings. Then Ladakh's Buddhist and Shi'a ensemble had something of the appearance of a modern nation, with different religions but a common culture.

It is also likely that the LBA knew this. It was a matter of making a "national" argument because anything "communal" and, in particular, religious, was very much frowned upon. (See the linguistic argument of the Sikhs below).

Sunnis of Suru valley

The Sunnis of the Suru Valley consider themselves to be related to each other through a common semi-mythical ancestor, who is believed to have come from Kashmir. Indeed, most Sunnis seem to be of outside origin on the paternal side (Grist 1998: 138), the only side that counts for a patrilineal society.

For the moment, let us note that the Sunnis, unlike the Shi'as (except for the descendants of the prophet, of course), consider themselves to be of outside origin. Around 1980, that was the end of the matter. Sunnis and Shi'as were not distinguishable from each other and often intermarried (Grist 1998: p. 138). "They [Sunnis] were also virtually indistinguishable from Shi'as in terms of dress, language, and day-to-day activities (...). They also used to attend Shi'a religious observances such as *Muharram*.[18] Besides, they were all poor, and, from this point of view too, there were no notable differences" (page 138).

The situation changed with the introduction of positions in the civil service or with the development of infrastructure. In the Suru block alone, in the 1930s, the literacy rate was low, and those few adults who were literate used Arabic and/or Persian (p. 143). When schools began to be built, only, or almost only, the Sunnis took advantage of them. And when job opportunities arose, only Sunnis took advantage of them.

In the 1970s, Grist explains, the Yogmapa faction was mostly interested in a millenarian movement. A "hidden imam," it was said, would return repeatedly. The Yokmapas showed little interest in secular education or the expanding state economy until the 1980s. Shi'as realized what was happening—or rather what had happened—too late because most of the jobs to be created had already been created. Why the Sunni success? Grist gives several reasons:

1) Shia's have a stronger ideological connection to the land than Sunnis do (pp. 135-136).

2) Sunnis have less land, so demographic pressure has led them to earn their livelihood using means other than agriculture.

3) The Sunnis quickly took up Urdu. This brought them closer to the Kashmiris and opened the doors to an administration built on Urdu. It seems that the Shi'as, more attached to Arabic and Persian, had a different approach to education.

The difference between the models promoted by the two branches of Islam is considerable. For Sunnis, there is nothing wrong with finding "secular" jobs. For Shi'as, it is the acquisition of merits through religious education (meaning Arabic and Persian), reading texts, making donations, making pilgrimages to holy places, and studying religious topics in the Middle East, that is important. If financial resources are limited, then the madrassa will suffice.

In 1993, all the boys and most of the girls in the district were attending school. Unfortunately for the Shi'as, it was too late. The Sunnis had established themselves as the administrative elite, had taken over all the posts, and had locked up the system through cronyism, nepotism, and corruption (p. 153).

We can now understand why, on this precise point of access to administrative posts, and on this precise point only, the Shi'as of Kargil and the Buddhists of Leh found each other. With the status of ST, they were given priority in access to administrative jobs. It is also clear why the Sunnis were excluded. It is likely that the Sunnis were not eliminated from the ST status because of a mistake or clumsiness on the part of the "experts." It was because they were a micro-minority in the two districts and had acquired a dominant position that justified not granting them ST status, especially since their dominance provoked the fury of the two majority communities.

Thus, the following points begin to become clear:

- That Ladakh does not constitute a cultural unit. Their common history, the element that could have united the Buddhist and Shi'a populations of the two districts, is rendered ineffective because of a radically opposed reading of it by the two communities.
- That a rapprochement could be made with a precise aim, which was for both Buddhists and Shi'as to have their share of the administrative and governmental cake. However, the circumstantial nature of such a rapprochement meant that it could not lead to a lasting alliance, much less a merger.

There is no Ladakhi identity

Popular culture

In her commentary on van Beek's article (2003) Dollfus writes, "Every year, since the creation of the Leh Cultural Academy in 1969, native scholars have published several volumes of folksongs, folktales, local history, and customs to preserve what they themselves call Ladakhi culture. But those publications do not have a wide audience. In fact, for various reasons (spelling difficulties, lack of clear guidelines in schools, usefulness in Indian administration and daily practices, etc.) a large proportion of Ladakhis—both Buddhist and Muslims—can read or write Urdu or English, but are illiterate in their own language." (p. 305). In fact, on the Kargili side, this is hardly surprising, since we have seen that the clerics reject epics, music, and songs.

This is fundamental. Modern nations have built their identity on songs, tales, epics, and the establishment of a national language. Thiesse (2001) is a valuable reference in this respect, providing information on Dalmatian songs (p. 43), Herder's *Volkslieder* (German songs) (p. 43), as well as the Serbian (p. 84), Greek (p. 87), and Bulgarian (p. 101) folk songs. Nations can also rely on fairy tales such as the Romanian tales (p. 16) and epics such as *Die Nibelungen* (p. 32) or those published by the Brothers Grimm (*The Heroic Legend, German Mythology*: 66). When no folk tales can be found, or there are not enough, false epics are created, such as Ossian's *Fingal* (p. 25), the songs of Igor's troop (p. 44), and the Czech epics (p. 106). The same is true for songs: the *Guzla*, a collection of Serbian folk songs published in 1827, was actually written by Mérimée. However, for Ladakh, it is unnecessary to produce forgeries—all the elements: songs, epics (the epic of Kesar), and tales are there. Moreover, much of this material had already been published by Moravian missionaries.

Language

It remains to look at the language. In some European countries, it was necessary to forge a new language based on dialects. This was the case with Norwegian (Thiesse 2001: 73-75), Albanian (p. 112), and Estonian (p. 118). It was sometimes difficult to achieve this because of a lack of inter-comprehension between the dialects (for example, in Albania). In other cases, it was necessary to create a modern language from an old written language—the most obvious example is Hebrew (pp. 76-80)—or adapt a written language as in Germany and Italy (pp. 71-72). In Ladakh, there would have been no difficulty with the dialects; Leh and Kargil speakers understand one another.

Language according to the Buddhists: In a fascinating article (Bray and al. 2020) four authors describe the release of textbooks for Ladakh in classical Tibetan. The project was a failure. Ladakhi people still do not know classical Tibetan and are much better at Urdu.

The underlying model is that of Germany and Italy before reunification, or the Arab model today, i.e., separate states speaking to each other in different dialects that are not written and having a written language that is common even though it is mastered only by a minority.

This model could not work. Why not? Ladakhis are not Tibetans, as they state repeatedly. They admit their religion is the same as Tibet's, but the original myth presents the Ladakhi civilization as the result of syncretism between Shina and Tibetan cultures.[19]

Language according to the Muslims: The Purigi have never learned a single word of classical Tibetan. They consider classical Tibetan to be the language of Buddhism. What they rely on is Arabic, the language of the Koran, and Persian. The main *rehbar*s studied in the major centers of Iraq and Iran. (Grist 1998: 26). Thus, of the two leaders of the Yogmapa faction, Agha Miggi Ort and Agha Bagir, the latter is much less influential: "He has not studied in Iran or Iraq" (ibid.: 78). Thus, the social hierarchy is largely based on knowledge of Arabic and Persian. It is the second criterion after the genealogy going back to the Prophet. Since then, with the opening of modern schools, Urdu and English have become increasingly important.

Zeisler summarized the situation well: "Like any minor language, the Ladakhi language, or *ladakse skat* and its dialects, spoken by about 180,000 speakers in Ladakh, is under strong pressure from the official state language (in this case, Urdu), the language of higher education (English), and the languages of mass media (Hindi and Urdu)." (Zeisler 2006: 2). "For many scholars, *phal-skat* [spoken Ladakhi] is but a deviation or even 'rubbish,' not worthy of being preserved, not to speak of being developed" (ibid.: 4). This is not exactly true. Kargilis recite religious hymns like *marsiya*s (elegies composed to recall the events at Karbala), *noha*s (dirges recited during *Muharram*), and *qasida*s (odes to the Prophet and Shi'i imams) written in Purigi dialect (Gupta 2012a). All this is obviously linked to religion, but poets are also important, and I will discuss them at the end of this article.

Lack of Ladakhi collective awareness

Some snippets of the ancient pre-Islamic culture can still be found. In Muslim law, there is a concept known as *'urf*. *'Urf* is a tolerance of local customs provided they do not contradict Islamic law. Thus, Gupta writes,"I had heard from other intellectuals in Kargil that *Mamani* is held during the coldest period of the winter between 21st December and 21st January, known as *Chile Kalan*; special food is cooked (usually a goat is slaughtered) and shared with relatives and friends. These feasts are held to mark the peaceful passage of winter. This festival was cited to me by several people in Kargil as an example of 'regional cultural' or a remnant of Kargil's Buddhist past"(Gupta 2013: 47).

For her part, Grist mentions that those who fetch the bride and bring her back during the wedding ceremony, the *nyopa* (*gnya'bo pa*), are accompanied by the maternal uncle, the *azhang* (*a zhang*) (Grist 1998: 205, 225, and Gupta 2022b). The procedure is the same as for Buddhist weddings

A religion-based identity

If it is not a nation based on language, what is it? Are we talking about two nations, each with a religious basis? Such nations exist. We even have an example in India. On November 1, 1966, the Akali Dal, the main Sikh party, obtained the creation of a Punjabi state after almost 20 years of struggle. The demand was made on a linguistic basis: the creation of a state for the speakers of the Punjabi language. But no one was fooled: the Akali Dal is a Sikh party, and what it was demanding was a Sikh state, which it finally got.

It is helpful to examine the case of Yugoslavia, which existed as a country from 1918 to 1992. Serbs, Croats, and Bosnians spoke the same language, and religion was the only difference. The Croats were Catholic, the Serbs Orthodox, and the Bosnians Muslim. Only the script differed: the Croats wrote in Latin characters, and the Serbs in Cyrillic characters (cf. Urdu and Hindi). The Bosnians, on the other hand, had used Arabic characters until 1878, when the Austrians, who had replaced the Ottomans, put an end to this practice. (To-day they use both Latin and Cyrillic characters). The division of Yugoslavia into three main states between 1990 and 1992 is all the more astonishing given that there were all the ingredients for creating a linguistically based nation.[20] Just as in Finland and Estonia, dialects had given rise to a common language, and collections of epics, stories, and songs had been published. Despite everything, religion reappeared. The Titist regime, not known for being religion-friendly, nevertheless granted Bosnian Muslims the status of a nation. To avoid confusion between Bosnian Muslims and Muslims, it was decided to spell the former with a capital M and the latter with a lowercase m. In 1974, the Yugoslav Constitution recognized these "Muslims" as the sixth constituent nation of the Federation (Glamocak 2007: 41; Garde 2007: 51-60). Later these "Muslims" adopted the term Bosnian. But, make no mistake, the words Croat, Serb, and Bosnian, serve to cloak a religious identity in a national identity.

In the case of Ladakh, can we specify what this religious identity is? It is not a question of theology. I doubt that many Buddhists know the Sarnath Sermon, or that many Muslims know what the *ijmā'* or the *ḥisba* is. No, it is something more practical that emerges, as this quote from Aggarwal) makes clear:

> My occupancy in both sides of Achinathang became a venue through which the intense competition between the Muslim and Buddhist communities was addressed. How did I cope, I was asked by people in Gongmathang, in the "land of the *phyi-pa*[21]?" Did I cover my face and hair behind a veil, did I eat fish as they did, did I see them prepare for a hunt, did they eat in the same plate as me and accept my food, was I treated as well? How had I existed, the Muslims asked, with those who drank beer all day, who slept with the wives of their brothers, who ate unhealthy meat after the animal had died if they ate any at all, who would not accept food from the hands of the castes they called lower? Food and marriage motifs recurrently emerged as points of difference. (...) Nonetheless, if one looks only for disparity, the evidence is considerable.

> There are noticeable differences in the orientation and décor of houses between Yogmathang and the rest of the village. The houses of the Muslims are seldom whitewashed (*dkar-rtsi*), the windows seldom ensconced in carved wooden frames (*shing-tsag*). No prayer flags (*dar-phyogs*) adorn their terraces. The rows and rows of barley growing fields are significantly less in Yogmathang because the cultivation of edible grass to feed livestock is a greater necessity here, etc. (1994: 256-257).

This ties in with the "do you burn or bury your dead?" mentioned by Grist. Identity is a ritual identity. It is manifested in a whole series of customs, especially rites of passage. This ritual identity is coupled with an origin myth that is clearly rooted in Buddhism, and is in the process of formation among Shi'as.

Recent events

The events of August 5, 2019

On August 5, 2019, Amit Shah, Minister of Interior, presented a text on the reorganization of J&K to both houses of parliament. The reorganization would split Jammu + Kashmir from Ladakh (Kargil + Leh) and make each of these two parts Union Territories (UT). This was the first time an Indian state had been stripped of its statehood.

Fearing the reaction of the Kashmiris, more than 90 percent of whom were Muslim, the government took preventive measures. All telecommunications were cut off, and 4,000 people were arrested or put under house arrest, including three former CMs[22] of J&K.

In Ladakh, the contrast between the reactions in Kargil and Leh was stark. While joy broke out in Leh, in Kargil there was consternation. "Status divides Leh and Kargil. Jubilation in one, howls of protest in other," observed *The Hindu* (August 7); and on August 31, the same newspaper wrote: "Celebrations in Leh, concerns in Kargil. And the *Times of India* wrote on August 22, "There was dancing in Leh, while there were protests in Kargil." *The Hindu* of August 31, 2019, summarized the situation well: "The two markets [Leh and Kargil] seem like they are located at two ends of the country." The disconnection was total. Gupta made the same observation: "While Ladakhi Buddhists celebrated the UT declaration, the Muslims of Kargil vociferously and unanimously rejected it" (2022: 195). She also talks about the war and the demonstrations and writes that the Kargilis "clearly expressed their allegiance to Kashmir" (2022: 195).

On August 5, demonstrations broke out in Kargil. A big meeting was organized during which it was decided to create a "*Joint Action Committee*" (JAC). It seemed that the rejection of the government decision was unanimous. The Kargili wanted to stay with Kashmir. The JAC called for a strike, signed by the presidents of the two *anjumans*. The strike lasted until August 20.

After August 5, 2019

Since September 2019, anxiety was rising in Leh. The inhabitants realized that from now on any Indian from the plains could come and settle in Ladakh, buy land, and get a job. For this purpose, an "*Apex Body of Peoples Movement for Sixth Schedule for Ladakh*" was created. The idea was to replace the HC status with the ADC (Autonomous Development Council) status provided for in the Sixth Schedule of the Constitution. This status implies greater autonomy than HC status. It was designed for the tribes of the Far East (Assam, Meghalaya, Tripura, Mizoram).

It should be noted that the Kargilis refuse this Sixth Schedule. Asghar Ali Karbalai, former president of the Kargil HC and former MLA, said, "We are not with the UT. We do not support the extension of the Sixth Schedule." Meanwhile, the president of the IKMT said, "We have decided neither to oppose nor welcome the promise made on the Sixth Schedule (...) We have already suffered due to the UT status, which was not Kargil's demand." This is a strange rejection because the problem has nothing to do with religion. Don't the Kargilis also have an interest in protecting their land and jobs? It is too early to draw any conclusions from this. Let us remember that it took the Kargilis eight years to accept the status of HC. What remains certain is that the disconnect between Leh and Kargil is total.

Since then, the debate in Leh about the Sixth Schedule of the Constitution has continued. Some people, like Phuntsok Stobdan, the only Ladakhi to have attained the rank of ambassador, are skeptical. While recognizing the need to protect local property and jobs, they consider the Sixth Schedule inappropriate for Ladakh, as it is designed for less economically developed societies. Others point out that the HC and UT statutes do not work well together.

In October 2020, the BJP won the Leh HC elections with fifteen out of twenty-six seats, nine going to the Congress and two to independents. This is the first election since the imposition of UT status. Is this a "thank you" to Prime Minister Narendra Modi's Bharatiya Janata Party?[23] The BJP is a Hindu party, and it is feasible that Buddhists feel closer to Hindus than to Muslims.

For their part, the Muslims of Kargil are sticking to their guns: "Union Territory status was never our demand—it was Leh's demand," explained Sheikh Nazir Ul Mehdi Mohammadi, President, Islamia School, one of the two influential religious schools in Kargil. We had demanded divisional status within the state, which was accorded to us before the abrogation of Article 370. We are no way going to accept the division of Jammu and Kashmir and loss of its special status. When we didn't demand a UT, how are we supposed to support or oppose the demand for Sixth Schedule? Neither we are in its favor, nor in its opposition".

Now that Ladakh has achieved UT status, Kargil feels marginalized from Leh. Mohammadi continues, "All the top offices of the Union Territory administration are in Leh. (...). There were other grievances: Leh had an airport, but Kargil did not. (...) Everyone knows that the road to Kargil is dangerous, and it remains cut off from the world for six months in winter. (...) We have been always ignored. Nobody from the Center is interested in coming here. They just come to Leh and leave from there. There's definitely a religious dimension to this treatment of Kargil."[24]

The same position is held by Karbalai, former MLA and twice president of the Kargil HC. "If the Center was really 'serious and concerned' about the development of Ladakh, it should restore statehood. The Centre, he pointed out, would discuss Sixth Schedule status with leaders from both Leh and Kargil. (...) We are definitely going to make our point to the Center," said Karbalai.[25]

As we can see, the positions of both sides remain anchored on religion. In October 2019, just after the transformation of Ladakh into a UT, a delegation had asked for the recognition of Bhoti as the official language of Ladakh. Bhoti is classical Tibetan and, therefore, has a Buddhist connection. Religion thus remains the determining criterion.

A difficult position

The violence of the Kargilis' reaction in fact conceals a much more nuanced position. Gupta summarizes it well.

The Kargilis never supported the Kashmiri rebellion against the central government that began in 1989. "In contrast to the calls for *azadi* (freedom) from India by the majority of Muslims in the Kashmir Valley, the people of Kargil have sought belonging in India. (...) Kargil has never extended support to separatist movements in the valley" (2022: 4). Then, she adds: "Muslim Kargilis never endorsed Ladakhi Buddhists' demand for Union Territory (UT) status first raised in the early 1990s, but they also remain deeply anchored in Ladakh" (ibid.). In brief, "Kargili Shi'as have sought to carve out a space for themselves that was neither subsumed within Kashmir nor overshadowed by Buddhist Ladakh."

> "The deployment of communal idioms in the struggle for UT status by radical Buddhists since the 1990s led the Shi'a

> Muslims of Kargil to seek a sense of psychological security in their ties with Kashmir. But the rise of insurgency in the Kashmir Valley in 1989 also led them to foreground their differences from the Valley to make clear their allegiance to India. Anxieties of being clubbed with the Valley Muslims, as they had often been before the Kargil War when their loyalty to India was still suspect, led to an emphasis on their territorial and cultural identification with Ladakh. Kargili Shi'as themselves have adopted the generalized framing of Shi'as as the 'good Muslims' as opposed to the Sunnis as 'bad Muslims.' Feeding the projection of Kargil as 'peaceful' in contrast to the Kashmir Valley is advantageous for it confers the concession of certain freedoms by the state" (p. 23).

The debate is reopened on pp. 113-114 concerning the Hill Council's refusal. "Although Kargil had shared the grievance in Leh that Ladakh was being marginalized within J&K, it rejected not only the demand for declaring Ladakh a UT but also the provision to set up a Hill Council in 1995. (...) A Kargili ex-member of parliament explained to me, 'At the time militancy in Kashmir was at its peak, and we feared that accepting the Hill Council might be construed as endorsing the separatists' demand for azadi [freedom]. There appeared to be confusion on the difference between autonomy within the nation-state and freedom from it.'"In the minds of the Kargilis, there would have been confusion between the demand for independence represented by the Kashmiri rebellion and the demand for autonomy represented by the UT rebellion. The Kargilis finally adopted the Hill Council (2003) after proving to the center their attachment to the Indian Union during the Kargil war (1999).

However, the Kargilis are not only rejecting Kashmir and Buddhist Ladakh; they are also rejecting Pakistan because they are not attracted by pan-Islamism. Moreover, the existence of anti-Shiite feelings in Pakistan seems to be another contributory factor: "An awareness of the persecution of Shi'as in Pakistan, the lack of political representation in Gilgit-Baltistan and prosaic material realities of life across the LoC formed a prism through which life on the Indian side was constantly refracted." (page 6)

You get the impression that these poor Purigi cannot define their own identity. In fact, that is what Gupta says. They are against the Kashmiris because they are Sunni, pro-Pakistani or pro-independence, against the Pakistanis, because they persecute the Shiites, against the Leh district because they are Buddhists.

So how do you explain their violent reaction against Leh's attachment to a UT and for keeping it with Kashmir? Indeed, the reaction was unprecedentedly violent. It must be said that if the Kargilis have an identity problem, if they are in contradistinction with all their neighbors, there are degrees of rejection. The Kashmiris, although Sunni and pro-Pakistani, are rejected less strongly than the Buddhists of Leh, because they are Muslims.

2024: A 180-degree turn

The Buddhists wanted UT status because the HC's finances were controlled by Kashmir. The idea was that the central state would pay the budget directly to the HC. But they were soon disillusioned. The central government simply abolished the HC budget. The amount allocated to UT Ladakh for the fiscal year 2024-2025 is Rs 59.58 billion. Of this, Rs 6.68 billion is allocated to the two HCs, or just over 10 percent[26]. In other words, it is the central government that manages Ladakh. The two HCs are a shadow of their former selves.

This is what led the Purigis to join the Buddhists. Especially as, with the repeal of Article 370, they realize the risk of Indians from other states coming to buy land, set up businesses, and so on. There is also a risk that Ladakhis will become a minority in their own region (some have mentioned Tibet as a case in point). The two communities are now calling for Ladakh to become a federal state of the Indian Union with the application of the 6th schedule.

Introduction of Tibetan script to Kargili country

A description of an important event will bring this article to a close. In 2024, an association from Leh, the *Himalayan Cultural Heritage Foundation*, signed an agreement with the *Jaffaria Academy of Modern Education* in Kargil, an English medium school attached to the Islamiya School, to establish the teaching of Tibetan script.

For the moment this may seem insignificant: a few courses in a single school. But the importance of the event can be seen by comparing it with what is happening on the other side of the LoC. In Skardu, another association is doing the same. This is the *Baltistan Cultural Foundation*. It has published a Tibetan writing manual for primary school pupils and installed a number of signs in Tibetan (Kenneth Iain Macdonald, 2006).

This is all the more important as literature already exists in the Kargili dialect but until now has been written in Arabic characters. The principal authors are Akhone Asgar Ali Basharat, Mohammad Ali Ashoor, and Haji Sadiq Ali Sadiq (who died in July 2020). Gupta mentions around ten names and even shows us a photo of a poets' club meeting (2022: 185).

If all these writers began writing in Tibetan characters, we would witness the birth of a national Ladakhi language. Is Ladakh in the process of becoming a nation that transcends religious divisions?[27]

Patrick Kaplanian is an independent researcher who has been working on Ladakh ethnology since 1975. In 1981, he published a monograph about Ladakhis and organized the second symposium on Ladakh in 1985, the proceedings of which he published twice. Moreover, he has written about 30 articles most of which are on hal. Kaplanian has also researched Greek mythology and the title of his thesis: "Analysis of the myth of Prometheus and Pandora, from Hesiod to the Caucasus."

Endnotes

1. On Anderson see Kaplanian 2020b.

2. *Kalhon* (*bka' blon*), is a high-ranking title in the traditional hierarchy. It follows the titles of "King" and "Prince".

3. The *rinpoche* (*rin po che*) of Spituk, the most important Buddhist hierarch at the time.

4. MP: Member of Parliament, member of the national assembly in New Delhi.

5. MLA: Member of local Assembly. Member of the local assembly of J&K.

6. To combat inequality, the Indian constitution provides for the reservation of a certain number of places in government and universities for members of the most disadvantaged castes and ethnic groups. This is known as Scheduled Cast (SC) and Scheduled Tribe (ST) status. The most "primitive" tribes and the untouchables are entitled to it.

7. All this is very well told by van Beek (1997). "Experts" came to divide the population of the two districts into tribes. There were 18 jeeps of "scientists" (ibid.: 32) that crisscrossed the country.

8. *History repeated in Ladakh (The Muslim viewpoint of the Ladakh agitation of 1989)*, published by the "Muslims of the Kargil district".

9. Zangskar is a landlocked valley where most of the population is Buddhist but which is attached to the Kargil district.

10. The HC of Kargil was not created until 2003.

11. It is necessary to specify that, after their conquest of Ladakh in 1834, the Dogra retained all the nobility and high clergy apparatus. The "king" no longer reigned, but it is clear from his appointment as deputy, a century later almost to the day, that the maharaja continued to rely on the old hierarchy. As for the *kalhon* of Leh, he was one of the most active in the "collaboration" with the occupation authorities. Consequently, he became the most powerful nobleman in Ladakh.

12. *lhonpo* (*blon po*) is another noble title.

13. In 1981,I wrote:

> "It is nevertheless remarkable that, after more than 130 years of Dogra, English, and then Kashmiri colonization, most attitudes remain unchanged, and that the monarchy and the nobility have retained their place: did not the Ladakhi elect their queen as a member of parliament in New Delhi in 1977? Do we not hear that in such and such a village the celebrations are more beautiful, because 'it is a village whose inhabitants are all servants of the palace', which is not true as the queen only has a few servants left?" (1981: 342, final paragraph of chapter XII, my translation).

14. Shina: an Indo-Aryan population. Most are Muslims; some Buddhist Shina are found in Ladakh.

15. Grist conducted the first part of her survey in 1993-1994.

16. The same is true for the consumption of alcohol, and the game of polo, which is nonetheless played in many Muslim courts.

17. When a *sayyid* leads a faction, he has the title of *rehbar*. Below him are the other *sayyid,* who are not faction leaders, and then the sheikhs and *akhun*s, who are Muslim scholars versed in the Koran. The most prestigious ones were educated in Iraq and/or Iran (see also Gupta, 2014: 379). The others were content with the local Koranic schools (madrassa).

18. The commemoration of the martyrdom of Hussain, the third Shiite imam, grandson of Muhammad and son of Ali and Fatima.

19. Tibetan refugees in Ladakh are considered foreigners and communicate with their hosts in Urdu.

20. Because Slovenes, Macedonians, and Kosovar Albanians are few in number, they carry little weight.

21. Musulman.

22. CM: Chief Minister, prime minister of the state of J&K as opposed to PM, prime minister of the central government in New Delhi.

23. For the record, in 2010 the Congress won 22 seats, the BJP 4.

24. Phrases quoted by Safwat Zargar, 6 October 2020. https://scroll.in/article/975010/ladakh-is-in-the-news-for-border-conflicts-but-its-residents-have-bigger-worries-than-china. Accessed April 18, 2022.

25. By *Reach Ladakh* Correspondent Leh, Oct 22, 2019 http://www.reachladakh.com/news/social-news/delegation-demands-bhoti-as-official-language-of-ut-ladakh?fbclid=IwAR3svRD8PHmnBo9dFKWIduXOIEiVjG1iiriCtXPsW4uNtAaKu6zOk48xvto.

26. Dr Gulam Mustafa, *Daily Excelsior*, 10 February 2024. According to the *Stawa* newspaper, of January 2024, only 5% is received by HCs.

27. The author is grateful to John Bray for providing important documentation of events after August 19, 2019, and to a correspondent, who wishes to remain anonymous, who brings to the author's attention the emergence of a sense of exasperation on the part of some young Buddhists with regard to the abusive behavior of some LBA leaders. The author is also grateful to Judith Biron, for correcting his English.

References

Aggarwal, Ravina. 1994. *From Mixed Strains to Barley Grains, Person and Place in a Ladakhi Village*. Typed dissertation: Bloomington, Indiana University.

Anderson, Benedict. 1991. *Imagined Communities. Reflections on the Origin and Spread of Nationalism.* London & New York: Verso.

Beek, Martijn van. 1996. *Identity Fetishism and the Art of Representation.The Long Struggle for Regional Autonomy in Ladakh.* Typed dissertation. Ithaca: Cornell University.

——. 1997. The Importance of being Tribal. Or: the Impossibility of being Ladakhis. In T. Dodin & H. Räther (eds), *Recent Research on Ladakh 7: Proceedings of the 7th Colloquium of the International Association of Ladakh Studies, Bonn/Sankt Augustin, held on 12-15 June 1995*. Ulm: Universität Ulm, Ulmer Kulturanthropologie Schriften 9, 21-42.

———. 1999. Hill Councils, Development, and Democracy. Assumptions and Experiences from Ladakh. *Alternatives* 24(4): 435-460.

———. 2003. The Art of Representation. Domesticating Ladakhi 'Identity,'in *Ethnic Revival and religious Turmoil. Identities and Representations in the Himalayas*, edited by P. Dollfus & M. Lecomte Tilouine, New Delhi/ New York: Oxford University Press.

Bertelsen, Kristoffer Brix. 1996. *Our Communalized Future: Sustainable Development, Social Identification and Politics of Representation in Ladakh*. Typed dissertation: Aarhus University.

Bray, John, Martijn van Beek, Tsering Gonkatsang, Phuntsok Wangchuk, 2020. Tsetan Phuntsog and Tibetan Textbooks for Ladakh in 1933. *Himalaya*, 39(2), Article II: 74-91.

Detienne, Marcel. 2010 [2008]. *L'Identité Nationale, une Énigme*. Paris: Gallimard.

Dollfus, Pascale. 2003. Answer to M. Van Beek : 'The Art of Representation : Domesticating Ladakhi Identity', in *Ethnic and Religious Revival and Turmoil: Identities and Representations in the Himalayas*, edited by M. Lecomte-Tilouine and P. Dollfus, Delhi: Oxford University Press.

Garde, Paul, 2007. Vrai et Faux Problèmes de Langue en Bosnie-Herzégovine et dans les Pays Limitrophes, *Cités*, 4(32): 51-60:

Glamocak, Marina, 2007. À la Recherche de l'Identité Bosniaque: Entre Religion, Nation et État. *Cités*, 4(32): 37-50.

Grist, Nicola, 1976-1977. Kinship, Marriage and Inheritance. In N. Grist, P. Farrington, M. Phylactou, P. Kaplanian, *Reports on Ladakh*. 1977-1979. Manuscript: Cambridge University.

———. 1979. Traditional Stratification, in N. Grist, P. Farrington, M. Phylactou, P. Kaplanian, *Reports on Ladakh*, 1977-1979. Manuscript: Cambridge University.

———. 1998. *Local Politics in the Suru Valley of Northern India*. Typed dissertation: London: Goldmiths, University of London.

Gupta, Radikha, 2013. The Importance of Being Ladakhi: Affect and Artifice in Kargil. *Himalaya* 32(1).

———. 2014. Experiments with Khomeini's Revolution in Kargil: Contemporary Shi'a networks between India and West Asia. *Modern Asian Studies*, March 2014:1-29.

———. 2022a. *Freedom in Captivity, Negotiations of Belonging along the Kashmir Frontier*, Cambridge University Press, Cambridge.

———. 2022b. Islam in the trans-Himalayan Ecumene. In *Routledge Handbook of Highland Asia*, Routledge, London.

Hobsbawm, Eric, 1990. *Nations and Nationalism since 1780*. Cambridge: Cambridge University Press, 1990.

Kaplanian, Patrick. 1981. *Les Ladakhi du Cachemire*. Paris: Hachette.

———. 1983. Quelques Aspects du Mythe et des Structures Mentales au Ladakh. *Recent Research on Ladakh*, Weltforum Verlag, Schriftenreihe Internationales Asienforum, 3 8039 0207 3. Also available on the web: hal-04675925.

———. 1991. Mythes et Légendes sur les Origines du Peuplement au Ladakh, in *Tibetan History and Language*, edited by Ernst Steinkellner. *Studies Dedicated to Uray Géza on his Seventieth Birthday*, Vienna: Arbeitskreis für Tibetische und Buddhistische Studien, Vienna University.

———. 2020a. Bakula Rinpoche's Family, in *Sounding in Ladakhi Everyday Life and Politics*, edited by Nawang Tsering Shakspo *International Conference on Padma Bhushan Kushok Bakula*, October 2016. Leh: Centre for Research on Ladakh. Also available on the web: hal-02319725.

———. 2020b. Une analyse de *Imagined Communities* de Benedict Anderson, https://hal.archives-ouvertes.fr/hal-02910376v1

Lamb, Alistair. 1993 [1991]. *Kashmir, a Disputed Legacy, 1846-1990*. Lahore: OUP.

Macdonald, Kenneth Iain. 2006. Transnationalism, Transculturation and the Production of Cultural Identity in Northern Pakistan. *Memories of Tibet India Review*, 5(2):190-219

Renan, Ernest. 1997 [1882]. Qu'est-ce qu'une Nation? (Conference, March 11, 1882, at the Sorbonne). Paris: Mille et une Nuits.

Sagaster, Klaus. 1989. *Die Balti*, Francfort: Museum für Völkerkunde.

Thiesse, Anne-Marie. 2001 [1999]. *La Création des Identités Nationales, Europe XVIII*[e]*-XIX*[e] *siècle*. Paris: Seuil.

Zeisler, Bettina, 2006. Why Ladakhi must not be Written: Being Part of the Great Tradition: As Another Kind of Global Thinking. In *Lesser-known languages of South Asia: Status and policies, Case Studies and Applications of Information Technology*, edited by Anju Saxena and Lars Borin, 175-194. Berlin: Mouton de Gruyter.

HIMALAYA
The Journal of the Association of Nepal and Himalayan Studies

Research Article

Building a Multilingual Republic: An Interview with Dr. Lava Deo Awasthi, Founding Chair of Nepal's Language Commission

Mark Turin
The University of British Columbia and Tokyo College, The University of Tokyo

Lava Deo Awasthi
Chairman, Language Commission, Nepal

DOI: https://doi.org/10.2218/himalaya.2025.9734

Abstract

This contribution is an edited version of a wide-ranging conversation between linguistic anthropologist and past co-editor of *HIMALAYA*, Mark Turin, and Lava Deo Awasthi, the first Chairperson of Nepal's Language Commission. In the course of the interview, Turin and Awasthi discuss the Commission's role and establishment, Awasthi's appointment to the position of Chairperson, his intellectual training and administrative preparation for the task, and the strategic goals and objectives that he brought to the portfolio. The conversation then moves on to a critical reflection of the challenges and achievements of Awasthi's term as Chairperson, concluding with his vision for mother tongue instruction and linguistic justice in Nepal.

Keywords

federalism, language, linguistic justice, mother tongue, Nepal, policy,

Recommended Citation

Turin, Mark and Awasthi, Lava D. (2025). Building a Multilingual Republic: An Interview with Dr. Lava Deo Awasthi, Founding Chair of Nepal's Language Commission. *HIMALAYA* 44(1): 164-174.

This work is licensed under a Creative Commons Attribution-Noncommercial-No Derivative Works 4.0 License.

1. **What is the role of Nepal's Language Commission and when was it formed?**
To fulfil the promises of the new federal state, the Constitution of Nepal (2015) created a Language Commission (LC) with the following four core mandates: (a) to develop eligibility criteria for gaining status as an official language and offer recommendations to the Government of Nepal about the official language(s) in each province; (b) to offer recommendations to the Government about measures to be taken for the conservation, promotion, and development of languages; (c) to suggest possible ways of using mother tongues in education by assessing their stage of development; and, (d) to conduct studies, carry out research, and perform monitoring functions on the response to the constitutional provisions for the federalization of languages in Nepal.
In addition, the Constitution made the Language Commission responsible for making recommendations on all matters regarding official languages. The Language Commission Act, 2017, elaborates on the functions as stipulated in the Constitution. The Commission was founded in 2016 (Kamat 2016).

2. **By what process and in what year were you appointed as its first Chairperson?**
As per the provision of the Constitution of Nepal, the Office of the Prime Minister and Council of Ministers, the Government of Nepal appointed me as the first Chairperson of the Language Commission. The process for the appointment was initiated by the Ministry of Culture, which is a liaison ministry for the Language Commission. Article 287 of the Constitution states that 'the Government of Nepal shall, no later than one year of the commencement of this Constitution, constitute a Language Commission…'. The Constitution came into effect on 20 September 2015, and it was therefore mandatory that the Government form the Commission within the constitutional timeframe. Recognizing the urgency of the matter, the Government searched for an appropriate candidate to be presented to the Council of Ministers. The qualifications stipulated in sub-clause (4) of Article 287 of the Constitution for the Chairperson or a member of the Commission were as follows: (a) a master's degree in a related subject from a recognized university; (b) at least twenty years of experience in the fields of study, teaching, and research on various languages of Nepal; (c) at least forty-five years old; and (d) high moral character (Constitution of Nepal 2015). Since I met all the criteria specified by the Constitution, I was encouraged to apply and advised by the Office of the Prime Minister and Council of Ministers to resign from my post as permanent secretary of the Government because the Chairperson of the Commission had an independent and constituent portfolio. The Cabinet of Ministers appointed me as the Chairperson of the Commission in September 2016. I assumed the post of Chairperson after resigning from my civil service post and receiving approval from the cabinet.

3. **What in your own professional and educational background helped to prepare you for the role?**
I have worked with the Government of Nepal for about thirty years, alongside holding teaching appointments at universities across Nepal. Prior to assuming the role of the Chairperson of the Commission, I served as permanent secretary to the Government of Nepal and worked as the Chief Administrator of the Central Development Region.
I was appointed as Director General of the Department of Education and completed my assignments as Joint Secretary at the Planning, Monitoring and Educational Administration Divisions of the Ministry of Education. I gained valuable experience working in different capacities at district, regional, and central level institutions while serving in the government system.
In addition, I have taught courses on the English language, language policy and

planning, English literature, linguistics, philosophy, diversity education, oriental cosmologies, and advanced research methodologies as a visiting professor at Tribhuvan University and Kathmandu University for more than three decades. Later, I also started supervising MPhil and PhD students at Far Western University in Mahendranagar, Kanchanpur. I have served on research committees and supported MPhil and PhD students at Tribhuvan University, Kathmandu University, Far Western University, Pokhara University, and Nepal Sanskrit University. I have served on various committees and task forces commissioned by the Government at policy and implementation levels and have attended professional courses and presented papers on language policy, language planning, linguistic diversity, curriculum designing, and classroom pedagogies at national and international forums.

I hold master's degrees in English literature from Tribhuvan University, Nepal, and in Applied Linguistics and TESOL from the University of Leicester, UK. I earned my PhD in language policy from the Danish University of Education, Denmark.

My PhD project was dedicated to making sense of Nepal's social construct of and commitment to multilingualism, exploring the persistence of monolingual school practices in the face of constitutional promises and state commitments to multilingualism (Awasthi 2004). I conducted a survey of Nepal's languages and carried out a qualitative study of the Tharu language in the district of Bardiya (Bellamy 2009). I analyzed language policy statements and explored classroom pedagogies in schools. I documented how local authorities (including education personnel), members of school management committees, head teachers, and parent representatives seemed to promote the Nepali language and English language even though the constitution enshrines mother tongue medium education as a fundamental right (Article 31). Furthermore, teachers seemed to show a tendency to resist change and maintain the status quo because they were not consulted when new educational language policies were introduced into schools.

Teachers also exhibited a deeply held adherence to the *Gurukul* education system, which appears to have been harnessed as a way to resist newer pedagogical ideologies imported from the West (Joshi and Gupta 2017). The *Gurukul* tradition is deeply connected to Nepal's ancient Vedic heritage and refers to the process by which a student stays in a teacher's home for an extended period until the disciple has accomplished mastery in the subject matter and has become an enlightened person. The core components of the *Gurukul* curriculum include competencies in Vedic knowledge, spirituality, self-discipline, empathy, compassion, and humanism. Historically, at least, the Sanskrit language played a major role in the transmission of knowledge from the master, or *guru*, to the *shiksya*, the disciple.

Recognizing how ingrained these rich traditions of knowledge transmission are, I wanted to understand why the students' engagement in the learning process appeared to have dwindled, creating a gap between children's home languages and the language(s) of the school. While statutory provisions for education in the mother tongue are oriented towards promotion, classroom pedagogies have remained resolutely monolingual and exclusionary. The result is that the multilingual education policies that have been introduced in Nepal have not resulted in meaningful changes in classroom practices.

My research was also a reflection of the childhood traumas I had experienced at the earliest stage of formal education. My home language, Baitadeli, has a strong oral tradition and no written literature (National Statistics Office 2021). English is my fifth language in terms of exposure and competence, and my home district of Baitadi is well-known for its loyalty to the local language. I had to drop out of school after completing my sixth grade. Staying at home, I received greater attention from my family and had much greater exposure to my native language, culture, and environment. My overall impression is that dropping out of school had a surprisingly positive impact on my life. The opportunity offered a surprising dividend for me as I gained mastery in my mother tongue and received extensive exposure to folk literature, Indigenous knowledge, and survival skills, thereby cultivating my interest in language, culture, literature, and local cosmologies.

Now that I reflect on it, I appreciate how language has always played a key role in my life. I grew up in a multilingual environment, brought up with Baitadeli, Hindi, Sanskrit, Nepali, and English. Language played a major part in my decision to leave school, and my later success is deeply linked to my competence in several languages. When I dropped out of school, I learned far more meaningful things from my grandparents, parents, and family members, as well as from the wider community. It was rewarding to be at home with my family as I gained mastery in my mother tongue, which in turn helped me to harness and refine my art of living. Languages mattered so much to me because they proved to be both software and hardware. Later, when I was in secondary school, I realized that my command of my home language contributed significantly to enhancing my English and Nepali. I used my mother tongue as a form of linguistic capital (Bourdieu 1991) to strengthen my competence in both English and Nepali. My deep connection with my family and community members provided me with a firm foundation for making headway in other languages. By networking with language communities, university professionals, government officials, and educational practitioners at local, national, and international levels, I gained the necessary confidence to embark on the daunting task of being the first Chairperson of Nepal's Language Commission.

4. **In your term as the Commission's first Chairperson, what were your strategic goals and objectives?**

My first strategic goal was to create an environment conducive to implementing the provisions of the Constitution of Nepal in relation to language. My priority was to prepare a detailed action plan for my six-year tenure in consultation with language stakeholders, including language experts, experienced professionals, language activists, Indigenous community members, and representatives of relevant national and local-level institutions. Likewise, the Commission formed a body of high-level advisors to ensure that the Chairperson's work was well-informed and credible. The advisors to the committee had highly visible professional and social reputations in Nepal and had much experience in the field of language conservation, promotion, research, and development. Another strategy we adopted was to establish close institutional linkages with federal, provincial, and local-level governments for collecting opinions and disseminating information across the country. In the beginning, only the Chairperson was appointed. Despite provisions for appointing members from all the provinces, it was a one-man Commission for almost two years. While this was a huge responsibility, I took it as an opportunity to prove my strength. I had to utilize all possible sources of knowledge, including the formation of the advisory body and rapport building with Ministers and Government officials. More importantly, the collaboration I had with language communities across the country was truly remarkable. I learned so much from them and set an agenda for the Commission based on the input we received from community members. I took up the challenge in the hope that I was not alone. In essence, whatever I could do at this early stage of my appointment as Chairperson might yield far-reaching results and provide a firm foundation for the years to come. Another member, Ms. Usha Hamal, a highly reputed author and an experienced professional, was appointed to the Commission in the second year of my tenure, and for more than five years, we two were the only appointed officials. In the sixth year, all members were finally appointed as had been envisioned in the Constitution. During my tenure, we had great difficulty carrying out the tasks stipulated in the Constitution as well as in the Language Commission Act. The expectations of stakeholders were so high, and we had to show quick results. The staff members and I faced considerable pressure due to the heavy workload, high expectations, and the urgency of the task at hand. We were fortunate to receive excellent support and cooperation from the stakeholders, enriching our journey and helping us to demonstrate results as envisioned in the Constitution.

5. **What critical issues did you have to consider while discharging your duty?**

When Nepal's new Constitution was drafted, a number of concerns raised by language stakeholders and members of the Constituent Assembly could not be adequately addressed. The major concerns were related to the conservation of languages, the recognition of official languages at the provincial level, and the use of mother tongues at federal, provincial, and local levels (Republica 2024). These unresolved issues and matters pertaining to the federalization of Nepal's languages were passed on to the Language Commission to address and resolve.

Regarding the recommendations for official languages, a five-year timeline had been set by the Constitution. As per the statutory provision, this matter had to be resolved within this time frame. The issue was linked with a decision to be made by each province for official recognition of specific language(s) (Sijapati 2021), alongside Nepali, which was and is the official language of Nepal. This proved to be a highly contentious issue. With great effort, we succeeded in having all provinces agree to recognize their official languages as per the recommendations of the Commission. The role played by Commission staff members was critical for the gains we were able to make within a relatively short period of time.

One of the challenges I faced at that time was the absence of legal instruments to support the work in which we were engaged. We needed Cabinet approval for the Language Commission's Executive Order, and this was essential to make the Commission functional. At the same time, the Parliament needed to pass the Language Commission Act as soon as possible to recognize the Commission as a competent and important entity. With considerable effort and advocacy, we finally succeeded in obtaining approval for these two basic documents to make the Commission institutionally functional. I deeply appreciate the support we received from the then Rt Hon'ble Speaker of the House of Representatives, Ms. Onsari Gharti Magar, and the Hon Minister for Culture, Mr. Jeetendra Dev. A dedicated session was held in Parliament, which is rare in Nepal, to debate the Language Commission Bill. The Bill formally received approvals from the Parliament in October 2017. Simultaneously, we had to work on developing a five-year Master Plan focusing on our constitutional mandate as well as articulating the terms of reference stipulated in the Act of Parliament. We then worked on annual action plans and prepared programs and budgets based on the resources allocated by the Government.

Recognizing the need for advisory input to the Language Commission for its engagement at federal, provincial, and local levels, a high-level Advisory Committee was formed, comprising Mr. Bairagi Kaila, Professor Chuda Mani Bandhu, Professor Yogendra

Prasad Yadava, Professor Tej Ratna Kansakar, Professor Madhav Pokharel, Professor Nobel Kishore Rai, Dr. Rudra Laxmi Shrestha, Professor Dan Raj Regmi, Professor Dubi Nanda Dhakal, and Professor Balram Prasai. All were renowned language advocates, linguists, language scientists, and scholars in Nepal. The formation of the Advisory Committee contributed significantly to first creating and then enabling an environment for the Commission to engage in a meaningful consultative process across the country.

Our first objectives included carrying out the four major mandates as articulated in the Constitution and outlined at the top of this contribution. The objectives were aligned with the milestones set in the Master Plan, and action steps were developed following our annual work plans and budget allocations. Elaborations were made on action steps for how official languages could be identified and recognized, how mediums of instruction for children could be reinforced at the local level, how language protection could be a priority, and how research could be carried out in collaboration with universities and relevant institutions as well as departments. Our plan also included developing monitoring tools and indicators alongside reporting mechanisms and feedback procedures.

6. **What were your greatest achievements during your term?**

After almost two years of solitary work as the Language Commission's only member, a new member was finally appointed. Staff members who were on the team from the beginning deserve particular credit for setting an agenda for conversations about language in the country. It was a real point of departure for the Commission to see language issues being debated so extensively with such a high level of enthusiasm across Nepal. Our team worked extremely hard to reach out to language communities and stakeholders in almost all parts of the country. Our advisory team and staff members were deeply dedicated and committed to carrying out consultations about the role and status of official languages, the use of mother tongues, and language conservation. Seven teams were formed to work at the provincial levels, drawing on speakers of local languages, language researchers, and key experts. Likewise, provincial-level conveners and team members worked day and night to produce reports on the language makeup and requirements of individual provinces. The consultative meetings we organized at the federal, provincial, and municipal levels, as well as at community levels with local stakeholders, municipality officials, political leaders, experts, and language activists, together with our distinguished advisors, proved to be truly rewarding and necessary for making recommendations on all areas of language work and policy as envisioned by the Constitution.

The provincial-level conveners who took the lead in organizing consultations and preparing reports on the official language(s) of Nepal's provinces included (1) Mr. Bairagi Kainla (Til Bikram Nemwang)—Koshi Province; (2) Professor Yogendra Prasad Yadava—Madhesh Province; (3) Professor Tej Ratna Kansakar—Bagmati Province; (4) Dr. Jagman Gurung—Gandaki Province; (5) Professor Hridaya Ratna Bajracharya—Lumbini Province; (6) Professor Jeevendra Dev Giri—Karnali Province; and (7) Professor Amma Raj Joshi—Far Western Province. In addition, the provincial task team members were senior-level professionals, linguists, language scientists, and researchers with strong reputations. I acknowledge with gratitude the support we received from the province-level conveners and members in accomplishing this task.

One of the greatest achievements of the Language Commission was that we succeeded in setting a language agenda at federal, provincial, and local levels. Nepal's language communities and other stakeholders expressed the view that this was the first time they felt their languages were being recognized and that their voices had been heard by the state. This was one of the most important successes for us. People participated in the debates and discussed issues relating to language, something that in all likelihood had never ever happened before in their lifetime, at least not in ways that were supported by the state. We encouraged people to speak in their own language(s) and provided translators during plenary sessions and group discussions.

A major achievement of the Commission was developing criteria for the status planning of languages at federal, provincial, and local levels and recommending eleven province-level official languages, in addition to the Nepali language.

In the federal context of Nepal, these recommendations signify a clear departure towards a federal language policy, with a focus on decentering language policy across the country (Tupas 2019). The languages recommended for official use (Pradhan, 2021) in Nepal's 7 provinces include (1) Avadhi (Lumbini province), (2) Bajjika (Madhesh province), (3) Bhojpuri (Madhesh and Gandaki provinces), (4) Dotyali (Far Western province), (5) Gurung (Gandaki province), (6) Limbu (Koshi province), (7) Magar (Gandaki and Karnali provinces), (8) Maithili (Koshi and Madhesh provinces), (9) Nepal Bhasa (Bagmati province), (10) Tamang (Bagmati province), and (11) Tharu (Lumbini and Far Western provinces).

Similarly, a notable achievement for us was the recognition of Indigenous languages spoken by smaller communities, all of whom faced ongoing marginalization and high levels of endangerment. The Commission identified 9 new languages (National Statistics Office 2021: 32) that had not been reported in the 2011 census, including Nawa Sherpa (Shankhuwa Sabha), Marek-Yakkha (Dhankuta and Ilam), Serake (Mustang), Poike (Dolpa), Nubri (Gorkha), Chum (Gorkha), Nar Phu (Manang), and Rana Tharu (Kanchanpur and Kailali). Furthermore, the Language Commission provided a framework for recognizing official languages within a municipality.

All languages spoken in Nepal were given a functional space to survive and thrive at the community, ward, municipal, provincial, and federal levels. The languages of historical importance, as well as classical languages, namely the Bhot language, Pali language, and Sanskrit language (Regmi 2021), were given recognition to support their protection, growth, and development. Recommendations were made for the conservation, promotion, and development of the marginalized languages of Nepal that were threatened by majority languages and for those languages that hold particular power at local and global levels. Recommendations were also made for how best to safeguard Nepal's languages from the ever-growing spread of English and other powerful, globalizing languages (Siwal 2021). In order to protect highly endangered languages facing real threat, the Commission took an initiative to digitize language corpora and provide such languages with a digital platform for inter-language connectivity and translation (Michailovsky 2006). The Language Commission plans to launch the portal within the 2024 fiscal year.

Another important aspect of the Commission's work was to emphasize mother tongue medium education and instruction in schools across the nation. Recognizing the role of language in children's cognitive and academic development, the Commission suggested strategies for linking schools with ward-level language clusters for use in the classroom. The importance of nurturing and respecting a child's first language was reiterated in the Commission's recommendations for children's learning and all-round development.

A foundation was laid for language research during my time at the Language Commission, in collaboration with university departments and other professionals. During my tenure, we stressed the need for publishing and disseminating research findings and language data, created and revised based on a database provided by the National Statistics Office, Nepal. District, municipality, and ward-level databases were developed for both macro- and micro-level language projection and planning. Our collaboration with UNESCO (UNESCO 2021) and other relevant partners gave impressive results. By the end of my term, a remarkable change could be observed in terms of building trust within and across Nepal's diverse language communities. A network of language groups and stakeholders across the country proved to be a powerful way of bringing all language communities under one roof for a collective review of and response to the process of federalizing language policy. The many language stakeholders across Nepal appreciated the opportunity to work within a coordinated framework and—feeling empowered by this—seemed genuinely enthusiastic about the initiatives taken by the Commission.

7. **What were the most significant challenges for you as Chairperson?**
One of the major challenges for me was to win people's trust in advocating for the mission of the Language Commission. I faced considerable resistance as I sought to emphasize the use of native languages in families and communities. While the Commission advocated for multilingualism and promoted linguistic diversity, the prevailing policy circles and central-level institutions had been deeply influenced by a one-language discourse and ideology (Yadav, 2013), that of Nepali only (Turin, 2006). The spread of English also poses a huge threat to Nepal's languages. However, people in power do not seem to see this as a problem. They tend to abandon their own languages in favor of English (Xue and Zuo 2013).
My work was very challenging because of how I needed to work with others who often held quite divergent positions. I could initiate something in my own capacity but could not advance anything at the structural or policy levels on my own. I had to coordinate and collaborate with stakeholders and partner agencies at federal, provincial, and local levels, many of whom held very different positions and ideologies about language. Until the establishment of the Commission, language had not been a government priority, nor had it received much attention from state institutions. Most intellectuals and politicians still believed that the Commission was ultimately irrelevant. Misconceptions were everywhere and remained rather entrenched.
The way that Nepal's municipalities are increasingly introducing English as a medium of instruction at the earliest stage of a child's school-based education has proven to be detrimental to their cognitive development and academic success (Ghimire 2024). Unfortunately, I could not do much about this and was unable to convince authorities in the center as well as at the local level to think otherwise. Most of Nepal's elites have been heavily influenced by the spread of English and remain unaware of its effects on their home languages as well as on the intergenerational transmission of Indigenous languages in the country. I wish that we could have produced more compelling evidence to show the consequences of making poor policy choices for our children's education. I now feel that I could have done better to offer concrete examples in favor of using the mother tongue as a medium of children's education at the earliest stages of a child's education (Stoop 2017; Wilson and Kamanā 2006).
Demystification calls for a collective response. To make change happen across a whole complex and federalizing country was daunting work and sometimes felt like a race against time. While to some extent, we have succeeded in bringing the agenda of the Language Commission to the consciousness of Nepal's citizens, we could have worked even more closely with language communities and municipalities to

cultivate a culture supportive of diverse language ecologies and bring about changes in stakeholders' attitudes and behaviors.

8. **What do you see the Language Commission achieving in the next 5-10 years?**
Within a five-to-ten-year time span, the Language Commission will have to ensure that all of its major recommendations are implemented at federal, provincial, and local levels. In ten years' time, all seven of Nepal's provinces will have their official languages in place. These languages will also be recognized as languages of federal business, alongside Nepali. I anticipate that all official languages in the federal and provincial systems will have a national portal for inter-language corpora using machine translation to fulfill their federal, provincial, and local level-language functions, and that all languages spoken in Nepal will be represented through a digital database in the national archive. By the end of the next decade, each municipality in the country will have recognized one or two official languages at the local level, based on speech populations. Other local languages will have received community-level legal recognition and official status to fulfill their functional roles. Languages that are highly endangered or at risk (Pine and Turin 2017) will be entitled to receive state grants for conducting language sessions to encourage families and young learners to speak the language. Incentive schemes that promote language within the family and at home will be introduced in municipalities (Sun 2019). Intergenerational transmission of languages will have received welcome and timely attention across Nepal.
It is my hope that all schools—public and private—will have introduced mother tongue medium instruction policies at the earliest stage of school education, at least up to class five. Nepali, English and other national as well as classical and foreign languages will be taught as subjects. The existing policy of English medium education at the early stage of education will be abolished. The Government of Nepal will be held accountable if the number of speakers of any language decreases or if local communities face language loss and greater endangerment.
I also imagine that language policies and Acts of Parliament will be in place at federal, provincial, and local levels. A digital database will be created in collaboration with the Government of Nepal and the Office of the Statistics, which will provide a basis for monitoring the status of Nepal's languages over time.
Under the aegis of the Language Commission, a Centre for Language Research and Innovation will be created with world-class facilities for language documentation and archiving in collaboration with Tribhuvan University's Central Department of Linguistics and other institutions. Harnessing the vastness of Nepal's linguistic diversity, the Language Commission will morph into a center of excellence for national and international communities to engage in collaborative language research, share experiences, and document best practices at all levels in service of both global linguistic diversity and Nepal's many Indigenous languages.

Lava Deo Awasthi has served as Joint Secretary at the Ministry of Education, Government of Nepal, and as the first Chairman, Language Commission of Nepal. Born in Baitadi district in the Far Western Province of Nepal, Awasthi earned MAs in English Literature from Tribhuvan University and in Applied Linguistics and TESOL from Leicester University, England, UK. He received his Ph.D. degree from the Danish University of Education, Copenhagen.

Mark Turin is an Associate Professor at the University of British Columbia. Turin previously served as the Director of the Yale Himalaya Initiative and Chief of Translation and Interpretation at the United Nations Mission in Nepal. In 2000, he co-founded the Digital Himalaya Project, a platform to make multimedia resources from the Himalayan region widely available online. From 2013-2020, together with Sienna Craig, he edited the journal *HIMALAYA*.

References

Awasthi, Lava. 2004. Exploring Monolingual School Practices in Multilingual Nepal. PhD thesis, Danish University of Education, Copenhagen, Denmark.

Bellamy, Briana. 2009. Tradition in Transition: Tharu Traditional Governing System in Post-Conflict Nepal. Independent Study Project (ISP) Collection. 798. https://digitalcollections.sit.edu/isp_collection/798/

Bourdieu, Pierre. 1991. Language and symbolic power. Cambridge, Massachusetts: Harvard University Press. https://archive.org/details/languagesymbolic0000bour

Constitution of Nepal. 2015. Constitution of Nepal, Article 31. https://lawcommission.gov.np/en/wp-content/uploads/2021/01/Constitution-of-Nepal.pdf

Constitution of Nepal. 2015. Constitution of Nepal, Article 287. https://lawcommission.gov.np/en/wp-content/uploads/2021/01/Constitution-of-Nepal.pdf

Ghimire, Khom Prasad. 2024. Perceptions on English as a Medium of Instruction in Community School in Nepal. KMC Journal 6(1): 176-191. https://doi.org/10.3126/kmcj.v6i1.62339

Joshi, Ankur, and Rajen K. Gupta. 2017. Elementary Education in Bharat (That Is India): Insights from a Postcolonial Ethnographic Study of a *Gurukul*. International Journal of Indian Culture and Business Management (IJICBM) 15(1): 100-120. https://www.inderscience.com/info/inarticle.php?artid=85390

Kamat, Ram Kumar. 2016. Language Commission Formed. The Himalayan Times. 9 September. https://thehimalayantimes.com/nepal/language-commission-formed (Accessed 16 July 2024).

Michailovsky, Boyd. 2006. Digitized resources for languages of Nepal. In Lesser-Known Languages of South Asia, edited by Anju Saxena and Lars Borin, 243-256. Berlin, New York: De Gruyter Mouton. https://doi.org/10.1515/9783110197785.3.243

National Statistics Office. 2021. National Population and Housing Census 2021 (National Report). https://censusnepal.cbs.gov.np/results/files/resultfolder/National%20Report_English.pdf

National Statistics Office. 2021. National Report on Caste/Ethnicity, Language and Religion. https://censusnepal.cbs.gov.np/results/files/resultfolder/Caste%20Ethnicity_report_NPHC_2021.pdf

Pine, Aidan and Mark Turin. 2017. Language Revitalization. In Oxford Research Encyclopedia of Linguistics, edited Mark Aronoff. New York: Oxford University Press. https://doi.org/10.1093/acrefore/9780199384655.013.8

Pradhan, Tika R. 2021. Adoption of Official Languages Recommended for Provinces Challenging, Experts Say. The Kathmandu Post. 18 September. https://kathmandupost.com/national/2021/09/18/adoption-of-official-languages-recommended-for-provinces-challenging-experts-say#:~:text=In%20the%20report%20presented%20to,and%20Awadhi%20for%20Lumbini%3B%20Magar (Accessed 17 July 2024).

Regmi, Dan Raj. 2023. Languages of Nepal: Sociolinguistic Typology, Census of the Languages and Sustainable Language Use. Nepalese Linguistics 37(1): 60-71. https://doi.org/10.3126/nl.v37i1.60013

Republica. 2024. Newari, Tamang to be Used as Official Languages in Bagmati Province. myRepublica. 5 May. https://myrepublica.nagariknetwork.com/news/newari-tamang-to-be-used-as-official-languages-in-bagmati-province/?categoryId=81 (Accessed 16 July 2024).

Sijapati, Alisha. 2021. Lost in translation. Nepali Times. 26 January. https://nepalitimes.com/here-now/lost-in-translation (Accessed 17 July 2024).

Stoop, Chrizell. 2017. Children's Rights to Mother-Tongue Education in a Multilingual World: A Comparative Analysis between South Africa and Germany. Potchefstroom Electronic Law Journal 20: 1-35. https://doi.org/10.17159/1727-3781/2017/v20i0a820

Sun, He. 2019. Home Environment, Bilingual Preschooler's Receptive Mother Tongue Language Outcomes, and Social-Emotional and Behavioral Skills: One Stone for Two Birds? Frontiers in Psychology 10. https://doi.org/10.3389/fpsyg.2019.01640

Tupas, Ruanni. 2019. Decentering Language: Displacing Englishes from the Study of Englishes. Critical Inquiry in Language Studies 17(3): 228-245. https://doi.org/10.1080/15427587.2019.1641097

Turin, Mark. 2006. Minority Language Policies and Politics in Nepal. In Lesser-Known Languages of South Asia, edited by Anju Saxena and Lars Borin, 61-72. Berlin, New York: De Gruyter Mouton. https://doi.org/10.1515/9783110197785.1.61

UNESCO. 2021. UNESCO celebrates International Mother Language Day 2021 in Nepal. February 25. https://www.unesco.org/en/articles/unesco-celebrates-international-mother-language-day-2021-nepal (Accessed 17 July 2024).

Wilson, William H. and Kauanoe Kamanā. 2006. "For the Interest of the Hawaiians Themselves": Reclaiming the Benefits of Hawaiian-Medium Education. In Hūlili: Multidisciplinary Research on Hawaiian Well-Being 3(1): 153-181. https://kamehamehapublishing.org/wpcontent/uploads/sites/38/2020/09/Hulili_Vol3_9.pdf

Xue, Jiao and Wenjing Zuo. 2013. English Dominance and Its Influence on International Communication. Theory and Practice in Language Studies 3(12): 2262-2266. Finland: Academy Publisher. https://www.academypublication.com/issues/past/tpls/vol03/12/16.pdf

Yadav, Raj Narayan. 2013. Language Planning and Language Ideology: The Majority and Minority Dichotomy in Nepal. Tribhuvan University Journal 28 (1-2): 197-202. https://doi.org/10.3126/tuj.v28i1-2.26242

HIMALAYA
The Journal of the Association of Nepal and Himalayan Studies

Book Review

Review of *Sustainability of Van Gujjars: A Transition of Muslim Pastoral Tribe in Himalayan Region* by Rubina Nusrat

Navneet Kaur
Jamia Millia Islamia, New Delhi

DOI: https://doi.org/10.2218/himalaya.2025.7433

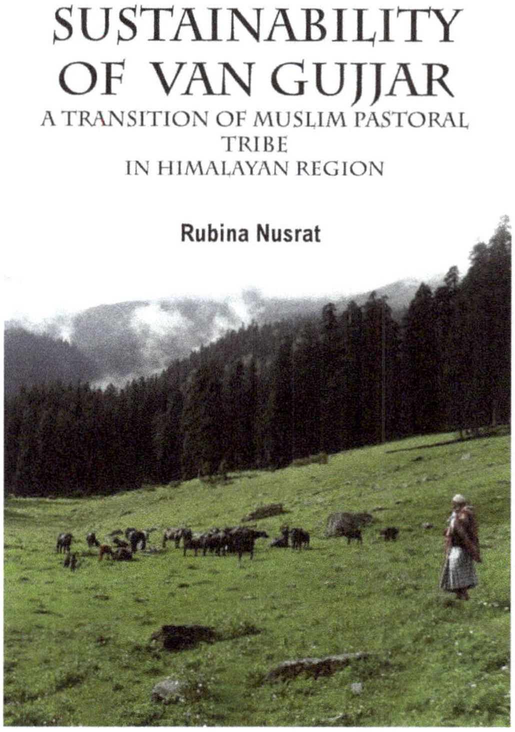

Recommended Citation

Kaur, Navneet (2025). Review of Sustainability of Van Gujjars: A Transition of Muslim Pastoral Tribe in Himalayan Region by Rubina Nusrat. *HIMALAYA* 44(1): 175-177.

cc BY NC ND
This work is licensed under a Creative Commons Attribution-Noncommercial-No Derivative Works 4.0 License.

Since India's independence, economic development and the interests of the country's tribal people have been in constant conflict. Displacement, marginalization, and vulnerability have been the fate of tribal people on the mainland. These people have suffered due to the adoption of neoliberal economic policies and exclusive development projects in the last few decades. In her book 'Sustainability of Van Gujjars,' the author highlights the tribal sustainability issues of the Van Gujjars of Uttarakhand. This book draws on the large body of literature about the "Forest Dwelling Gujjars" who originally migrated from Gujarat to Jammu and Kashmir and later to Uttarakhand (then Uttar Pradesh). The book covers three main themes: literature about the historical and socioeconomic conditions of Van Gujjars, cultural extinction, marginalization, and the vulnerability caused by displacement (later resettlement), as well as future strategies for sustainable livelihood and development using a sustainable livelihood framework.

At the start of the book, the author reviews information about the origin of the Gujjar tribe. Various past records have been ingeminated to present accounts of Gujjar history. Further, the spatial settings and socio-cultural perspectives of this mobile Muslim tribal community have been described. The author asserts that globalization has adversely affected the Van Gujjars in both economic and cultural terms. (p.65). These issues are also highlighted by Suratha Kumar Malik in his book *Land Alienation and Politics of Tribal Exploitation in India* (2020). Industrialization has destroyed pastoral lands and disrupted the Van Gujjars' mobility patterns. Later, as a nomadic tribe, they became "victims of conservation" due to political marginalization in the absence of permanent addresses and cultivation lands. Historical marginalization dating from the British era and lack of social, legal, and human rights ultimately led to the displacement of these tribals. Exclusion from development policy-making, the attitudes of villagers, and lack of cooperation by forest authorities have ensured the political marginalization, vulnerability, and cultural extinction of Van Gujjars. These factors have constrained their economy and damaged their region's unique cultural heritage, as well as affecting the community's rich experience in creating conservation-based livelihoods.

Nusrat, in the chapter "Examining Gender Roles in Gujjar Community," explores gender roles in pastoralist livelihoods and examines the factors determining these roles in Gujjar communities. Women work with men in livestock management, but due to the *Islamic* (religious identity) custom of *pardah* (veil), the social mobility of women is restricted to the proximity of *dera* (house). Women are zoophilists as they love and give veterinary care to animals, and they are naturalists due to their dependence on nature for *dera* building materials, traditional medicines (ethnoveterinary), and animal fodder. Women understand nature. As the author writes,

> *Gujjar women seem to depend on natural resources to even interweave the dead aspects in their living aspects. (p.98)*

Marriage is usually arranged through a barter system: i.e., "your daughter for my son" and "my daughter for your son." The husband gives livestock as *mehr* (dowry) to his wife at the time of marriage, which ensures that the majority of the livestock are under the ownership of the Gujjar women, and inheritance laws follow *Sharia* (Islamic) law. Sharia law dictates that women should have restricted mobility and social interaction. Such practices predominantly reflect religious norms rather than tribal rules.

Nusrat further argues that marginalization during the British era has led to the Van Gujjar's persistent exploitation as they are denied access to the forests and are branded as "forest destroyers." The resulting sedentarization and conflicts with the locals have brought an end to their traditional lifestyle, and they are compelled to work as wage laborers to survive. Food insecurity, reduced income, and loss of animals have become the new normal for this tribal community. (p.104).

In the chapter, "Indigenous Knowledge of Van Gujjars," the author explains that the traditional lopping technique of the Van Gujjars is equivalent to leaf fall. Similar arguments have been suggested by Clarke et al. (1986) in their study of Rajaji National Park. These cases demonstrate that the tribals use their indigenous knowledge to create strategies to coexist with nature (p.143). The seasonal migration of the Gujjars and their buffaloes to higher *bugyals* (pasturelands) allows the grass to regenerate, contributing to the carrying capacity of the forests (p.148). This sustainable practice of the Van Gujjars is reflected in the prefix to their name—*Van (*forest).

In the final chapter, "Strategy of Development," Nusrat emphasizes the urgent need for this tribal community to be included in mainstream development policies on a social and political level, explaining that they have fallen behind because they are socio-economically vulnerable and lack political representation. The author emphasizes the need for workable State Government schemes for the settlement of this semi-nomadic tribe. Properly implemented, such schemes could pave the way for the Van Gujjars' socioeconomic development (p.171). Nusrat's book is a pioneering work that disseminates information about the socio-cultural as well as the economic status of Van Gujjars in Uttarakhand. It is highly recommended for scholars and students of Himalayan Studies, Political Ecology, Indigenous Studies, Anthropology, and Rural Development, as it provides a comprehensive understanding of the challenges and dynamics faced by indigenous communities in the region.

Navneet Kaur holds a Ph.D. in Geography from Jamia Millia Islamia, India, specializing in gender and land rights issues among tribal communities in the North Himalayan States of India. Her academic journey began with a Bachelor's in Geography Honours from Banaras Hindu University, India, followed by a Master's degree at Jamia Millia Islamia, India, which deeply informed her research focus. Her Ph.D. work, adopting an intersectional framework, explores maternal healthcare among the Gujjar and Bakarwal tribes in Jammu and Kashmir, highlighting how geographic inaccessibility affects their health-care-seeking behaviors.

HIMALAYA
The Journal of the Association of Nepal and Himalayan Studies

Book Review

A Borderland's Soul: Through the India–China Border and the Hidden Histories of Kalimpong

Review of *Through the India–China Border: Kalimpong in the Himalayas* by Prem Poddar and Lisa Lindkvist Zhang

Tanka Subba

Indian Institute of Technology, Gandhinagar

DOI: https://doi.org/10.2218/himalaya.2025.10881

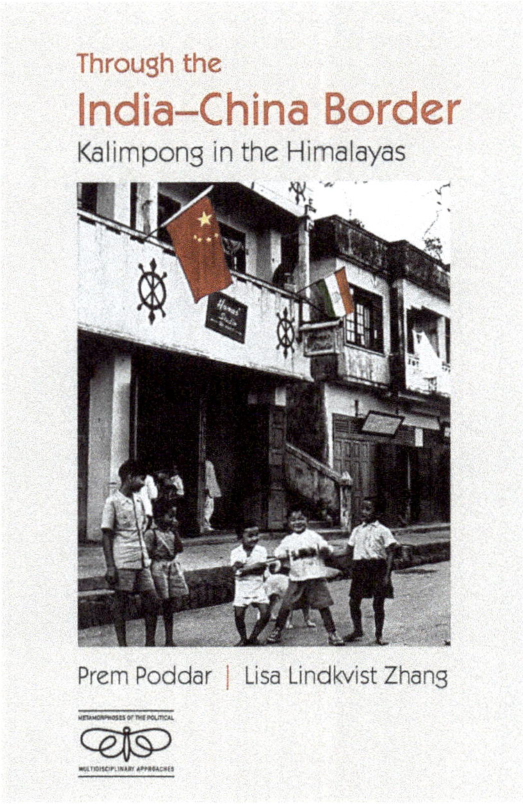

Recommended Citation

Subba, Tanka (2025). Review of *Through the India–China Border: Kalimpong in the Himalayas* by Prem Poddar and Lisa Lindkvist Zhang. *HIMALAYA* 44(1): 178-181.

This work is licensed under a Creative Commons Attribution-Noncommercial-No Derivative Works 4.0 License.

Kalimpong has long been a place of passage, where history lives through the stories strewn across its gentle hills, where multiple cultures coexist. In *Through the India–China Border*, Prem Poddar and Lisa Zhang bring to life a landscape that is as enigmatic to insiders as it is to outsiders. As a native of this borderland—and as someone privileged to call Prem Poddar a friend—I can attest to the depth of his insight and the lyrical precision with which he, together with Lisa Zhang, unveils Kalimpong's layered past. I was also impressed by Lisa Zhang when I met her in Kalimpong during one of my winter sojourns.

From the outset, I felt the pulse of Kalimpong—the bustling trade routes that once hummed with Tibetan and Marwari traders, the Tibetan muleteers, British explorers and administrators, and the many people who gathered there from around the world. Poddar and Zhang trace the journey of Kalimpong with historical finesse, revealing how this small town became a crucial node in British imperial ambitions, Chinese geopolitics, and Indian frontier administration. The book does more than narrate a history of the town—it resurrects voices and moments that might otherwise fade into obscurity. As a son of Kalimpong, I take pride in this monumental book, which taught me much about the history and geopolitics of my hometown.

What makes this work exceptional is the way it intertwines grand political narratives with the intimate details of local life. The book pulses with the stories of Kalimpong's people—the traders with their lingering nostalgia for a vanished trade, the Chinese shoemakers who made it their home, the monks from Sikkim and Bhutan walking with rosaries or prayer wheels in hand, the autochthonous Lepchas paying respects to their religious specialists called Muns and Bongthings, and a host of others shaping the town's cultural tapestry. It is through their voices that Kalimpong's vibrancy shines, and Poddar and Zhang capture this uniquely.

Throughout the book, there are reflections on Kalimpong as both a place of convergence and a site of tension. The spectres of World War II, shifting borders, and territorial uncertainty linger in the background. Yet there is also resilience—a quiet determination among its people to preserve their way of life. The authors do not merely recount the past; they allow us to feel its weight—every diplomatic manoeuvre, every exile's longing, every trader's dream, every spy's imagination.

One of the most poignant aspects of the book is the way it frames Kalimpong as a space of imagination and belonging. It is not just a town perched on geopolitical fault lines; it is a home, a crossroads of cultures, a testament to human endurance. If one walks through its winding paths, one still sees traces of lost caravan trails. Poddar and Zhang have given Kalimpong a voice that speaks of its past with honesty, of its present with subtlety, and of its future with hope—as seen in the possible reopening of the Jelep-La pass.

Nestled in the Eastern Himalayas, Kalimpong has historically served as a crucial interface between India, Bhutan, Sikkim, and Tibet. Its strategic location made it a hub for trade, diplomacy, and cultural exchange, particularly during British colonial rule and the early years of India's independence. The town has remained a focal point for geopolitical tensions, such as the Doklam standoff in 2017 and the Galwan Valley confrontation in 2020, underscoring its continued relevance in India–China relations.

Kalimpong has also been conceptualized as a metonymic space, representing broader India–China relations, particularly in the mid-20th century. Historically, it was a British trade post strategically positioned on the Lhasa–Kolkata trade route, which later became a vital corridor for the People's Liberation Army (PLA) in the early 1950s. The town housed a sizeable Tibetan population, including refugees and influential members of the Kashag (Tibetan governing council), making it a focal point for political manoeuvring in Tibet. Additionally, a diasporic Chinese community lived in Kalimpong, many of whom were later interned in Deoli, Rajasthan, following the 1962 Sino-Indian War. Even today, some Chinese families remain part of the town's social fabric.

Through archival research and fieldwork, the authors examine how Kalimpong functioned as both a symbolic and geopolitical node, shaping narratives in Chinese and Indian official circles during the 1950s and 1960s.

Kalimpong has long been a crossroads of espionage, political intrigue, and covert operations. During the 1950s, it was infamously labelled a "nest of spies" by Indian Prime Minister Jawaharlal Nehru. Chinese authorities and media, including *People's Daily*, denounced Kalimpong as a command centre for Tibetan rebels and espionage.

Its proximity to Tibet made it a crucial intelligence outpost for various nations with interests in the region. British intelligence maintained networks in the town, particularly during World War II, when operatives like Frederick William "Bill" Bailey and Lawrence "Laurie" Waddell gathered intelligence from Tibet and Burma (now Myanmar). Of the two, Waddell was a well-known author, notably of *Among the Himalayas* (1899).

After the British departure, Kalimpong remained vital to Indian intelligence efforts monitoring Chinese movements and Tibetan resistance. The town was a key transit point for Tibetan refugees fleeing the Chinese occupation—among them informants and operatives working for various governments. The CIA-backed Tibetan resistance movement had deep ties to Kalimpong; some volunteers were recruited from the town itself. It was also a meeting ground for Tibetan exiles, traders, and monks—many of whom engaged in intelligence gathering. Gyalo Thondup, the elder brother of the 14th Dalai Lama, lived in Kalimpong and played a crucial role in diplomatic negotiations between Tibet, India, and the West. His death in February 2025 is rightly described as "the end of an era."

Chinese intelligence was also active in Kalimpong, closely monitoring Tibetan activists and Indian border personnel. The town's vibrant trade routes provided cover for spies posing as merchants, scholars, and travellers.

The authors employ a rigorous, multidisciplinary approach to uncover the historical and geopolitical significance of Kalimpong. Drawing on rarely used documentary materials from British, Chinese, and Indian archives, they shed new light on the "Tibet Question" (pp. 85-86) in India–China relations. Their framework—blending historical analysis, cartographic studies, and oral histories—demonstrates how Kalimpong's past continues to shape contemporary geopolitics. As John Keay notes on the book's "Advance Praise" page, it is a "model of international scholarship."

The book's methodology is grounded in postcolonial and transcultural theory, enabling the authors to treat Kalimpong not merely as a geographical entity, but as a political and ideological flashpoint. This approach permits a nuanced reading of imperial histories, postwar politics, decolonization, and frontier cultures. The authors also integrate trade records and intelligence reports, offering a comprehensive view of Kalimpong's role in espionage and diplomacy.

Overall, Through the India–China Border stands out for its innovative theoretical engagement, which enriches our understanding of Kalimpong while contributing to broader discussions on border studies, postcolonialism, and transcultural interaction. It is a seminal work that challenges dominant historiographical frameworks and offers a fresh, interdisciplinary perspective on one of Asia's most politically charged regions.

I believe it should be read by every person who feels they belong to Kalimpong—or who has visited this rather unruly (Prem might prefer to call it "dystopian") town that it has become in recent years, where there is nowhere to park a private vehicle or walk without being pushed or jostled.

Tanka B. Subba retired as Professor of Anthropology from North-Eastern Hill University in 2022. He also served as Vice-Chancellor of Sikkim University from 2012 to 2017. He is currently Visiting Professor at the Indian Institute of Technology, Gandhinagar, Palaj, Gujarat 382355, India. Email: tanka.subba@iitgn.ac.in

HIMALAYA
The Journal of the Association of Nepal and Himalayan Studies

Book Review

Review of *Nepal's Dalits in Transition* by David N. Geller and Krishna P. Adhikari

Ina Zharkevich

King's College London

DOI: https://doi.org/10.2218/himalaya.2025.10048

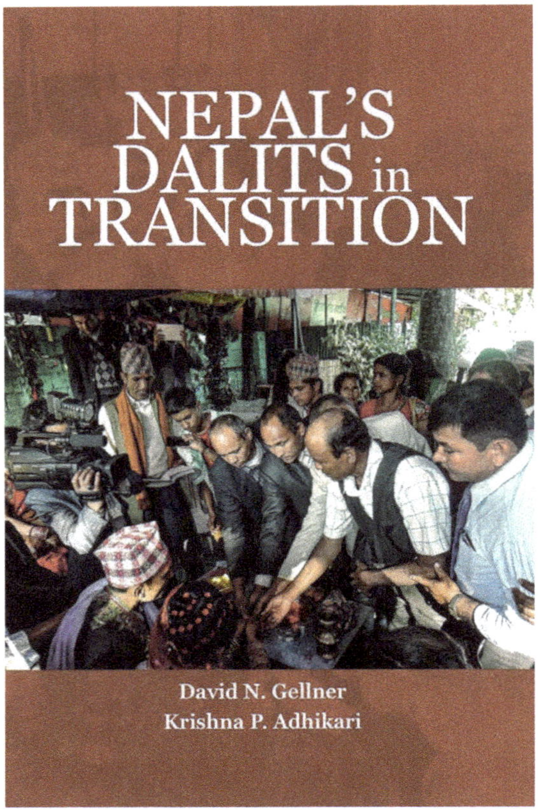

Recommended Citation

Zharkevich, Ina (2025). Review of *Nepal's Dalits in Transition* by David N. Geller and Krishna P. Adhikari. *HIMALAYA* 44(1): 182-184.

This work is licensed under a Creative Commons Attribution-Noncommercial-No Derivative Works 4.0 License.

Due to the paucity of research on Nepal's Dalits, *Nepal's Dalits in Transition* can be read as a handbook of Dalit studies in Nepal, providing a much-needed introduction to this field. Comprising thirteen chapters and an introduction, *Nepal's Dalits in Transition* provides comprehensive coverage of the wide range of issues that the Dalit population in Nepal faces, ranging from the psychological effects of belonging to the Dalit category (Ch.3) and the tension inherent in different strategies of dealing with this identity—for example, claiming vs. concealing it (Intro, Ch.6, Conclusion)—to the history of the term (Ch.2) and changes in the material conditions of Dalit lives (Ch.5,7,8). With several chapters focusing exclusively on the Tarai Dalits (Ch.9 and 10), the volume shows the diversity of Nepal's Dalit population as well as inequalities not only between Dalits and non-Dalits but also within the Dalit community (Ch.10).

Several core themes run through the volume. The first reflects the contradiction between public recognition and the claiming of Dalit identity, often characteristic of the activist path, and identity-based effacement or "strategic passing" (Ch. 13), which is chosen not only by ordinary people but also, as shown by Pfaff Czarnecka (Ch.6), by some highly educated and upwardly mobile young Dalits. Thus, many university-educated Dalit youth are reluctant to be organized based on collective identity. They dislike reservations and refuse to base their identity on suffering, choosing instead to conceal it, which is often taken as betrayal by fellow Dalits (Ch.6).

As Pfaff Czarnecka shows, despite university being a space relatively free from caste discrimination, Dalit students must grapple not only with the lack of social and cultural capital—or, as Gellner and Adhikari call it, "negative cultural capital" (p.300)—but also with dilemmas about how to reconcile their individual life paths and aspirations with the collective struggle for Dalit identity, which is still associated with low status (ibid). Furthermore, as shown by Arjun BK (Ch.4), there is no consensus among Dalits about the term, with many arguing that it stigmatizes and reinforces the boundaries between Dalits and non-Dalits. As Arjun BK demonstrates, the refusal of some Dalits to be called "Dalits" causes resentment among non-Dalits, who insist that people receiving state benefits based on the legal category should own it: "If you feel offended by the term, you should not take allowances" (p.74). Gellner and Adhikari (Ch.13) discuss five ways in which Dalits come to terms with their identity: assimilation, reparation, revolution, ethnicizing identity, and exit (conversion to Christianity).

The second theme running through the volume is the change in the material conditions of Dalit lives. While the chapters provide ample statistical and survey data demonstrating that Dalits remain the most economically disadvantaged group (with the exception of Muslims)—43 percent of Hill Dalits and 38 percent of Madhesi Dalits live below the poverty line as compared to the national average of 25 percent (p.148)—the volume also explores advances made by Dalits in the last decade due to outmigration abroad (Ch.5), affirmative action policies (Ch.12), refusal to perform *balighare* (services to former high-caste patrons) (Ch.5) and increased representation in the public sphere (Ch.13). However, as shown by P. Nepali in Ch.7, land ownership, or, rather, Dalit landlessness, remains a key impediment to Dalit social and political empowerment. Although they comprise 12.9 percent of the population, Dalits own only 1 percent of the land (p.146)—which demonstrates the material basis of the symbolic domination that Dalits endure.

The volume also reveals that discrimination against Dalits goes well beyond the economic domain. By taking a phenomenological approach to the process of *being*, *belonging*, and *becoming* a Dalit, the chapter by Folmar (Ch.3) poignantly shows the psychological burden borne by those inhabiting the Dalit category and the totalizing effects of living at the bottom of the hierarchy. Folmar explores what it means "psychologically to *be* a Dalit person" (p.37), demonstrating the symbolic violence exerted by the ascribed low status, which people do not choose yet must inhabit and embody. The chapter develops a carefully researched and nuanced argument about the association between belonging to the Dalit category and mental health vulnerabilities. The psychological weight of the Dalit category is such that many parents, according to Folmar, do not tell their children about caste. Contrary to the common assumption that one is born a Dalit, Folmar persuasively demonstrates that becoming one is a "daunting psychological and social process" (p.58) that happens over time during encounters with neighbors, joining a school, or other social interactions.

The tenacity of caste in today's Nepal, especially in the private domain, is powerfully illustrated by Biswakarma (Ch.12). Based on the analysis of twelve inter-caste marriages in the Dhanusa district in the Tarai, Biswakarma demonstrates that caste is rooted in power relations based on birth and kinship. The harrowing cases of physical, psychological, and mental torture inflicted on young people who marry outside their caste and transgress the hierarchical order (ibid.) demonstrate that caste remains a lived reality, despite changes in the public domain. Biswakarma demonstrates that in the Tarai, unlike in the Hills, all cases of inter-caste marriage must go through Mainjan ("caste head" or literally honourable person), who can upgrade caste and excommunicate "upgraded" Dalits from their families. Thus, in cases of hypergamous marriages (non-Dalit males and Dalit girls), the girls must go through a ceremony of caste upgrade to become a non-Dalit.

According to Biswakarma, the double standards inherent in this ceremony—upgrading someone from the status of untouchable to a higher caste while forcing them to treat their own family as untouchable and, more importantly, upgrading only those Dalits whose status would imperil the purity of higher castes—is a clear example that the "caste system is a traditional ploy to retain power" and maintain caste hegemony (p.198). It is also a striking example of how inter-caste marriages, envisioned as the only way to break down boundaries between Dalits and non-Dalits (p.297), might, under certain conditions, reinforce and strengthen the separation.

While the range of themes covered in the volume is impressive, none of the chapters except Ch.11—which takes a gendered perspective on the Dalit social movement—and the chapter by Biswakarma, with its focus on kinship, explore the intersection of gender and caste. This is surprising, given the centrality of gender for understanding caste, as shown by Cameron (Mary Cameron, 1998. *On the Edge of the Auspicious. Gender and Caste in Nepal.* University of Illinois Press).

Having said this, *Nepal's Dalits in Transition* makes an important and much-needed contribution to scholarship on Nepal's Dalit population, with much of the previous scholarship on Nepal having predominantly focused on *janajati* groups. It will be of interest to researchers working on Nepal and on caste in Nepal and South Asia, with individual chapters speaking to scholars working on social mobility and social stratification, social justice and inequalities, structural/symbolic violence, and social movements/activism.

Ina Zharkevich is a Senior Lecturer in Social Anthropology and Development, King's College London. Ina has worked on issues around the Maoist civil war, migration, and social change in Nepal. She is the author of *Maoist People's War and the Revolution of Everyday Life in Nepal* (2019).

www.ingramcontent.com/pod-product-compliance
Lightning Source LLC
LaVergne TN
LVHW072241140825
818608LV00020B/384